ASEAN-China
Relations
Realities and Prospects

The **Institute of Southeast Asian Studies (ISEAS)** was established as an autonomous organization in 1968. It is a regional centre dedicated to the study of socio-political, security and economic trends and developments in Southeast Asia and its wider geostrategic and economic environment.

The Institute's research programmes are the Regional Economic Studies (RES, including ASEAN and APEC), Regional Strategic and Political Studies (RSPS), and Regional Social and Cultural Studies (RSCS).

ISEAS Publications, an established academic press, has issued more than 1,000 books and journals. It is the largest scholarly publisher of research about Southeast Asia from within the region. ISEAS Publications works with many other academic and trade publishers and distributors to disseminate important research and analyses from and about Southeast Asia to the rest of the world.

ASEAN-China Relations
Realities and Prospects

EDITED BY

Saw Swee-Hock • Sheng Lijun • Chin Kin Wah

ISEAS

Institute of Southeast Asian Studies
Singapore

First published in Singapore in 2005 by ISEAS Publications
Institute of Southeast Asian Studies
30 Heng Mui Keng Terrace
Pasir Panjang
Singapore 119614

E-mail: publish@iseas.edu.sg
Website: <http://bookshop.iseas.edu.sg>

This book is published under the ASEAN-China Study Programme funded by Professor Saw Swee-Hock.

The responsibility for facts and opinions in this publication rests exclusively with the authors and their interpretations do not necessarily reflect the views or the policy of the publisher or its supporters.

ISEAS Library Cataloguing-in-Publication Data

ASEAN-China relations : realities and prospects / edited by Saw Swee-Hock, Sheng Lijun and Chin Kin Wah.
1. Southeast Asia—Foreign relations—China.
2. China—Foreign relations—Southeast Asia.
3. Southeast Asia—Foreign economic relations—China.
4. China—Foreign economic relations—Southeast Asia.
5. Sea-power—Southeast Asia.
6. National security—Southeast Asia.
7. Great powers—Southeast Asia.
8. Economic development projects—China—Yunnan.
9. Chinese—Southeast Asia.
10. South China Sea—Strategic aspects.
I.   Saw, Swee-Hock, 1931–
II. Sheng, Lijun.
III. Chin, Kin Wah.
DS525.9 C5A842   2005

ISBN 981-230-342-1

Typeset by Superskill Graphics Pte Ltd
Printed in Singapore by

Contents

The Contributors

BAVIERA, Aileen S.P. is an associate professor and dean of the Asian Center, University of the Philippines. Her research covers Asia Pacific regional security, China-Southeast Asian relations, Asian regionalism and community building, and maritime security. She has been a member of the East Asia Vision Group, headed the Center for International Relations and Strategic Studies of the Philippine Foreign Service Institute, and served as Executive Director of the Philippine-China Development Resource Center. Her recent books include *China's Relations with Southeast Asia: Political, Security and Economic Interests* (1999); *Comprehensive Engagement: Strategic Issues in Philippines-China Relations* (2000); *Bilateral Confidence Building with China in Relation to the South China Sea Disputes: A Philippine Perspective* (2000). She has also co-edited several books and published articles in *Asian Studies* (2000) and the *Australian Journal of International Affairs* (July 2003).

CAI Bingkui is a major general (Rtd.) of the People's Liberation Army (PLA) in China and vice-chairman of the China Institute for International Strategic Studies. He was defence attaché to Thailand and Pakistan.

CAO Yunhua is a professor and the chair at Department of International Relations, and director of the Institute of Southeast Asia Studies, Jinan University, Guangzhou, China. He is also vice president of the Chinese Association for Southeast Asia Studies. His research focuses on economics and politics in Southeast Asia, regional international relations and ethnic Chinese studies. He has authored six books and edited two, both in Chinese, and published more than one hundred academic papers in China and other countries.

CHIN Kin Wah is deputy director of the Institute of Southeast Asian Studies (ISEAS), Singapore. He was formerly associate professor in the Department of Political Science, National University of Singapore. He is a specialist on regional affairs. His recent publications include *Southeast Asian Affairs 2005* (co-editor) and *Michael Leifer: Selected Works on Southeast Asia* (co-editor/co-compiler 2005).

CHINWANNO, Chulacheeb is an associate professor and head of the International Relations Department of the Faculty of Political Science, Thammasat University, Bangkok, Thailand. He was former director of the Institute of East Asian Studies, and also the Human Resource Institute at Thammasat University. He is the senior expert of the Committee on Foreign Affairs, House of Representatives, Thailand. His research focuses on Asia-Pacific security and China and other major powers in Southeast Asia.

CHIRATHIVAT, Suthiphand is an associate professor of economics and former dean of the Faculty of Economics, Chulalongkorn University. He has previously served as assistant to the dean of the Faculty of Economics and Business Administration at Kasetsart University as well as director of the Center for International Economics and the Center for European Studies at Chulalongkorn University. He is advisor to the Minister for Foreign Affairs, Member of Thailand's Committee on International Economic Policy, and Corresponding Editor of *Journal of Asian Economics*. His recent publications include *Asia-Europe on the Eve of the 21ˢᵗ Century* (co-editor, 2001), *ASEAN-EU Economic Relations: The Long-term Potential beyond the Recent Turmoil* (co-editor, 1999).

GAO Zhiguo is executive director of the China Institute for Maritime Affairs and adjunct professor at the China University of Oceanography, and Research Centre for Eco-environmental Science, Chinese Academy of Sciences. He is also deputy to the National People's Congress (MP) and member of the Foreign Affairs Committee of the Congress. He was the principal drafter of China's major marine and maritime laws, including the law of the territorial sea and contiguous zones, and the law of exclusive economic zones and continental shelf. His research focuses on international law, law of the sea and natural and environmental law and maritime cooperation and security.

HAN Feng is a professor and deputy director of the Institute of Asia-Pacific Studies, Chinese Academy of Social Sciences, Beijing. His research covers contemporary international relations in the Asia-Pacific region including ASEAN.

HE Shengda is a professor and vice president of the Yunnan Academy of Social Sciences, Kunming, China. He is also the vice president of the Chinese Association for Southeast Asian Studies. His research focuses on relations between China and Southeast Asia, especially Yunnan and mainland Southeast Asia. His publications include *Southeast Asia Toward the 21ˢᵗ Century and its Relations with China* (co-author, 1997); *ASEAN and China at Turn of the Centuries* (co-author, 2001); *Construction of the ASEAN-China Free Trade Area and Yunnan's Opening to Southeast Asia* (co-author, 2003).

HEDRICK-WONG, Yuwa is MasterCard International's economic advisor for Asia/Pacific, monitoring and forecasting economic growth and emerging business development trends in the region. He also conducts research on the dynamics of the growth of the payments industry in all key markets in the region.

HU Shisheng is an associate professor and director of the Institute of South & Southeast Asia Studies, China Institutes of Contemporary International Relations. His research focuses on South Asia politics, India's foreign relations, including its relations with China and ASEAN. He has published extensively with many book chapters, among which are "Perspectives on the Ethnic & Religious Issues of China's Surrounding Regions" in the book *The Ethnic and Religious Situation of Nepal and Sri Lanka* (2002) and "Focus on the Global Religious Problems" in the book *The Role of Tibetan Buddhism in the Internationalization Process of the Tibetan Issue* (2002).

KAO Kim Hourn is Secretary of State, Ministry of Foreign Affairs & International Cooperation, Royal Government of Cambodia and president of the University of Cambodia. He was formerly executive director of the Cambodian Institute of Cooperation and Peace.

KRAFT, Herman Joseph S. is a research fellow at the Institute for Strategic and Development Studies, Manila, specializing in Philippine security issues, particularly its relations with the United States, and regional security in Southeast Asia. He is also a faculty member at the Department of Political Science at the University of the Philippines.

LI Yaqiang is naval captain of the People's Liberation Army (PLA) in China.

LIU Xuecheng is a senior fellow and director of American Studies, China Institute of International Studies. He is also director of the Beijing Center for American Studies, director of the Asia Program, China Reform Forum, member of the CSCAP-China National Committee, and an ARF Expert/ Eminent Person. His research focuses on China-US relations and Asia-Pacific political and security issues. He has written over 100 academic articles and research papers in leading Chinese journals or at international conferences and authored two books: *Sino-Indian Border Dispute and Sino-Indian Relations* (1994) and *China and U.S.: Rivals or Partners* (2001).

MOHAMED JAWHAR HASSAN is director-general of the Institute of Strategic and International Studies (ISIS), Malaysia. His research focuses on international relations, security and nation-building. In July 2002 he was nominated as ASEAN Regional Forum (ARF) Expert and Eminent Person. He is also co-chair of the CSCAP Working Group on Cooperative Security and Comprehensive Security.

ONG Keng Yong is Secretary-General of ASEAN. He joined the Singapore Ministry of Foreign Affairs in 1979 and held senior positions including the director in charge of American and European affairs, Singapore's High Commissioner to India and ambassador to Nepal. He was seconded to Singapore Prime Minister's Office as the press secretary to the Prime Minister and concurrently to the Ministry of Information, Communications and the Arts as deputy secretary.

RICHARDSON, Michael is a visiting senior research fellow at the Institute of Southeast Asian Studies, Singapore. He was Asia Editor of the International Herald Tribune. He has a longstanding interest in relations between Southeast Asia and Australasia. His recent research for ISEAS has focused on maritime security and his book is, A Time Bomb for Global Trade: Maritime-related Terrorism in an Age of Weapons of Mass Destruction (2004).

SAW Swee-Hock is Professorial Fellow and Adviser of the ASEAN-China Study Programme at the Institute of Southeast Asian Studies. He was formerly Professor of Statistics at the University of Singapore and the University of Hong Kong. He is a Council Member of the National University of Singapore, and a recipient of its Distinguished Alumni Service Award. Among his major publications are *Economic Problems and Prospects in ASEAN Countries (co-editor), ASEAN Economies in Transition (editor), Growth and Direction of*

ASEAN Trade (co-editor), Malaysia: Recent Trends and Challenges (co-editor), Population Policies and Programmes in Singapore, Investment Management, and A Guide to Conducting Surveys.

SHEN Danyang is a senior economist and vice president of the Chinese Academy of International Trade and Economic Cooperation, Ministry of Commerce. He is also secretary-general of the China Foreign Trade Award Inspection Committee and a council member of the China International Trade Society. He is editor-in-chief of *Foreign Trade Review* (Beijing).

SHENG Lijun is a senior fellow and coordinator of the ASEAN-China Study Programme at the Institute of Southeast Asian Studies, Singapore. His research focuses on China's foreign relations in East Asia. He has written extensively, with articles published in numerous journals including the *Washington Quarterly,* the *Journal of Strategic Studies, Cambridge Review of International Affairs, Security Dialogue, Asian Perspective, Journal of Northeast Asian Studies, Contemporary Southeast Asia,* and *Pacific Focus.* He is the author of *China's Dilemma: The Taiwan Issue* (2001), and *Cross-Strait Relations under Chen Shui-bian* (2002).

SISOWATH, Doung Chanto is assistant dean and lecturer, Faculty of Social Sciences & International Relations, Pannasastra University of Cambodia. He was formerly deputy executive director and a senior research fellow for the Cambodian Institute for Cooperation and Peace. He previously served in the Council of Ministers' Legal Coordinating Unit of the Royal Government of Cambodia.

SURYADINATA, Leo is a senior research fellow at the Institute of Southeast Asian Studies. He was formerly professor of political science at the National University of Singapore. He has published extensively on ethnic Chinese in Southeast Asia as well as China-ASEAN relations. His books include: *China and the ASEAN States: Ethnic Chinese Dimension* (1985), *Pribumi Indonesian, the Chinese Minority and China* (1993) and *Ethnic Relations and Nation-Building in Southeast Asia: The Case of the Ethnic Chinese* (editor 2004).

TEO, Eric Chu Cheow is council secretary of the Singapore Institute of International Affairs and managing director of Savoir Faire Corporate Consultants, Singapore. He specializes in political and economic risk analysis and the political economy of East Asian countries and has written extensively for numerous local and international academic publications. He has also undertaken consultancy projects for the World Bank. He was conferred the title of *Chevalier de l'Ordre National du Mérit* by the President and Government of the Republic of France on 1 December 2003.

WANANDI, Jusuf is a senior analyst of Southeast Asian regionalism and the politics and foreign policies of Indonesia and the United States. He is a co-founder of Indonesia's Centre for Strategic and International Studies. He has co-authored or co-edited more than a dozen books, including *Europe and the Asia Pacific* (1998), *Security Cooperation in the Asia-Pacific Region* (1993), and *Asia and the Major Powers* (1988)

WANG Gungwu is director, East Asian Institute, National University of Singapore.; professor in the Faculty of Arts and Social Sciences, National University of Singapore; and emeritus professor of the Australian National University. He was Vice-Chancellor of the University of Hong Kong in 1986–95.

WANG Zhongchun, is a senior colonel of the People's Liberation Army (PLA), professor and deputy director of the Training and Research Division for Foreign Officer Students, PLA National Defense University (NDU). He was a senior fellow in the Institute for Strategic Studies of NDU for more than 10 years. His research focuses on China-U.S. relations, particularly in the field of security. He has authored several books, including *The Pentagon's Secret Plan for the Use of Nuclear Weapons; On Modern U.S. Army; The U.S. Nuclear Armament and Nuclear Strategy; International Disarmament and Arms Control;* and *The Nuclear Weapons, Nuclear Powers, and Their Nuclear Strategies.*

ZHANG Xiaoji is a senior research fellow and director-general of the Research Department of Foreign Economic Relations, Development Research Centre of the State Council of the PRC. He is also standing member of the China Association of International Trade, China Association of International Economic Cooperation and professor of Beijing Normal University. His research focuses on China's macroeconomic management, foreign economic policy and regional economic integration.

ZHANG Youwen is professor and director at the Institute of World Economy, Shanghai Academy of Social Sciences. He is also a member of the expert team for Financial and Economic Committee of the Standing Committee of Shanghai People's Congress, editor-in-chief of the *Journal of World Economic Studies*, a council member of the China Association of World Economy and vice chairman of the Shanghai Association of World Economy.

Foreword

The rise of China is one of the most critical developments in the world today. Some are reflective on its meaning and implications. Others ponder over the long-term impact on the region's security landscape while exploring security cooperation with this major power. The regional business community seeks to adjust to this change, wondering how to ride the tide of benefits that can come with the creation of an ASEAN-China Free Trade Area. There will be the downside but, for the present, the focus is on the immense opportunities that will come with the rise of China. Both ASEAN and China are hoping for a win-win outcome. For better or worse, the rise of China is a development we can ill afford to ignore.

To provide a comprehensive understanding of China's rapid rise and explore the impact and implications for ASEAN, the Institute of Southeast Asian Studies (ISEAS) organized the first ASEAN-China Forum from 23 to 24 June 2004 in Singapore. The forum brought together more than thirty reputable experts and scholars from China and ASEAN countries. They included strategic thinkers, senior economists and policy advisers from leading research institutions and think-tanks. Among the Chinese participants were representatives from the State Council, Ministry of Commerce, Ministry of Foreign Affairs, Ministry of Defence, and Chinese Academy of Social Sciences.

HE Ong Keng Yong, ASEAN Secretary General, delivered the keynote address on how to develop ASEAN-China relations, while Professor Cai Bingkui, PLA Major General and Vice Chairman of China Institute for International Strategic Studies, delivered the luncheon speech on "China's Peaceful Development and Relations with Its East Asian Neighbours".

Issues discussed at the forum included ASEAN and China assessments of the evolving security environment in Southeast Asia; the role of other major powers; the prospects for ASEAN-China maritime security cooperation;

strengthening cooperation in the ARF; the proposed ASEAN-China FTA; cooperation in human resources development; cooperation for Greater Mekong Sub-Region (GMS) development; moving beyond confidence-building in the South China Sea; the ethnic Chinese factor in ASEAN-China relations; and strengthening East Asian cooperation through the ASEAN+3 process.

ISEAS hopes that this publication, which contains the essence of the discussions at the two-day forum, will contribute towards a greater understanding of ASEAN-China relations.

I would like to acknowledge, with thanks, Professor Saw Swee-Hock's sponsorship of the ASEAN-China Study Programme which funded the holding of the forum and the publication of this book.

K. Kesavapany
Director
ISEAS

Opening Remarks

On behalf of ISEAS, let me welcome all of you to ASEAN-China Forum 2004. ISEAS is only slightly younger than the original ASEAN first established in 1967, but ISEAS has, of course, not grown together with ASEAN in every respect. For one thing, ISEAS did not admit five new partners. For another, I am delighted to add ISEAS did not experience the financial crisis that almost paralysed some of the members of ASEAN. I say this only in jest in order to emphasize how presumptuous it is for me to mention ISEAS and ASEAN in the same breath. But, seriously, there is one link between the two that I am not afraid to point to. The founders of ASEAN, like those of our institute, would not have expected ASEAN to grow as quickly and as dramatically as it did during this past decade. The fact is that, despite the crises for some members and for the region as a whole, ASEAN proved to be more than viable under great stress and the Secretary General's office in Jakarta is now busier than ever before.

Among ASEAN's many changes, there were a few that were exceptional. One of them was something that the founders of our institute would hardly have dared to dream of. I refer to the fact that ASEAN, the organization that the ISEAS as a research centre began to study almost from day one of its foundation, would one day have the People's Republic of China as one of its warmest supporters. I think it would have been inconceivable for any of our founders that we can now expect concrete plans to be drawn up for ASEAN and China to develop a Free Trade Area.

It is humbling to think how far ASEAN has come. You can thus imagine how proud our institute is to hold this forum today on "Developing ASEAN-China Relations". We are indeed grateful that the Secretary General Mr Ong Keng Yong has found it possible to come and support our efforts and give us this keynote address.

I also want to thank the large number of paper writers and discussants who have agreed to help us explore the many realities that this relationship will have to face. We have many expert essays here on how ASEAN-China relations might be developed in the coming years and there are even more ideas there about the prospects for the relationship to progress smoothly. Needless to say, we look forward to the discussions that these papers will stimulate.

However, there is one set of realities that we should not forget. ASEAN began under conditions of insecurity and threat but sought to focus initially on the possibilities of economic cooperation. The leaders of the five original members and their officials spent a lot of time tracing the ways and means for such cooperation to take effect. But, until the late 1980s, progress in intra-regional economic relations was exceedingly slow with each member depending mainly on extra-regional trading relations for their development. In contrast, economic growth *within* each country into the first half of the 1990s was more dramatic. It has been explained that this had to do directly with the fact that the U.S. economy was doing so well during that period. Perhaps the sharp entrepreneurship of many of the region's businessmen has something to do with it, too. We may even have to thank the cultural values that we have been so fortunate to have inherited.

But the explanations that take us back to some major political decisions are those that attract me most of all. I do feel that they really made the difference between sluggish and cheeseparing talk and the readiness to take decisive steps forward. Let me mention a few obvious examples. In 1978, Chinese leaders turned away from an ideology that made the country poorer and that changed the background for ASEAN's position. Another, ASEAN and its allies acted together to help rebuild the Cambodian nation and that was remarkable. Also, American political leaders pushed the Soviet Union to a state of collapse and ended the Cold War, indirectly giving ASEAN fresh fields to conquer. Yet another, ASEAN leaders decided to invite the remaining four Southeast Asian countries to join ASEAN; that was a decision not without pain but it was one that has led to other very promising possibilities.

None of these decisions is related to the feeble efforts before the 1990s among ASEAN members to cooperate economically. I cannot help but think that, where there is no political will, economic relations will always develop at the slowest allowable pace. ASEAN's recent relationship with China reminds us how true this observation can be. Out of the blue came a decision by China's leaders to seek a Free Trade Agreement with ASEAN as a whole. For boldness, the region has rarely seen anything like this since the organization was first mooted. Suddenly, a new configuration emerged. All kinds of gears had to be changed in the ASEAN vehicle and also in some of our neighbours' machines. I therefore underline one of the realities for the conference to ponder on, the need for political will to be exercised by ASEAN leaders.

Such an emphasis, of course, suggests that the prospects of ASEAN-China relations developing smoothly, and according to the time hoped for, may also depend on bold political decisions in the future. We note that ASEAN has acted firmly several times before. This has been possible whenever ASEAN gave more weight to the organization as a whole and softened its insistence on each member's absolute sovereignty. Whenever the mantra of non-intervention in each other's affairs is silenced because of an urgent need that most members can see, ASEAN as an entity has taken a step forward. That is what I am inclined to see. Even if this observation is only partly true, I hope that past experiences will encourage ASEAN members to be bold from time to time.

Today, this forum is pursuing the consequences of China's first moves, the fact that China made the initial difference. But I see no reason to doubt that ASEAN too could do the same the next time round. It may be that, for the relationship to take the next great step forward, more will depend on ASEAN. I do not know if that will be so, but I do expect the sessions today and tomorrow to provide us with some evidence that ASEAN has reached the point when the organization will now do some of the leading. What I do know is that when the secretary general and his colleagues in Jakarta identify the way that ASEAN should next go, they would expect the leaders of ASEAN to have the will to move along with them.

Wang Gungwu
Chairman
ISEAS

1

An Overview of ASEAN-China Relations

Saw Swee-Hock, Sheng Lijun and Chin Kin Wah

INTRODUCTION

Before the 1990s, there was no official relationship between ASEAN as a grouping and China, although China had official bilateral relations with certain individual ASEAN member states. From the late 1980s, China intensified its efforts to establish diplomatic relations with all the remaining ASEAN states leading eventually to official relationship with the ASEAN grouping.

In his visit to Thailand in November 1988, Chinese Premier Li Peng announced four principles in establishing, restoring and developing relations with all the ASEAN states. After establishing diplomatic relations with Singapore on 3 October 1990, China pushed for official ties with the ASEAN grouping. On 19 July 1991, Chinese Foreign Minister Qian Qichen attended the opening session of the Twenty-Fourth ASEAN Ministerial Meeting (AMM) in Kuala Lumpur as a guest of the Malaysian Government, where he expressed China's interest in cooperating with ASEAN. The latter responded positively. In September 1993, ASEAN Secretary General Dato' Ajit Singh visited Beijing and agreed to establish two joint committees, one on cooperation in science and technology, and the other on economic and trade cooperation. An exchange of letters between the ASEAN secretary general and the Chinese foreign minister on 23 July 1994 in Bangkok formalized the establishment of the two committees. At the same time, ASEAN and China agreed to engage in consultations on political and security issues at senior official level. In July 1996, ASEAN accorded China full Dialogue Partner status at the Twenty-ninth AMM in Jakarta, moving China from a Consultative Partner, which it had been since 1991.

By early 1997, there were already five parallel frameworks for dialogue between ASEAN and China: (1) the China-ASEAN political consultation at senior official level; (2) the China-ASEAN Joint Committee on Economic and Trade Cooperation; (3) the ASEAN-China Joint Cooperation Committee (ACJCC); (4) China-ASEAN Joint Committee on Scientific and Technological Cooperation; and (5) the ASEAN Beijing Committee. China participated in a series of consultative meetings with ASEAN, which include the ASEAN Regional Forum (ARF), the Post Ministerial Conferences (PMC) 9+1 and 9+10, the Joint Cooperation Committee (JCC) Meeting, the ASEAN-China Senior Officials Meeting (SOM) and the ASEAN-China Business Council Meeting.

In December 1997, Chinese President Jiang Zemin and all the ASEAN leaders had their first informal summit (ASEAN+1) and issued a joint statement of establishing partnership of good neighbourliness and mutual trust oriented towards the twenty-first century, thus putting into place the framework and charting the course for the all-round growth of their relations.

Relations between China and ASEAN countries have since developed rapidly, highlighted by the frequent exchange of visits by top leaders of the respective countries. In 1999, China signed framework documents on bilateral cooperation oriented towards the twenty-first century with Thailand and Malaysia, and signed joint statements on future cooperation with Vietnam and Brunei. By 2000, China had signed similar framework documents with all ASEAN states. It established official relations with the first non-socialist party in Southeast Asia (the Malaysia National Front) in 1994 and since then, the Communist Party of China (CPC) has built official relations with thirty-nine political parties there (including both socialist and non-socialist parties, in office and out of office).

China's ASEAN security relations with ASEAN countries in the 1990s were marred by territorial disputes in the South China Sea, especially with the Philippines over the Mischief Reef and Scarborough Shoal, and with Vietnam over their sea and land borders. But by 2000, the tension had cooled down. China and Vietnam signed the Treaty on the Land Border on 30 December 1999. In 2000, the two countries signed a historic agreement demarcating maritime territory in the Gulf of Tonkin. On 15 March 2000, senior officials from China and ASEAN met in Thailand to discuss, for the first time, their respective draft Codes of Conduct for the South China Sea. In November 2002, they signed the Declaration on the Conduct of Parties in the South China Sea. Relations between China and the Philippines have greatly improved since late 1990s and reached a new height with the state visit to China by Philippine President Gloria Macapagal-Arroyo in early September 2004.

China and ASEAN countries also cooperate on transnational non-traditional security threats such as dealing with drug-trafficking, with the Beijing Declaration signed in August 2001 between China, Laos, Myanmar and Thailand. In November 2002, China and ASEAN signed the Joint Declaration of ASEAN and China On Cooperation In the Field of Non-Traditional Security Issues.

China has also improved its military ties with individual ASEAN members, with high-level visits by their military leaders, military training and assistance of weapons and military technology, and naval port visits.

An important milestone in the development of ASEAN-China relations was China's signing in 2003 of a key ASEAN security protocol, The Treaty of Amity and Cooperation (TAC), and their declaring each other as strategic partners of peace and prosperity.

ASEAN-China trade also expanded fast, with an average growth rate of 20.8 per cent from 1990 to 2003. In 2003, China-ASEAN trade reached a record high of US$78.3 billion, with a growth rate as high as 42.9 per cent. The goal of US$100 billion might be achieved in 2004, instead of 2005 as previously expected. ASEAN is now the fifth largest trade partner of China while China is the sixth of ASEAN.

Mutual investment has also expanded. From 1991 to 2000, ASEAN investment in China increased at an average annual rate of 28 per cent. In 1991, ASEAN investment in China was only US$90 million, and increased to US$26.2 billion by 2001, accounting for 6.6 per cent of total FDI utilized by China. China's investment in ASEAN was comparatively small, but also increased sharply to US$1.1 billion by 2001, accounting for 7.7 per cent of China's overseas investment.

The proposed China-ASEAN Free Trade Area (CAFTA) marks another milestone in the ASEAN-China relations. China's push for the formation of a free trade area (FTA) embracing China and all the ten ASEAN members started from the ASEAN+3 Summit in November 2000. At the ASEAN-China Summit in November 2001, China formally raised the proposal for the formation of the CAFTA in ten years. ASEAN leaders at the meeting accepted this Chinese proposal. The Framework Agreement on ASEAN-China Comprehensive Economic Cooperation was signed at the ASEAN-

China Summit in November 2002 to establish the CAFTA. Formal talks on CAFTA started in 2003, with the year 2010 set for China and the six original ASEAN states — Brunei, Indonesia, Malaysia, the Philippines, Singapore and Thailand — and 2015 for the less developed ASEAN members of Cambodia, Laos, Myanmar and Vietnam. But an "early harvest" programme of tariff cuts on agricultural products was launched immediately.

The past decade has thus witnessed the rapid development in ASEAN-China relations. Both sides now have more in common than before though differences still exist, as indicated below. It is important to know the areas of convergence and divergence as expressed in the ASEAN-China Forum, which will be discussed in the rest of this chapter.

REGIONAL SECURITY CHALLENGES

ASEAN's Internal and External Challenges

As for ASEAN's internal security challenges, ASEAN scholars who participated in the Forum generally take the view that ASEAN countries are faced with two internal challenges: The first challenge is due to the financial crisis and globalization, which has not only economic but also social, political and even cultural dimensions. The second challenge is the pressure on the new relations among the Southeast Asian countries that have come from the expansion of ASEAN's membership from six to ten, resulting in divergent expectations within the expanded ASEAN. Chinese scholars generally believe that Southeast Asia will be largely stable, but with some potential challenges from ASEAN's economic instabilities, their domestic political and social changes, some lingering historic disputes, and threat of terrorism.

As for ASEAN's external security challenges, ASEAN scholars view potential instabilities in East Asia as coming from potential conflict across the Taiwan Straits, and nuclear proliferation in the Korean peninsula. In addition, there are new threats and challenges, that is, terrorism and the proliferation of weapons of mass destruction (WMD). What is most important in dealing with international terrorism is to raise the threshold against any attack in the future through regional and international cooperation in intelligence, policing, immigration, financial control, and sometimes among the military, when it is needed. Efforts should also be made to identify the root causes and to win the hearts and minds of the Muslim community. In the longer term, the strategic challenges to Southeast Asia will include a rising China and the evolving relationship between China and Japan and that between China and the United States.

How is the region going to cope with a rising China? Although there is no consensus among ASEAN countries about the impact of the rise of China, most of them prefer to "ride the Chinese wave" as best as they can. They have differing views on the extent to which China could become a potential "threat". One optimistic note is that China's main objective in Southeast Asia is to preserve a regional security and economic environment conducive to its domestic development and regime stability. If so, this peaceful rise of China can enhance security and stability of the Southeast Asian region.

However, the unease over China's aspirations in Southeast Asia, though more muted now than it was a decade ago, remains. Interestingly, a significant part of the unease has less to do with how China deals with the ASEAN states as it does with China's relationship with the other partners of ASEAN. China's competition with Japan over economic leadership in the region and, even more, its strategic rivalry with the United States has placed the ASEAN states in an awkward situation. Therefore, a new paradigm, for example, the formation of an East Asian Community (EAC), is needed to help bring about the rise of a responsible and peaceful China, which will be a positive development for China and the East Asian region as a whole.

As for the relationship between China and Japan, ASEAN scholars notice that Japan is becoming increasingly assertive while there has been a resurgence of Chinese nationalism. The normalization between the two powers is a condition for East Asia to make real progress towards deeper cooperation, especially in the political-security field. ASEAN can assist the normalization, especially through the process of the East Asian community-building.

As for the future relationship between China and the United States, some believe that their potential confrontation could happen while others believe that some conflicts are possible though not a full confrontation.

On the North Korean issue, ASEAN and Chinese scholars believe that it is important for both ASEAN and China to support a non-nuclear Korean peninsula.

Chinese scholars generally take an approving attitude towards regional security environment and China's relations with its East Asian neighbours, except on the Taiwan issue and China's relations with Japan, which they attribute the current difficulties to Japan's attitude on Taiwan and the historical baggage. As for its economic relations with Japan, they, while being positive in general, hope that Japan will work harder with both China and Korea as equals to promote Northeast Asian economic cooperation, which will lead to an East Asia FTA instead of intensifying the "hub and spokes" effect that will cause negative trade diversion in the region.

The Taiwan Issue

ASEAN scholars agree on the "one China" position. Taiwan should try to work within this parameter and neither Taiwan nor China should do anything that would destabilize the cross-strait situation. The Taiwan situation is potentially explosive because of the legacy of mistrust between Beijing and Taipei. The danger is that misunderstandings could lead to a possible military confrontation across the Taiwan Straits. Chen Shui-bian's administration is using "salami-style" step-by-step tactics to stealthily move Taiwan towards independence. ASEAN has a vested interest in that the cross-strait situation does not spin out of control. ASEAN can use the ARF mechanism to help reduce the regional tensions over both the Korean peninsula and the Taiwan Straits.

Chinese scholars notice that ASEAN has been playing a role, albeit a minor one, on the Taiwan issue and hope that China, ASEAN and other countries will work together to keep Taiwan from making further provocations and creeping further into independence.

U.S. Anti-Terrorist Effort in Southeast Asia

As for enhanced U.S. military presence in East Asia in the name of anti-terrorism, Chinese scholars point out that the regional security threat in Southeast Asia does not mean terrorism alone. It should also include many other non-traditional security threats, against which China and ASEAN should cooperate. They question the U.S. notion of terrorism and, in their view, the best way to deal with this threat is through multilateral cooperation. They suspect that the Bush administration is using its anti-terrorism strategy to regain U.S. dominance in Southeast Asia. They have raised three "No's", that is, the current U.S. anti-terrorist efforts in Southeast Asia should not be permanent, should not be large-scale, and should not change the current international relations in the region.

Chinese scholars notice the difference between ASEAN's multi-layered approach and the United States' military approach in dealing with regional terrorism. They point out that a successful anti-terrorism strategy requires non-traditional thinking, that is, including a focus on the socio-economic conditions that provide fertile ground for breeding terrorists. ASEAN scholars agree with this point and acknowledge that there is a need to tackle the root causes. ASEAN can help moderate Muslims to reconcile Islam with economic development and modernization. They also note that ASEAN does not have a united response to recent U.S. policy initiatives in Southeast Asia, for example, the recent U.S. proposal for external great power involvement to ensure safety in the Straits of Malacca. Similarly, there are differences among ASEAN states regarding the U.S.-led war against terrorism.

ASEAN-China Strategic Partnership for Peace and Prosperity

Many ASEAN scholars (with some exceptions) take an upbeat view of the ASEAN-China relationship. They note that ASEAN and China are tapping the opportunities and complementarities offered by each other and acting as catalyst for one another to achieve higher development goals while maintaining peace, security and stability. Chinese foreign policy has undergone changes, giving way to more pragmatic and proactive strategies. The result is more focused, nimble and engaging policy on Asia involving enhanced diplomatic, economic, and military exchanges, and increased Chinese participation in regional and multilateral mechanisms and tactical flexibility on bilateral disputes.

The signing of the Joint Declaration on the Strategic Partnership for Peace and Prosperity in Bali in 2003 has elevated the ASEAN-China relations to a new height. But the word "strategic" does not mean ASEAN and China are developing a defence alliance or a military pact. Both sides are determined not to characterize their relationship as exclusive and aimed against any particular country. It will also enable ASEAN to continue its dynamic relations with other dialogue partners, namely, Australia, Canada, the EU, India, Japan, New Zealand, the ROK, Russia and the United States.

Some Chinese scholars also take an optimistic view and have high expectations of the development of ASEAN-China relations. They stress the common interests and multilateral cooperation and would like to see stability in Southeast Asia. They support ASEAN's enlargement and believe that it will help peace and stability in the region. They hope to see further regional integration through institutionalization.

But they also point to other issues that may affect the smooth development of relations, such as the deep-rooted geopolitical perception of the "China threat", territorial disputes, economic barriers, similar exporting structures and markets, and competition for FDI.

ASEAN AND MAJOR EXTERNAL POWERS

ASEAN scholars generally take the view that ASEAN's relationship with China is increasingly becoming one of its most important strategic relations, particularly over the long term. However, its relations with Japan and the United States are equally, if not more, important at present. It is commonly perceived that ASEAN's relations with Japan and the United States are part of a strategy of balancing the increasing power of China in the region. While this concern cannot be denied, it should also be pointed out that ASEAN's relations with Japan and the United States, and certainly with China, are all part of ASEAN's self-identification as an honest broker in regional politics with the ultimate goal of maintaining peace and stability and promoting prosperity in Southeast Asia.

Chinese scholars are convinced that ASEAN's strategy is to use the competition among big powers for regional balance of power, to obtain regional security, stability and prosperity. ASEAN intends to enlarge America's and Japan's presence and influence in Southeast Asia to balance a rising China.

ASEAN-Japan Relations

ASEAN's approach towards Japan since the early 1990s has been based on two considerations, pushing for greater regional economic integration with Japan and making sure that Japan did not transform its enormous economic power into greater military capacity. But much has changed since then.

The official premise behind their current relationship is laid out in the 2003 ASEAN-Japan Plan of Action. There are three main areas of cooperation: (1) strengthening the ASEAN integration; (2) enhancing ASEAN competitiveness; and (3) cooperation against transnational issues, particularly terrorism and piracy, through institutional and human capacity building with particular emphasis on law enforcement agencies. ASEAN now accepts Japan's continued importance of economic cooperation, as always, and also its increasing prominence in security cooperation.

Any increase in economic dynamism on the part of Japan is welcomed by the ASEAN states. However, Japan is increasingly using a regional multilateral framework for its greater acceptance into the regional partnership. This is evident also in the area of security cooperation. ASEAN states have generally become more relaxed about the idea of Japan becoming a political power, even a military one. The possibility of joint patrols of the sea lanes of the Straits of Malacca involving Japanese MSDF ships have been broached, though the topic seems to be a controversial one. An overlapping concern is the possible conflict over the South China Sea and the potential Japanese involvement.

The increasing importance of Japan as a partner in regional security is one of the most important developments that revolve around ASEAN-Japan relations. While sensitivities between China and Japan make it imperative for the ASEAN states to navigate carefully their relationship with these two powers, the institutionalization of cooperative mechanisms and the support that both China and Japan have given to the process of regionalization make the work of ASEAN easier.

Chinese scholars are concerned over the Japanese expansion into the security area of Southeast Asia. For historical reasons, China is unwilling to see a re-armed Japan in Southeast Asia. China will face a new "security dilemma", if ASEAN-Japan military and security cooperation develops further.

ASEAN-U.S. Relations

The U.S.-ASEAN relationship has since 9/11 been dominated by concerns over terrorism, which call for security cooperation. The U.S. war on terror has placed the ASEAN states on a very difficult position in their relationship with the United States. While some ASEAN states value their security relationship with the United States, others, particularly those with large Muslim populations, are concerned with the adverse reactions of their citizens. Some ASEAN scholars are concerned that if the United States increases its pressure, a danger will occur to the unity of ASEAN. The rivalry between Japan and China has served indirectly to improve China-ASEAN relations, and created the push for enhancing economic institutionalization through the ASEAN+3 process. It is the relationship between the United States and ASEAN that has the greatest potential for creating problems between China and ASEAN.

U.S. relations with Taiwan, particularly the U.S. guarantee of its security, has created a clear area of conflict with China. It will be a conflict, wherein choice-making could be disastrous for ASEAN unity. The balance between China and the United States has important implications for ASEAN, which must be able to navigate between these two powers and hopefully guide them towards less confrontational situations.

ASEAN-India Relations

The economic relations between India and ASEAN increased significantly in the past decade, though, from the ASEAN's viewpoint, India's trade with ASEAN is still in its infancy. But India's thrust is not only in the economic area, but also on security issues. In the past, different security perceptions kept the two sides apart. At present, there are more similarities than differences. China and India could develop into partners as well as competitors in the economic and security arenas in Southeast Asia. ASEAN must manage the two rising powers and two other major powers, the United States and Japan, in such a way that they will complement each other and learn to respect one another.

In the view of Chinese scholars, India's effort to strengthen its relations with ASEAN is based on the following considerations: (1) for its economic growth; (2) for stability in its north-eastern region, especially in dealing with insurgency at the India-Myanmar border; (3) against terrorism; (4) to balance China's growing influence; (5) for its great power ambitions. Close India-ASEAN relations will be in the interests of ASEAN, especially in the economic field. ASEAN has benefited and will still continue to benefit much from India's "Look East" policy. Nevertheless, the "China factor" exists in nearly every development of India's "Look East" strategy, by which, India hopes to balance China and to ease the geographic and psychological pressure brought about by the warming of China-ASEAN relations. China is not alarmed by the so-called Indian challenge or India-U.S. collaboration to contain China, as it believes that India's greatest strategic challenge is from the Indian Ocean (that is, from its south), but not from the land (that is, from its north), and therefore China stand ready for diplomatic improvement and strategic cooperation with India.

ASEAN-CHINA MARITIME SECURITY COOPERATION

China is concerned over maritime security in the Straits of Malacca. Chinese scholars have raised six principles and nine forms for China-ASEAN cooperation in the regional maritime security. The six principles are (1) mutual respect;(2) mutual recognition of interests; (3) mutual trust and mutual benefit; (4) equal negotiation and coordination; (5) effectiveness; and (6) steady advancement.

The nine forms of cooperation are (1) maritime security dialogue; (2) consultation on shipping security; (3) maritime anti-terrorism operation; (4) maritime search and rescue; (5) building up maritime military communication channels; (6) marine environment protection; (7) joint law enforcement against transnational crimes; (8) joint military exercises; and (9) regional peace-keeping operations and humanitarian assistance.

In the absence of a regular formal mechanism for security dialogue and consultation, Chinese scholars support a dialogue between governments, but through Track II. ASEAN and China can consult each other on how to safeguard the safety of navigation, such as through exchange of information and technical training. China would like to make maritime anti-terrorism cooperation a major field of China-ASEAN maritime security cooperation. The two sides can, first of all, carry out substantive cooperation in such areas as anti-terrorism intelligence exchange, cooperation and coordination in handling legal cases, and deportation of suspects.

Chinese scholars also call on ASEAN cooperation to build maritime military communication channels. Maritime joint military exercises may first take search and rescue, humanitarian assistance, mine-sweeping, and cracking down on drug trafficking as its main forms, and subsequently include counter terrorism/piracy, and other maritime criminal activities. It is possible that at the request of the United Nations, the Chinese Navy will attend necessary regional peace-keeping operations especially some operations of humanitarian assistance. But ASEAN scholars seem to be concerned that China and ASEAN may not be equal partners in maritime security cooperation because of their power asymmetry. The status of U.S.-China security cooperation would be a major consideration in ASEAN's willingness to cooperate with China on maritime security.

ASEAN REGIONAL FORUM

Many ASEAN scholars take the view that the ARF should emphasize institutionalization and capacity-building, reform of organizing concepts for promoting collaborative security, norm-building, strengthening work in the "non-traditional" security sphere of security, and redressing imbalances in the ARF's security agenda. Despite some successes of the ARF, its shortfalls are also evident:

(1) It has played no significant role in managing or resolving any of the traditional conflicts afflicting the region. It has explored non-traditional security problems more extensively, but has yet to adopt any binding substantive region-wide measure.
(2) It is perceived to be less sensitive to problems in Northeast Asia.
(3) It is too slow in responding to unfolding situations.

Therefore, some ASEAN scholars have made the following proposals to strengthen the ARF:

(1) There is a need to develop ARF-dedicated institutional capacity either within the ASEAN Secretariat or outside it, with adequate capacity to undertake its responsibilities and the longer-term vision of establishing a full-fledged ARF Secretariat, led by an ASEAN national but staffed by personnel from other countries as well.
(2) The ARF should continue to be "driven" by ASEAN for the time being, until there is consensus for a co-chair system involving a non-ASEAN co-chair as well. It is suggested that the ARF start thinking about co-chairing with non-ASEAN partners.

(3) The involvement of defence and security officials in the ARF process should be further upgraded, with defence ministers and ministers responsible for internal security also attending meetings annually. Security officials should include the military and the police, and others involved in non-traditional security work as well, such as the immigration authorities.

(4) To have ARF Summits, initially informally, which can be held back-to-back with the APEC Leaders' Meetings.

(5) To adopt the new concept of cooperative and comprehensive security, in replacement of the current "realist" approach, to underpin ARF approaches to regional security.

(6) To revisit the idea of a Pacific Concord as proposed by Russia and ASEAN-ISIS, and develop a set of norms unique to the Asia-Pacific region that will draw inspiration from the universal norms as well as from the ASEAN Treaty of Amity and Cooperation.

(7) In addressing "non-traditional" security issues, ARF should acknowledge the inapplicability of the three-stage nomenclature, confidence-building, preventive diplomacy and conflict resolution, and conduct activities outside this conventional framework.

(8) A bold effort must be made to redress the imbalance in the ARF security agenda between non-proliferation of nuclear weapons and the reduction and elimination of existing nuclear weapons.

(9) Given the massive militarization underway in the region, especially on the part of the United States, it is important that the ARF address the critical issue of arms control.

However, there are reservations among other ASEAN scholars regarding the proposals, such as the setting up of an ARF Secretariat or ARF Summits. They are concerned over potential weakening of the efficiency of the ASEAN Secretariat.

Chinese scholars note that China and ASEAN have nurtured a considerable sense of common identity and share similar values. Both sides prefer the use of informal, consultative process and emphasize the importance of inclusiveness in the process of security dialogue and cooperation. The principle of mutual trust, making gradual progress, moving at a pace comfortable to all, consensus in decision-making and non-interference in the internal affairs of member states is in conformity with China's foreign and security policy. They hope that these principles will continue to guide future ARF process. The ARF, in their view, needs to address (1) security cooperation for economic development; (2) multilateral cooperation against common threats; (3) coordination and cooperation of big powers; and (4) balance between institution-building and issues-orientation.

They stress China's New Security Concept as the "foundation" for China-ASEAN cooperation in the ARF. They emphasize that the concept of threat does not mean only terrorism, but also non-traditional threats, which ARF should cover. China attaches importance to the leading role played by ARF in pushing forward regional security dialogue and cooperation. Therefore, it is against the proposal of co-chairing because ASEAN may lose its leadership and become divided. With two chairs, it is difficult to reach consensus. It hopes to see more China-ASEAN cooperation at ARF in the non-traditional security field and in gradually expanding the participation of defence officers in ARF.

CHINA-ASEAN FTA

Both ASEAN and Chinese scholars generally agree that China's economic growth is largely internally driven and can act as a driving force for economic growth of the ASEAN region. Some ASEAN scholars see China as not only a locomotive for regional economic development but also the new locomotive of the world economy, as developed countries may not be able to strive for a new source of growth so soon. China-ASEAN FTA (CAFTA) is an important vehicle in strengthening ASEAN-China economic linkages, promoting trade, investment and the trans-border flows of goods and services. While China is ready to be liberal with offers, especially in agriculture, ASEAN needs to better synchronize its moves towards the CAFTA.

ASEAN-China trade has developed rapidly. From 1990 to 2003, the average annual growth rate in trade between ASEAN and China was 20.8 per cent. The trade structure has also improved. In 1993, the top five ASEAN exports to China were oil and fuel, wood, vegetable oils and fats, computer/machinery and electrical equipment and the top five ASEAN imports from China were electrical equipment, computer/machinery, oil and fuel, cotton and tobacco. Compared with the early 1990s, the strongest growth has been in the trade of manufactured products, especially the five categories of (1) office machines and automatic data-processing machines; (2) electrical machinery, apparatus and appliances, and electrical parts; (3) tele-communications and sound-recording and reproducing apparatus and equipment; (4) petroleum, petroleum products and related materials; (5) general industrial machinery and equipment, and machine parts. The fact that these products are both the leading exports and imports of both ASEAN and China suggests the importance of intra-industry trade, brought about by product differentiation and economies of scale.

Business Opportunities from China and the CAFTA

China's GDP in 2000 was one quarter of that of Japan, and one half if calculated in PPP. Some Chinese scholars expect China's GDP to be the same as Japan's in the next ten to fifteen years. By 2003, China had bypassed Japan and the United States as the main trading partner of many countries in the East Asian region and accounted for almost one quarter of the increase in total world trade in 2003 and passed Japan as the world's third largest importer. In 2003, China accounted for 5.3 per cent of the total world import, an increase of 40 per cent over the previous year, the fastest growth rate among all the thirty leading importers. ASEAN's share in China's import increased from 6 per cent in 1991 to 11.5 per cent in 2003. China's rapid economic growth will provide opportunities for ASEAN.

It is forecast that the CAFTA, when completed, will increase ASEAN's exports to China by 48 per cent and China's exports to ASEAN by 55 per cent. However, Chinese economists believe that this forecast does not reveal their exports to the whole world markets, which the CAFTA will enhance. They are optimistic that Chinese companies' investment in ASEAN will increase with the CAFTA and encouragement by the Chinese Government.

China would like to make economic concessions to ASEAN states through the "early harvest" programme. It has been running deficits in its total trade with ASEAN. But in the "early harvest" products since 1992, except for 2000 and 2001, China had trade surpluses. If the "early harvest" programme is fully implemented, according to their simulation analysis, by 2006 China's export of "early harvest" products to ASEAN will increase by US$784–946 million, and its import from ASEAN will increase by US$838–1017 million, and China will run a trade deficit of US$125–157 million. China seems to be more politically than economically motivated and conscious of its offer of the CAFTA.

Some ASEAN scholars are concerned over China's economic attractiveness which makes ASEAN's outlook vulnerable. They cautioned that it is still too early to claim any substantive achievements out of the CAFTA. The acceptance of these Chinese overtures by the ASEAN states cannot be said to be wholehearted, but guarded, in spite of their leaders' endorsement. The economic initiatives of China cannot erase the fact that China and most of the ASEAN states are competitors in the export markets. ASEAN is concerned about Chinese competition for foreign direct investment (FDI). Although the decline of ASEAN-bound FDI has been overstated, the perception in Southeast Asia is nevertheless that FDI to China is having a "hollow out effect" and this perception has contributed to a growing sense of threat across much of the Southeast Asian region. They are also concerned that such a free trade area could create significant costs with regard to rules of origin and its administrative surveillance and implementation. This can cause more complications as different countries in ASEAN, and perhaps China, get involved in an increasing number of separate but overlapping FTAs.

THE SOUTH CHINA SEA ISSUE

ASEAN scholars generally take a positive view of the Declaration on the Conduct of Parties in the South China Sea (hereafter cited as the Declaration). Although the Declaration does not automatically prevent conflict, it nevertheless reduces the opportunities for conflict. More significantly, although the sovereignty issue remains a sticking point, some breakthroughs on the bilateral level have been made, namely, the joint development negotiations between China and the Philippines over the South China Sea (SCS), and the maritime delimitation agreement between China and Vietnam.

China is happy to see that the long-standing jurisdictional claims and territorial disputes in the South China Sea have yielded to the attention over comprehensive security in the region, tackling the non-traditional security issues such as economic and environmental security, piracy, transnational crimes, and maritime terrorism. But it feels that after the September 11 terror attacks, the SCS policy of the United States has evolved slowly but steadily from neutrality to active neutrality, and will continue to evolve into one of active concern. It might be even willing to intervene on sovereignty issues. It is concerned over the recent U.S. attempts to station troops in the Straits of Malacca. Chinese strategists are also studying the implications of the increasing security role by both Japan and India in the SCS.

China pays special attention to the Declaration, which provides ASEAN and China with a formal framework for understanding and cooperation on the SCS issue and serves as a safety valve. China has no problem in making it legally binding, that is, to have a code of conduct rather than simply a declaration as it is now. However, some ASEAN countries are unwilling to develop the Declaration into a code of conduct.

The Chinese scholars criticize the continued sporadic actions and counter-actions taken by the claimants to bolster their respective maritime jurisdictional claims to the disputed islands and waters in the SCS. They have strong views over the recent event of Vietnam organizing boat tours to Spratlys Islands. They call it an open violation of the spirit and letter of the Declaration, poisoning the current understanding and cooperation between ASEAN and China. They emphasize that since China signed the Declaration, not with Vietnam but with ASEAN as a group, such a violation by Vietnam should be seen as a group violation by ASEAN as a whole. They call for the establishment of a review mechanism for the implementation of the Declaration.

ASEAN scholars notice that the SCS dispute was once a source of worry, but has since improved significantly with the signing of the Declaration. However, the current bilateral confidence-building measures still fall short in preventing unilateral activities from taking place. There have been multilateral ASEAN-China efforts to defuse tensions, but the progress has been rather slow. ASEAN claimants have not been able to sustain solidarity on the matter of how to deal with China on the SCS issue. For that matter, tensions among the ASEAN claimants have also surfaced occasionally, such as between the Philippines and Vietnam, the Philippines and Malaysia, and Malaysia and Vietnam.

Some ASEAN scholars urge the parties to push forward the process beyond confidence-building into the next stage of preventive diplomacy, eventually paving the way for claimants to explore together cooperative approaches to the management of the sea and its resources. But they also point out that the construction of a true and lasting peace between China and ASEAN over the SCS must proceed by building on what little progress that has already been made, moving with patience but with persistence to achieve "peace by pieces".

ASEAN+3 AND EAST ASIAN COOPERATION

ASEAN and Chinese scholars are studying and promoting the process of ASEAN+3 and East Asia integration. In their view, there are three models for East Asia integration: (1) FTAs (knitting or weaving a web of existing FTAs together in the region to create a huge East Asian Free Trade Area; (2) Japan savings-based; and (3) China-centred economic integration.

ASEAN scholars argue that with the shift from "flying geese" to "bamboo capitalism", the Japanese model of regional integration is now called into question as production networks have expanded horizontally and as the social dimension has increased in the East Asian economic model. As the state-led and SME-led East Asian models converge, the social dimension is again highlighted, especially in post-SARS Asia today. It appears therefore that the East Asian model is fast integrating the social dimension into its economic model, thus reducing the influence of the "pure" U.S. model, based solely on productivity and shareholders' value. The ultimate economic integration model for East Asia, or a combination of all three integrative models in varying doses and degrees, will also need a firm social dimension. Otherwise, Asian socio-economic development, given its traditional communal base, will not be truly sustainable in the long run. Given these factors, China and ASEAN can play key roles in shaping this integrative economic model.

The strategic convergence of interests between ASEAN and China is obvious at this stage, thus guaranteeing their respective key roles in "driving" ASEAN+3 forward, at least in the foreseeable future.

ASEAN needs ASEAN+3 for the following strategic objectives:

- A bigger and more diversified market for ASEAN to stimulate growth;
- A new challenge for "laggard" countries within ASEAN to enhance their own national competitiveness through reforms *via* a bigger and liberalized market;
- A new impetus in crisis and HRD management;
- To absorb a great power such as China in a regional institution and therefore strengthening the new paradigm of the peaceful rise of China;
- To assist in the normalization of China-Japan relations and make the East Asian region much more conducive for peace and stability; and
- To prevent, in the longer term, a China-U.S. confrontation.

On the other hand, China realizes that it needs a peaceful regional environment and external stability in order to concentrate on its own development and has therefore supported the ASEAN initiative of creating a viable ASEAN+3 to "balance" America and Europe. China needs ASEAN, as much as ASEAN needs China, in their respective developments. In fact, this mutual convergence of interests constitutes China's and ASEAN's driving force for ASEAN+3 as East Asia's emerging regionalism. This driving force of "mutual interests" should propel ASEAN+3 forward as the main pillar of East Asian regionalism.

Both ASEAN and China realize that while market forces will remain fundamental in bringing about a *de facto* East Asian Community, it is the exercise of political will and a real sense of community and commonality in East Asia that will actualize a "common East Asian house". An East Asian Community can be based on the principles of mutual benefit, trust, and common interests and supported by three pillars: political will, active involvement of the business community, and engagement of civil society.

However, differences also exist here. Chinese scholars would like to see greater institutionalization of this regional economic integration in order to avoid another APEC-like forum in Asia. While some ASEAN scholars take a similar approach and even call for accelerating the process of ASEAN+3 into an earlier and institutionalized East Asian Community, other ASEAN scholars, out of the concern that ASEAN may lose its driver's seat in a premature acceleration, prefer to maintain a gradual and long-term process of ASEAN+3.

CONCLUDING REMARKS

This chapter provides a brief overview of the rapid development of ASEAN-China relations since the early 1990s and concludes that ASEAN and China have now established a promising strategic partnership ensuring the peace, stability, cooperation as well as prosperity of the region. New challenges will, however, continue to emerge to test the resolve of the partnership. It is important for ASEAN and China to understand the new challenges and take them in their stride as they move forward. In this respect, the discussion of the possible trajectories of the development of ASEAN-China relations, and the assessments and proposals from both ASEAN countries and China presented in this book, are most timely and important.

2

Securing a Win–Win Partnership for ASEAN and China

Ong Keng Yong

INTRODUCTION

Let me begin by defining the word "win-win partnership" in the context of ASEAN-China dialogue relations. As the Chinese saying goes, "benevolent government and friendship with neighbouring countries are the good fortune of a country", ASEAN and China are tapping the opportunities and complementarities offered by each other and acting as catalyst for one another to achieve higher development goals while maintaining peace, security and stability crucial for economic growth and prosperity. It means forging substantive cooperation based on the principles of mutual trust, respect, equality and mutual gains to create conditions that will benefit the people of both regions. The Joint Declaration on Strategic Partnership between ASEAN and China signed by the leaders of ASEAN and China in October 2003 called for the securing of such a partnership in the political and security, economic, social and cultural, and regional and international cooperation fields.

REPOSITIONING CHINESE POLICY *VIS-À-VIS* ASEAN

ASEAN-China relations in the last decade have not always been easy. In fact, the relationship has seen its ups and downs. Before ties between ASEAN and China were formally established in 1991, they were marked by mutual suspicion, mistrust and animosity largely because of China's support for the communist parties in ASEAN countries.

The normalization of relations with China in 1990 by Indonesia and then Singapore and Brunei Darussalam acted as a catalyst to set the path for China's admission into the ASEAN Regional Forum (ARF) in 1994 and eventually the granting of ASEAN dialogue partnership in 1996. Since then, the partnership grew from strength to strength resulting in the expansion and deepening of cooperation in the economic, political and security, social and cultural and development cooperation areas.

My Chinese friends have often said to me, "a close neighbour means more than a distant relative". ASEAN recognized that it would have to work with China, its most populous neighbour in East Asia, to address the issues and challenges in the region.

On the other hand, China was receptive to the friendly initiatives of ASEAN. This was largely due to the reorientation that the Chinese foreign policy went through. The Chinese foreign policy underwent changes giving way to more pragmatic and proactive strategies. The result is a more focused, nimble and engaging policy on Asia involving enhanced diplomatic, economic, and military exchanges; increased Chinese participation in regional and multilateral mechanisms (APEC, ACD, FEALAC); and tactical flexibility on bilateral disputes.

This Asia policy is premised on the "calculative strategy" of China to build a strong foundation for a vibrant and modern state. The key elements of this strategy are to promote market economy for economic growth, to refrain from the use of force while pursuing military modernization, and to expand international political influence. At the same time, China generally avoids explicit competition with the United States or its allies, notably Japan.

STRENGTHENING ASEAN-CHINA COOPERATION

Even though ASEAN-China cooperation was formalized in 1996, substantive cooperation only picked up pace in 2001 when the leaders of ASEAN and China endorsed a proposal for a framework on economic cooperation and to establish a free trade area (FTA) in ten years as well as identified five priority areas to move cooperation. This was in the areas of agriculture, information technology, human resource development (HRD), mutual investments and Mekong cooperation.

Political and Security

In the political and security realm, China is an active participant in the ARF. It is also a key member of many of the regional processes that ASEAN has been instrumental in initiating, particularly the ASEAN+3 process.

ASEAN and China have concluded a number of agreements ensuring the peace and security of the region and establishing a tranquil regional environment to pursue economic development. ASEAN and China signed the Declaration on the Conduct (DOC) of Parties in the South China Sea in November 2002 in Cambodia, which signalled the mutual desire to promote trust and confidence to establish a regional code of conduct in the area. Discussions will be intensified in the coming months between ASEAN and China to move forward the implementation of the declaration.

ASEAN and China concluded a Memorandum of Understanding (MOU) in the Field of Non-Traditional Security Issues in November 2002 in Cambodia, which sets the stage for substantive cooperation in the field of combating transnational crime, including terrorism, drug trafficking, sea piracy and trafficking in persons. An annual plan to implement the declaration was agreed to by both sides in January 2004 and efforts are underway to implement concrete cooperation activities.

In 2003, a milestone was achieved in ASEAN-China relations, when China became the first Dialogue Partner to accede to ASEAN's Treaty of Amity and Cooperation (TAC) in Southeast Asia. By acceding to the TAC, China provided further reassurance to the peace and security of the region and for the treaty to become eventually a code for inter-state relations in the region. China is now keen to sign with ASEAN the Protocol to the Treaty on Southeast Asia Nuclear Weapon Free Zone (SEANWFZ).

Another milestone was the signing of the Joint Declaration on the Strategic Partnership for Peace and Prosperity in Bali last year. This formal document elevated the ASEAN-China relations to new height: we are now partners. An extended range of activities will bring ASEAN and China closer and more substantively. Both sides are now working on a five-year plan of action to implement the declaration.

Economic

ASEAN-China cooperation in the economic field has grown rapidly since the signing of the Framework Agreement on Comprehensive Economic

Cooperation in November 2002. Both sides have targeted to realize the Free Trade Area in 2010 for the ASEAN-6 and 2015 for Cambodia, Laos, Myanmar and Vietnam. The "early harvest" plan under the FTA commenced in January 2004. Negotiations for the trade in goods component of the ASEAN-China Free Trade Area are expected to be concluded by end June 2004. The negotiations for services, investment, and the dispute settlement mechanism (DSM) have commenced.

Trade between ASEAN and China had grown by double digits since 1995. In 2003 alone, it grew by 43 per cent to a new high of US$78.2 billion in which China imported US$47.3 billion from ASEAN, which is a 50 per cent increase. ASEAN and China are targeting to hit the US$100 billion mark in two-way trade by 2005 and this benchmark seems achievable given the current dynamics in the ASEAN-China trade ties.

Bilateral trade cooperation between ASEAN countries and China is intensifying. For example, Thailand and China had initiated a zero tariff for vegetables and fruits in October 2003 through the China-Thailand Early Harvest Programme Acceleration Agreement resulting in a 143 per cent increase for Thai exports to China. Thailand is now actively pushing for zero tariff for fish and milk products for 2004 and industrial products for 2005.

Similar trends are witnessed in bilateral investments between ASEAN and China. In 1999, two years after the financial crisis, total foreign direct investment (FDI) into ASEAN from China stood at US$78 million and this has doubled to US$150 million in 2001. The potential for the inflow of Chinese investments is promising due to the Chinese Government's policy of encouraging its businesses to go global with priority given to its neighbouring countries. On the other hand, ASEAN continues to be an even more important source of FDI for China. In 2003, contractual FDI flows into China amounted to US$6.5 billion and the actual paid-up capital was US$2.9 billion. By the end of 2003, accumulated contractual FDI from ASEAN was US$64.3 billion and the actual paid-up capital was US$32.3 billion.

Development Cooperation

Development cooperation with China now covers an expanded and intensified number of areas, apart from the five priority areas mentioned earlier. These include science and technology, tourism, public health, youth, and culture. MOUs have been concluded in the areas of agriculture, non-traditional security issues and information and communications technology. More are being planned, including one in transport cooperation and another in cultural cooperation. More than forty projects have been implemented since 1999 supported by the ASEAN-China Cooperation Fund.

China continues to assist ASEAN in narrowing the development gaps through the Initiative for ASEAN Integration and other sub-regional programmes such as the Mekong Basin cooperation and the Brunei Darussalam-Indonesia-Malaysia-Philippines East ASEAN Growth Area (BIMP-EAGA).

SECURING A WIN-WIN STRATEGIC PARTNERSHIP

What do we mean by securing a strategic partnership in the context of the ASEAN-China dialogue relations? Some may say that "strategic" means ASEAN and China are developing a defence alliance or a military pact. Let me assure you that this is not what both sides are looking for. Both sides are determined not to characterize their relationship as exclusive and aimed against any particular country. It is and will be based on trust, understanding, neighbourliness and a mutually beneficial and comprehensive partnership premised on the underlying philosophy of "prosper thy neighbour", a notion very much shared by the leaders of ASEAN and China.

Why do ASEAN and China need to develop a strategic partnership? I cannot speak for China. For ASEAN, we see ASEAN and China as part of a contiguous geographical landscape in East Asia. China shares common borders with ASEAN and has historical and cultural linkages with many ASEAN countries. Both face similar challenges and opportunities and share aspirations, as developing countries, to achieve economic prosperity and higher living standards for their people. At the same time, they want to tackle the emerging transnational issues, which may have an adverse impact on their economy and society. Putting it another way, ASEAN and China must co-exist and share the responsibility of making our region a better place and be better global citizens.

Most analysts have forecasted that ASEAN will grow by 5–6 per cent a year up to 2008 with Vietnam tipped to be the fastest growing with a 7 per cent annual expansion. The Chinese economy is expected to grow between 8 and 9 per cent. Thus, there is a huge potential to tap. Our "prosper thy neighbour" philosophy is not based on an illusion.

China is weighing more and more on the world economy. Let us review some facts and figures. China is now the fourth largest trading nation in the world. With the accession of China into the WTO, its share of foreign trade in 2003 was almost 5 per cent of world trade or about US$620 billion. In terms of FDI, China now receives more than two-thirds of all FDI flowing into East Asia compared to the beginning of the 1990s. It is predicted that FDI will reach an annual utilized rate of US$100 billion in 2005. In international finance, China has become a major player, as it possesses more foreign exchange reserves than any country, except Japan. It is a creditor to the U.S. holding billions of dollars in U.S. government securities.

ASEAN has been watching the developments in China and has taken the prudent step of engaging China instead of treating it as a competitor. While China is a competitor in one sense, it also shares complementarities with ASEAN, which have to be capitalized by both sides. At the same time, ASEAN's services industry is developing faster than that of China, and therefore could help to support the Chinese economic boom. If Saudi Arabia is for oil and Brazil for coffee, China is certainly the world's factory and ASEAN can be the service support for this global factory.

How to take this partnership between ASEAN and China forward? I have six proposals to share with this ASEAN-China Forum.

One, ASEAN and China will have to intensify cooperation in the political and security arena, starting with cooperation in less sensitive non-traditional security issues while building confidence in sensitive areas. For example, the implementation of the DOC in the South China Sea. Also, ASEAN and China should implement the annual plan to implement the MOU on cooperation in non-traditional security issues without further delay.

There should also be a conscious effort to promote security dialogue so that both sides can understand each other's positions on issues of common interest in the region and in the world. ASEAN should use the opportunity to encourage China to play a more active role in regional issues through existing multilateral processes. China, being a strategic partner of ASEAN and a permanent member of the UN Security Council could help to represent the views and concerns of ASEAN to a wider audience.

China is a key player in the Six-Party Talks and it could use the ARF to discuss issues concerned. The DPRK is also in the ARF.

Second, ASEAN and China should continue to promote high-level exchanges and visits and people-to-people contacts. This is crucial to develop a better understanding among government leaders, top policymakers, bankers, and bureaucrats as well as experts in the various fields. As for people-to-people contacts, tourists, students, and general workers from China have already started to fan out in Southeast Asia bringing about new opportunities and revenue for ASEAN countries. Promising youths from ASEAN must also be given more opportunities to study and stay in China to better understand the "friendly giant" so that a crop of future leaders who are well versed in China, not only in terms of language but the mindset and nuances, will be ready to further the mutually beneficial partnership.

Both sides should strengthen the soft side of cooperation such as arts and culture. The "soft power" will provide the gel to bring ASEAN and China even closer together, which will be necessary to building a sustainable partnership as ASEAN and China enhance their relations in a comprehensive manner. This could include the promotion of arts and culture, cuisine, cinema, curios, calligraphy, acupuncture, herbal medicine and fashion fads.

Third, ASEAN and China should place emphasis on strengthening the economic partnership by keeping within the timelines for the realization of the FTA and ensuring that a high standard FTA, covering not only commodities but also services and investments, is achieved to serve as a benchmark for other FTAs being negotiated in the Asia-Pacific region. Both sides should be flexible and accommodating in the negotiations towards the FTA due to the different levels of economic development and readiness of ASEAN countries to embrace the FTA. Creative ways to resolve outstanding issues in the negotiations should be considered.

China can do more in terms of investments into ASEAN. The flow of FDI from China is low compared to the size of its economy. In terms of investments, the EU, the United States, and Japan continue to be the top three investors in ASEAN. China could invest in the manufacturing sector in ASEAN as well as the services sector since the services industry in ASEAN is more mature, and will be able to support the buoyant manufacturing sector in China and the overall Chinese economy. Clustering of industries between ASEAN and China could also be considered to tap on the comparative advantages in manufacturing or undertaking certain services with the participation of the private sector. This will provide a wider choice of goods and services at competitive prices, which will benefit the consumers from ASEAN and China.

Fourth, ASEAN and China cannot ignore the deepening cooperation in addressing transnational issues such as combating terrorism, communicable diseases, trafficking in drugs and women and children, and protecting the environment.

Fifth, ASEAN and China should increase the collaboration in helping ASEAN integrate. China's prominent participation in the Initiative for ASEAN Integration (IAI) will be inspiring and catalytic. When ASEAN narrows the gaps in national development, a bigger market for Chinese goods and services will consolidate. China could be actively involved as a strategic partner in supporting the successor plan to the Hanoi Plan of Action to implement the ASEAN Vision 2020 to be adopted by the ASEAN leaders this November in the Vientiane Summit.

Finally, ASEAN and China should work towards the realization of the East Asian community in the long run by actively driving the ASEAN+3 process with Japan and the Republic of Korea (ROK). Implementing the East

Asia Study Group's seventeen short-term measures by 2006 will be crucial as well as strengthening the sectoral cooperation in the fields of monetary and finance cooperation, energy, public health and so on. Both sides should also start looking at possible ways to implement the other nine medium- to long-term measures. This will not only help to speed up East Asian cooperation but also bring China closer to Japan and the ROK.

The initiation of a tripartite cooperation among China, Japan and the ROK, as a part of East Asian cooperation last year in Bali through their joint declaration, had helped to generate new momentum in cooperation among them. The "Plus Three" countries could use the new momentum to come together and implement joint activities with ASEAN to assist in ASEAN's economic integration and narrowing the development gaps crucial for promoting greater East Asian economic integration. Perhaps, as a start, the "Plus Three" countries could pool their resources in implementing more IAI projects.

ENSURING A GREAT FUTURE

ASEAN and China have established a more fruitful partnership ensuring the peace and stability as well prosperity of the region. However, new challenges and problems are emerging that will continue to test the resolve of the partnership. ASEAN and China should take them in their stride as they move forward together in the new millennium. The challenges may have an impact on the cooperation but both sides will steadily endeavour for the common good, as wise friends from China would say: "Be not afraid of growing slowly, be only afraid of standing still."

As you can see, there is so much in the ASEAN-China partnership. But the one essential element for this partnership to endure and be even more mutually beneficial is to ensure a healthy and open environment where ASEAN is able to continue its dynamic relations with other dialogue partners, namely Australia, Canada, the EU, India, Japan, New Zealand, the ROK, Russia and the USA. This is especially so since ASEAN continues to be an outward-looking organization and inclusive in its approach to economic cooperation and external relations. The strengthening of relations with the ASEAN dialogue partners will secure a peaceful, prosperous and vibrant Southeast Asia.

3

China's Peaceful Development and Relations with its East Asian Neighbours

Cai Bingkui

CHINA'S PEACEFUL DEVELOPMENT

China adheres to the road of peaceful development. It will take full advantage of the good opportunity that world peace affords to develop and strengthen itself, and at the same time safeguard world peace with its development.

China's development will be mainly based on its own strength and self-reliance, the vast domestic market, rich human resources, abundant accumulation of capital as well as the systematic innovation triggered by reform.

China's development could not be achieved without the rest of the world. China adheres to its opening-up policy and develops economic and trade exchanges with other countries on the basis of equality and mutual benefit so as to realize common prosperity.

China's development will require a very long time. Though China's GDP already ranks sixth and its total import and export trade volume ranks fourth in the world, China's per capita GDP is only a little over US$1,000, ranking behind the hundredth in the world. It requires long-term and unremitting efforts of probably several generations for China to realize its goal to rise.

China's rise will definitely bring positive impact on the peace, stability and development of Asia and the world. It will not create obstacles or threats to anybody. China unswervingly pursues an independent foreign policy of peace, adheres to the Five Principles of Peaceful Co-Existence and advocates a new security concept featuring mutual trust, mutual benefit, equality and coordination. It does not seek hegemony now, nor will it seek hegemony even after it becomes powerful in the future.

CHINA'S POLICY OF GOOD-NEIGHBOURLINESS AND FRIENDSHIP

China's development requires a sound peripheral environment.

China persists in building a good neighbourly relationship and partnership with its neighbours. It has formulated a basic framework of developing relations with its neighbouring countries in the new century by the establishment of various types of partnership.

The Chinese Government has always attached great importance to confidence-building measures with neighbouring countries and has worked hard for their adoption. It has energetically advocated the conclusion of border treaties or agreements through talks and consultations with the parties concerned, so as to safeguard equal security for all parties, and for regional peace and stability. The relevant government departments and frontier forces of China have faithfully implemented the stipulations of the treaties and agreements, and actively promoted exchanges and cooperation with their counterparts in the neighbouring countries. They have dealt with boundary affairs in a timely manner and cracked down on illegal activities in the border areas together with their counterparts through communication and consultation mechanisms, and frontier talks and meetings.

It is a component part of China's policy of good-neighbourliness and friendship to conduct multilateral dialogue and cooperation with Asian countries. China is extensively involved in the various mechanisms of Asia-based regional cooperation, makes its efforts to promote regional economic integration and conducts security dialogue in various forms. It has worked hard to boost the formation and development of the Shanghai Cooperation Organization (SCO). It has taken an active part in the activities of "Boao Forum for Asia" and the Asian Cooperation Dialogue (ACD) foreign ministers' informal meeting. It has supported and participated in the ASEAN Regional Forum (ARF), Conference on Interaction and Confidence-Building Measures in Asia (CICA), Council on Security Cooperation in the Asia-Pacific Region (CSCAP) and other activities for multilateral security dialogue and cooperation. During the recent year

China has made its important contributions to the successful tripartite and Six-Party Talks on the nuclear issue in the Korean peninsula.

CHINA'S RELATIONS WITH ITS EAST ASIAN NEIGHBOURS

Since it came into being, ASEAN-China "Ten+1" cooperation mechanism has developed rapidly. In the political and security field, the Declaration on the Conduct of Parties in the South China Sea and Joint Declaration on Cooperation in the Non-traditional Fields were successively signed. With China's formal accession to the Treaty of Amity and Cooperation in Southeast Asia in 2003, the political and legal basis of China-ASEAN relations is strengthened. In the same year, China became ASEAN's first strategic partner, marking a new stage of the bilateral relations. That was the first time for China to sign a document on establishing strategic partnership with a regional organization. China has been taking an active part in the ARF process and supporting ASEAN to play the leading role in the forum. In the economic and trade field, the Framework Agreement of China and ASEAN on the Comprehensive Economic Cooperation signed in 2002 marks a new historical stage of the economic and trade cooperation between the two sides. The China-ASEAN Free Trade Agreement to be ready in 2010 will encompass the most populated economic area in the world with 1.7 billion consumers.

In October 2003, the leaders of China, Japan and the Republic of Korea (ROK) signed the Joint Declaration on the Promotion of Tripartite Cooperation on China's initiative, which formulated a basic framework and orientation for the cooperation. Since the establishment of diplomatic ties in 1992, cooperation between China and ROK has achieved much progress in all fields with fruitful results. The annual trade volume between the two countries has increased from US$5 billion in 1992 to more than US$60 billion in 2003, and will reach US$100 billion within next five years as a set goal. China is devoted to constant deepening of the Sino-ROK partnership of comprehensive cooperation in the new century, and to realization of their common prosperity. Sino-Japanese relations are generally good. Since the normalization of diplomatic ties between the two countries, exchanges in political, economic, cultural and other fields have increased. The annual trade volume exceeded US$130 billion in 2003. At the same time, there exist some problems for bilateral relations. The Japanese side should respect China's stand and reasonable proposition on the questions of Taiwan, history, etc. and abide by the three political documents concerning bilateral ties, take history as a mirror and face the future, and push forward Sino-Japanese relations of friendship and cooperation with actual deeds.

The Sino-Russian relations have gained momentum. The Sino-Russian Good-Neighbourly and Friendly Cooperation Treaty signed in 2001 has laid a solid legal foundation for the long-term and stable development of the relations between the two countries and marks a new stage of development in the Sino-Russia strategic cooperation partnership. The political mutual trust has consistently deepened, the economic and trade relations rapidly developed and the consultation and coordination in international affairs become closer.

China also maintains good relations with the Democratic People's Republic of Korea (DPRK) and Mongolia. There exists traditional friendship between China and DPRK. It is the firm and consistent policy of the Chinese Government to develop relations of friendly cooperation with DPRK. The two sides keep close and friendly exchanges, and maintain sound cooperation in the fields of economy, trade and culture, and on regional and international issues. China and Mongolia share a common boundary of more than 4,600 kilometres. During the recent years the two sides have made concerted efforts for developing partnership of good neighbourliness and mutual confidence on the basis of mutual respect, mutual understanding and mutual trust, which have yielded fruitful results.

China's peaceful development and its maintaining relations of good neighbourliness and friendship with the East Asian neighbours are conducive to the progress of East Asian regional cooperation with "Ten+3" as its main channel, to the integral development of East Asia as well as to the peace and stability of the region.

4

Strengthening Cooperation in the ASEAN Regional Forum: An ASEAN View

Mohamed Jawhar Hassan

INTRODUCTION

The ASEAN Regional Forum (ARF) is now a decade old. During this period it has not progressed much beyond Stage One, namely, the promotion of confidence-building measures. It has begun to discuss preventive diplomacy, but has not developed or implemented any. As for Stage Three, the development of conflict-resolution measures, the ARF has even decided to be more cautious, renaming it "elaboration of mechanisms for conflict settlement". Ten years into its formation, it is perhaps fair to note that the ARF is at a stage where it is deeply engaged in confidence-building, and is testing the ground for preventive diplomacy.

Assessing the ARF's record through the nomenclature of confidence-building, preventive diplomacy and elaboration of mechanisms for conflict settlement, however, does not do justice to the substantive preliminary work done by the ARF in the fields of counter-terrorism especially, but also on maritime security and transnational crime. Lumping this work under the terminology of "confidence-building" or "preventive diplomacy" just to conform to conventional ARF ideology is both largely erroneous as well as doing an injustice to the work done. This aspect will be discussed further below.

To some, especially those in the non-government sector, this progress in the ARF has been slow. To others, particularly government officials engaged in the process, the progress has been satisfactory although they concede that more needs to be done. Criticism regarding the slowness of the ARF which was initially expressed by officials from some Western countries has since abated, perhaps because they are more sanitized now of the complexities involved in the ARF, and perhaps also because they are relatively satisfied with the numerous activities that are being done by the ARF.

This chapter focuses on some of the areas where the ARF could be strengthened, areas where ASEAN and China could perhaps work together to advance the mission and agenda of the ARF further. It begins with a discussion of some of the factors that need to be borne in mind when considering the subject, followed by an assessment of the achievements and shortfalls of the ARF to-date.

STRATEGIC FACTORS IMPINGING UPON ARF'S DEVELOPMENT

These may be summarized as follows:

1. The members of the ARF have some widely diverging security perspectives and interests. They also have different political and security cultures. There is much greater congruence in the political and security cultures of Europe, especially Western Europe for instance, than in the Asia-Pacific. These differences need to be recognized and catered to by the ARF. The situation requires flexibility and maximum accommodation, especially in the initial stages when the ARF process is still in the delicate formative phase. Pushing the ARF too hard and too fast in one direction or the other may cause severe stresses, and some countries may find their continued participation untenable.

2. The Third ARF Meeting in July 1996 confined the "geographical footprint" of the ARF for key activities to Northeast Asia, Southeast Asia and Oceania. The footprint does not include the United States (and Canada). This is unfortunate for various reasons. It does not conform to the realities of the strategic environment, where the United States is an important and integral player. The U.S. is a key part of the

equation, a major protagonist, in several of the most critical security issues confronting the region, including the Korean problem, cross-strait issues, terrorism and WMD. The greatest matter for security concern in the region is in fact Sino-American relations, and this cannot be addressed by merely looking at one of the players; the policies of the U.S. need to be scrutinized too.

Confining the footprint to the countries of East Asia and Oceania also tends to make them the "object" of security deliberations that involve other participating states. This situation makes some of the "subject" countries sensitive and wary to perceived intrusion and "management" by outside powers. There is no reciprocity, and the situation is not conducive to equal relationships.

3. There is no powerful defining and overarching conflict involving the Asia-Pacific countries like the Cold War in Europe, that impelled both sides to come together to construct a strong and institutionalized common security mechanism in the form of the CSCE/OSCE to manage and contain conflict between them. In the Asia-Pacific there is no such powerful impulsion. The region instead has a number of essentially localized conventional security problems like the Korean and the South China Sea issues and some common non-traditional security concerns like international terrorism and lethal contagious diseases that do not carry the same weight for all members as the Cold War did in Europe.

4. There are a number of essentially bilateral disputes especially with regard to territory that the states concerned feel no particular compulsion or usefulness to submit to a regional multilateral mechanism for resolution. The option of the International Court of Justice also makes recourse to a regional alternative less compelling.

5. There are several bilateral mechanisms for security management among many countries to address essentially bilateral problems that reduces the worth and relevance of multilateral mechanisms.

6. On the other hand, there are also several overarching matters of regional security concern, even if this concern is not overwhelming, that make a pan-regional process useful and beneficial. The Korean and South China Sea issues, though essentially localized, are of great security interest to the regional community as a whole. Non-traditional security problems like

AIDS, SARS, illicit drugs, international terrorism and transnational crime also benefit from a region-wide cooperative security process.

7. Suspicion and lack of trust is still a marked feature in the region, a legacy of past bitter conflicts as well as ongoing disputes in some cases. This is particularly so in the case of the states of Northeast Asia and between the United States on the one hand and North Korea and China on the other. This situation makes confidence-building initiatives still exceedingly relevant and important for the region.

8. Many weaker developing countries that recently emerged from colonial bondage and occupation are sensitive and jealous about their hard-won sovereignty, and are concerned about intrusion by the big powers. They are also hesitant about giving too much authority to the ARF. A similar reluctance also exists in the U.S., which still prefers unilateral space and relies heavily upon its bilateral alliances.

9. China is concerned that the ARF process will be used by the U.S. and like-minded states to contain her and intervene in disputes that involve her fundamental interests, such as the cross-straits problem and Tibet.

THE ARF ASSESSED

Although the ARF has a number of shortcomings, its worth and achievements to-date should not be underestimated. The achievements include the following:

1. It has been able to assemble under a single security umbrella not only the United States and China, two large powers not too well disposed towards the constraints of multilateral processes, but also the entire Asia-Pacific community of major, middle and lesser powers. It has also successfully engaged two major out-of-region entities, India and the European Union. That the ARF has been able to do this despite the fact that many of these countries have divergent and sometimes conflicting security perceptions and interests, adds to the ARF's success.

2. A habit of consultation and dialogue essential to confidence- and trust-building has been successfully fostered over the years. This consultation and dialogue has recently extended into some sensitive and domestic areas as well, such as Myanmar, Indonesia, the Korean peninsula and the South China Sea as comfort levels have grown.

3. Some CBM measures like the Annual Security Outlook are already being implemented. In addition, the forum through its many ISG and ISM events, seminars, workshops and other meetings has delved into several substantive areas of potential security cooperation. These include new measures for "CBM" such as regional cooperation on maritime security, coordination and cooperation in search and rescue, peacekeeping, disaster relief and counter-terrorism.

4. The ARF has established a register of experts and eminent persons, and procedures will soon be adopted regarding the utilisation of this resource for preventive diplomacy and conflict resolution.

5. Moves are afoot to engage military officials more directly and extensively in the ARF process.

SHORTFALLS

Some of these are as follows:

1. The ARF has not been able to progress much beyond the confidence-building stage. It has played no significant role in managing or resolving any of the traditional conflicts afflicting the region. It has explored non-traditional security problems more extensively, but has yet to adopt any binding substantive region-wide measure.

2. There is a great institution deficit in the ARF process. There is no full-fledged ARF Secretariat to support and organize the many ARF activities.

3. Though the annual ARF meetings never fail to reiterate their support for ASEAN's leading role in the forum, some members, especially those from the West and some Track Two organizations, question ASEAN's ability to "drive" the ARF, or prefer to see the process at least co-chaired by a non-ASEAN country. Some also allege that the ASEAN-driven process is less sensitive to problems in Northeast Asia.

4. The ARF is perceived to be too slow in responding to unfolding situations, because it is not organized or equipped to respond in a more timely fashion.

PROPOSALS

This chapter highlights the following proposals for strengthening the ARF and cooperation within it. A number of these subjects (though not all) have also been discussed in the forums organized by the ARF and by others such as ASEAN-ISIS and CSCAP, and some of the points below are more in the nature of this author's commentary upon them.

1. There is a need to build an ARF-dedicated institutional capacity either within the ASEAN Secretariat or outside it. ASEAN and the ARF have already agreed to the establishment of an ARF Unit in the ASEAN Secretariat. The ARF should ensure that the unit is provided adequate capacity to undertake its responsibilities. In the longer term a full-fledged ARF Secretariat should be established, led by an ASEAN national but staffed by personnel from other countries as well. This is considered a necessary measure if the ARF is to shoulder and expand its already heavy responsibilities. The engagement of personnel from non-ASEAN member states will both help enrich capacity in the ARF Secretariat as well as enhance the sense of shared ownership among them.

2. The ARF should continue to be "driven" by ASEAN for the time being, until there is consensus for a co-chair system involving a non-ASEAN co-chair as well. This position is not only supported by ASEAN but by China as well. "Driven" is actually a misleading word, for non-ASEAN members have a healthy share of the ideas that drive the ARF, and they also share in the leadership of the ISGs, ISMs, workshops and seminars organized by the ARF.

3. The involvement of defence and security officials in the ARF process should be further upgraded, with defence ministers and ministers responsible for internal security also meeting annually. Security officials should include not only the military and the police, but also others involved in non-traditional security work such as the immigration authorities.

4. In the medium term (three to five years), the ARF should also think about organizing ARF Summits, initially informally. They could be held back-to-back with the APEC Leaders' Meetings.

5. Far from being the best option for maintaining inter-state security, the so-called "realist" approach to inter-state security with its heavy emphasis on the development and utilization of military power has actually brought untold and repeated suffering to humankind. The relevance of the military

instrument has been further undermined by rapid globalization and economic interdependence, where the security of states has become increasingly common and intertwined. An adversarial approach is becoming increasingly untenable and costly. Resting essentially on the rationale of an anarchic international environment, it encourages especially the militarily strong with a vested interest in perpetuating the system to constrain the development of a strong law-based international order with strong international security institutions, thereby fortifying the self-serving and self-fulfilling rationale.

The region and the world are in need of an alternative doctrine that is more relevant to the evolving global environment. Responding to this challenge, CSCAP in its Memorandum No. 3 (The Concepts of Comprehensive Security and Cooperative Security) has advocated the concept of cooperative and comprehensive security, where security is perceived in comprehensive terms and is best advanced through cooperative means. It is proposed that the ARF task Track II institutions like CSCAP to carry out a dispassionate study of the relevance and benefits or otherwise of the so-called "realist" approach to international relations and inter-state security in the current context, and similarly undertake an objective study on the feasibility of the region adopting and pursuing the principles of cooperative and comprehensive security in its approach to security management.

In this regard, it may be noted that the First ASEAN Regional Forum in July 1994 agreed to study the comprehensive concept of security. A cooperative and comprehensive security underpinning the ARF approaches to regional security would greatly facilitate the fostering of sustainable security in the region.

6. Regional security will benefit greatly from the adoption of a body of norms to govern member behaviour in their management of inter-state relations and security. While many of the principles will be universal principles already codified in documents such as the United Nations Charter and the Five Principles of Peaceful Co-existence, a formulation unique to the Asia-Pacific region and consistent with the universal principles will help lend a sense of identity and concrete guidance for the ARF community.

Russia and ASEAN-ISIS have already done substantive work in this area and submitted a draft Pacific Concord for the consideration of the Seventh and Eighth ARF. However, besides welcoming the draft and calling upon the two parties to continue consultations with one another, no firm decision has been made. The ARF needs to revisit this idea positively and develop a set of norms for the Asia-Pacific region that draws inspiration from the universal norms as well as from the ASEAN Treaty of Amity and Cooperation.

7. The ARF has begun to give greater attention to the so-called "non-traditional" security issues, which in truth are as traditional as traditional can be. This move is timely and welcome, because for too long the world has been obsessed with the military dimension of security at the expense of the non-military dimension. In addressing "non-traditional" or non-military security problems however, there is a tendency for the ARF to group them under the rubric of confidence-building or preventive diplomacy in conformity with the ARF Concept Paper's three stages. These three stages are actually irrelevant and inapplicable to non-traditional security issues, except where cooperation between countries in the non-traditional sphere contributes directly towards confidence-building. It is ridiculous, for instance, to consider measures to fight contagious lethal diseases or environmental threats and transnational crime or even terrorism as falling within the ambit of preventive diplomacy, when political or diplomatic tools to avert or constrain conflict are absent and are wholly irrelevant to the issues at hand.

    The ARF should abandon this abuse of terminology just to conform to the prescribed three-stage roadmap of the ARF Concept Paper. The inapplicability of the three-stage nomenclature for addressing non-traditional security problems should be acknowledged, and the ARF should recognize that it is conducting activities outside this conventional framework.

8. A gross imbalance in the ARF security agenda is the ferocious focus upon non-proliferation of nuclear weapons while studiously avoiding the other, no less important, half of the Nuclear Non-Proliferation Treaty, which is the reduction and elimination of existing nuclear weapons. Any reference to reduction and elimination is mere lip service, with hardly any concrete measures to address them, in contrast to non-proliferation. The fact that

non-nuclear weapons states themselves are largely quiet on this issue is testimony to how uncritically acquiescent some of them can be to this hypocrisy. A bold effort must be made by these states to redress the imbalance, and introduce equally rigorous measures to reduce and ultimately eliminate nuclear weapons in the interests of regional security.

9. Arms control, once so fashionable when it was some East Asian states which were perceived as being engaged in an arms race, has disappeared completely from regional security discourse. It never made an appearance in the ARF agenda. Given the massive militarization underway in the region, especially on the part of the United States which is already continents (not streets) ahead of the others, it is urgently important that the ARF address this critical issue.

CONCLUSION

Assessments of the progress of the ARF vary, depending upon the criteria and the standards employed, as well as the expectations entertained by the parties concerned. This chapter is of the view that given the many challenges and constraints confronting security cooperation in the region, the ARF has performed reasonably well. Much, however, can still be done to improve and strengthen regional security cooperation through the ARF. The priorities are in the area of institution and capacity-building, reform of organizing concepts for promoting collaborative security in the region, norm-building, strengthening of work in the "non-traditional" sphere of security, and redressing imbalances in the ARF's security agenda.

5

Strengthening ASEAN-China Cooperation in the ASEAN Regional Forum

Liu Xuecheng

The ASEAN Regional Forum (ARF) is the most important governmental forum for multilateral security dialogue and cooperation in the Asia-Pacific region. It was officially initiated by ASEAN and the inaugural ARF Ministerial Meeting was held in Bangkok on 25 July 1994. For the past decade, all the annual ARF ministerial meetings have been hosted by ASEAN as the driving force. All the participants have exchanged views on security issues of common concern in a spirit of candour, thus reducing each other's suspicions and differences, enhancing mutual understanding and trust, and accelerating the process of security cooperation in the fields of common concern.

The Second ARF Ministerial Meeting adopted the Concept Paper in 1995, designing the three-phase process of security dialogue and cooperation. They are the promotion of confidence-building, development of preventive diplomacy, and elaboration of approaches to conflict. ASEAN is the driving force for this process with other participants as dialogue partners.

ARF has made substantial progress in promoting confidence-building and developing preventive diplomacy in the region for the past ten years.

ARF has sought to increase mutual confidence and trust through dialogue and to promote peace and stability through multilateral cooperation on an equal footing. Such an approach is in line with the new security concept coming into shape in the course of security dialogue and cooperation in the Asia-Pacific region since the end of the Cold War.

In 2001, ARF made substantive progress. All participants reached consensus on the three documents about the enhanced role of the ARF Chair, Experts/Eminent Persons (EEP), and Preventive Diplomacy (PD), which signifies an important achievement in the transitional process as ARF moves from confidence-building measures to preventive diplomacy.

In response to the situation after the terrorist attacks of 11 September 2001, the ARF has placed greater emphasis on anti-terrorism, non-proliferation of WMD and non-traditional security issues, and it has started substantive discussions on and collaboration in their solution. All this has added to the vitality and dynamism of the ARF process.

China has valued ARF and became its dialogue partner at the time of its founding. China has worked hard to strengthen its cooperation with the ASEAN countries within the ARF framework for regional security and stability.

NEW SECURITY CONCEPT: COMMON FOUNDATION FOR COOPERATION IN ARF

Since the end of the Cold War, the trend toward economic globalization and regional grouping has brought the Asia-Pacific region unprecedented opportunities for cooperation as well as new challenges to regional security. The region is facing more and more diverse security threats with traditional and non-traditional security factors intertwined. The recent events in international affairs have demonstrated that security threats tend to be multi-faceted and global in scope. Interdependence and cooperation among the regional countries are ever deepening. A new security concept has evolved to be multi-fold, with its contents extending from military and political to economic, social, environmental, and many other areas. Therefore, many countries have realized that they share more common security interests and are more interdependent in maintaining peace and stability. Regional security problems should be solved through multilateral cooperation and comprehensive measures. Only in this way can a peaceful and stable security environment be created for economic development in the region.

Since the 9/11 attacks, the Asia-Pacific security situation has been undergoing major and profound changes. Unstable and uncertain factors have increased tremendously with terrorism and other non-traditional security issues getting more salient. Against this backdrop, Asia-Pacific countries have adjusted their domestic and foreign policies to adapt themselves to the evolving situation and meet the new security threats and challenges.

While the threat of international terrorism is on the rise in the region, the basic contradictions have not been resolved and some deep-rooted problems remain. Traditional security concepts still dominate in the strategic perspectives of certain countries. Efforts to develop military strength and attempts to use military means to solve new security issues would probably lead to arms race and regional tensions. New security challenges have brought into question traditional security concepts and security strategies. Under such circumstances, fighting the common threats makes it possible for the countries to seek common ground while preserving differences. New security situations have strongly called for a new security concept and approaches to emerging threats and challenges. The ARF responds to such a call and puts the perspectives of cooperative security on its agenda for security dialogue in the region.

Approaches to security have been diversified. Dialogue and cooperation have been featured as the fundamental approach of cooperative and common security concepts. If the Shanghai Cooperation Organization (SCO) is a fruitful case for common security, ARF is the testing ground for cooperative security. Their common feature is the promoting of mutual trust through dialogue on an equal footing and seeking security through multilateral cooperation. The new security concept is formulated essentially on the basis of the basic principles of these two security concepts. These two security concepts are not exclusive from each other but complement each other. It is the common aspiration of peoples in the region to discard the old way of thinking and replace it with new perspectives to seek cooperative and common security.

ARF has been dedicated to fostering trust through dialogue and promoting security through cooperation in the Asia-Pacific region. Such an approach is based on a cooperative security concept. Advocates of cooperative security believe that with the end of the Cold War, the bipolar confrontation would be replaced by multilateral dialogue and cooperation. The nature of security is conceptualized as diversified or comprehensive, with traditional and non-traditional threats intertwined. Given such assessments, the traditional security concept or theories formulated during the Cold War become irrelevant to the changing security situation in the Asia-Pacific region. Within this framework of security cooperation, security issues are no longer the privileged domains of big powers playing power politics, and small and medium-sized countries can also talk to big countries as equals in the security field.

China and ASEAN have nurtured a considerable sense of common identity, and share similar values. Both sides prefer the use of the informal consultative process and emphasize the importance of inclusiveness in the process of security dialogue and cooperation. The principle of mutual trust, making gradual progress, moving at a pace comfortable to all, consensus in decision-making and non-interference in the internal affairs of member states is in conformity with China's foreign and security policy, consistent with China's new security concept and the Five Principles of Peaceful Co-Existence. These principles will not only guide future ARF process but also serve as reference for other regional organizations. These modalities have been credited as "the ASEAN Way". ARF has made substantial progress in promoting confidence-building measures and preventive diplomacy in 2001, with three documents adopted, giving a new impetus to future development.

China has attached importance to the leading role played by ASEAN in pushing forward regional security dialogue and cooperation. China has supported ARF in further exploring and developing dialogue and cooperation in non-traditional security field, including counter-terrorism, in gradually expanding the participation of defence officials in ARF.

In the course of the discussion on ARF reforms for the past years, China has taken a constructive attitude. It has consistently supported ASEAN's leading role within the ARF process, and firmly adhered to the existing and effective modalities and principles of the ASEAN Way, with confidence-building at the core. China has initiated position papers on non-traditional security issues and a new security concept. It has also initiated the ARF Security Policy Conference, accelerating the dialogue and cooperation of defence and security officials within the ARF framework. It has taken an active part in the discussions and formulation of the definition, concept and principles of preventive diplomacy.

Since the end of the Cold War, China has consistently advocated that countries in the region jointly cultivate a new concept of security, which focuses on enhancing trust through dialogue and promoting security through cooperation. The new security concept has become an important component of China's foreign policy, and mutual trust, mutual benefit, equality, and cooperation constitute the basic principles of such a new security concept. China has been working hard to put the new security concept into practice. It has been seeking settlement of disputes with its neighbours through peaceful negotiation, and resolved the land boundary question with most of its neighbouring countries. It has vigorously supported and worked for the establishment and development of a regional security mechanism of dialogue and cooperation, believing that the key guarantee for the regional security comes from a regional security framework featuring cooperation instead of confrontation. Thus, China has attached great importance to and taken an active part in the ASEAN Regional Forum.

SOLID BILATERAL RELATIONS: RELIABLE FOUNDATION OF COOPERATION IN ARF

Sound relationships with neighbouring countries constitute the strategic backing and shield of China's national security. Based on the policy of good-neighbourliness and cordiality, the Chinese Government has put forward the policy of "neighbours as partners and with cordiality". Premier Wen Jiabao interpreted this policy as "good-neighbourhood, common security and prosperity shared with neighbours" at the East Asian Leaders' Meeting in 2003.

The development of the China-ASEAN relationship is an important pillar of China's foreign and security strategy since the end of the Cold War. The China-ASEAN dialogue process has witnessed rapid development since its launch in 1991. There have been constant exchanges of high level visits, markedly increased mutual trust in the political arena and continuously strengthened economic cooperation.

Normalization of the relations between China and ASEAN began in 1991 when China attended the ASEAN Post-Ministerial Conference (ASEAN PMC). China's attitude toward the ARF has changed from sceptic to observer to participant as a dialogue partner. Since 1994, it has become a full dialogue partner of ARF. Since the later half of the 1990s, the China-ASEAN relationship has improved steadily. Substantial progress has been made especially within the "Ten+1" and "Ten+3" frameworks.

Deepened cooperation between China and ASEAN has been based on mutual trust in the political field. China and ASEAN countries signed the China-ASEAN Joint Statement in 1997, which put forward principles of good neighbourliness and mutual trust between China and the ASEAN countries.

China's overall relationship with ASEAN attained a new momentum of development in 2002. At the eighth ASEAN Summit in Phnom Penh, China and ASEAN reached four agreements, including cooperation in various areas ranging from comprehensive economic cooperation to non-traditional security cooperation. The signing of these agreements demonstrated that political trust between China and the ASEAN countries has reached new heights.

The Declaration on Conduct of Parties in the South China Sea was a milestone for renouncing the use of force on both sides and maintaining the *status quo* in the disputed sea. China has persistently advocated the policy of "shelving the dispute (on sovereignty) and carrying out joint development". It appreciates and supports the purposes and principles enshrined in the Treaty of Amity and Cooperation in Southeast Asia. China's accession to this treaty has also consolidated the base of the China-ASEAN strategic partnership for peace and prosperity. China is also positive about signing the protocol of the Treaty on Southeast Asia Nuclear Weapon Free Zone.

Despite volatility in the regional economic environment following the financial crisis in 1997, China-ASEAN bilateral trade volume has maintained an average annual growth rate of 15 per cent, and has been growing steadily. Both sides have made agriculture, IT, human resources development and the development of Mekong River Basin key areas of their cooperation in the years to come. Now both sides have also signed the agreement on China-ASEAN Business Council, adding a new mechanism of their cooperation. China and ASEAN have signed the Framework Agreement on China-ASEAN Comprehensive Economic Cooperation, committing them to establish an FTA before 2010 and speed up the process of China-ASEAN economic cooperation and integration under the China-ASEAN strategic partnership for peace and prosperity. For the first time, China became the largest export market of the ASEAN countries in 2003.

The goal of China's good-neighbourliness policy is to make efforts to pursue a non-zero sum or win-win game in forging mutual relationships with its ASEAN neighbours. In the coming years, China will adhere steadfastly to the amity policies and improve China-ASEAN relationship more actively. China will continue to support strongly and participate actively in the ASEAN integration process. China and ASEAN signed the joint declaration on the establishment of the China-ASEAN strategic partnership for peace and prosperity in 2003. All these have not only further substantiated the China-ASEAN Partnership of Good Neighbourliness and Mutual Trust, but also demonstrated the huge potential for developing China-ASEAN comprehensive cooperation in all the fields. A solid bilateral relationship has laid a reliable foundation for cooperation in the future process of the ARF dialogue and cooperation.

STRENGTHENING COORDINATION AND COOPERATION IN THE FUTURE ARF AGENDA

The ARF process is essentially a mechanism for security dialogue and cooperation in the Asia-Pacific region. The nature of security threats is comprehensive. The means of coping with the security threats is cooperative. The goal of security dialogue and cooperation is to seek common security.

Looking back to the dynamic development of the ARF process, we need to address the following four main issues to promote the healthy development of the ARF process in the future.

1. Security Cooperation for Economic Development

Peace and development are closely linked with each other. Security and prosperity have their inherent logic. Peace is the fundamental requisite for development and shared development is conducive to regional peace. Since the end of the Cold War, countries have given top priority to their economic growth. After the Asian financial crisis, all the countries in the region have attached greater importance to economic security. The economic factor is increasingly becoming an important prerequisite for the maintenance of regional security.

The history of economic development in the region has shown that economic development needs a peaceful external environment and stable internal conditions. It also indicates that economic development would enhance the social welfare and be conducive for political stability in a country. In a certain sense, economic security is a reliable basis of political security. Successful economic cooperation could foster political confidence and mutual trust. Political confidence and trust can become a catalyst for creating a favourable environment for common security. While we are promoting security cooperation within the ARF framework, we need to keep in mind its implications for economic development.

2. Multilateral Cooperation for Common Threats

Non-traditional security issues are now a real threat that all nations must face and cope with. They are gaining importance in regional security affairs and there has been a greater desire among the countries for joint efforts to address these issues. Transnational or transregional in nature, these issues are difficult for one or several countries to deal with. Multilateral cooperation is the only effective way to resolve them. After the 9/11 terrorist attacks, many countries have carried out active bilateral and multilateral dialogues, coordination and cooperation on counter-terrorism. Coordination and cooperation among major countries in this respect are particularly noteworthy. Such cooperation in these fields has not only checked terrorism and other transnational crimes effectively, but also led to positive changes in the relations between the regional countries and promoted the development of multilateral security cooperation.

3. Diversity and Coordination of Multilateral Processes

Since the end of the Cold War, a number of mechanisms of multilateral security cooperation have taken shape in the Asia-Pacific region. In terms of security dialogue and cooperation, there have emerged ARF, CSCAP, Shangri-La Dialogue, Asia Cooperation Dialogue, and the Asia-Pacific Roundtable Dialogue, NEACD and so on. The economic cooperation-oriented organizations like APEC and "Ten+3" have also touched upon political and security issues in the region. Their functions are overlapping but complementary. With the evolution of all these cooperation mechanisms, we should recognize their diversity and we also need effective coordination among them.

4. Coordination and Cooperation of Big Countries

China and India are the two largest developing Asian countries in the region. Japan is the second largest economic power in the world. Russia is re-emerging from the collapse of the Soviet Union. The United States is the only superpower in the world. China, Russia, India, Japan and the United States are major countries with significant influence in the Asia-Pacific region. They have great stakes in regional stability and economic development. Their economies have grown quite interdependent. These countries have developed very strong economic links with the other countries in this region. Their relationships will, to a great extent, shape the future of Asia-Pacific cooperation and integration. To develop cooperative relations among the big countries is of vital importance to peace and prosperity in the region.

INSTITUTION-BUILDING VERSUS ISSUES–ORIENTATION

The ten years of the ARF dialogue have seen three processes of norms-making, institution-building and issue-orientation. Disputes and differences have emerged in the deliberations and consultations. They have involved the priority of the three processes in the ARF dialogue. Indeed, in the course of establishing the ARF dialogue mechanism, we need to take into account all these three processes. However, for the time being, some participants put institution-building or mechanization of the dialogue process as the top priority on the ARF agenda. For example, some participants were eager to change ASEAN's status as the driving force in the ARF process, ignored the CBMs and urged mechanization of the ARF dialogue by taking the OSCE model. In order to push ahead the process of institution-building, some participants tried to change the norms characterized by the ASEAN Way, such as decision-making by a flexible consensus or "Ten minus X" principle, and humanitarian intervention in internal affairs. Since the 9/11 attacks, the issue-oriented process has been highlighted and emphasized at the last three annual meetings. Although three documents related to institution-building were deliberated and adopted, more issue-related topics were raised and discussed, such as anti-terrorism, non-traditional security threats, non-proliferation, maritime security, and so on.

At the Tenth ARF Ministerial Meeting held at Phnom Penh in 2003, the Chairman's Statement raised the nine recommendations endorsed at the Ninth ARF Ministerial Meeting in Brunei Darussalam on 31 July 2002 for the development of the ARF process and its future direction. They are:

1. As an immediate step, consolidate and strengthen measures to combat international terrorism.
2. Enhance intelligence-sharing, police cooperation and financial measures against international terrorism.
3. Establish Inter-sessional Group on International Terrorism and Transnational Crimes.
4. Enhance the role of the ARF Chair and assign the ASEAN Secretariat to assist the ARF Chairman in co-ordinating the work of the ARF
5. Develop and utilize the Register of Experts/Eminent Persons.
6. Strengthen CBMs.
7. Widen engagement and involvement of security and defence officials, building upon the Singapore Concept Paper on Defence Dialogue within the ARF.
8. Enhance linkages between ARF and ASEAN-ISIS, CSCAP and other organizations.
9. Provide substantive follow-up to the Paper on Concept and Principles of Preventive Diplomacy adopted last year.

At the meeting, the ministers welcomed China's proposal on convening an "ARF Security Policy Conference" in which high military officers and government officials will be invited to take part. Some participants also proposed the establishment of ISG on the proliferation of WMD.

All these proposals have demonstrated that the ARF process has entered the issue-oriented process with the steady evolution of institution-building. Whether in the fields of anti-terrorism, non-proliferation, anti-transnational crimes or in the field of necessary institution-building, China will vigorously work together with ASEAN in the future development of the ARF process.

6
ASEAN+3: The Roles of ASEAN and China

Eric Teo Chu Cheow

East Asia is in the throes of an important socio-economic evolutionary process, after three waves of monumental transformation since the late 1980s. Each wave of change and transformation moulded East Asia incrementally and helped forge an East Asian economic model, which is becoming discernable today. In turn, the emergence of this "new" model is dictating East Asia's challenges and opportunities, as new socio-economic and political trends emerge and as East Asian regionalism take off.

In this regional context, ASEAN and China are playing important roles in shaping ASEAN+3 in socio-economic development, regional peace and cooperation, and the cultural affirmation of an Asian identity. This chapter focuses on three aspects.

1. The East Asian socio-economic transformation in three waves (liberalization/globalization, the 1997–98 Asian financial crisis and the Severe Acute Respiratory Syndrome or SARS epidemic) has prompted China and ASEAN to develop an East Asian model of socio-economic development;

2. The fundamental geopolitics is based on a shifting ASEAN-China relationship, thanks to China's pragmatism and ASEAN's changed threat perception of China;

3. The eventual affirmation of an Asian identity or "Asian-ness", especially with the rise of China's "soft power" and ASEAN's acquiescence of this rise, has in turn contributed to the consolidation of ASEAN+3.

THREE WAVES OF TRANSFORMATION AND CHANGE: TOWARDS EAST ASIAN REGIONALISM AND A NEW EAST ASIAN SOCIO-ECONOMIC MODEL

First Wave of Liberalization/Globalization: Opening Up and Export Orientation

Like the rest of the world, East Asia was profoundly affected by the trends of liberalization and globalization, as it was "opened up" and its economies liberalized, at the behest of the United States and Western powers.

In the early 1990s, the Reaganite and Thatcherite revolutions brought sweeping changes to the mentality of the post-Cold War order. When the Soviet Empire ultimately collapsed under the weight of inefficient communism and China became progressively engaged in a successful "socialism *à la chinoise*" experiment, liberalism's final triumph was hailed and communism's demise ultimately sealed. Daniel Yergin emphasized that the most important phenomenon and transition in post-War modern times was undoubtedly this "free market revolution that changed the world".[1]

Neo-liberalism and liberalization engaged the world in a frantic race towards the globalization of four key elements, *viz.* the massive and rapid circulation of goods and services, capital, ideas and human resources worldwide. The IT revolution was instrumental in "partnering" effectively the liberalization trend in enhancing globalization. In this context, East Asia was actively engaged in this first wave of liberalization and the globalization of goods, services and capital. But some East Asian countries were better prepared to "open up" and thus handled liberalization in a much better way than others. For example, most of Southeast Asia opened up haphazardly without rigorous planning, creating a bubble economy in production, stocks and property, as "easy money" flowed in during the early 1990s.[2] These countries then took an enormous beating during the Asian crisis, with stupendous quantity of capital outflow.

The circulation of ideas and information was also impressive, as we are plugged into the world information web; no information can be deliberately hidden or denied for long, as media giants (though still dominated by the West) feed information by the seconds across the globe. East Asia and its societies have thus been "forced" to "open up" progressively to the world. Worldwide, it can be discerned that the rapid flow of information had indeed helped ensure better governmental and corporate accountability and transparency, which in turn had promoted an acceleration in the flow of goods, services and capital across East Asian economies. However, the flow of human resources remains truly globalized, as the more developed and richer countries resist free flow of human capital across the globe for obvious reasons. Though talents and professionals now criss-cross the world in search of better value and profit creation, lower levels of labour and mass migration of population in search of a better life are still strictly monitored and controlled. Thus, although ideas have been circulating more freely across East Asia and have undeniably contributed to boosting East Asian economies and moulding a new East Asian socio-economic model "of a certain openness", these countries still maintain tight and effective control over foreign labour across the region.

East Asian economies were liberalized in varying degrees of depth and speed by the liberal revolution; the basic problem was the state of readiness of these economies to meet the future challenges of globalization. More fundamentally, East Asian financial systems were liberalized and "opened up" without the necessary regulation, consolidation or safeguards, which then made them intrinsically "bubble economies" before June 1997. This first wave of transformation had therefore helped bring East Asian economies into the mainstream of international economics and finance, especially encouraging them to be "export economies", as they benefited enormously from trade liberalization.

The East Asian economic model clearly shifted in the 1980s and 1990s towards a liberal and export-oriented one, in order to benefit from the fruits of globalization; Asian exports became the hallmark of these economies' unprecedented success, in what was then triumphantly termed as "the age of the Asian economic miracle".

The Second Wave: The 1997–98 Asian Crisis and Realizing Asia's Vulnerabilities

The 1997–98 Asian crisis constituted the second wave of change and transformation in East Asia. It has left till today many important political, economic, financial and social consequences on most of the ASEAN countries and South Korea. The crisis provided force and impetus to the region's transition process and changed the basic foundations of East Asian societies to an even greater degree than liberalization and globalization; the East Asian economic model was also severely modified by the Asian crisis, as Asians realized the extreme vulnerabilities of their economies and the critical economic, financial and social "failure" of their social structures during the crisis.

Indonesia, Thailand and Malaysia (within ASEAN) and South Korea bore the brunt of the Asian crisis; in fact, they faced a "total crisis" of huge financial, economic, social and political proportions in 1997 and 1998. Beginning as a financial crisis, it soon became an economic one; the crisis then engendered a social crisis, which finally spilled over into the political realm. The economic and social fabrics of these societies were savagely torn apart during the crisis, as plunging currencies, bad loans, shaky financial systems, corporate bankruptcies, rising unemployment and social instability engulfed them. Loans from the IMF, related financial agencies and other governments were pledged on condition for economic, financial and social reforms; Thailand was pledged US$17.5 billion, South Korea took US$55 billion and Indonesia had US$43 billion in bailouts. The crisis also aggravated ethnic and religious tensions, as well as the uneven distribution of wealth within countries and amongst ethnic-cum-religious communities, like in Indonesia or even in the Philippines (which was still under IMF care then), but to a lesser extent, in Malaysia or Thailand. Indonesia, Thailand and South Korea were then "forced" into political upheavals and reforms, just as crucial political and social reforms are still haunting the Philippines and Malaysia today. Like its "affected" neighbours, Singapore and Vietnam had to also contend with profound economic and social reforms as well as a serious rethink of their own future, as a direct or indirect result of the Asian crisis. Cambodia, Laos and Myanmar are also finally learning the ropes of transition from central-planned to market economies and societies in the post-crisis context.

The East Asian economic model was then forced to take on a more social dimension after the first wave of liberalization and export-orientation, as Asians suddenly realized during the Asian crisis how vulnerable they were to the effects of globalization and "easy money". Most East Asian economies had no social safety nets in 1997; many of the "new poor" in the cities were thus encouraged to find solace in the lush and rich countryside then, so as to prevent crime and other social evils in congested cities.

The Asian crisis thus ended the "bubble economic state" of most Asian economies and tragically brought these economies "back to earth", after their ephemeral, euphoric and vertiginous rise in the early 1990s. Forces of reform were then unleashed in many of the affected countries, as democracy and reforms had become key slogans in the affected countries by 1998. In fact, the nexus of the Asian political economy was also shifting from the previous duo-pole of "big government-big business" to a new triangular nexus of "government-private sector-civil society".[3] Civil society, comprising lobby groups (which include labour unions, student groups and human rights activists), NGOs and environmental lobbies began taking their governments to task openly on an array of issues; there then also appeared a real need to redefine the *contrat social* (social contract) *à la Jean-Jacques Rousseau* within these societies, between the governed and the governing. The old social order was crumbling and a new one had to be founded.

With the need to renegotiate such *contrats sociaux* in East Asian societies, the East Asian economic model clearly took on a more social dimension, when socio-economic reforms were perceived to be necessary and critical, thanks to the tragic social consequences of the Asian Crisis and increasing pressure from the emerging civil societies and lobbying groups across the region.

The Asian crisis also became a crisis in governance for the affected countries. Democracy was the new tool of governance; democratic aspirations ran high, just as calls for drastic economic and social reforms rang out across the region. Decentralization became *à la mode* across Asia, from Indonesia to Thailand, as grassroots democracy took root across East Asian countries. Governmental accountability became the new code word for governance, as governments are now checked not only by a mushrooming of political parties and bolder politicians (as well as emerging opposition forces, which have since developed substantially), but also by the rising civil society and people's groups. New power centres sprang up, as these Asian democracies became complex political entities with multiple power centres. The Asian crisis had therefore contributed to a reform of the political foundations of the affected Asian countries; for example, political volatility has become the name of the game in Jakarta after the fall of Suharto, whereas political power has become democratically "normalized" in Seoul and Bangkok. The Asian crisis had indeed provoked a crisis of governance in some form; as democracy was being installed, many of the affected countries had in fact to build or rebuild crucial political and social institutions, which unfortunately had led to some instability.

In parallel with increasing "pent-up" calls for more democracy, reforms and governmental accountability, consumer power rose in East Asia after the crisis. The East Asian economic model clearly shifted from its previous "sole" export-oriented tilt towards an upsurge in consumer demand and the rising power of the middle class; consequently, owing to the region's exposed vulnerability to globalization (thanks to the Asian crisis), the East Asian growth model shifted "inwards" towards building and consolidating domestic demand and growth. As Asian economies try to find "their own internal economic strengths", instead of relying too heavily on exports and external markets alone, a "new" Asian economic nationalism emerged. To cater to rising consumer demands of the middle class, Asian governments have had to contend with rising democratic aspirations in their emerging electorate. The Asian crisis had thus helped infuse the *contrat social* dimension into the East Asian socio-economic model, which has become domestic demand and growth-driven; the private sector and middle class are clearly encouraged to play a greater economic, social and political role, as accountability and transparency are now clearly gaining importance.

The Third Wave: Consequences of SARS and The Re-Emergence of the State

Five years after the tragic Asian crisis, East Asia could be said to have witnessed yet another socio-economic transformation, thanks to the ravage of the SARS epidemic. This transformation was of course more acute in the countries affected by SARS, owing to the severity of the epidemic in China, Hong Kong, Taiwan, Singapore and Vietnam; a total of more than 600 deaths were registered in these countries, with hundreds hospitalized (but with many recovered as well) and thousands on home quarantine at some stage. SARS had dealt huge blows to the affected economies in varying degrees, but by repercussion, all Asian economies were affected through "richochet" socio-economic effects. This was especially true, as SARS hit China hard; as China is the region's economic locomotive and social force, all Asia became affected economically "by contagion", just like the financial crisis that began with the Thai baht in 1997. The SARS epidemic had undeniably left severe marks on the society and politics of East Asia, as SARS had in fact consolidated or even aggravated the monumental transformations, which had begun and taken place during the first two waves of changes in East Asia. SARS thus pioneered a "third-wave revolution" in East Asia in the socio-economic arena, as well as in terms of political changes and regional mindset; as such, SARS has helped mould the evolving East Asian socio-economic model even further. Being major entities, China and ASEAN became much closer after the SARS epidemic, just as their socio-economic development became intertwined even more tightly together.

The economic impact of SARS has been three-fold on East Asia. It tested the maturity of East Asian consumers and their governments' economic strategy of encouraging domestic consumption and growth as a "second pillar of sustainable economic growth", like "Thaksinomics" in Thailand; China's domestic consumption was severely tested in Beijing and Guangzhou during the epidemic. With SARS, the confidence to consume, invest, trade, service and interact was seriously at stake. It also emphasized the critical importance of confidence and morale (both internally and externally), as East Asia's "maturing" economies seek to build a consumption-based strategy, a more services-oriented and IT-based economic structure and an "exports-to-balance-domestic-consumption" economy. Domestic demand and consumption, and consequently investments and employment, especially in the services sector, plunged, affecting growth and even social stability, as was widely feared in China. SARS had thus hit hard at the vibrancy and dynamism of East Asian economies, and especially, in testing domestic markets and confidence. Finally, it underscored the growing importance of China as East Asia's main engine and locomotive of growth; East Asia's "economic dependence" on China was highlighted during the SARS epidemic. Any dampening of China's domestic consumption would in turn have serious repercussions on Southeast Asian countries, whose trade with China totalled US$55 billion in 2002, as they increasingly "hedge" their own economic growth on China's spectacular growth. ASEAN acknowledged this fact even more in 2003 and look to China as their locomotive of growth and development.

SARS had also revolutionized the sociology of work and play. The SARS epidemic underscored the quality of life and changed work habits; health and a less stressful lifestyle could have become the ultimate "silver lining" of SARS, as healthy lifestyle, stress alleviation and regular exercises now take on a new dimension in East Asia. Furthermore, sociological changes are also taking place too; supported by IT, many service industries are already experimenting with flexible work hours and formats; East Asian worker may increasingly benefit from IT to work smarter, less stressfully and chalk up less work-hours in the office, whilst maintaining productivity, just as the virtual world becomes more popular.

Sociologically, SARS had also underscored the importance of social stability as serious cleavages and tensions within Asian societies could have a strong destabilizing effect. SARS had divided urban societies in East Asia, as the traditional community and communal spirit flagged initially in urban cities like Singapore or Hong Kong. Social cohesion was in danger, both within urban communities, as well as between urban and rural communities, as was the case in China. Ironically, it was the state (as in China, Singapore and Vietnam), which had ensured that communal solidarity ultimately prevailed after serious initial concerns, thanks to the governments' vigilance and efforts. Given the authorities' strengthened hand in dealing with the SARS epidemic, and with greater public backing for governmental action and the generous financial relief packages, the state has undoubtedly become sociologically more powerful and determinant today. Social cohesion has become a critical issue for regional governments and their citizens, as the social dimension gains further ground regionally. The SARS epidemic has thus crystallized the role of the state versus individuals; more importantly, the post-crisis social dimension has gotten a further boost after the SARS epidemic and will definitely find an even greater place within the East Asian socio-economic model.

Added to the socio-economic sphere, SARS has also transformed the region in three political aspects, which would contribute to a consolidation of the "new" East Asian model. They include the "opening up" of more political space through greater governmental transparency and accountability, effective communication of the authorities (or a new form of "communicative governance") and reaffirming the place and role of the state, effective statecraft and governance of an emerging new Asian leadership. A new style of communicative governance is clearly the first step towards this *contrat social* and governmental transparency and accountability. After the winds of liberalism and the philosophy of "the less state the better" had swept through the planet, SARS has reminded East Asians that the state could and should still play a primary role in managing epidemics, national crises and public services. East Asians would ultimately expect a more efficient and powerful state (and not a "lesser" one, as previously advocated by Western liberals) to look after their well-being. The "winds of liberalism" would now have to contend with a "re-emerging" state in East Asia, just as the art of effective statecraft and communications take on new importance and dimensions in managing the rising aspirations of East Asians. East Asia's socio-political dimension (especially China and ASEAN) should take on an increased importance, thanks to SARS.

East Asia (especially China and ASEAN) has been duly transformed through three waves of transformation. Globalization had brought East Asians "closer" as the region liberalized and became more "integrated" through the increased flow of goods, services, capital, ideas and human exchanges (through tourism and expatriates). The Asian crisis then brought East Asian nations "closer", as they experienced common vulnerabilities during the attack on their currencies, economies and societies. The SARS epidemic re-emphasized the two above facts, as East Asia was tested economically and socially, as well as the region's interdependence and its common vulnerabilities.

The East Asian economic model has also been subjected to three waves of changes, transition and transformations too. The first wave of globalization and liberalization shook the fundamentals of "closed" East Asian economies and "opened" them up to benefit from the fruits of globalization; it clearly confirmed the "export" vocation of East Asia. The second, which came with the 1997–98 Asian crisis, affected the East Asian model profoundly, thanks to this "total crisis" effect (for the affected countries), as the political, economic, financial and social ramifications were seismic. A certain economic nationalism began to take shape in East Asia and the social dimension became specifically highlighted in the tumult of the crisis. Last year, a third wave hit Asia, as a result of the recent SARS epidemic, and is beginning to radically transform the East Asian socio-economic model further. The model has undoubtedly taken on an even greater social dimension and "resurrected" the power and importance of the state.[4]

More importantly, these three waves of socio-economic change have helped cement East Asian regionalism and "concretized" the ASEAN+3 framework, within which both ASEAN and China have played significant roles.

EAST ASIAN ECONOMIC MODEL, ASEAN+3 AND BUDDING REGIONALISM

As the spread of SARS (and then the avian flu epidemic this year[7]) has shown, the longer-term goal of an East Asian Community may already be crystallizing much faster than was initially thought, because of increasing people-to-people contacts and the freer movement of goods, services, tourists and expatriates across the whole region. Liberalization and globalization had indeed already transformed East Asia into one *de facto* community to a huge extent. SARS has indeed helped create a new East Asian bonding and awareness. East Asians now also realize that they have a common destiny with a region that is fast becoming interdependent and borderless. Secondly, for the region to really take off, East Asians have become, after the SARS and avian flu epidemics, more aware of a better and greater redistribution of wealth, development, social and health benefits within the region. Otherwise, richer regions would never be exempt from social problems and diseases, which could originate from poorer and lesser-developed areas in East Asia and infect the richer and more developed areas. Development, growth and social equity must therefore be more quickly and effectively redistributed across East Asia, and Singaporeans have clearly a role to play in this regional endeavour. Third, East Asians now understand that their economic growth and recovery could be seriously stalled, if regional countries had succumbed to excessive fears of contagion, close their borders and restrict the movement of people, goods and investment flows. Furthermore, besides physical or geographical borders, East Asians should be careful not to close their minds to each other too. Indeed, discrimination based on nationalities or race, as the SARS epidemic had shown, could be very dangerous, especially for callous, irrational or emotional reasons. Confidence, closer economic coordination and cooperation are thus necessary; a regional mindset change is thus shaping up, as the SARS and avian flu epidemics have helped cement East Asia firmer together as a closer-knit and non-discriminatory community in the longer term.[5] SARS (and avian flu) may therefore have positively fuelled East Asian regionalism.

East Asian regionalism has increased in recent years, due to not only the three waves of changes and transformations, but also to three other economic and financial regional facts, as follows:

- Firstly, intra-regional trade has substantially increased for East Asia-13, from 36 per cent in 1985 to about 50 per cent in 2000 and to almost 55 per cent in 2002, especially as China becomes a greater trading partner for all the East Asian economies.
- Secondly, in East Asia's trade, current account surpluses of the thirteen nations amount to more than US$200 billion per year, this despite a shift towards more domestic-led growth in East Asian economies, thereby signifying a trend towards more matured economies in the region. These economies have also become more important competitors amongst themselves, besides being increasingly important markets for their neighbours too. Deflationary trends exist across East Asia today, as over-capacity may constitute a growing problem in many of the East Asian economies, although China, South Korea and most ASEAN countries are currently experiencing some doses of inflation. Moreover, China is also showing the way to ASEAN in stressing the need for greater redistribution of wealth and equity in order to secure socio-economic sustainability in the longer term, as Beijing ensures to "uplift" its 900 million peasants amidst a booming economy.[6]
- Lastly, East Asia has become an enormous pool of foreign reserves, as it is estimated at some US$1.2 trillion or more than 50 per cent of the world's total reserves. China's foreign reserves are now estimated at some US$440 billion, whereas Japan top the world's reserves with more than US$500 billion (or some 10 per cent of its GDP). East Asians are therefore the world's top savers (which is clearly recognized by Asians themselves), although a big chunk of these reserves are sustaining the US deficit through Japanese (and increasingly Chinese) purchase of American T-bonds. In a way, this Asian wealth is unfortunately "parked" outside Asia and thereby, not necessarily helping to build East Asia itself.

Attempts at regional coordination and cooperation have begun timidly. Although Malaysian Prime Minister Dr Mahathir Mohamad's East Asian

Economic Grouping/Caucus idea was shot down in the early 1990s, this grouping has been *de facto* created, thanks to efforts of coordination on the Asian side during preparations for the Asia-Europe Meeting or ASEM. Since then, this grouping of East Asia (thirteen states) has been dubbed "ASEAN+3" and is evolving as a regional framework. In turn, the habit of coordination and cooperation amongst the thirteen is facilitating a freer flow of ideas, and even in unofficially adopting an "appropriate" economic model for Asia, as Asian policymakers exchange notes on and discuss the "best" socio-economic model for Asians.

There is also a slow shift away from the "flying geese model of vertical East Asian economic integration", which was centred on Japan (vertically) through capital flow, technological transfer and supply of manufacturing parts and based on market exchange and a clear regional division of labour and production networks (thanks primarily to the expensive cost of production in Japan and the strength of the yen after the Plaza Agreement). Today, according to an ADB Institute Research Paper,[7] this regional model appears to be shifting towards that of "bamboo capitalism" or "parallel development", based on FDI flows in the region, which create intricate intra-regional production networks, based on the exchange of parts, components and other intermediate products, and hence a "horizontal network of trade and capital", with China at its core. This FDI-driven supply chain has indeed created diverse and vibrant local industries around the East Asian region, and the further the supply chains are decomposed and extended geographically, the faster and the more profuse would be the proliferation of new entreprises and FDI flows across East Asia. There is therefore a new division of labour and production across East Asia.

As a region and for the creation of a future East Asian (ASEAN+3) community, it is believed that there are currently three "regional integration models", which are being discussed. East Asian integration could either be done through:

- Firstly, knitting or weaving a web of existing bilateral free trade areas (or FTAs) together region-wide to create a huge East Asian Free Trade Area;
- Secondly, finding the means to effectively use the mass of "unproductive" Japanese savings more efficiently (instead of letting them "fallow" in the banks with sub-zero interest rates or "lie" massively in T-bonds in the United States) in urgently developing the weaker economies of Asia through a sort of "Japanese Marshall Plan for Asia", although the latter should also create the conditions for fruitful and sound investment in their weak economies; and

- Lastly, creating an integrated East Asian region, centred on China and its enormous potential economic development, through trade (in both goods and services) and investments in both ways (China-East Asia, as well as East Asia-China), as well as through a new integrated China-centred production chain-cum-demand network in the whole region; the current "ASEAN-China" FTA could be "expanded" both geographically and intellectually to Japan and Korea, as well as "deepened" beyond a mere FTA.

Based on the shift from "flying geese" to "bamboo capitalism", the Japanese model of regional "integration" is now called into question, as production networks expand horizontally, and as the social dimension increases in the East Asian economic model. As the state-led and SME-led East Asian models "converge", the social dimension is again highlighted, especially in post-SARS Asia today. It appears therefore that the East Asian model is fast integrating the social dimension into its economic model, thus reducing the influence of the "pure" U.S. model, based solely on productivity and shareholders' value. The ultimate "economic integration model" for East Asia, or a combination of all three integrative models (FTAs, Japan savings-based or China-centred economic integration) in varying doses and degrees, would also need a firm social dimension; otherwise, Asian socio-economic development, given its traditional communal base, would not be truly sustainable in the long run. Given these factors, China and ASEAN would play a key role in shaping this integrative economic model.

The *contrat social* aspect of the Old Continent appears to be making some waves in East Asia too, after the initial euphoria of liberalization and globalization had pushed Asian economies to a frantic rush towards an exports-alone strategy as the principal pillar of Asian economic growth. But it was certainly the Asian crisis and then SARS/terrorism that had helped push and emphasize the social and "state" dimensions in Asian economies (especially in China and most ASEAN countries), although there are doubts that they would ultimately become welfare states. The greatest concern today in the more matured economies of East Asia is the impact of a "jobless economic recovery" on the social fabric and systems of these countries, as in the cases of Japan, Singapore, South Korea, Taiwan and Hong Kong. On the other hand, the "rising tigers" in Asia would have to urgently institute some form of social safety nets and wealth-distribution systems in order to "support and sustain" their domestic-demand based growth (and not solely as export-based economies), just as "people's power" and popular aspirations rise in their political systems. China appears to be at the cutting edge of experimenting with a new socialist revolution in its countryside, based on the "three *nong's*" (agriculture, peasants and rural villages), which many of the lesser-developed ASEAN economies would most likely follow and develop as well.

China and ASEAN's role in ASEAN+3 could in fact be attributed to the modelling of East Asia's socio-economic development, on account of their common experiences in the three waves of transformation and change, as well as China's progressive emergence as the region's premier economic force and locomotive.

THE EMERGENCE OF A "BENIGN CHINA" PERCEPTION IN SOUTHEAST ASIA AND THE BUILDING OF ASEAN-CHINA FOUNDATION AS A CORNERSTONE OF ASEAN+3

The second aspect of ASEAN and China's role in shaping ASEAN+3 is undoubtedly in the geopolitical and diplomatic arena, as their relationship is today firm and consolidated. This in turn would help build the foundations of ASEAN+3.

ASEAN-China relations are fast consolidating, as Beijing "advances" into Southeast Asia to "balance" the region's relations with Japan and the United States. This successful strengthening of ASEAN-China relations, despite recent historical animosities and initial economic "hang-ups", could be attributed to China's successful political, economic and cultural cultivation of ASEAN. But more importantly, China's "soft power" has risen substantially in Southeast Asia, which in turn has boosted Beijing's clout, influence and standing in ASEAN countries.[8] At the close of the annual parliamentary (NPC-CPPCC) session in Beijing in early March, Chinese Premier Wen Jiabao described China as "a friendly elephant", which poses no threat to ASEAN.

From a historical perspective, China used to pose two sorts of threats to Southeast Asia, viz Beijing's "communist threat" in the 1960s/1970s (as experienced by Indonesia, Thailand, Malaysia, Singapore, Philippines and Burma), as well as a "war threat" to Vietnam in 1979, when Chinese troops crossed the Sino-Vietnamese border to "teach Vietnam a lesson" after its "invasion and occupation of Cambodia".

Today, all ASEAN countries embrace unequivocally, acknowledge publicly the "one-China" policy and engage Beijing in all aspects of regional cooperation. ASEAN countries also acknowledge China's "peaceful rising", as expounded by China's leaders.

Added to this historical dimension, Southeast Asian countries have also witnessed a major perception change of China, from what was termed a

"China threat" (in economic, trade, investment, social/job terms) just three years ago, to one of a "benign China with opportunities (for ASEAN)", thanks to three factors.[9]

Firstly, Beijing's pragmatic policy of "political stabilization" has assured ASEAN countries, instead of its previous "ideological destabilization" of the region through communism.

Secondly, China is perceived today as an economic opportunity for ASEAN, thanks first to Beijing's "political" decision not to competitively devalue the renminbi (RMB) during the 1997–98 Asian crisis, and to China "according" trade surpluses to ASEAN countries.

Lastly, this reduced threat perception of China is also due to Beijing's new and active "sophisticated diplomacy", from Deng Xiaoping through the Jiang Zemin–Zhu Rongji team to the present Hu Jintao–Wen Jiabao leadership. ASEAN countries are constantly assured of a "benign China", in its outlook and national strategy, which subsequently reduced the "China threat". This shift in Southeast Asia mirrors a similar change in the international perception of China, as it emerges not only as an economic and political power, but also as a responsible player on the world stage.

Key to this perception shift in ASEAN has been China's strategic policy of "down-playing ideology, moving towards pragmatism", which ASEAN countries have detected in both China's domestic policies and external relations; ASEAN countries appreciate the "normalization" of Beijing's relations with the region. With greater "sophistication", Beijing has deliberately changed its strategic engagement with ASEAN and extended a hand of "strategic friendship". Ideology has been abandoned both domestically and externally, thus assuaging the fears and concerns of ASEAN countries. A more pragmatic and "normalized" China has therefore helped redefine the geopolitical relationship between Beijing and ASEAN, as the former seeks stability for its own economic development, based on its current *tryptique* of "stability, development, reforms". The common feeling in ASEAN is that they could now do business with a more pragmatic generation of Chinese leaders and the "new" China. China has thus successfully wooed and courted ASEAN countries, in order to stabilize relations and the region, for economic development and social progress.

Economically, the ASEAN-China Free Trade Agreement (FTA) or "Ten+1" has effectively bound China closer to ASEAN; furthermore, China is "according" unprecedented surpluses to ASEAN economies and increasing Chinese investments to ASEAN, like in oil and gas in Indonesia (through CNOOC) or in manufacturing in Vietnam and Thailand. Potentially, Chinese investments could fuel further economic growth in ASEAN, but competition could also increase for natural resources worldwide, thanks to China's growing appetite for oil, gas, steel, minerals and agricultural products, with potential negative repercussion on world prices, especially for non-commodity-producing ASEAN economies. Similarly, China's human resources are moving to Southeast Asia in a progressive, but not insignificant way. Chinese tourists, students, expatriates and lower-level workers are flocking to ASEAN countries, bringing new opportunities and revenue to their economies. Chinese growing presence could thus have an increasing financial and social impact on ASEAN. Moreover, Chinese economic and social assistance will increase to the region, like in the Greater Mekong Sub-Region (GMS), or in the "regional fight" against SARS and avian flu.

ASEAN and China have contributed enormously to laying the foundation of ASEAN+3, through the consolidation of relations for 1.8 billion people living in East Asia; this in turn should lay the foundation for the whole East Asia of thirteen countries, as the ASEAN-China cornerstone "embraces" Japan and South Korea, the other two key partners in the region.

THE RISE OF CHINA'S "SOFT POWER" AND ITS CULTURAL AND SOCIAL INFLUENCE IN ASEAN

Commensurate with China's rise as an economic and political power, there has been a concurrent rise in China's "soft power" in Southeast Asia.[10] Chinese culture, cuisine, calligraphy, cinema, curios, art, acupuncture, herbal medicine and fashion fads have penetrated into regional culture.

Fascination for popular Chinese culture amongst ASEAN youth in film, pop music and the television has been noticeable, even though such popular culture may in fact emanate from Hong Kong (films, actors, actresses and "canto-pop") or Taiwan (like the "Meteor Garden" television series or boy-bands, such as F4 or 5566), and not necessarily, China. Joint "Chinese" film production, such as "Hero" or "Crouching Tiger, Hidden Dragon" (which "pool" together acting talents from China, Taiwan and Hong Kong) have hit international box-offices and given Chinese culture a big boost. Mainland Chinese cinema idols, like Zhang Yimou and Gong Li, are beginning to command an artistic following, although they still lack a popular following. But Mainland Chinese consumer brands (like Hai-er, TCL or Huawei) are becoming increasingly popular in ASEAN societies, especially in lower-end electronic and telecommunication products in Indonesia and Philippines today.

But more importantly in Southeast Asia today is the rise in the role and influence of ethnic Chinese. Formerly, resolute anti-communist and anti-Beijing, this group has swung towards a "more benign China", as these communities ride on the coat-tails of this emerging China. In Thailand, there is undoubtedly a rise in Thai-Chinese power and influence, not only in commerce and business (as it had always and traditionally been the case), but also in politics (with PM Thaksin Shinawatra and his ruling Thai Rath Thai Party), the bureaucracy and intelligentsia. Indonesia has "rehabilitated" its Indonesian-Chinese community, as the Lunar New Year or "Imlek" has, since 2003, been designated an official Indonesian public holiday; public "Metro TV" has even some of its news bulletins ("*xin wen*") read in Mandarin. In the Philippines, Filipino-Chinese movies have captured top prizes in the annual Metro-Manila Film Festival for the past two years. There are also more "*chinovelas*" (Chinese serials) on local television stations in the afternoon, and Taiwanese boy-band F4 is currently Philippines' biggest craze, as its songs fill Manila's mega-malls. Vietnam is undoubtedly following the "China model" economically and even politically, as returning *viet kieu* (or overseas Vietnamese) are leading Vietnamese economic recovery, like overseas Chinese fifteen years ago. In Malaysia, Chinese tycoons are playing an increasingly prominent role in leading the current economic boom, and may even "inspire" reforms to Malaysia's *bumiputra* policy. In Southeast Asia, the "*pai hwa*" (or anti-Chinese) sentiment has undoubtedly subsided to a large extent, and many ethnic Southeast Asian Chinese now want to "rediscover" their (Chinese) culture and identity, in line with the emerging China to the north; Mandarin classes have thus boomed in ASEAN countries.

One of the most significant changes in Southeast Asia has been the attitude of ethnic Chinese, who have become less biased, less anti-communist and less anti-Beijing. But an "overplay" of their "China connection" could be a double-edged sword, if they do not "share" their acquired wealth in their own countries, especially if they are perceived to have prospered thanks to their "China connection". Therein lies a potential danger for the ethnic Chinese (in better integrating with their Southeast Asian "homeland") and Beijing, which must be aware of such a potential "ethnic Chinese" danger in ASEAN.

The twin factors of ASEAN acknowledging the rise of China's soft power in Southeast Asia and the recognition of the role and contributions of ethnic Chinese in the region have helped China affirm its cultural identity and prowess in the region, which in turn is helping consolidate an Asian identity within ASEAN+3.

THE DEVELOPMENT OF ASEAN+3 AS A COOPERATIVE EFFORT: CHINA'S AND ASEAN'S ROLES

ASEAN had indeed done a lot to shape ASEAN+3 in its initial stages, primarily as a means to help reform ASEAN from within and give ASEAN more clout on the international stage. ASEAN+3 has evolved into a formal regional framework today, thanks to ASEAN's driving power, but also due to the three Northeastern powers accepting ASEAN's primary role in formulating and leading the ASEAN+3 framework.

ASEAN+3 was in fact kicked off at the Informal ASEAN Summit meeting in Singapore in November 1999, where the East Asian Community concept was "sealed", although the three Northeast Asian countries did not meet the ten ASEAN countries together as a group, but separately in three "Ten+1" formats. The following year at the formal ASEAN Summit in Hanoi, China, Japan and South Korea inaugurated and institutionalized their breakfast meetings at the summit level involving the prime minister of China, the prime minister of Japan and the South Korean president. Then in Brunei in 2001, the ASEAN countries, China and Japan endorsed President Kim's idea of inaugurating the "ASEAN+3" Summit from that year onwards in Phnom Penh, Cambodia (at their next summit) and also commissioned an "ASEAN+3" study group to come out with a blueprint for the future East Asian grouping. Then at the Bali Summit in October 2003, the Northeastern component of ASEAN+3 issued for the first time a joint statement after their "institutionalized" breakfast meeting, hence concretizing the ties amongst the Three in a more formal way for the first time. It is believed that China had played a key role in recognizing the Northeast Asian-Three, which resulted in this joint statement. ASEAN on one hand, and the Three in the Northeast of Asia on the other hand, are hence developing well simultaneously and would hence consolidate ASEAN+3 as a true regional framework.

Besides these summits and since 2001, the foreign, finance and trade ministers of the "ASEAN+3" countries having been meeting separately, at least twice a year for each of the three groups of ministers and a sense of East Asian regionalism is consolidating slowly in the region. As the "ASEAN+3" grouping is institutionalized, there is a possibility that functionally in the future, the thirteen countries would be holding ministerial meetings in all areas, ranging from the social to the cultural and environmental fields. A process akin to the European cooperation (minus the Union) would probably gather steam across the East Asian region, although the idea of a union is still probably far over East Asia's horizon.

The strategic convergence of interests between ASEAN and China is obvious at this stage, thus guaranteeing their respective key roles in "driving" ASEAN+3 forward, at least in the foreseeable future.

Strategically, ASEAN has therefore come to a conclusion that it needs a bigger Asian entity to spark a revival of and constitute a stimulus for ASEAN and the greater East Asian region. There are at least three principal reasons why the "ASEAN+3" goal is now more acutely vital for ASEAN, namely:

- A bigger and more diversified market for ASEAN to stimulate growth through greater ASEAN exports and foreign investments. A subsidiary but equally important question is whether Japan could also revive its own moribund economy through such a regional "Ten+3" stimulus.
- A new challenge for "laggard" countries within ASEAN to enhance their own national competitiveness through reforms via a bigger and liberalized market, as ASEAN countries face a real "challenge from within", that is, the so-called "China threat".
- A new impetus in crisis and HRD management, as the region "pulls" its resources together, ranging from a potential financial pool of more than US$1,000 billion in total reserves to increased monetary cooperation (Chiang Mai Initiative) and the Human Resource Development and IT uplift programmes.

On the other hand, China realizes that it needs a peaceful regional environment and external stability in order to develop itself internally and have thus embarked on supporting the ASEAN initiative of creating a viable ASEAN+3 to "balance" America and Europe. China needs ASEAN, as ASEAN needs China to succeed in their own development; this mutual convergence of interests in fact constitutes China's and ASEAN's driving force for ASEAN+3 as East Asia's emerging regionalism.

This "mutual interests" driving force should propel ASEAN+3 forward as the main pillar of East Asian regionalism. Both sides have realized the importance of contributing towards modeling a "new" socio-economic development in East Asia, consolidating political and diplomatic relations and accepting the rise of China's soft power in the region (as *versus* American and Japanese soft power), within the framework of ASEAN+3.

CONCLUSION

Market forces will undoubtedly be fundamental in the *de facto* creation of an East Asian Community one day. What is critically needed is political will and a real sense of community and commonality in East Asia, which both China and ASEAN profoundly share and push for today, as they continue to play key roles in modelling this "common East Asian house" of tomorrow.

NOTES

1. Daniel Yergin and Joseph Stanislaw, *The Commanding Heights: The Battle for the World Economy* (New York: Simon and Schuster, 2002).
2. Paper presented by Eric Teo Chu Cheow at the Alpbach Europaische Forum, Austria, August 2003.
3. Paper by Eric Teo Chu Cheow to the Asia-Pacific Roundtable in Kuala Lumpur, June 2002.
4. Eric Teo Chu Cheow, "The East Asian Socio-Economic Model", paper presented at the Alpbach Europaische Forum in Austria, August 2003.
5. Eric Teo, "Asian Reactions to the Avian Flu Crisis", *China Brief*, The Jamestown Foundation, 3 March 2004.
6. Eric Teo, "Healthy Growth Key to Political Stability", *China Daily*, 19 March 2004.
7. ADB Research Paper, published by the ADBI, Tokyo, January 2003.
8. Eric Teo Chu Cheow, "China's Go South Policy", *Taiwan Perspective*, 8 March 2004.
9. Eric Teo Chu Cheow, "Solidifying China's Regional Partnerships", *China Daily*, 15 May 2004.
10. Eric Teo Chu Cheow, "China's Rising Soft Power in Southeast Asia", PACNET, #19A, 3 May 2004.

7

Ways Towards East Asian FTA: The Significant Roles of ASEAN and China

Zhang Xiaoji

INTRODUCTION

East Asia is an area where new emerging market economies are very dynamic, intra-regional economic links are closely knitted and highly reliant on external markets. Faced with the rapid growth of regional trade arrangements around the globe and especially the expansion of the two trade blocs of EU and NAFTA, the various countries in this region are reformulating their strategies of foreign economic relationship, and actively carrying out intra-regional and cross-regional free trade negotiations. Under the established "ASEAN+3 (Japan, China and Korea)" framework for cooperation, the Framework Agreement on Comprehensive Economic Cooperation between ASEAN-China was signed at the ASEAN-China summit held in Phnom Penh, and currently the Free Trade Area negotiations have entered an intensive period. Japan has signed a Japanese-Singapore Economic Partnership Agreement (JSEPA), and has issued a joint statement with ASEAN concerning the establishment of the Comprehensive Economic Partnership and the conducting of bilateral FTA negotiations with some members. FTA negotiations between Korea and

Singapore are also underway. China, Korea and Japan have issued a joint statement to set up a three-party committee to promote cooperation between the three countries. The final report submitted by the "East Asian Study Group" to the "ASEAN+3" Summit laid out proposals on how to boost the prosperity and stability of the East Asian region.

Against such a backdrop, how to maintain the cooperative tendency of the East Asian region and bridge the ideal and reality has become a common challenge to the "Ten+3" leaders. Through a multi-scheme comparison of East Asian regional cooperation, this chapter attempts to analyse the possibilities for EAFTA to be realized as a mid-term objective for ASEAN, Japan, China and Korea to promote regional economic integration.

NEW TENDENCIES OF FREE TRADE RELATIONSHIP IN EAST ASIA

In the 1990s, a wave of regional economic integration swept through the whole world. By the end of 2002, the World Trade Organization had received formal notifications of 250 Regional Trade Arrangements (RTAs). Most WTO members have participated in one or more RTAs, and the trade volume between RTA members accounted for forty-three per cent of the global trade in 2001. With various forms of RTA, institutional arrangements with Free Trade Area (FTA) at the core are winning over more and more acceptance by various countries. The establishment of trade blocs *via* trade agreements between countries is more often driven by political motives. For instance, countries can depend on free trade agreements to prevent possible military conflicts or to keep peace in the region. However, along with economic globalization, the expansion of internal markets *via* free trade areas to attract foreign investment and enhance international competitiveness has become a new driving force for regionalism.

All countries in East Asia are members of APEC, where its trade liberalization scheme applies the Principle of Unilateral Willingness, which is not binding upon its members. Therefore, prior to the Asian financial crisis, East Asian countries mostly abided by the unilateral liberalization policy based on the Most Favoured Nation (MFN) status as an important force supporting the multilateral trade system. The economic ties between the East Asian countries were mainly based on market forces rather than inter-governmental institutional arrangements.

The Asian financial crisis in 1997 changed the policy orientation of the East Asian countries, after which regional economic integration was driven onto the fast track of institutional arrangements. The strengthening of regional economic cooperation to jointly safeguard against the impacts of economic globalization has become a consensus of the East Asian countries. The ten ASEAN countries established a regular summit meeting arrangement with Japan, China and Korea (Ten+3), thus forming the regional cooperative framework in East Asia.

On the global scale, new regional trade arrangements kept increasing, driven not only by the interests of the members themselves, but by external pressure as well. Since multilateral trade systems cannot ensure all countries will share the benefits of economic globalization, intra-regional trade within the EU and the NAFTA, the two largest trade blocs, now accounts for one third of the global trade, and EU is still expanding its intra-regional market through its eastern enlargement. Under the active promotion of the United States, economic integration on the basis of the NAFTA will be expanded to the whole American continent, forming the Free Trade Area of America (FTAA). The internal trade of these two emerging largest trade blocs has exceeded forty per cent of the global trade (see Table 7.1 for details). In order to avoid damage from the trade diversion effect of the two largest trade blocs or to seek shortcuts into the two largest markets, various countries are seeking regional cooperative partners, forming a domino effect of regionalism around the globe. If the "Doha Round" agenda fails to bring into full play the role of promoting trade liberalization under the multilateral trade mechanisms and to enable the developing countries to share the benefits of economic liberalization, more and more countries will resort to regionalism so as to

Table 7.1
Comparison between ASEAN+3 and Major Regional Trade Blocs

	Percentage of Intra-regional Exports			Percentage of Intra-regional Exports in Global Export Volume
	1990	1995	2001	2001
EU-15	64.9	64.0	61.9	22.9
NAFTA	42.6	46.1	55.5	10.3
MERCOSUR	8.9	20.5	17.3	0.2
ASEAN	20.1	25.5	23.5	1.5
EU-25	67.4	65.7	68.9	27.1
Free Trade Area of America	45.7	52.6	60.8	13.1
ASEAN+3	27.1	36.8	32.0	5.4

Note: The percentage data of Intra-regional Exports of ASEAN+3 in 1995 and 2001 use figures of 1996 and 2000.

depend on regional trade liberalization to promote and complement the role of multilateral trade mechanisms.

EXPANSION OF INTRA-REGIONAL MARKET — KEY TO EAST ASIAN ECONOMIC INTEGRATION

Under the economic globalization, industrial transfers driven by cross-border investment are changing the intra-regional layout of the division of labour in East Asia, and the economic connections between the various states are becoming closer and closer. However, the growth pattern of depending on external demand as the driving force in East Asia is now facing the challenges presented by the two trade blocs in Europe and North America. In order to improve efficiency and to maintain stable growth, it has become a new option for East Asian regional economic integration to expand intra-regional markets and to strengthen self-supported growth capabilities through trade liberalization arrangements.

1. Characteristics of East Asian Intra-Regional Trade Development

For quite some time, East Asia has always been a global manufacturing base with a high dependence on external markets such as Europe and the United States. Although the percentage of intra-regional trade in East Asia has risen somewhat in the 1990s, yet distinct from the feature of the EU single market and the NAFTA with the U.S. market as the core, the expansion of internal trade in East Asia mainly depended on the extension of the production link and value link resulting from the medium products trade based on industrial transfers.

Since the 1990s, the Four Tigers of Asia followed Japan in speeding up their industrial transfers, resulting in changes to the traditional patterns of division of labour in East Asia. In the first place, some formerly backward countries narrowed the industrial gap between countries by implementing a catching-up strategy and promoting industrial upgrading. Secondly, multinational corporations have changed the patterns of industrial transfer and division of labour between East Asian countries by implementing global manufacturing and procurement strategies. For instance, the globalization development of such newly emerging industries as the IT industry sets the enterprises in various countries as suppliers in the production chain to participate in the division of labour within the industries. Thirdly, the intra-regional production layout is not only dependent on resource, cost, and market scale advantages, but also on the assembling effect of industry as well.

The new industrial division of labour and production layout has brought about changes in the trade structure of East Asian countries, which can be demonstrated in the gradual decrease in the proportion of primary products in intra-regional trade and gradual increase in the proportion of capital-intensive products and medium products. The comparative advantages of the various countries are not only evident in the commodities trade between different industries, but also in the intra-industrial trade. For instance, the export of machinery equipment, steel, and chemical products from Japan and Korea still maintains an obvious advantage, while ASEAN and China is more competitive in exporting labour-intensive light industry and textile products. What deserves attention is that IT products and components have become the most important commodities in mutual exports between Japan, Korea, China and ASEAN. Japan and the NIEs shifted industries and production links that are no longer of competitive advantage to other East Asian countries, thus expanding the mutual trade in components and spare parts between East Asian countries. Japan still leads the other countries in producing capital-intensive products and key spare parts, while the developing countries possess obvious advantages in labour-intensive production and assembling links. The value chains resulting from the changes of industrial division of labour and industrial layout has not only brought closer the economic relations between East Asian countries, but also fiercer competition.

2. Increasing Importance of Cross-Border Direct Investment in East Asian Intra-Regional Trade

In the early 1990s, Japan used to be one of the three largest sources of global FDI together with EU and the United States, and the ASEAN countries and Korea were major investment destinations for Japan at the time. Later, since the Japanese economy stagnated and the growth rate of overseas investment slowed down, capital primarily flowed out to Europe and the United States. The percentage of Japanese investment in the FDI inflow in East Asia fell from 26 per cent in 1996 to 8 per cent in 1999, while that of the United States and EU increased from 14 per cent and 10 per cent respectively to 18 per cent, according to IMF figures. Since 2000, however, Japanese investment in China grew rapidly, accounting for an increasing percentage of its FDI in East Asia. As both capital inflow and outflow countries, Korea and ASEAN concentrated their foreign investments in the East Asian region, and China is also an important target for Korean and ASEAN investments. The 1997 Asian financial crisis dramatically reduced capital inflows into Korea and ASEAN, currently restored to the pre-crisis levels. China, which pulled through the financial crisis with relatively minor disturbance, absorbed over 40 per cent of FDI inflows in Asia. In recent years, China has adopted the "going out" strategy, and overseas investments by Chinese enterprises have increased rapidly. In 2003, officially approved investment abroad amounted to US$2 billion, 60 per cent of which went to Asian countries and regions. FDI is the most important factor affecting the industrial division of labour and industrial distribution in the past ten years in the East Asian region. The industries and location selected by FDI sources exert significant influences over the trade within and outside East Asia. For instance, Japan and Korea transferred their industries to China through FDI, resulting in changes in the places of origin for exports. But this has not only reinforced the two countries' status as suppliers of capital-intensive and medium products, but has expanded Japanese and Korean exports to China. In the meantime, the percentage of trade volume of Foreign Investment Enterprises (FIEs) in China-Korea and China-Japan trade has exceeded 50 per cent, of which enterprises with Japanese and Korean investments played a leading role. Between 1991 and 2001, the annual growth rate of FIE exports to and imports from Japan were 32.8 per cent and 42.7 per cent respectively, much higher than that of bilateral trade between China and Japan during the same period (17.3 per cent and 16.9 per cent). Of Chinese imports from and exports to Korea in 2001, the percentage of foreign enterprises was as high as 59 per cent and 49 per cent respectively. The practices of the three countries suggest that the promotion effect of investment on trade is much larger than the substitution effect. In recent years, trade between ASEAN and China has been growing rapidly, and is closely related to the import and export of spare parts by FIEs in China, including ASEAN-invested enterprises.

3. Striking Contradictions between Expanding Supply Capabilities in East Asia and Slow Growth of Intra-Regional Market Demand

For a long time, the various countries in East Asia have adopted the outward development strategy, and their economic growths have been driven by external demand with a high degree of dependency on the exports to European and American markets. Most East Asian economies only have small domestic markets and lack the capabilities to upgrade their industries. Since global technologies are speedily upgrading and the life cycles of the products are being shortened, these countries are in an unfavourable position in receiving international industrial transfers, thus resulting in identical industrial structure and tough competition. In 1996, the falling of electronic products prices resulted in the reduction of export revenues in East Asian countries and deteriorating international balance of payments, which is also one of the major reasons for the outbreak of Asian financial crisis.

With the formation of the two trade blocs of EU and NAFTA and their continuous expansion into the peripheries, a trade diversion effect has already affected the East Asian countries. The market in EU and the United States of some East Asian countries is squeezed by their member states, so their market shares are reducing gradually. Between 1993 and 2001, East Asian imports from North America fell from 33.5 per cent to 28.5 per cent. In order to enhance competitiveness, various countries are transferring more and more commodities to China for processing and exporting. Since China is at the end of the production chains in East Asia, such triangular trades have resulted in an ever-increasing trade deficit of China to East Asian countries (see Figure 7.1 for more details). At the same time, China's trade surplus and friction with the United States have been on the rise.

East Asian economies have a high degree of dependency upon external markets and relatively weak capabilities to achieve self-supported growth within the region. After the Asian financial crisis, East Asian countries had to maintain large quantities of foreign reserves to safeguard against the risks brought about by globalization. But such an action has not only increased the costs for macro-economic management and asset management, but has also resulted in the draining of resources as well. Faced with such pressures, East

Figure 7.1
Trade Volume between China and Asia (excluding HK) (1991–2003)
(US$100 Millions)

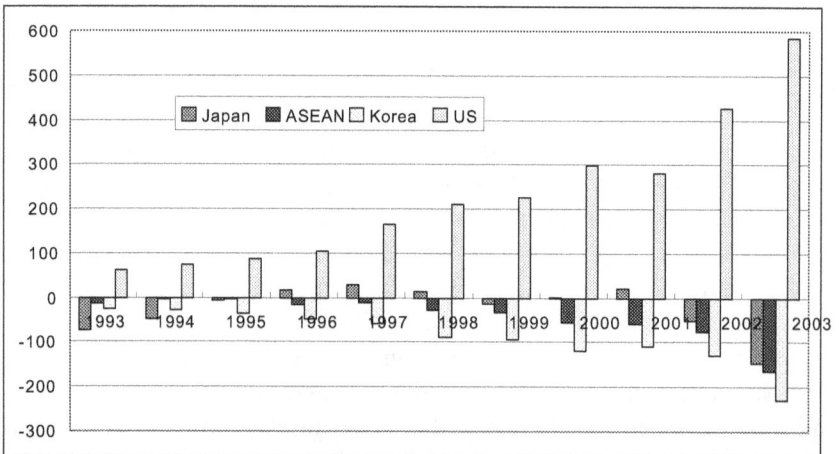

Asian countries have to reconsider the multilateral and bilateral trade policies. The short-term effects to realizing the liberalization and facilitation of intra-regional factors lie in the reduction of production costs and the improvement of efficiency. The long-term effect of intra-regional trade liberalization is the expansion of market scale and the increase of intra-regional demands so as to optimize resource allocation, to attract more foreign investments and to improve their capabilities of self-supported growth. This is more important for countries with small domestic markets and is one of the major driving forces to establish a free trade area.

SIMULATION AND COMPARISON OF OPTIONS OF FTA UNDER THE "TEN+3" FRAMEWORK

1. Benefits and Costs of Establishing the Free Trade Area

Whatever option is adopted to establish an FTA between ASEAN, China, Japan and Korea, different economic influences will emerge between the member and non-member countries, as well as between the free trade area members. Overall, the elimination of tariffs within the FTA will result in trade creation and trade diversion effects between members. Trade creation is mainly derived from the expansion of market scale and the improvement of competitive efficiency, but the reduction of tariff revenues, the adjustment of industrial structure and trade diversion within and outside the region are likely to harm certain members. Under normal circumstances, the complementarities between members are stronger in a free trade area composed of developed countries and a number of members, and the benefits derived by the participating countries from the trade liberalization are larger. The preferential arrangements between the FTA members are almost bound to generate a trade diversion effect on non-members, for the exporting enterprises in the non-participating countries will face unequal terms of competition with enterprises within the FTA. Therefore, during the course of regional trade liberalization, each country will have to weigh their choices from the economic, political and security perspectives, whether or not to establish or join an FTA.

2. Macro-Economic Simulation on the Free Trade Area in East Asia

The research project entitled "Options for the Free Trade Area in East Asia", completed by the Development Research Centre of the State Council of the PRC (DRC) last year, adopted the computable general equilibrium model

(CGE) to make simulation analyses of the FTA options under the "Ten+3" framework. The results analysed the effects of prospective FTAs on the various countries in comparison with the baseline scenario. Since China has reached a framework agreement with ASEAN, China, and Japan and Korea have started to research the possibilities to establish a China-Japan-Korea FTA (CJKFTA). We will only analyse the schemes of the China-ASEAN (CAFTA), CJKFTA and East Asian Free Trade Area (EAFTA) here.

1. China-ASEAN FTA (CAFTA)

As can be seen in Table 7.2, the establishment of a China-ASEAN FTA will boost the economic growth of each other and add to their welfare gains. Compared with the baseline scenario, the GDP growth of ASEAN will grow by 1.95 per cent (US$50 billion), China by 0.78 per cent (US$22.3 billion) in terms of overall welfare increases.

The aforementioned simulations are based on the 1997 statistics. With

Table 7.2
Simulation Results of CAFTA (Scenario One)

Country/Region	GDP %	Welfare (US$ Billions)
ASEAN	1.95	49.5
China	0.78	22.3

Source: Simulation results from the CGE model by the DRC research team.

China's accession into the WTO in 2001, the level of tariffs has been greatly reduced. Therefore, the research team revised relevant parameters in accordance with China's WTO commitments, attempting to make the results closer to the reality. Table 7.3 is the simulation results after the adjustment. Through the comparison, we can see that, since the unilateral liberalization commitments have been realized, China's GDP growth has increased from 0.78 per cent in "Scenario One" to 2.4 per cent, but the total welfare gains have fallen from US$22.3 billion to US$7.4 billion correspondingly. The economy of ASEAN has grown by 1 per cent more and the welfare benefit is US$47 billion. This may result from the share of ASEAN's exports to China being significantly larger than the share of China's exports to ASEAN.

Table 7.3
Simulation Results of CAFTA (Scenario Two)

Country/Region	GDP %	Welfare (US$ Billions)
ASEAN	3.0	47
China	2.4	7.4

Source: Simulation results from the CGE model by the DRC research team.

2. China-Japan-Korea FTA (CJKFTA)

According to the consensus reached by the leaders of China, Japan and Korea, the three representative research teams carried out joint researches on the "Economic Impacts of a Possible FTA among China, Japan and Korea", adopting the CGE model to make a simulation analysis of the macro-economic impacts by the CJKFTA. Although the three countries established models separately, yet the conclusions were basically identical. As indicated by Table 7.4, first of all, the establishment of CJKFTA is significant in boosting economic growth in the three countries, expanding foreign trade and improving welfare. Due to the influences of trade liberalization of the three countries, the lifting effect of GDP growth is 1.1–2.9 per cent to China, 0.1–0.5 per cent to Japan, and 2.5–3.1 per cent to Korea (the most obvious one, since the exports to output ratio is substantially higher for Korea). The total welfare gain increases of the three countries will amount to US$4.7–US$6.4 billion, US$6.7–US$7.4 billion and US$11–US$26.3 billion respectively. The conclusions of the tri-party joint research are as follows: First of all, from an overall perspective, according to these macro-economic figures, China, Japan and Korea will all benefit from the CJKFTA, and the establishment of the CJKFTA will produce a win-win situation. Secondly, the economic effects or welfare gains from any bilateral FTA among the three countries will be less remarkable than the CJKFTA. And any bilateral FTA will make the excluded country sustain great losses because of the trade diversion effect. Thirdly, given that the CJKFTA is established, benefits brought about by the capital aggregation effect (including the FDI) will be much higher than the static efficiency benefits from trade liberalization.

The leaders of China, Japan and Korea appraised the research results in their Joint Declaration positively: "Appreciating the progress of the joint study on the economic impact of a free trade agreement (FTA) conducted by

Table 7.4
The Impacts of CJKFTA on Welfare and GDP

	Welfare (Unit: US$ billions)	GDP (%)
China	4.7 – 6.4	1.1 – 2.9
Japan	6.7 – 7.4	0.1 – 0.5
Korea	11.4 – 26.3	2.5 – 3.1

their respective research institutes, the three countries will explore, in a timely manner, the direction of a closer future economic partnership among the three countries".

3. East Asian Free Trade Area (EAFTA)

As indicated in Table 7.5, compared with the China-ASEAN Free Trade Area, the GDP of all members in an EAFTA will experience faster increases. The GDP growth of ASEAN is the greatest at about 4 per cent, China at 3.4 per cent, and Korea at the same pace. Although Japan will only experience a GDP growth of 0.78 per cent, yet owing to its huge economic aggregation, its absolute welfare is larger than that of the other members.

Since welfare effects include the transfer of producer surplus to consumer surplus, members with higher levels of income or larger scales of demand will be affected more greatly during the course of regional economic integration. Although the GDP growth of China, Japan and Korea are not high, yet their welfare gains increased by US$54.7 billion, US$118.8 billion and US$34.7 billion respectively, obviously much larger than any single member of the ASEAN.

Table 7.5
Macro-Economic Impacts of the EAFTA

Country/Region	GDP %	Welfare (US$ Billions)
ASEAN	4.0	55.0
China	3.4	54.7
Japan	0.8	118.8
Korea	3.4	34.7

Source: Simulation results from the CGE model by the DRC research team.

The virtue of the CGE model is its ability to make simulations over the macro-economic effects of a possible FTA, but the simulation results can only reflect the economic benefits at the time of the FTA establishment in comparison with the baseline scenario. Since the hypothesized conditions of the model itself are at variance with the real economy (for example, all factors within one country can flow freely between the industries, but cannot flow across the border), the simulation results can only be used in analysing the direction of effect by regional trade liberalization on the economic development of the various countries.

3. Comparison of Macro-Economic Simulation Results between FTA Options

As indicated by the comparisons of the macro-economic simulation results, the larger the market scale covered by the FTA and the stronger the economic complementarities, the more benefits can be yielded. In terms of economic gains of each country, the order of FTA options is ranked as follows: East Asian Free Trade Area, China-Japan-Korea Free Trade Area and China-ASEAN Free Trade Area. Nonetheless, it is not hard to imagine the difficulty of negotiations for the thirteen countries with different economic development levels to establish a free trade relationship. As the experience of APEC may suggest, it would be very hard for multi-party trade liberalization negotiations to achieve substantial progress given the lack of mutual trust. Therefore, the choice of the optimal scheme must take into account the efficiency of the negotiations and the cost.

PATH CHOICE FOR THE ESTABLISHMENT OF THE EAST ASIAN FREE TRADE AREA

1. Competition for Core Status in East Asian Regional Cooperation

Reviewing the FTA strategies within the East Asian region, it can be said that, although Japan has signed a framework agreement of Comprehensive Economic Partnership with ASEAN, it is not eager for the initiation of formal negotiations but places the establishment of bilateral free trade relationship with Korea, Thailand, Malaysia, the Philippines as a priority. According to the strategic conception of Japan, East Asian economic cooperation will be dominated by Japan, China, Korea plus ASEAN, but Japan has not yet made a final decision on the Sino-Japanese relationship, and is still ambivalent in its attitude towards the establishment of a CJKFTA.

Figure 7.2
The Impact of Different FTA Options on the GDP of Various Partners

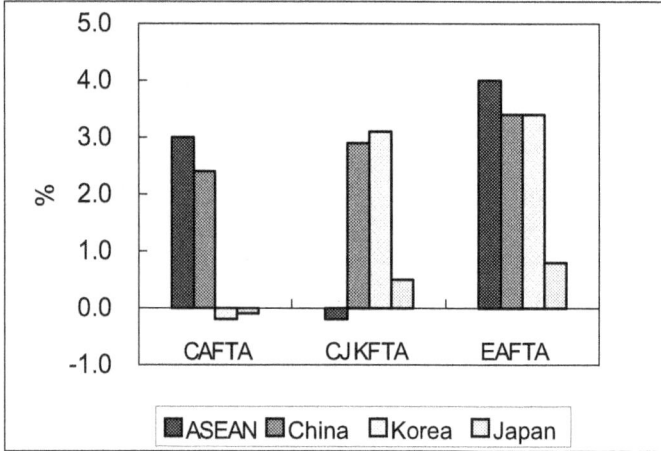

Source: Simulation results from the CGE model by the DRC research team.

It is obvious that Japan wishes to copy the "Japan-Singapore Pattern", that is, to push East Asian economic integration towards the direction of reinforcing Japan's core status through bilateral EPA negotiations.

The FTA negotiation between Korea and Japan has already started, but Korea still desires to play a hub role of sub-regional cooperation in Northeast Asia and maintains an active attitude towards the CJKFTA. On the issue of establishing free trade relationship with ASEAN, Korea seems to be imitating Japanese tactics: On the one hand, it has initiated negotiations with Singapore, and on the other, it is consulting with ASEAN on signing the "Comprehensive Economic Partnership" framework agreement.

Under the Ten+3 framework, ASEAN has been playing the core role. Since AFTA is a test case for developing countries to implement regional integration, the ASEAN experience will be of important significance to East Asian regional cooperation. However, the overall economic strength of ASEAN is far weaker than the three countries in Northeast Asia. If the major ASEAN members establish partnership relationships with Japan, China and Korea respectively, the negotiating status of ASEAN as a whole will be indubitably weakened. On the one hand, ASEAN is continuously pushing forward the AFTA process, while on the other, ASEAN has established partnership relationships with China, Japan (and maybe Korea later) respectively, and is consulting with the United States, India and other countries on the establishment of free trade relationships. By doing so, it wishes to maintain its hub status in East Asian regional cooperation by taking advantage of the power balances between the great powers.

2. The Hub-Spokes Pattern to East Asian Regional Integration: Propeller or Stumbling Block?

Judging from the current situations, two "hub-spokes" sub-regional integration patterns are likely to emerge in East Asia. One would be the respective establishment of free trade areas with China, Japan and Korea by ASEAN, through which ASEAN will become the hub for regional cooperation, with China, Japan and Korea without any free trade relationship with each other, as the "spoke countries". The other pattern would be with Japan as the hub, and Korea, Singapore, Malaysia, Thailand, the Philippines as the "spoke countries".

From the perspectives of geoeconomic and trade relationships, the economic relationship between China, Japan and Korea is obviously closer than that between ASEAN and the three countries (See Figure 7.1). At least for China, Japan and Korea, the "hub-spokes" pattern is not an optimal choice. Although the three countries can derive benefits from establishing FTAs with ASEAN, yet the three countries can not only fail to obtain any liberalization benefits among themselves, but their mutual trade and investment relationship is likely to be harmed by the trade diversion effect as well.

As the hub, ASEAN can attract more investments and obtain more market opportunities by establishing FTAs with China, Japan and Korea respectively. Nonetheless, since the "consensus decision-making principle" is implemented inside ASEAN and every member is able to veto the resolutions, the coordinating capabilities of the ASEAN Secretariat are greatly curtailed. In reality, respective FTA negotiations by ASEAN with China, Japan and Korea are ten separate negotiations with the ten ASEAN countries. If any negotiation with any member is not smooth, the negotiating process with other members will be affected. The difficulty of negotiating with China, Japan, Korea or even more powers at the same time is not hard to imagine. Moreover, since a unified market has not been formed inside the AFTA, the management costs concerning the rule of origin would also be higher in trying to establish FTAs with numerous countries.

In terms of economic strength and influence, Japan is the second largest economic power in the world and by far the most powerful in East Asia.

Figure 7.3
Percentage of Mutual Exports

Percentage of Mutual
Exports between China, Japan
and Korea in
Their Total Exports (%)

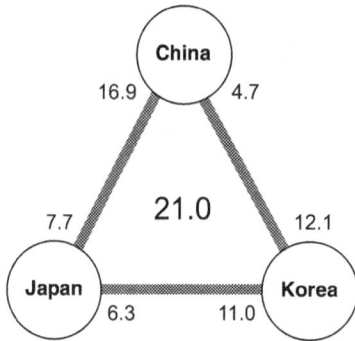

Percentage of Mutual
Exports between China, Japan,
Korea and ASEAN in
Total Exports (%)

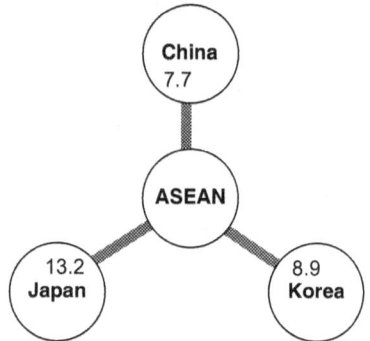

Note: The figure at the centre of the left diagram stands for the percentage of intra-regional exports for China, Japan and Korea.
Source: WTO, ASEAN Secretariat.

However, weak political status, mercantilism and conservative agricultural trade policies have kept Japan from playing such a core role in East Asian regional cooperation like Germany, France and the United States. The strategy of Japan in establishing an EPA with Korea and ASEAN members can bring to full play the advantages of Japan as a great power. Although it seems to be quite advantageous to Japan, the Japan-Singapore FTA pattern does not necessarily apply to other bilateral negotiations. If Japan refuses to make concessions on the issue of agricultural trade, it would be hard for the bilateral negotiations to achieve any substantial progress. If the bilateral FTAs put excessive products into the List of General Exceptions, it is also likely to raise the suspicion or objection of other WTO members.

The negotiation costs of bilateral or sub-regional institutional arrangements are relatively lower and can offer accumulated experience as well as promote the trade liberalization process on a larger scale. However, the mutual competition between "hub-spokes" FTAs may result not only in the trade diversion effect, but the complicated preferential policies and ROOs are also likely to disrupt the original production layouts and dissever the intra-regional supply chains towards the global market, thus harming the overall vigour of the East Asian economy.

3. The Role Played by China, Korea and Japan in East Asian Regional Economic Cooperation

The total population of China, Japan and Korea was 1.5 billion in the year 2002. According to World Bank statistics, the total GDP of the three countries amounted to US$5,700 billion, accounting for 20 per cent of the world total. In 2001, the exports from the three countries accounted for 11.9 per cent of the global market, and the service imports accounted for 12.4 per cent of the world total (see Table 7.6 for more details). Although the intra-regional trade between China, Japan and Korea rose from 11 per cent in 1990 to 21 per cent in 2001, it is still quite low compared with the EU, the NAFTA, the MERCOSUR, the ASEAN and other regional trade blocs.

Currently, China, Japan and Korea are seeking to establish free trade relationships with their respective trade partners, yet the process of institutional cooperation between the three countries is relatively slower. This can no longer be reasoned, with the ever-closer economic link between the three countries, nor will it be conducive to the development of East Asian regional economic cooperation. As mentioned above, if China, Japan and Korea establish bilateral free trade relationships with ASEAN or certain ASEAN members respectively, while the three countries themselves fail to boost mutual cooperation and coordination, each country can only derive limited benefits, and will be unable to play an active role in the trade liberalization

Table 7.6
Economic Survey of the China-Japan-Korean FTA, EU and NAFTA

	CJKFTA	EU	NAFTA
GDP percentage in the world total	18.5	26.4	33.6
Percentage of commodity trade in the world total	11.9	37.1	21.6
Percentage of service imports in the world	12.4	41.9	17
Percentage of intra-regional trade	21	61.4	46.2
Percentage of intra-regional investment	11	52	21.2

Note: The figure of intra-regional investment in NAFTA is calculated according to the inflow volume in 1994.

process in East Asia. Therefore, speeding up the establishment of a free trade relationship among China, Japan and Korea is of great significance to the East Asian regional economic integration.

4. China's Active Stance on East Asian Regional Cooperation

China has established a long-term strategy to develop a partnership relation with its neighbouring countries. Its leaders have stated the Chinese stance on various occasions that China will continue to consolidate its harmonious relationship with its neighbours, to stick to the principle of "Doing Good to the Neighbours and Building a Good-Neighbourly Relationship and Partnership", to strengthen regional cooperation, to keep peace and stability in the region, and to push to a new level of exchanges and cooperation with neighbouring countries.

China does not seek any special status in regional cooperation. Some regard its active stance in promoting East Asian regional cooperation as "struggling with Japan for leadership or dominating status in East Asia", but such a view is a misunderstanding. Chinese leaders have repeatedly stated that China welcomes a more important role played by Japan in East Asian regional economic integration. As a member of East Asia and the largest developing country in the region, China is willing to participate actively in regional cooperation and support any proposal that is beneficial to developing regional cooperation in the common interests of the East Asian countries. China is willing to study the plan for establishing an East Asian FTA and holding the East Asian Summit. It is of the view that, with the constant development of regional cooperation in various fields, it is necessary to plan and coordinate the "Ten+3" cooperation, and welcomes any active discussion in this regard.

With the fast development of the Chinese economy, China will play two roles in the region with unusual prominence. First, it is likely to strengthen its export competitiveness in a wider range of products. Second, the size of China's growing internal market will make it the largest East Asian importer of East Asian goods. The market scale advantage of China is becoming increasingly obvious. As can be seen in Figure 7.4, since the early 1990s, the degree of dependence of East Asian exports on China has obviously been on the rise. It can be attributed to the increase in medium products trade resulting from speedy industrial transfers, but in the meantime, it also reflects the expansion of domestic market demands in China. East Asian neighbours will be among the first to benefit from China's WTO commitments to opening up its market. In 2003, the total volume of imports in China increased by 39.9 per cent, and imports from Japan, Korea and ASEAN

Figure 7.4
Degree of Dependence by East Asian Exports on China

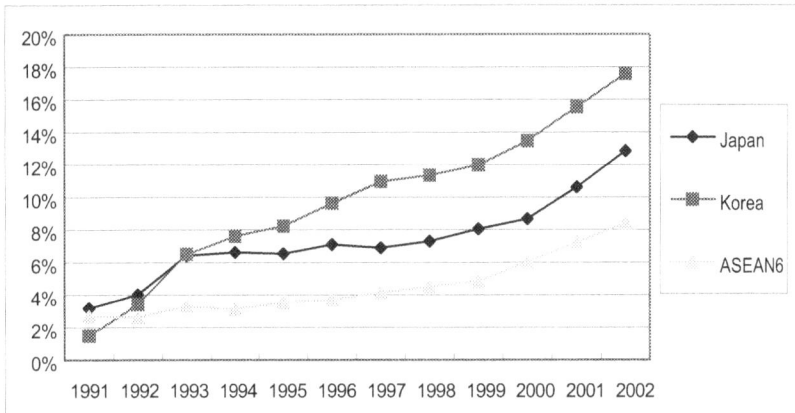

Note: ASEAN-6 refers to Singapore, Malaysia, Indonesia, Thailand, the Philippines and Brunei.
Source: Calculated according to the statistics of WTO and China's Ministry of Commerce.

increased by 38.7 per cent, 51 per cent and 50 per cent respectively. More and more people realize that the rise of China is an opportunity rather than a threat. The fast economic development in China has become an important driving force for East Asian exports.

China's active stances under the "Ten+3" framework promoted the process of East Asian regional cooperation. It signed the Framework Agreement on Comprehensive Economic Cooperation with ASEAN as the first ever country to do so. In order to benefit from the free trade area as soon as possible, the two parties formulated an "early harvest" plan, deciding to reduce tariffs for more than 500 products since 1 January 2004. Since the three ASEAN countries of Vietnam, Laos and Cambodia have not yet joined the WTO, China agreed to grant non-WTO members of ASEAN with Most Favoured Nation status so as to help with these countries' development, that is, the WTO commitments made by China in her accession will also apply to these countries. The Chinese leaders also took the initiative to put forward proposals to Japan and Korea on initiating researches into the possibilities of a trilateral FTA, with the aim to boost trade and economic cooperation between the three countries and to realize greater economic integration in East Asia.

5. Implementation of the China-ASEAN FTA Way towards EAFTA

The levels of economic development in East Asian countries are quite different, which, together with the great diversity of politics, culture and religion, are often deemed barriers to the establishment of a regional free trade area. People of such an opinion often regard the EU and NAFTA as the model for East Asian economic integration. However, the objectives of regional economic integration are to encourage and respect diversity rather than to eliminate diversity. The ever-closer economic links between the East Asian countries prove that, instead of hindering regional integration, diversity will turn into an active factor enabling the various countries to bring into full play their comparative advantages and disadvantages. It will also be able to promote intra-regional trade, industrial transfer, specialization and division of labour. One of the major aims of establishing the East Asian FTA is to narrow the income gaps between the various members by sharing the benefits of economic integration.

Although the role of large countries in promoting East Asian regional economic cooperation is quite important, at present, the interests of the smaller countries and the less developed countries require more attention. The challenges to the establishment of the East Asian FTA lie not in the relationship between China and Japan, but in how large countries can win over the trust of small countries and form a common political will among the thirteen states.

Currently, of all bilateral and sub-regional FTAs that have been implemented or are under negotiation in East Asia, the China-ASEAN FTA is the most influential one involving the most members. A unified market with 1.8 billion people, US$2 trillion of GDP, US$1.7 trillion total trade volume and more than US$600 billion of foreign reserves will undoubtedly constitute a huge attraction to, and produce an exemplar effect on, East Asia and the other countries around the globe. Measured in terms of GDP, FTAs with Japanese participation are without question more influential. But, the potential for development of the populous new emerging market economies cannot be ignored, for the greatest challenge to the self-supported growth capabilities in East Asia lies in the inadequate intra-regional market demands. With the participation of Japan, the country with the greatest domestic purchasing power in the East Asian region and entering into an aging society, it is not enough to depend only on Japan to absorb the huge productive capabilities of the manufacturing sectors in the region. China's exports to other East Asian economies are significantly smaller than its imports from these economies. By contrast, Japan runs large trade surpluses with other East Asian economies. This might create incentives for the rest of East Asia to form an FTA with China rather than with Japan, particularly if the Japanese Government is reluctant to open its agricultural market.

Currently, the numerous FTA plans in East Asia reflect the wills of the statesmen. If these FTAs or EPA plans can be implemented in a short period of time, they are very likely to bring about benign interaction between the sub-regional cooperation and to boost regional economic integration in East Asia. The China-ASEAN FTA will enhance the integration of trade liberalization networks, resulting in the establishment of an East Asian FTA rather than discriminate against the other forms of free trade arrangements in East Asia.

Although there could be multiple roadmaps to the establishment of the East Asian FTA, market forces and choices by enterprises are not to be ignored. For instance, in order to safeguard the already formed industrial chains and markets, no entrepreneur in any country would give up the huge business opportunities brought about by the China-ASEAN FTA and wait for the slow decisions made by politicians. The FTA initiative between China and ASEAN will not only expand intra-regional trade and investment, but also attract large investments from Japan, Korea and other countries or regions as well as enhance self-supported economic growth capabilities and export competitiveness within the region. Perhaps restricted by the pace of adjustment of the domestic agricultural sector, Japan and Korea will not join the China-ASEAN FTA within the foreseeable future. But with the outbound transfers of the manufacturing industry and the service industry, Japan and Korea will adjust their trade policies on agricultural products as soon as possible to remove barriers to their integration into the East Asian Free Trade Area. Therefore, although the final formation of the EAFTA may require ten to fifteen years, the initiatives taken by the China-ASEAN FTA will indubitably accelerate the process.

CONCLUDING REMARKS

The promotion of economic integration among the East Asian countries through institutional arrangements is based on multiple motivations. With the two largest trade blocs of the European and American continents starting to exert the trade diversion effect on East Asia, the strengthening of regional economic cooperation to jointly safeguard against the impacts brought about by economic globalization, has become the consensus of the various East Asian countries.

Regional economic integration of East Asia based on market forces is the internal driving force behind the creation of free trade relationships in East Asia. Over the last ten years, the value chains formed as a result of the industrial division of labour and the industrial distribution in East Asia have expanded medium products trade within the region and made the economic links among the relevant countries closer. FDI is the most important factor affecting the industrial division of labour and the industrial layout within the East Asian region. The short-term effect of the liberalization and facilitation of factors flowing within the East Asian region is the reduction of production costs and the improvement of efficiency. The long-term effect of regional trade liberalization will be the expansion of market scale, increase in demand within the region, the optimization of resource allocation, the attraction of foreign investments, and the enhancement of self-supported economic growth capabilities. For countries with limited domestic markets, this appears all the more important.

By comparing the macro-economic simulation results of the three options including the EAFTA, the China-Japan-Korea FTA and the China-ASEAN FTA, the larger the scale of the market covered by the Free Trade Area and the stronger the economic complementarities, the greater the benefits will turn out to be. Nonetheless, it is quite difficult for the thirteen countries with great discrepancies of economic scale and levels of development to negotiate on the free trade relationship.

The negotiation costs of bilateral or sub-regional institutional arrangements are relatively lower, through which much experience can be accumulated and the trade liberalization process within a larger scale can be boosted. Nonetheless, the competitions between the "hub-spokes" FTAs are likely to result in trade diversion effects. Moreover, the complicated preferential policies and ROOs are also likely to disrupt the original production layouts and dissever the intra-regional supply chains towards the global market, thus harming the overall vigour of the East Asian economy.

Although the role of the large countries in promoting East Asian regional economic cooperation is quite important, yet at present, the interests of the smaller countries and the less developed countries deserve more attention. The challenges to the establishment of the EAFTA lie not in the relationship between China and Japan, but in how large countries can win over the trust of the smaller countries and form a common political will among the thirteen states.

Although there could be multiple roadmaps to the establishment of the East Asian Free Trade Area, yet, besides the political wills, the development potentials of the new emerging markets and the choices by enterprises to maintain stable production chains are important decisive factors as well. Since China does not seek any special status regarding East Asian regional cooperation and has always taken an active, reciprocal, open and pragmatic stance on the issue, the China-ASEAN FTA will enhance the integration of trade liberalization arrangements networks, ultimately forming the East Asian Free Trade Area.

8

Japan and the United States in ASEAN-China Relations

Herman Joseph S. Kraft

INTRODUCTION

Descriptions of the relationship between China and the ASEAN states range from one of inevitable hegemony[1] to one of greater openness, comfort and cooperation.[2] At first glance, these perspectives seem to reflect different points of emphasis. From a security standpoint, the effects of China's growing military and economic strength on the medium- and long-term stability and prosperity of the ASEAN states is seen as a cause for concern. Increased economic cooperation, however, is being institutionalized through the ASEAN+3 process as well as through multilateral and bilateral free trade agreements. These apparently diametrically opposed tendencies are not necessarily mutually exclusive as it is quite possible to look at the increasing "openness, comfort and cooperation" between China and ASEAN as part of an ASEAN policy of accommodation in the face of the inexorable growth of Chinese power. The reality behind it, however, is probably closer to somewhere in between. Relations between China and the ASEAN states are tinged with elements of both heightened cooperation and continuing unease.

From an ASEAN standpoint, the relationship with China is increasingly becoming one of its most important strategic partnership particularly over the long term. The ASEAN states, individually and collectively, need to balance between the dichotomy of competition and cooperation. It is, however, not purely a matter of exploring and finding common interests with China that could be exploited. ASEAN has two other strategic relationships with other major partners which are both more long-standing and enduring. While ASEAN's relationship with China may develop into its most significant partnership over the long-term, its relationship with Japan and the United States are equally, if not more so, important in the present term. It is commonly perceived that ASEAN relations with Japan and the United States are part of a strategy of balancing the increasing power of China in the region. Doing so, however, reduces the importance of the evolving partnership between ASEAN and China, and attenuates the complexity of ASEAN relations with Japan and the United States to a mere strategy of balancing China. While the idea of seeking a surety against a future of Chinese hegemony over the region is certainly part of ASEAN's concern, its relationship with Japan and the United States, and certainly with China, are all part of ASEAN's self-identification as a honest broker in regional politics with the ultimate goal of maintaining peace and stability and promoting prosperity in Southeast Asia. In this context, the ASEAN states' relations with their partners are all inter-related; thus, how they manage their relationship with both Japan and the United States will largely define the direction that their relationship with China will take.

This chapter looks into three main areas. First, is the current state of relations between ASEAN and China. It is basically argued here that this relationship has increasingly moved towards greater cooperation at the initiative of China. Fundamentally, China has been concerned with the strategic partnerships that the ASEAN states have been building with the United States and, to a lesser extent, Japan. American preoccupation with the war on terror and Japan's long economic economic recession has offered China the opportunity, which it has taken with both hands, to improve its relationship with the ASEAN states. It has done this by taking the initiative on economic cooperation while at the same time pushing policies that are directed at reassuring the ASEAN states that the long-standing notion of the "China threat" is exaggerated. Second, this chapter looks into the trends and directions of the relationship between ASEAN and Japan, and between ASEAN and the United States. It explores these developments in the context of the role of ASEAN as the hub of inter-connected relationships. Despite the damage done to the reputation and international standing of the association by the 1997 financial crisis, ASEAN remains the most acceptable mediator in a region where the competing interests of China, Japan and the United States are fully at work. Third, the chapter looks at how these trends and directions in ASEAN-Japan and ASEAN-United States relations impact on the growing relationship between ASEAN and China. Ultimately, any development in the latter relationship will have to take into consideration how ASEAN also deals with Japan and the United States.

ASEAN-CHINA: BALANCING BETWEEN COOPERATION AND COMPETITION

One of the most notable developments in the last ten years is the initiative taken by China to improve and strengthen its relationship with Southeast Asia. Exchanges of visits and the signing of substantive agreements, including trade and even security cooperation, are clearly geared towards a political outcome intended to send reassurances to the ASEAN states of the peaceful and non-threatening intentions of China.[3] In 2001, Chinese Premier Zhu Rongji proposed a free trade agreement between China and ASEAN that was endorsed by the ASEAN leaders at their meeting in Brunei that same year. The proposal intended to push China and the ASEAN states towards a free trade area within a five-year period. Due to structural asymmetries between China and ASEAN, and among the ASEAN states themselves, this was modified to a timetable of ten years. John Ravenhill described the result of the initiative as a diplomatic coup that placed other countries in the region, especially Japan, "on the defensive".[4] It illustrates, however, the growing importance of ASEAN in China's strategic perspective. This is also shown by the strong support that China has given to the ASEAN+3 process, and its involvement in a number of development projects in the Mekong River basin area. Successful bilateral partnerships are also encouraged to continue. At a meeting with Singapore's Senior Minister Lee Kuan Yew, Vice Premier Huang Ju suggested that the successful Suzhou Industrial Park (SIP) project should be replicated in the development of China's western region.[5] Not only would this help narrow the development gap between China's western provinces and its coastal region, but it will also further bilateral relations between China and Singapore. Outside of these successes, however, China's initiatives on the economic front are driven more by political than purely economic calculations. As one analyst noted, these developments may be the reaction of a Chinese leadership concerned with the possible re-emergence of a U.S.-led Asian security alliance in the context of a "global war against terror".[6] China needs ASEAN support or at least neutrality in a region increasingly subject to the power of American global hegemony.

China's policy of reassurance is even more palpable in the realm of security. On 21 March 2003, China acceded to the Treaty of Amity and

Cooperation (TAC) in Southeast Asia (TACSEA), a few months ahead of Japan. This was a very clear signal of the heightened importance that China accorded to ASEAN and, again, of the policy of reassurance that China was pursuing. Accession to the TACSEA underscored its willingness to subject its behaviour to standards the institutionalization of which it was not a party to. At the Sixth ASEAN+3 Summit held in Phnom Penh on 4 November 2002, it was China which suggested that the process be expanded to include regional political and security issues such as terrorism and transnational crime, which resulted in the institutionalization of the ASEAN+3 Ministerial Meeting on Transnational Crime which first met in Bangkok on 10 January 2004. In the aftermath of that meeting, ASEAN and China signed a memorandum of understanding to cooperate in non-traditional security issues. This MOU laid out the intention of all the parties to cooperate over the medium- and long-term on information exchange, personnel exchange and training, law-enforcement cooperation and joint research. Some results have already emerged from this as joint operations between the Malaysian and Chinese police led to the crippling of a major drug ring that was shifting its operations to Malaysia from China.[7] An indication of the seriousness of China's push towards acceptance by ASEAN as a partner can be seen in this MOU's financial arrangement, which states that:

> Expenses of workshops and training courses organized by China in accordance with this Memorandum of Understanding shall be covered by the Chinese side, including meals, accommodation and local transportation for the participants sent by ASEAN Member Countries during their stay in China and fees for inviting experts, while the expenses of international travel shall be covered by the sending Countries, except when it is agreed otherwise.[8]

While this is a normal arrangement for activities of this kind, the MOU shows no commitment on the part of the ASEAN states to organizing similar activities.

China's effort at reassurance is perhaps most clearly seen in the case of the South China Sea. China has had a history of having resorted to force to settle its differences with other claimants. One analyst described the issue as a "litmus test" for ASEAN on the realities behind a "China threat".[9] This reflected the continuing thorn that the disputed Spratly Islands archipelago represents in ASEAN-China relations. Again, the Chinese have been using diplomacy to try to reduce ASEAN concerns over this. In November 2002, China and the ASEAN states signed a Declaration on the Conduct of Parties in the South China Sea in Phnom Penh. This document was a compromise that took into consideration the demands of those states that were most in favour of pinning China down to a standard of behaviour over the disputed territory over the South China Sea. Vietnam had wanted to include the Paracel Islands to the area covered by the document but it was limited only to the immediate area around the Spratlys archipelago. The Philippines, another claimant that had had encounters with the Chinese short of military confrontation over the area, had wanted a document which was to be couched as a formal treaty and which committed the parties involved to refrain from occupying new islands, reefs, or shoals. The final document committed the parties to refraining from "action of inhabiting uninhabited (sic) islands, reefs, shoals".[10] It was the first time that China had agreed to a multilateral declaration over the South China Sea. It also worked in China's favour since the document limited the risk of conflict arising in the area and thereby ensured that it would not provoke the involvement of the United States in the dispute.[11] The document has become important in imposing a behavior of self-restraint not only on China but also on the other claimant states. In May 2004, China referred to the declaration in condemning a decision on the part of Vietnam to renovate an old airstrip on Spratly Island.[12] China pointed out that this action violated the Declaration on a Code of Conduct. Vietnam was also criticized by the Philippines for allowing a tour group to operate in the area.[13]

The establishment of all these new institutions and activities indicates that ASEAN and China relations are undergoing some form of institutional consolidation, with most of the initiative recently coming from the Chinese side. These help to provide a fulcrum for the relationship (what Mark Beeson refers to as "institutional ballast"), building confidence, and eventually becoming bulwarks of an effective regional architecture. It is, nonetheless, still too early to claim any substantive achievement for any of them.[14] One thing that is clear, however, is the evident acceptance of these overtures by the ASEAN states, a trend that perhaps signals the kind of pragmatic calculations taking place among the foreign policy elites of ASEAN. It may even be that the interest exhibited by the ASEAN states towards the Chinese proposal for a free trade area suggests "a willingness to contemplate bandwagoning with a rising power".[15]

The increasing acceptance by the ASEAN states of China's role in the region is not wholehearted. The enthusiasm of the ASEAN states for these proposals, in spite of their leaders' endorsement, remain guarded. The economic initiatives of China cannot erase the fact that it is the competitor of most of the ASEAN states in the export market — a situation that has made more difficult any projected intensification of the process of economic integration between the two parties.[16] Then Prime Minister Mahathir Mohamad of

Malaysia was quoted as warning the ASEAN states that they "must make sure the influx [of Chinese goods] will not cause our industries to shut down".[17] Much has also been said about the dramatic change in power distribution in the region, which the rapid economic growth of China has created,[18] as well as China's success in capturing the lion's share of foreign direct investment flows into the region.[19]

Clearly, the uneasiness felt by the ASEAN states regarding the perceived hegemonic aspirations of China in the region is more muted now than it was a decade ago. Overall, China's efforts at mollifying perceptions of a Chinese threat that even now continue to colour ASEAN perceptions of itself has advanced ASEAN-Chinese relations further than was expected a decade ago. The modernization of the Chinese People's Liberation Army, an issue that caused a number of ASEAN states to look into the idea of strengthening defense ties within ASEAN and with other external powers in the early 1990s, no longer attracts as much attention. The launching, for example, of the first of two modified Sovremenny-class destroyers in April 2004 and the importation of what is projected to be more than US$2 billion worth of arms from Russia by the end of 2004 have not gained that much attention from the region.[20] The unease, however, remains. Interestingly, a significant part of the unease has less to do with how China deals with the ASEAN states as it does with China's relationship with the other partners of ASEAN. China's competition with Japan over economic leadership in the region and, even more, its strategic rivalry with the United States has placed the ASEAN states in very awkward situations. They have, however, also been a balancing factor in ASEAN's relationship with China.

JAPAN: THE INCREASING CONCERN OVER SECURITY

Japan's relations with ASEAN and China has, especially since the early 1990s, always had to deal with two competing issues. The first involves trying to push greater regional economic integration with Japan taking the lead. The East Asian Economic Community (EAEC) concept that Malaysia proposed could only work if Japan was willing to take an active part in it. Its eventual refusal (in deference to the position of the United States) led to the Community becoming a caucus within APEC. Similarly, in the aftermath of the 1997 financial crisis, attempts to push for the establishment of an Asian Monetary Fund had to be abandoned when Japan, the originator of the idea, backed out of it again due to opposition from the United States. The second issue has had to do with making sure that Japan did not transform its enormous economic power into greater military capacity. Even the seemingly innocuous idea of

Japan participating in peace-keeping operations overseas invited much debate within Southeast Asia and China. Much has changed since then, particularly regarding Japan's relations with ASEAN.

The official premise behind the current relationship between the ASEAN states and Japan is laid out in the 2003 ASEAN-Japan Plan of Action.[21] Three main areas of cooperation are emphasized here. First is strengthening the process of integration being undertaken within ASEAN. This includes reducing the gaps in capacity and economic development between the older members of ASEAN (Brunei, Indonesia, Malaysia, the Philippines, Singapore, and Thailand) and the newer ones, also referred to as the CLMV (Cambodia, Laos, Myanmar and Vietnam) countries. Second, cooperation between Japan and ASEAN is being geared towards enhancing the competitiveness of the ASEAN countries. In this context, economic partnerships are being established with assistance provided by Japan in order to promote education, human resource development and institutional capacity building within ASEAN itself. Finally, events since 11 September 2001 have accentuated the significance of transnational issues, particularly terrorism and piracy. ASEAN and Japan have agreed on enhancing cooperation in this area primarily through institutional and human capacity building with particular emphasis on law enforcement agencies. The issues given prominence here indicate two things: the continued importance of economic cooperation, which has always been the fulcrum of ASEAN-Japan relations, and the increasing prominence of security cooperation in this relationship.

Japan remains the second most important trading partner of the ASEAN states and the most important source of Official Development Assistance. The Miyazawa Plan of 1998 made available US$30 billion as a liquidity provision to help the recovery of crisis economies. A series of bilateral swap arrangements with Malaysia and Thailand have helped fortify the currencies of these countries.[22] This is not likely to change in the short-term although Japan's decade-long economic malaise has allowed China to take the initiative in pushing economic cooperation with Southeast Asia. The competition for leadership in the region between the two powers has given impetus to what John Ravenhill calls "the new regionalism". He noted that:

> the two countries have increasingly vied to play a role in identifying ideas that an East Asian grouping might pursue. Although Japan was first to seize the initiative, with its proposals for an Asian Monetary Fund, more recently China has led the debate in the trade field with a proposal at the ASEAN Plus Three summit in 2000 for the creation of a free trade zone between China and ASEAN.[23]

Japan would like to pursue a more dynamic role in the region and its apparent economic upturn is a positive sign. High oil prices in the international market, however, could harm that recovery process.[24] Nonetheless, the revival of the idea of an Asian Monetary Fund gives Japan an opportunity to push this role especially as the idea has received indications of becoming more acceptable to the United States.[25] Monetary union is also being promoted with Malaysian Prime Minister Abdullah Badawi strongly recommending the adoption in Asia of a single currency to further promote regional economic and cultural cooperation.[26]

A more controversial issue is the plan linking future aid to countries in the region to a "series of benchmarks" which include respect for human rights, the environment, positive moves towards democracy and a market economy. This was made clear when Japan laid out its new aid policy towards Vietnam.[27] Aid conditionalities have always been a problem in relations between Japan and Southeast Asia, more so as the benchmarks being set by Japan can be deemed to be intrusive and constitute interference in the internal affairs of a sovereign nation. William Long argues that this is part of a "new security manifesto" that indicates a new role for Japan as an international actor.[28] At the same time, recent debates within ASEAN concerning the lack of responsiveness of Myanmar to calls from within ASEAN itself to ease up on opposition groups may indicate that this policy may not necessarily be seen as overly intrusive. It is more likely that there will be some statements that criticize Japan from some ASEAN states, particularly the newer members, but it will not lead to harsh condemnation from the rest of ASEAN. These benchmarks can also be seen as part of the Japanese strategy of strengthening its bilateral relations with Southeast Asia.[29] In a speech he gave in Singapore, Prime Minister Junichiro Koizumi pointed out that the fundamental basis for cooperation between ASEAN and Japan should be based on "undertaking reforms in our respective countries" to ensure that "we will advance individually and jointly toward increased prosperity."[30] This indicates that Japan will deal with each ASEAN state individually but within a multilateral framework. This seems to hark back to the duality of national and regional resilience that the ASEAN states had always referred to in the early years of the association. It is, however, much more than this as it implies a more active involvement of Japan in enhancing processes of cooperation. While the issue of human rights and democracy may continue to be controversial concerns across most of the ASEAN member states, the emphasis on market reform is universally acceptable.

Any increase in the economic dynamism of Japan is welcomed by the ASEAN states, particularly if this facilitates the strengthening of East Asian regionalism. Julie Gilson argues that this is precisely the direction that Japan is taking. Japan is increasingly using a *regional* multilateral framework (even as aspects of it demand a bilateral approach) made feasible by "the greater acquiescence of [its] regional partners".[31] It is this idea of greater acceptance by its regional, in this case Southeast Asian, partners that is new in this environment of cooperative endeavour. And this is more evident in the area of security cooperation.

One of the most important developments in ASEAN-Japan relations is the decreasing centrality of history as a factor.[32] Jian Yang noted that the ASEAN states have generally become more relaxed about the idea of Japan becoming a political power, even a military one. He warns though that ASEAN should remain sensitive to China's sensitivities on this issue and "not take a strong position on the historical dispute between China and Japan".[33] This may become more difficult as members of Japan's ruling Liberal Democratic Party (LDP) have begun to urge the removal of a self-imposed ban on weapons exports even as it also considers the pursuit of technology that would allow it to target missile bases in foreign countries.[34] China will certainly react to this development and some countries in Southeast Asia will probably seek greater reassurance from the United States to ensure that Japan will continue to behave peacefully. It would not be surprising if countries such as the Philippines, Singapore and Thailand will continue to call for the continued maintenance of its military presence in the region. It will push at least these ASEAN states towards even closer security relations with the United States and invite tension with China.

Japan has, nonetheless, increased its involvement in security with the ASEAN states eliciting only positive reactions from them. It was reported that Japan invited and trained officials from Cambodia, Indonesia, Malaysia, the Philippines and Thailand on how to stop the spread of weapons of mass destruction at a two-week seminar in Japan on 16–30 May 2004. This was particularly important with regard to the spread of WMDs via sea routes.[35] Japan's interest in the security of the sealanes always goes back to its economic interests, with over 80 per cent of its crude oil requirements passing through the Straits of Malacca in Southeast Asia. This concern for the sealanes makes it imperative for Japan to seek cooperation with the ASEAN states. The possibility of joint patrols involving Japanese MSDF ships have been broached though the topic seems to be a controversial one.[36] An overlapping concern is the threat of possible conflict over the South China Sea. Jian believes that Japan will not stay idle in the event of conflict.[37] It will nonetheless stay out of the issue even as it continues to encourage the continuation of multilateral talks. The dispatch of two Maritime Self-Defence Force ships for the Arabian Sea to support anti-terrorist efforts was hardly a factor in ASEAN-Japan relations.[38] As Paul Midford contends, it seems that Southeast Asian countries have now become more "comfortable with, and accepting of, Japanese troops sent overseas for non-combat missions".[39] At the same time, Japan is increasingly looking at broadening its role in international politics.[40]

Prime Minister Koizumi's reassurance in 2001 that he will adhere to the Fukuda Doctrine helped persuade the ASEAN states to accept the inevitability of overseas deployment of Japanese SDF members.[41] The other factor is probably the nature of Japan's commitments. The concern over terrorism is a shared concern and makes it easy for Japan's neighbours to understand, even sympathize, with the deployment. In Japan itself, there is a debate over the constitutionality of this deployment. The need for it, however, is brought home by reports of a senior Al-Qaeda member being based in Japan for more than a year trying to establish a terrorist cell.[42]

The increasing importance of Japan as a partner in regional security is one of the most important developments that revolve around ASEAN-Japan relations. The nature of the relationship is such that it continues to build on what is evidently growing confidence and trust. The obvious competition between Japan and China for regional leadership has been beneficial to the growth of regionalism in East Asia in general, and Southeast Asia in particular. While sensitivities between China and Japan make it imperative for the ASEAN states to carefully manage their relationship with these two powers, the institutionalization of cooperative mechanisms and the support that both China and Japan have given to the process of regionalization makes the work of ASEAN lighter.

THE UNITED STATES IN THE ASIA-PACIFIC: GLOBAL TERRORISM AND REGIONAL COOPERATION

The relationship between ASEAN and the United States has, since the attacks on the World Trade Centre and the Pentagon on 11 September 2001, been dominated by concerns over terrorism. Jonathan Pollack noted that in President George Bush trip to the region for the 2003 APEC Summit in Bangkok, he dealt primarily with international terrorism.[43] He did renew the commitments of the United States to the economic development of the region but indicated the primacy of the war on terror in emphasizing that greater security collaboration especially against terrorism will lead to increased trade and investment.

In the wake of the events of 11 September 2001, the Bush administration met collectively with the ASEAN states on 26 October 2002 to discuss the Enterprise for ASEAN Initiative (EAI). The idea behind the initiative was to promote the growth of free trade in the region and the strengthening of the involvement of the United States in the region.[44] Closer ties with the region were seen as a means towards opening up markets and help redirect investment into Southeast Asia. The United States has already established trade and investment agreements with Indonesia, the Philippines and Thailand with Brunei indicating its interest. As well, it has concluded a Free Trade Area (FTA) agreement with Singapore that it hopes will be a model for other FTAs around the region. According to one report, the main purpose behind these network-building activities is the idea of intensifying the process of economic integration in East Asia and "bind the United States more tightly to the region, *strengthening the fight against terrorism* (italics are mine)".[45]

The primacy of the war on terror has focused ASEAN-US relations on the issue of security cooperation. In investigations that followed the 11 September attack on the World Trade Centre towers and the Pentagon, the links between local terror groups with a domestic agenda such as the Abu Sayyaf in the Philippines, and regional networks such as the Jemaah Islamiyah (JI) and the Al-Qaeda network of Osama bin Laden, began to come out in the open. To illustrate how these links evolve, the initial stages of the development of the Abu Sayyaf saw bin Laden sending a brother-in-law to coordinate with them. Money was provided and an attempt was made to arrange a merger between the Abu Sayyaf and the Moro Islamic Liberation Front (MILF), a secessionist group which claimed the island of Mindanao and other adjoining islands for Muslims.[46] Similar activities took place in Indonesia, Malaysia, and Singapore. By 2002, reports of connections between the Abu Sayyaf and the Jemaah Islamiyah had surfaced.[47] The involvement of the Jemaah Islamiyah meant that the local secessionist movements were no longer domestic in nature. The JI is a network of radical Islamists with a stated goal of establishing an Islamic state that would encompass the whole of Indonesia, the islands of Palawan and Mindanao, and the Malay peninsula. It was declared a terrorist organization by both the United States and the United Nations after its involvement in a number of terrorist activities including the bombing of a Bali nightclub which killed more than 180 people.

The growth of regional terrorist networks aligned with the Al-Qaeda made it imperative for the ASEAN states to intensify cooperation among themselves and with the United States. On 1 August 2002, ASEAN and the United States signed a Declaration for Cooperation to Combat International

Terrorism. It emphasized cooperation in five areas: intelligence and terrorist financing information sharing; enhancement of liaison between law enforcement agencies; strengthening capacity-building efforts through training and education, consultations, and conferences; mutual assistance on transportation, border and immigration control challenges; and compliance with all UN resolutions and declarations on international terrorism. Intelligence exchanges (including real time intelligence in some cases), training, investigative assistance and military assistance have been provided by the United States to its allies in the region. In 2001, President Gloria Macapagal-Arroyo declined an offer from President George Bush of direct U.S. military support in the Philippines but accepted US$90 million in military aid.[48] Part of this assistance has been a training team composed of between 200 to 600 personnel that have been in Mindanao since 2002 working with different units of the Armed Forces of the Philippines. In 2004, Indonesia was assisted by the Federal Bureau of Investigation (FBI) in its investigation into a bomb found in a Medan grocery store.[49] A number of JI operatives captured in Indonesia, the Philippines and Singapore were caught with the assistance at various levels of intelligence from the United States.

The relationship, however, is a touchy one. On one hand, the United States feels that some of its allies are not doing enough. Thailand was criticized for its refusal to recognize the danger of terrorism until the capture of Hambali in Bangkok dashed their claim of the unlikelihood of terrorist attacks. The Arroyo administration was quietly warned by the U.S. Government that it had not been doing enough to crack down on terrorist groups in the Philippines.[50] Singapore and the United States are involved in talks over joint maritime patrol over the Malacca Straits to prevent possible acts of maritime terrorism. Deputy Prime Minister Tony Tan said that the matter will eventually have to be resolved with Malaysia and Indonesia.[51] The initiative, however, was rejected by Malaysia and Indonesia which felt that the presence of American forces in the region could cause a backlash and radicalize even the moderate Muslim community. Malaysian Defence Minister Najib Razak pointed out that "a foreign military presence will set us back in our ideological battle against extremism and militancy."[52] In Indonesia, the perceived high-handedness with which the United States deals with its allies in pursuit of its anti-terror campaign is being criticized. Hasyim Muzadi, a Muslim cleric chosen by incumbent President Megawati Sukarnoputri to be her running mate said that the United States "has to let Indonesia deal with terrorism its own way, and trust that the people and the government of Indonesia are all anti-terrorism".[53] The criticisms and strategies advanced by the Bush administration clearly showed its lack of sensitivity to the local political situation faced by governments that have to deal more directly with terrorism in their own countries. In the case of the Philippines, for instance, the backlash from the direct involvement of the Philippine Government in the international war on terror could lead to an increase in terrorist activities. Before his death in 2003, Hamsiraj Sali, one of the five leaders of the Abu Sayyaf on the U.S. wanted list of terrorists, had warned that the Philippine Government's support for the U.S.-led global war on terror and its new military agreement with the United States made the country a prime target for terrorist attacks.[54]

The problem became even worse when the United States went to war against Iraq. While the Philippines, Singapore, and, eventually, Thailand supported the invasion, Indonesia and Malaysia made clear their opposition to it. Some analysts believe that these differences will not seriously undermine the security relationship between these countries and the United States,[55] but it does reflect concern over U.S. unilateralism and how this has harmed the UN system.[56] Pressure from civil society groups also created problems for those governments that had supported the United States. When President Arroyo openly set her government on the side of the Americans in its war against terrorism,[57] nationalists in the Philippines criticized her over the renewed military relations between the two countries and the possibility of increased U.S. military presence in the country.[58] The importance of this domestic political opposition to the participation of the Philippines in the war in Iraq became evident in the decision of the Arroyo administration in July 2004 to withdraw its small humanitarian contingent ahead of schedule when one of the militant armed groups in Iraq threatened to kill a Filipino overseas worker it had kidnapped. The withdrawal was less a response to the threat from the militant group as it was a reflection of the strength of the popular clamour to save the life of the kidnapped worker. Despite criticism from the United States and other allies involved in the war in Iraq, the Arroyo administration decided that the survival of her administration and the political stability of the country demanded that it withdraw the Philippine humanitarian group. The episode, however, shows in very stark terms how domestic political conditions get in the way of alliance considerations. As Barry Wain had correctly pointed out at the start of the global war on terror, U.S. action may destabilize fragile administrations and disturb religious and ethnic sensitivities.[59]

Even as the United States and the ASEAN states have disparate appreciation of how the common concern over terrorism should be approached, it is clearly an issue which has facilitated an increase in security cooperation between the two parties[60] — a development which has both been advantageous and problematic for China.[61] On one hand, the focus on counter-terrorism has shifted American attention away from the human rights front in China. The latter has supported the global war against terrorism as it can conveniently invoke a parallel case in its domestic security issues involving separatist movements in Xinjiang province and Tibet, especially the former. At the same time, however, the Chinese Government cannot take lightly the increased security relationship between the United States and some of the ASEAN states, a development which might have spillover political implications over its own differences with the United States especially on issues like the latter's support for Taiwan. Taiwan has become bolder in its desire to move towards independence and China has been consistent in its warning that this is unacceptable. Although the United States has been discouraging the Taiwanese Government from proceeding along lines that would only increase tensions with China, they have nonetheless done little to support this. They continue to work with Taiwan in enhancing its military capability.[62] This has already affected relations between ASEAN and China at the unofficial level. China has refused to attend the Seventeenth Asia-Pacific Roundtable, an annual conference on regional security matters held in Kuala Lumpur in 2003, and the Shangri-La Dialogue held in Singapore in 2004, due to the presence of scholars from Taiwan. The Taiwan issue is clearly an area where the ASEAN states can find themselves in an awkward situation in their relations with China.

Again, the case of the United States and the ASEAN states show two conflicting tendencies at work. The war on terror places the ASEAN states on a very difficult position in their relationship with the United States. On one hand, the United States has been instrumental in the thus far successful campaign to fight terrorism in Southeast Asia. In this context, its allies in the region give value to the security relationship that they share with the United States. At the same time, however, a number of ASEAN states, particularly those with large Muslim populations, are concerned with the reaction of their citizens to the close relationship with the United States. David Capie points out that the response of the ASEAN states towards the United States have largely been dictated by pragmatic considerations that have their origins in the domestic conditions of the different ASEAN states.[63] This has been true to some degree, but only because the United States has not yet pushed hard. In the event of increased U.S. pressure, however, a danger exists to the unity of ASEAN. If choices are made on the basis of pragmatic considerations in the face of greater U.S. pressure, it could very well create fissures within the association. The United States has to be careful not to make the members of ASEAN make choices that will be self-destructive.

CONCLUSION

The situation between ASEAN and its major partners show great improvement that could well be the building blocks for greater regional integration. The rivalry between Japan and China has only served to improve ASEAN-China relations, and creates the push for enhancing economic institutionalization through the ASEAN+3 process. It is the relationship between the United States and ASEAN that has the greatest potential for creating problems between China and ASEAN. The enhanced security relationship facilitated by the war against terror may be problematic, but it nonetheless shows the importance of keeping the United States engaged in the region. The U.S. Government's obsession with terrorism has made it imperative for the United States to maintain good relations with the ASEAN states. Its relations with Taiwan, however, particularly the U.S. guarantee of its security creates an clear area of conflict with China, one which has already involved the ASEAN states if only at the non-governmental level. It is a conflict which has long-term significance for ASEAN in much the same way as the war on terror. Either case is a situation wherein choice-making could be disastrous for ASEAN unity. Over the short-term, it is the balance between China and the United States which has important implications for ASEAN. It must be able to navigate its relationship with these two powers and guide them towards less confrontational situations. This is going to be the challenge for ASEAN.

NOTES

1. Martin Stuart-Fox believes that the ASEAN states are inadequately equipped to deal with China strategically as a bloc because of the absence of a single guiding principle. Any attempt to do so will ultimately lead to the weakening, if the not completely break-up, of ASEAN. In any case, the ASEAN states will have to deal with a China in a *de facto* position of hegemony. Martin Stuart-Fox, "Southeast Asia and China: The Role of History and Culture in Shaping Future Relations", *Contemporary Southeast Asia* 26, no. 1 (2004): 136.
2. This observation was made by Eric Teo of the Singapore Institute of International Affairs at the Eighteenth ASEAN-ISIS Asia-Pacific Roundtable at Kuala Lumpur in June 2004.
3. Jian Yang, "Sino-Japanese Relations: implications for Southeast Asia", *Contemporary Southeast Asia* 25, no. 2 (August 2003): 314; and Joseph Y.S. Cheng, "Sino-ASEAN Relations in the Early Twenty-first Century", *Contemporary Southeast Asia* 23, no. 3 (December 2001): 422–24.

4. John Ravenhill, "A Three Bloc World? The New East Asian Regionalism", *International Relations of the Asia-Pacific* 2 (2002): 182. Kavin Cai is more explicit when he pointed out that the ASEAN-China FTA announcement in November 2001 "came as a major shock to the region and beyond". See Kevin G. Cai, "The ASEAN-China Free Trade Agreement and East Asian Regional Grouping", *Contemporary Southeast Asia* 25, no. 3 (December 2003): 388. Interestingly, representatives of the ASEAN states themselves were initially shocked by the proposal. See Alice Ba, "China and ASEAN: Renavigating Relations for a 21st-Century Asia", *Asian Survey* 43, no. 4 (July/August 2003): 641–42.
5. *The Straits Times* (Interactive), 16 June 2004.
6. Cheng, op. cit., 426–30.
7. *Bernama*, 28 April 2004.
8. See Article 4, Section 1 of the "Memorandum of Understanding Between The Governments of the Member Countries of the Association of Southeast Asian Nations (ASEAN) and the Government of the People's Republic of China On Cooperation in the Field of Non-traditional Security Issues", signed in Bangkok, Thailand, on 10 January 2004.
9. Cheng, op. cit., p. 443.
10. Quoted in Leszek Buszynski, "ASEAN, the Declaration on Conduct, and the South China Sea", *Contemporary Southeast Asia* 25, no. 3 (December 2003): 357.
11. Ibid.
12. *ABC News*, 19 May 2004.
13. *ABC News*, 20 May 2004.
14. Beeson wrote similarly of the ASEAN+3 process. See Mark Beeson, "ASEAN Plus Three and the Rise of Reactionary Regionalism", *Contemporary Southeast Asia* 25, no. 2 (August 2003): 264.
15. John Ravenhill, op. cit., p. 176
16. John Wong and Sarah Chan note that the degree of integration and interdependence between ASEAN and China have not increased proportionally to the growth of the two parties' total trade because of the naturally competitive structures of their economy. See John Wong and Sarah Chan, "China-ASEAN Free Trade Agreement", *Asian Survey* 43, no. 3 (May/June 2003): 516–17.
17. *BBC News Online*, 6 November 2001.
18. China's tremendous economic growth has been sustained over a fairly long period of time. The expansion of the economy by 9.7 per cent in the first quarter of 2004 was the third consecutive quarter of at least 9 per cent growth. See *Japan Today*, 16 April 2004.
19. See Stuart-Fox, op. cit., p. 132; and Wong and Chan, op. cit., p. 523. Jian Yang and Joseph Cheng, however, contend that the threat to ASEAN of China's ability to attract FDI may be exaggerated. See Jian, op. cit., p. 315; and Cheng, op. cit., p. 447.
20. See *Jane's Defence Weekly*, 12 May 2004; and *Moscow Times*, 16 April 2004. A study released by the U.S.-China Economic and Security Review Commission

pointed out that China's military was being modernized with the help of Russia and Israel. This would make it more difficult to defeat an invasion of Taiwan. The release of the report and other reports indicating that China was enhancing its mobilization capability hardly caused a ripple in Southeast Asia. See *The Straits Times* (Interactive), 16 June 2004 and 21 June 2004.

21. See "The ASEAN-Japan Plan of Action", available at <http://www.aseansec.org/15503.htm>.

22. Ravenhill, op. cit., p. 187.

23. Ravenhill, op. cit., p. 179.

24. *Straits Times* (Interactive), 16 June 2004.

25. *Far Eastern Economic Review*, 22 April 2004.

26. *ABC News*, 3 June 2004.

27. *Channel News Asia*, 3 June 2004.

28. William J. Long, "Nonproliferation as a Goal of Japanese Foreign Assistance", *Asian Survey* 39, no. 2 (March–April 1999): 329.

29. See Julie Gilson, "Complex Regional Multilateralism: 'Strategising Japan's Responses to Southeast Asia", *The Pacific Review* 17, no. 1 (March 2004): 90.

30. Junichiro Koizumi, "Japan and ASEAN in East Asia: A Sincere and Open Partnership", speech delivered in Singapore on 14 January 2002.

31. Gilson, op. cit., p. 91.

32. Jian, op. cit., p. 317.

33. Ibid., pp. 317–18.

34. *The Age*, 25 March 2004.

35. *Japan Today*, 4 May 2004.

36. Suggestions that the United States could participate in joint patrol of the Malacca Strait was strongly rejected by Indonesia and Malaysia despite Singapore's strong support for the idea. See *Jakarta Post*, 7 July 2004.

37. Jian, op. cit., p. 319.

38. *Japan Today*, 18 May 2004.

39. Paul Midford, "Japan's Response to Terror: Dispatching the SDF to the Arabian Sea", *Asian Survey* 43, no. 2 (March/April 2003): 344.

40. Paulo Gorjao argues that Tokyo's approach to the issue of East Timor between 1999 and 2002 showed this particular trend in Japan's foreign policy. See Paulo Gorjao, "Japan's Foreign Policy and East Timor, 1975–2002", *Asian Survey* 42, no. 5 (September/October 2002): 765–69.

41. The Fukuda Doctrine assures Japan's neighbours that Japan will not be a military superpower even as it became an economic superpower.

42. *CNN*, 20 May 2004. There had been reports of Al-Qaeda planning to carry out attacks during the 2002 World Cup in Japan.

43. Jonathan Pollack, "The United States in Asia 2003: All Quiet on the Eastern Front?" *Asian Survey* 44, no. 1 (January/February 2004): 10–11.

44. *International Herald Tribune*, 4 November 2002.

45. Ibid.

46. The Philippine intelligence community and that of the United States believe that the relationship never really developed though there were reports of joint operations in Zamboanga and joint training in Camp Abubakar which was taken by the Armed Forces of the Philippines through military operations in 2001.
47. *International Herald Tribune*, 2 December 2002.
48. *Far Eastern Economic Review*, 6 December 2001.
49. *Jakarta Post*, 17 March 2004.
50. *New York Times*, 11 April 2004.
51. *Jakarta Post*, 20 May 2004.
52. *The Age*, 6 June 2004.
53. *Jakarta Post*, 31 May 2004.
54. *Manila Standard*, 26 November 2002, p. 1.
55. Noel M. Morada, "The Fight Against Terrorism in Southeast Asia after the American War in Iraq", *Panorama: Insights into Southeast Asian and European Affairs* no. 1 (2003): 33–34.
56. In Indonesia, for example, public sentiment against the U.S. action against Iraq was based primarily on the absence of a UN Security Council resolution for war. See Anthony Smith, "A Glass Half Full: Indonesia-U.S. Relations in the Age of Terror", *Contemporary Southeast Asia* 25, no. 3 (December 2003): 462–63.
57. *Philippine Star*, 5 July 2002, p. 1.
58. Walden Bello, for example, argues that the continued presence of U.S. forces in the Philippines are part of U.S. hegemonic aspirations. See Walden Bello, "America's War in the Philippines," *Frontline* 19, no. 9 (27 April to 12 May 2002). See also *Far Eastern Economic Review*, 31 January 2002, p. 20.
59. *Far Eastern Economic Review*, 31 January 2002, p. 19.
60. An interesting case here is Malaysia which has been, in spite of its very vocal and strong criticism regarding the American-led invasion of Iraq and how the aftermath has been handled by the Bush administration, developing closer security relations with the United States even prior to the September 11 attacks. See Pamela Sodhy, "U.S.-Malaysian Relations during the Bush Administration: The Political, Economic, and Security Aspects", *Contemporary Southeast Asia* 25, no. 3 (December 2003): 376–81.
61. See Ba, op. cit., p. 641.
62. See *The Straits Times* (Interactive), 16 June 2004.
63. David Capie, "Between a Hegemon and a Hard Place: The 'War on Terror' and Southeast Asian-U.S. relations", *The Pacific Review* 17, no. 2 (June 2004): 223–25.

REFERENCES

"The ASEAN-Japan Plan of Action". <http://www.aseansec.org/15502.htm>.

Ba, Alice. "China and ASEAN: Renavigating Relations for a 21st-Century Asia". *Asian Survey* 43, no. 4 (July/August 2003): 622–47.

Beeson, Mark. "ASEAN Plus Three and the Rise of Reactionary Regionalism". *Contemporary Southeast Asia* 25, no. 2 (August 2003): 251–68.

Bello, Walden. "America's War in the Philippines". *Frontline* 19, no. 9 (27 April to 12 May 2002).

Buszynski, Leszek. "ASEAN, the Declaration on Conduct, and the South China Sea". *Contemporary Southeast Asia* 25, no. 3 (December 2003): 343–62.

Cai, Kevin G. "The ASEAN-China Free Trade Agreement and East Asian Regional Grouping". *Contemporary Southeast Asia* 25, no. 3 (December 2003): 387–404.

Capie, David. "Between a Hegemon and a Hard Place: The 'War on Terror' and Southeast Asian-U.S. Relations". *The Pacific Review* 17, no. 2 (June 2004): 163–77.

Cheng, Joseph Y.S. "Sino-ASEAN Relations in the Early Twenty-first Century". *Contemporary Southeast Asia* 23, no. 3 (December 2001): 420–51.

Gilson, Julie. "Complex Regional Multilateralism: 'Strategising Japan's Responses to Southeast Asia". *The Pacific Review* 17, no. 1 (March 2004): 71–94.

Gorjao, Paulo. "Japan's Foreign Policy and East Timor, 1975–2002". *Asian Survey* 42, no. 5 (September/October 2002): 754–71.

Koizumi, Junichiro. "Japan and ASEAN in East Asia: A Sincere and Open Partnership". Speech delivered in Singapore on 14 January 2002.

Long, William J. "Nonproliferation as a Goal of Japanese Foreign Assistance". *Asian Survey* 39, no. 2 (March–April 1999): 328–47.

"Memorandum of Understanding Between The Governments of the Member Countries of the Association of Southeast Asian Nations (ASEAN) and the Government of the People's Republic of China On Cooperation in the Field of Non-traditional Security Issues". Signed in Bangkok, Thailand, on 10 January 2004.

Midford, Paul. "Japan's Response to Terror: Dispatching the SDF to the Arabian Sea". *Asian Survey* 43, no. 2 (March/April 2003): 329–51.

Morada, Noel M. "The Fight Against Terrorism in Southeast Asia after the American War in Iraq". *Panorama: Insights into Southeast Asian and European Affairs* no. 1 (2003): 23–36.

Pollack, Jonathan. "The United States in Asia 2003: All Quiet on the Eastern Front?" *Asian Survey* 44, no. 1 (January/February 2004): 1–13.

Ravenhill, John. "A Three Bloc World? The New East Asian Regionalism". *International Relations of the Asia-Pacific* 2 (2002): 167–95.

Smith, Anthony. "A Glass Half Full: Indonesia-U.S. Relations in the Age of Terror". *Contemporary Southeast Asia* 25, no. 3 (December 2003): 449–72.

Sodhy, Pamela. "U.S.-Malaysian Relations during the Bush Administration: The Political, Economic, and Security Aspects". *Contemporary Southeast Asia* 25, no. 3 (December 2003): 363–86.

Stuart-Fox, Martin. "Southeast Asia and China: The Role of History and Culture in Shaping Future Relations". *Contemporary Southeast Asia* 26, no. 1 (April 2004): 116–39.

Wong, John and Sarah Chan. "China-ASEAN Free Trade Agreement". *Asian Survey* 43, no. 3 (May/June 2003): 507–26.

Yang, Jian. "Sino-Japanese Relations: Implications for Southeast Asia". *Contemporary Southeast Asia* 25, no. 2 (August 2003): 306–27.

9

U.S.-ASEAN, Japan-ASEAN Relations and Their Impacts on China

Cao Yunhua

Since the end of the Cold War, and especially after the Asian financial crisis and the September 11 terrorist attacks, the presence and influence of some world powers including the United States, China, and Japan in Southeast Asia have greatly changed. Because of these changes, ASEAN has been readjusting its policy and trying to seek a balance of these powers to maintain peace, stability and prosperity in Southeast Asia. The readjustment is a strategic choice for ASEAN to meet the new situation in the region after the Cold War, as its members consider that ASEAN is not able to safeguard its security by its own efforts. At the same time, great powers driven by their own interests are sure to expand and compete in Southeast Asia. If ASEAN takes advantage of the competition of these great powers, it may achieve the balance of power and meet the ends of maintaining regional security, stability and prosperity. ASEAN believes that China's influence on Southeast Asia tends to be increasing as an ambitious regional power, whereas United States is a "moderate superpower". In this case, it is necessary to enlarge America's and Japan's presence and influence in Southeast Asia to balance China. This chapter mainly analyses the development and changes in the U.S.-ASEAN relations, Japan-ASEAN relations and their impact on China.

ASEAN-US RELATIONS: STRENGTHENING THE MILITARY AND SECURITY COOPERATION

After the Cold War, the United States has continued to reinforce economic and trade relations with Southeast Asia. Ever since the Clinton administration defined Southeast Asia as an important new market, U.S. investments and trade in Southeast Asian countries have risen steadily. In addition, Southeast Asian countries have come to depend on American capital and export market even more since the Asian financial crisis. At present, the United States is the largest export market for most of the ASEAN countries, and ASEAN is the fourth largest trade partner of the United States (only after Canada, Mexico and Japan). The volume of trade between the United States and ASEAN accounts for 20 per cent of the total trade volume between the United States and Asia, more than that between the United States and China. What is equally important is that ASEAN's commitment to free trade is beneficial to the establishment of an open and multilateral trade system which is promoted actively by the United States. With the ASEAN Free Trade Area (AFTA) and other measures, ASEAN is accelerating the liberalization of the regional economy, which is expected by the United States.

But what kind of role would the United States play in Southeast Asia's security after the Cold War? Does Southeast Asia need a U.S. military presence? These questions are in dispute among ASEAN countries. Most Southeast Asian countries believe that the presence of great powers in Southeast Asia has changed much since the end of the Cold War. New regional powers have risen around Southeast Asia and they are trying to fill the power vacuum left by the United States and the Soviet Union, two superpowers during the Cold War. If the United States withdraws from Southeast Asia completely, the situation in Southeast Asia would be much more unstable. Thus, the maintenance of U.S. military forces in this region is a basic guarantee of its stability, prosperity and development. Goh Chok Tong, the premier of Singapore, once made a speech on "ASEAN-U.S. Relations: Challenges" during his visit to America in September 2000. He pointed out:

> The U.S. presence has been a determining reason for the peace and stability which Asia enjoys today. It has helped turn an unstable region of tension and strife into a booming and dynamic southeastern Asia.

He admitted that there were disagreements among the ASEAN countries on whether it was necessary for the U.S. presence in Southeast Asia after the end of the Cold War, especially its military presence. He went on:

> There is a grudging acceptance of each ASEAN country that the U.S. continues to be a stabilizing factor in the region.... In the coming years, the issues that will arise in Asia will be far more complex and difficult to manage than during the Cold War. They demand greater cooperation between U.S. and ASEAN countries, at the bilateral, regional and even global level.... Regional stability and prosperity are better served with greater and closer U.S.-ASEAN cooperation, and conversely, both sides stand to lose if ties between the U.S. and ASEAN are weakened . We must both play our part to strengthen this extremely important relationship.[1]

In fact, ASEAN countries have already reached a consensus which considers U.S. military and security presence in Southeast Asia an important and indispensable counterweight for the balance of power and stability in this region. As a senior ASEAN official once said:

> During the past fifty years, U.S. presence played a dominant role in the stability of this region. Anti-terrorism has brought ASEAN and the U.S. together again. It indicates that ASEAN, which consists of ten small countries, hope to balance its diplomacy with China by cooperating with the U.S.[2]

In recent years, the rise of China and Japanese pursuance of political and military power have increased ASEAN's sense of insecurity. It has fallen into a security dilemma. To get rid of such a dilemma, it found that the best way was to maintain U.S. presence in this region to achieve the balance of power. As a Southeast Asian scholar said:

> If China is regarded as the regional power with the most suspect intentions, then the United States must be regarded as the country with the most benign intentions.... No country in ASEAN specially views the United States as a source of threat, even if Indonesia has always articulated a preference for an independent and neutral foreign policy. There are a number of issue areas such as press freedom, human rights, democracy, and deforestation when the interest of ASEAN member states may not be congruent with that of the United States. Alternatively, certain members of ASEAN's political establishment, such as Prime Minister Mahathir Mohamad of Malaysia, may express occasional anti-American rhetoric. However, apart from these irregular and often issue-specific irritants, most ASEAN member states view the U.S. role as inevitable and positive.[3]

The following statement by Tommy Koh, former Singapore ambassador to the UN, appropriately reflects the present psychology of Southeast Asian countries:

> What do Southeast Asians want to get from U.S.? Firstly, they hope U.S. continue to maintain its military presence in this region, and to keep the force at a level of 100,000. It highly inspires the Southeast Asian countries who hope U.S. to be the counterweight of balance and stability in Asia-Pacific, for they consider U.S. as a moderate superpower.... Southeast Asian countries hope that U.S. would cooperate with them to nourish the ASEAN Regional Forum together, so that it could in time become an equal organization with APEC.[4]

After 2001, the ASEAN-U.S. relations had the following new characteristics.

1. U.S. Military Presence in Southeast Asia is Accepted by Most ASEAN Countries

To the Southeast Asian nationalists, the presence of the U.S. military is not pleasant, but it is beneficial to their fight against international terrorism and increasing threats from other powerful countries. So, from these aspects, the enforcement of a U.S. military and security presence in this region is somewhat positive. Among Southeast Asian countries, the Philippines' attitude is very typical. President Gloria Macapagal-Arroyo has reinforced political, economic, military and security cooperation with the United States, especially on issues of anti-terrorism. As she has said, Philippines has always stood in the forefront in support of America's anti-terrorism actions.

For the U.S., it has also focused much attention on Southeast Asia because one-third of the world's Muslim population live in this region. The geographic, religious and ethnic mix is the most ideal hiding place for international terrorists. In the attempt to win the cooperation of ASEAN, the United States promised to provide more economic and military aid to ASEAN countries, on condition that they support the United States and engage in the U.S.-led international coalition against terrorism actively. Laerfu Aimos considered that "September 11 made Southeast Asia valued again. It seems that the anti-terrorism war is the most important thing for Washington. They put lots of problems aside."[5] For example, the United States no longer made harsh comments on Southeast Asian countries on the issue of human rights and stopped asking Southeast Asian countries to implement economic reform and open up their markets on the basis of the IMF standards.

Through the ASEAN Regional Forum, a multilateral security cooperation organization, together with the bilateral military and security cooperation with Philippines, Thailand, Singapore, Malaysia, and Indonesia, the United States has refilled the power vacuum which was left by its withdrawal from the military base in the Philippines in 1992.

Rommel C. Banlaoi, a professor at the National Defence College of Philippines, once pointed out that:

> The reestablished presence of US in southeast Asia has refilled up the perceived power vacuum created after the American withdrawal in 1992. ... The reinvigorated Philippine-American relations enhance American network of strategic bilateral alliances in Southeast Asia. When tied-up together, this network of bilateral strategic alliances could pose a counterweight against potential aggressors in the region. ... The reinvigoration of Philippine-American security alliance has also strengthened American defense posture in Southeast Asia, for US security policy in Asia is strongly anchored on its bilateral alliances in the region.[6]

2. US-Philippines Relations at a New Best

After September 11, the United States sent several thousands of American soldiers to launch the "Balikatan 02-1" U.S.-Philippines joint military exercise to assist the Philippines in fighting against terrorist forces, such as the Abu Sayyaf terrorist group.

In November 2001, during President Arroyo's state visit to the United States, the Bush administration promised that the United States would give the Philippines a total of US$92.3 million military aid to strengthen its ability to fight terrorists and the local insurgents. On 3 August 2002, after the talks between U.S. Secretary of State Colin L. Powell and Philippine President Arroyo, the former announced that the Bush administration would fulfil its commitment to provide military and economic aid, and would provide another US$55 million to enhance the Philippine Government's ability to enforce the law and get rid of poverty. The United States would provide the Philippine military with various technical assistance, such as training the Philippines to use new military equipment made by the United States to carry out psychological warfare and night warfare, to enhance the exchange of intelligence between the U.S. and Philippine military. Furthermore, it would also send technicians to help the Philippines to construct highways and airports and provide professional training of municipal anti-terrorism. In October 2003, U.S. President Bush visited five Asian countries and Australia as well, four of which were Southeast Asian countries, including the Philippines

(8 October), Thailand (18–21 October), Singapore (21–22 October) and Indonesia (22 October). His first choice in Southeast Asia was the Philippines, which indicates the importance of the Philippines to the United States.

3. U.S.-ASEAN Joint Forces Against Terrorism

During the period 29 July to 3 August 2002, U.S. Secretary of State Colin Powell called on six countries when he attended the 2002 ASEAN Regional Forum. The greatest gain from his Southeast Asian visit was that he persuaded all ASEAN countries to sign the U.S.-ASEAN Joint Declaration on Combating Terrorism. The declaration shows that the United States is determined to work together with ASEAN to strengthen cooperation at bilateral, regional and international levels, in order to combat terrorism in a comprehensive manner. The main purpose of this cooperation is to enhance the efficacy of those efforts to combat terrorism. The scope and fields of cooperation are as follows: to continue and improve intelligence exchanges and terrorist financing information sharing on counter-terrorism measures, including the development of more effective counter-terrorism regimes. This declaration set a new basis for joint anti-terrorism between the United States and ASEAN. It shows that the United States and ASEAN have achieved greater mutual understanding on anti-terrorism, and would take more united actions to strengthen their joint anti-terrorism efforts.

4. Improved U.S. Relations with Indonesia and Malaysia

The Bush administration considers that bilateral anti-terrorism cooperation with Indonesia and Malaysia, the two most important Islamic countries in the region, has strategic significance to the U.S. anti-terrorism strategy at the global level. Thus, since September 11, the Bush administration has taken a series of actions to show its friendliness to Indonesia and Malaysia, which also grasped this good opportunity to improve their relations with the United States.

Indonesian President Megawati paid a state visit to America in November 2001. She was the first leader of the Islamic world to visit America after September 11. She showed her support for the U.S.-led anti-terrorism war. Such a stand was praised and well accepted by the Bush administration. An important outcome of Powell's Southeast Asian visit during the end of July and beginning of August in 2002 was that he successfully improved the bilateral military cooperation between the United States and Indonesia. Powell noted that the military cooperation between America and Indonesia would be deeper. Powell also announced that in the coming years, America may provide US$50 million for Indonesia to help its anti-terrorism efforts and other activities. Thus, U.S.-Indonesia military cooperation has been enhanced, in spite of the "Leahy Amendment"which was legislated by the U.S. Congress in 1999 to restrict the military cooperation between America and Indonesia, because the Indonesian Army conducted a crude and violent campaign against the independence supporters in East Timor in 1999.

The relations between Malaysia and America have always been unstable. After the Anwar Ibrahim case, relations between them declined sharply. However, after September 11, both sides had the desire and made some efforts to improve their relations. In May 2002, Prime Minister Mahathir was invited to visit the United States. During the visit, Malaysia and the United States signed the Declaration for Cooperation to Combat Transnational Terrorism. The declaration calls for Malaysia and the United States to enhance their cooperation in intelligence sharing, cutting off the funding sources of terrorism, etc. They would also enhance liaison relationship amongst their law enforcement agencies, and strengthen capacity-building efforts through training and education. In response to Malaysian cooperation on anti-terrorism, the Bush administration promised to purchase US$1.3 billion of Malaysia's national debt by U.S. companies as the first phase of economic aid in 2002. During the Thirty-fifth ASEAN Ministerial Meeting held in July 2002, the United States promised to provide aid for logistics, personnnel training, infrastructure and information technology. Furthermore, Malaysia and the United States also improved their military exchange and cooperation.

However, while improving its relations with the United States, Malaysian and Indonesian governments hold some reservations. On the one hand, both want to take advantage of anti-terrorism to improve their relations with the United States. On the other hand, they are unwilling to go too far in this direction to avoid alienating domestic Islamic opposition groups, for the majority of their population is Muslim.

5. Singapore Strengthens Its Traditional Friendly Relations with America

Singapore's leaning towards America has always been obvious. America is the second largest trade partner for Singapore (only after Malaysia), and its largest foreign investor. By the end of 2002, the total investment of America in Singapore had reached US$23 billion. On 6 May 2003, America and Singapore signed a free trade agreement which came into effect on 1 January 2004. Furthermore, they also cooperated closely on military and security issues. The

U.S.-Singapore Free Trade Agreement indicated that the U.S.-Singapore economic and trade relations had entered a new era. The agreement enabled Singapore to expand its market share in America on a wider scale and to attract more American capital. It would benefit Singapore's future economic recovery and development. The agreement was also highly valued by the Bush administration, for it was the first of such agreements signed with an Asian country. In addition, Singapore enjoys a very unique position in Southeast Asia. Such a treaty would provide the United States with a strategic stand in Southeast Asia. U.S. officials considered the agreement an example for other Southeast Asian countries to start FTA talks with the United States.

ASEAN-JAPAN RELATIONS: AT A SUBTLE TURNING POINT

Most Southeast Asian countries were seriously hit by the 1997 Asian financial crisis. Even now, some of them still have not recovered from it yet. Taking advantage of this opportunity, Japan has strengthened its economic ties and expansion into Southeast Asia, and promoted its economic relations with ASEAN at a wider and deeper level. Japan hopes to establish a "Comprehensive Economic Partnership" with ASEAN in order to expand its influence and consolidate its leadership role in Southeast Asia.

During the Asian financial crisis, Japan provided more aid to Southeast Asia than any other country. According to statistics, since the outbreak of the Asian financial crisis, the Japanese administration has issued the "Asian Aid Programme" and "New Miyazawa Initiative" to provide Southeast Asian countries with a total of US$80 billion aid. By the end of 1999, Japan had implemented US$43 billion of its programmes. A Japanese scholar suggested that the various aids provided by Japan to Southeast Asian countries during the Asian financial crisis could be regarded as the Marshall Plan provided by the United States to Europe after World War II. He concluded that "Japan is the greatest supporter for the economic recovery of Southeast Asian countries."[7]

Taking Thailand as an example, it was hit extremely seriously by the Asian financial crisis. Japan provided a great amount of aid to Thailand to help it overcome the crisis. Japan's Foreign Ministry considered that "Japan [was] the largest donor country for Thailand in the midst of the economic crisis." According to statistics issued by the Japanese Foreign Ministry, Japan has provided Thailand with a total of more than US$12.6 billion in financial and technical aid. Apart from the US$4 billion loan in August 1997 under IMF, Japan offered to provide US$8 billion trade insurance aimed at export promotion, to help the Thailand Government conduct its economic reform and other measures including sending 1,000 experts and an emergency grant of US$950,000 for Thai students to pursue their studies in Japan.[8]

Because of the long recession of its domestic economy and less enthusiasm to invest than before the middle of the 1990s, Japan's direct investments in ASEAN countries has decreased. However, Japan is still the largest foreign investor and is playing an extremely important role in the foreign capital flow in ASEAN countries. In the seminar held in 2002, Raymond Lim Siang Keat, the Minister of State for Trade & Industry and Foreign Affairs of Singapore, pointed out that although Japanese investments in China have increased rapidly at an average rate of 45 per cent during 1999 to 2001, Japanese companies continued to invest in Southeast Asia vigorously. From 1996 to 2001, the annual Japanese overseas investments in Singapore, Indonesia, Malaysia, Thailand and Philippines amounted to US$4 billion, which is much more than US$1.5 billion in China.[9]

Thailand is an example again. It is one of the early ASEAN countries to receive Japanese direct investment. In the 1980s, Japanese companies moved vigorously into Thailand. At present, there are more than 1,000 registered Japanese companies in Bangkok, of which 39.9 per cent are direct investments in Thailand. Based on the accumulative sum of foreign investment capital, Japan is the largest direct investing country in Thailand. In 2000, Thailand had 427 foreign direct investment projects worth a total of 243.2 billion baht, of which 184 are from Japan accounting for 43.1 per cent of the total projects and 39.3 per cent of total sum of foreign direct investment. Moreover, during the years after the Asian financial crisis, Japanese direct investment in Thailand has not declined, on the contrary, it has increased somewhat to 81.4 billion baht in 1998, 89 billion baht in 1999 (9.2 per cent more than 1998), and 95.6 billion baht in 2000 (7.5 per cent more than 1999).[10]

In Malaysia, Japan is the second most important source of foreign direct investment after Singapore. In 2001, Japan applied for 116 direct investment projects in Malaysia, with a total volume of 1.7 billion Malaysian ringgit. The same data recorded 68 projects and 460 million Malaysian ringgit from January to June 2002.

In terms of trade, the pattern which has been established since the 1980s is still stable today. Japan is still the most important trade partner for ASEAN countries.

In terms of bilateral official development aid (ODA), since the 1970s, Japan has replaced America as the largest aid country for ASEAN. One of the features of Japanese ODA for ASEAN countries is that it chose Indonesia as the main target country. In 1997, the bilateral official development aid provided by foreign countries for Indonesia amounted to US$790 million, of which Japan accounted for US$497 million or 62.8 per cent of the total, followed by Germany's US$115 million accounting for 14.5 per cent and Australia's US$79 million accounting for 10 per cent. In the same year, Indonesia received a total of US$52 million multilateral official development aid (by Asian Development Bank and other international organizations). Japan also played a dominant role in it. That year, Indonesia was the second largest recipient of the Japanese bilateral ODA only after China.[11] In 1998, the bilateral ODA provided by Japan for Indonesia amounted to 187 billion yen, equal to US$1.56 billion according to the exchange rate of that year. It was more than three times that of 1997. In addition, Japan also provided 700,000 tons of rice to Indonesia under the food aid plan. Furthermore, in October 1998, under the "New Miyazama Initiative", Japan provided US$900 million for Indonesia to keep the balance of payments (of which US$670 million has already been paid).[12]

Table 9.1
The ODA Provided by Japan for Indonesia, 1996–2000

Type	The Amount of Aid (US$ Billions)
Government Loan	137
Free Aid	12
Technique cooperation	230

Source: Foreign Affairs of Japan, <http://www.mofa.go.jp>.

Another feature of the Japanese ODA is to expand its aid to the new members of ASEAN including the three Indochinese countries and Myanmar. Japan pledged to promote the integration of old and new ASEAN members and help the new members of ASEAN catch up with the development pace of the old ASEAN members. The amounts of aid provided by Japan to the four new countries were as follows: Vietnam 100.5 billion yen in 2001–02, Myanmar 2.06 billion yen in 2002, Laos 104.6 billion yen in 1996–99 and Cambodia 19.65 billion yen in 1992–99.[13]

In terms of helping ASEAN countries to overcome the difficulties caused by the Asian financial crisis and recover their economies, the ASEAN countries consider that Japan has played the most important role. Furthermore, the economic leadership of Japan in East Asia is also irreplaceable. As the second largest economic country in the world, Japan has made a great contribution to help ASEAN overcome the Asian financial crisis and achieve economic recovery as soon as possible. The successive recession of the Japanese economy also severely affected the ASEAN economy. Thus the ASEAN countries expect Japan to revive its domestic economy as soon as possible and recover its vitality as the leader of Asia's economy. Just as Bhubhindar Singh, associate research fellow at the Institute of Defence and Strategic Studies, once said:

> Despite ASEAN's severe criticisms of Japan's role during the economic crisis, ASEAN countries continue to perceive Japan as an important economic partner. ASEAN countries realize the need for the economic presence of Japan in the region, not only to help revive their ailing economies, but also to help restore their previously dynamic growth rates.[14]

With regard to what kind of role Japan should play in the military and security fields, ASEAN's opinion has been changing with the situation. Japan's long-time investment in Southeast Asia has begun to gain huge repayment in politics and other fields. Before the 1990s, most ASEAN countries expected Japan to only play a role in the economy. As Lee Kuan Yew said: "We'd rather let Japanese concentrate on the research of high-resolution TV, not to let it rub sword."[15] However, in recent years, things have begun to change. More and more ASEAN countries began to agree that Japan could play an important role in politics and security of Southeast Asia in order to balance the other rising powers. Wong Kan Seng, former Foreign Minister of Singapore, once said, "Japan has participated actively in ASEAN's politics and security, it means that Japan-ASEAN relations are becoming more and more mature."[16] Domingo Siazon, former Foreign Affairs Secretary of the Philippines, expressed that "the regional cooperation between Japan and ASEAN must exceed economic field, it should include peace and security."[17] These words are representative. They reflect the significant changes in the opinions on Japan. Bhubhindar Singh noted:

> Recently, more and more ASEAN countries have begun to accept that ASEAN should enhance its cooperation with Japan on politics and security. …Southeast Asian countries are working together with Japan to keep the peace of this region. Especially in the fight against piracy, they have reinforced bilateral cooperation, for the pirates have become more rampant, and have threatened the security of sea transport in this region. …Apart from the bilateral security cooperation, ASEAN also permits Japan to play an active role in Southeast Asian multilateral security cooperation regimes, such as the ASEAN Regional Forum. Moreover, ASEAN also welcome Japan to play a positive role in other regional security affairs, such as, peace-keeping, preventive diplomacy, prevention of nuclear proliferation, and so on.[18]

Responding to China's active diplomacy in Southeast Asia, Japan initiated a series of actions in 2003, two of which are influential. The first was to launch the "ASEAN-Japan Exchange Year 2003". In November 2002, at the Japan-ASEAN Summit, Japanese Prime Minister Junichiro Koizumi suggested 2003 as the "ASEAN-Japan Exchange Year 2003", which aims to push ASEAN and Japan to "go forward together, improve together". According to the agreement, Japan was the key coordinator in January and worked together with Thailand as coordinator in April and December. The other nine member countries were designated key coordinator for each of the rest of the nine months respectively. "ASEAN-Japan Exchange Year 2003" involves various fields including politics, economics, society, culture and so on, with government and private partnership of central and local governments and non-governmental organizations. In Japan, an organizing committee headed by Hirosi Okuda, Chairman of Japan Business Federation (Nippon Keidanren) was established. The ASEAN-Japan Centre was responsible for the activities of non-governmental organizations. Japan carried out a series of activities such as organizing a variety of performance and exhibition, issuing commemorative stamps, publishing the Japan-ASEAN booklet, introducing the geography, history and culture of ASEAN countries through websites, newspapers, cartoons, pictures and so on.

Japan's other step was to enhance its relations and deepen consultation on economy, politics, security and cultural exchanges with ASEAN countries. They signed a series of treaties and agreements on the above basis. On 10 March 2003, the first conference of the Comprehensive Economic Partnership between Japan and ASEAN was held in Kuala Lumpur. The second one was held in Tokyo in 25–26 April 2003. On 18 November 2003, the ASEAN-Japan Vice-Ministerial Meeting was held in Tokyo.

The most important was the Japan-ASEAN Commemorative Summit held in Tokyo in 11–12 December 2003. They issued the Tokyo Declaration for the Dynamic and Enduring Japan-ASEAN Partnership in the New Millennium, which aims to strengthen and broaden their cooperation in politics and economy, and the Japan-ASEAN Plan of Action which was drafted to implement the aims of the above declaration. Japan also signed the Treaty of Amity and Cooperation in Southeast Asia. At the Tokyo conference, Japanese Prime Minister Koizumi indicated that in the coming three years from 2004, Japan would accept foreign students from ASEAN and send Japanese technical personnel to ASEAN, totalling 40,000 in number. Furthermore, Japan would also provide US$1.5 billion to help the ASEAN countries develop Mekong River Valley.[19]

IMPACT ON CHINA

In recent years, ASEAN-China relations developed very quickly and dramatically. However, ASEAN is still suspicious of China. A Philippine scholar wrote:

> From Southeast Asia's perspective, there is fear that growing nationalism in China might cause it to try to dominate its smaller neighbors. The worst manifestation of nationalism thus far is China's ambitions to become an Asia-Pacific military power. China has, among other actions, been expanding naval activities in the South China Sea. This appears to be done both in pursuit of its sovereignty claim over islands and waters of the entire area, and also presumably to develop capacity to counter US-Japan military strategy against China. ... By virtue of its proximity and size, not to mention its growing economic power, political influence and military reach, China may naturally be deemed a threat or at least a potential threat by smaller and weaker states living in its shadow. Among the ASEAN states, there are differences in the degree with which they perceive China to be a threat, and perhaps even some differences in the approaches they are inclined to take in order to neutralize any such threat as may be perceived. Among the founding states, Indonesia and Malaysia have historically been most suspicious of China, while Thailand has been the closest to Beijing in terms of convergence of strategic interests. Next to Thailand, Singapore and the Philippines in the past appear to have been least concerned with the prospect of China's flexing of muscles. In the case of the Philippines, however, this was true only until the Chinese occupation of Mischief Reef in its claimed area of the Spratlys in 1995, which raised great alarm in Manila.[20]

However, at present, what the ASEAN countries worry most is not the direct military and security threat, but the economic competition from China. Some Southeast Asian politicians have said that ASEAN products had been squeezed out of the European, American and Japanese markets by low-priced Chinese products. Furthermore, China attracted a great amount of foreign capital which should have flowed into ASEAN countries. Malaysian Prime Minister Mahathir once said in an international conference held in Tokyo, on May 2002:

> We don't consider that China will take military risks, thus, there is no need for Southeast Asia to worry about China's military force. However, China is an economic threat to Southeast Asia, with regard to the foreign investment, China has already been a threat, worse, it would be a threat to the world trade of Southeast Asia. We could calculate in advance that Chinese products not only would squeeze that of Japan and Korea, but also that of Southeast Asian countries. China is not likely to carry out military threat, not to

mention military occupation, however it is likely to control the economy in this region. Though the control is not likely to be thorough, it is highly likely to damage the economy of Southeast Asian countries.[21]

Although the Singaporeans are very mild towards China, they also worry about China. George Yong-Boon Yeo, Minister for Trade and Industry of Singapore said:

> To ASEAN countries, Chinese economic growth is not a threat but a challenge. … I'm not worried about Singapore. However, we are not willing to see most manufacturing industries squeezed out of Southeast Asia. If the profits of the manufacturing industry in this region decline, it will put Singapore on the second-line. Singapore is faced with challenges in keeping a high rate of economic increase, but the challenges are worldwide, not merely from China.… I never use the word "threat", China's economic growth brings challenges to Southeast Asia, especially the industries which face fierce competition from China. However, on the whole, the growth of the Chinese economy also creates some opportunities to Southeast Asian countries. … To some degree, the threat from China can stimulate the improvement of ASEAN.[22]

Enhancing military and security cooperation with the United States to restrict China is an important step for ASEAN to practise its strategy of balance of power. Thus, ASEAN will strengthen its military and security cooperation with the United States especially on anti-terrorism, for both parties have the desire and need to cooperate. Presently, the United States has bilateral military and security cooperation with each of the main members of ASEAN, thereafter, U.S.-ASEAN military and security cooperation will mainly take the form of bilateral cooperation. The United States has been trying to establish multilateral cooperation with ASEAN, and the U.S.-ASEAN anti-terrorism agreement which was signed in July 2002, was an important attempt. In addition, the United States hopes to play an important role in the ASEAN Regional Forum, but ASEAN is vigilant about it. ASEAN insists that the ASEAN Regional Forum is only a mechanism for dialogue and consultation on security; it is not fit to play the same role as NATO.

The need for the United States as a balancer is unprecedented for ASEAN. ASEAN considers that only the United States has enough power to balance an increasingly powerful China. Lee Kuan Yew pointed out in a speech in 2001:

> China will develop rapidly in the following decades. By 2040, China and Japan's combined GDP will exceed that of the United States. These developments will shift the economic center of gravity of the world from

the Atlantic to the Pacific. China will be a formidable player in the region. No combination of other East Asian economies — Japan, South Korea, Taiwan and ASEAN will be able to balance China. The Russian Federation will not be a major player for at least another 20 years. Therefore the role of America as the balancer is crucial if we are to have elbow room for ourselves.[23]

Japan also plays an important role in ASEAN's strategy of balance of power. ASEAN expects Japan to be more active in the political, military and security fields, as it continues to play an important role in economy. ASEAN hopes that Japan will speak for ASEAN at the G-7 Summit, and ASEAN is willing to support Japan to become a permanent member in the UN Security Council. Some of the ASEAN countries also believe that Japan need to be not only introspective about its history; it has much room to cooperate with ASEAN countries on politics, military and security.

Presently, ASEAN countries view China with mixed feelings. On the one hand, the rapid growth of China's economy provides them with more opportunities. They hope to work together with China to overcome the difficulties caused by the Asian financial crisis. On the other hand, they are afraid that a rising China will fill the power vacuum in Southeast Asia. China's efforts to accelerate its national defence modernization leave them with a sense of insecurity and put them in a "security dilemma". As an American scholar once said:

> As each state seeks to be able to protect itself, it is likely to gain the ability to be a menace to others. When confronted by this seeming threat, other states will react by acquiring arms and alliances of their own and will come to see the rest of the states as hostile. A common search for security thus results in a situation in which all powers are less secure.[24]

So for ASEAN countries, enhancing cooperation with the United States and Japan might be the best way to get rid of this "security dilemma".

The reinforcement of the ASEAN-U.S. and ASEAN-Japan economic cooperation will promote the development and prosperity of the Southeast Asian economies. It is also in China's interest to see a stable and prosperous Southeast Asia, which is the essence of the "Good Neighbour, Safe Neighbour and Rich Neighbour" policy proposed by Chinese Premier Wen Jiabao. However, the influence of the reinforcement of ASEAN-U.S. military and security cooperation on China should be analysed specifically.

How should the U.S. military and security presence in Southeast Asia be judged? Presently, some Chinese scholars hold the pessimistic view that China is confronting its worst peripheral environment, as the United States has completed its strategic encirclement of China by returning to Southeast Asia with the justification of anti-terrorism, in addition to its penetration and expansion in the Middle Asia. However, personally I do not agree with such a view. I think that there are three positive meanings for the enhancement of U.S. military and security presence in Southeast Asia.

First, it is beneficial to maintain the balance of power in Southeast Asia. The American withdrawal of its last troop from the Philippines in 1992 left a huge power vacuum in Southeast Asia. The countries which have their own interests in this region competed to fill this vacuum and their actions led to the imbalance of power in this region. If this situation exists for a long period of time, it would undoubtedly affect the stability and peace of this region.

Second, it could contain the "counter-disarmament" which has emerged in Southeast Asian countries since the end of the Cold War. At the beginning of the 1990s, as the U.S. military presence decreased, Southeast Asian countries felt an increasing sense of insecurity. They accelerated their national defence modernization programmes respectively. The military expenditure of some countries have increased to a great extent. All these phenomena caused a contrary situation to the global disarmament, which was called "counter-disarmament". Since the outbreak of the Asian financial crisis, owing to internal economic difficulties, most Southeast Asian countries have slowed down their national defence modernization. However, with the recovery of their economy, the trend of "anti-disarmament" seems to be re-strengthened. In this sense, the reinforcement of a U.S. military and security presence in this region can somewhat contain this tendency.

Third, a U.S. military and security presence in this region can promote Southeast Asian countries' fight against terrorism, contain Islamic fundamentalism, and safeguard their unification and social stability. Peace and prosperity in Southeast Asia fit China's interests as it also needs a peaceful, stable and prosperous Southeast Asia just as America does. It is often said that China needs a stable peripheral environment to develop its economy. The fact is that if Southeast Asia attains stability, then a large part of China's neighbours will be stable. On this point, the strategic interests of the United States and China are mutual.

It remains a new research topic on what impact it will have on China if ASEAN cooperates with Japan in the military and security field. Generally speaking, China is vigilant and anxious about Japanese military and security presence in Southeast Asia. For example, a writer named Liang Ming, once wrote in an influential Chinese magazine, *Outlook*, to criticize Japan's attempt to control the military and security of Southeast Asia by expanding its military activities to Southeast Asia, in the name of attacking pirates and anti-terrorism. He also criticized this as an attempt to revive Japan's dream of "Greater East Asia Co-prosperity Sphere". Liang Ming pointed out:

> Japan will rely on its military expansion to realize its expansion in Southeast Asia. There is no doubt that Japan holds the attempt to establish a new "Greater East Asia Co-prosperity Sphere", and what is more important is that the core of its attempt is to protect its so-called economic interests in Southeast Asia by military means. What we should pay more attention to is that Japan's new expansion in Southeast Asia occurs when it does not introspect its previous invasion history in Southeast Asia.[25]

This point of view is well accepted by many scholars and common people. Jin Xide, an expert at the Institute of Japanese Studies of the Chinese Academy of Social Science, pointed out that we should be vigilant about Japan's attempt to enhance its military and security presence in Southeast Asia and even the whole of Asia:

> If Japan insists on its military rise, it undoubtedly will destroy the stability and balance of East Asia, induce the upheaval and readjustment of its neighbour relations and even the international pattern, for it already is a power with huge economic and technological potential. With regard to the "international contribution", Japan is able to contribute to the non-military fields to promote the world peace and development. The status and function for Japan as a world power should be based on the premise that Japan must introspect deeply that period of history of invasion to gain the understanding, trust and support of Asian countries as well as international society.[26]

In view of the historical reason, China is not willing to see a re-armed Japan in Southeast Asia, since China will be trapped into a new "security dilemma" if ASEAN-Japan cooperation on military and security is further developed.

NOTES

1. Goh Chok Tong, "ASEAN-U.S. Relations: Challenges". Keynote speech at the ASEAN-United States Partnership Conference, New York, 7 September 2000, <http://www.aseansec.org>.
2. "The Role as Leader for U.S. and China Is More Obvious", *Xinhua News Agency*, 2 August 2002.
3. N. Ganesan, "ASEAN's Relations with Major External Powers", from *Contemporary Southeast Asia* 22, no. 2 (August 2000). Published by Institute of Southeast Asian Studies, Singapore.
4. Tommy Koh, *The Investigation into World Order*, trans. by Men Honghua (Central Translation and Edition Press, 1999), pp. 349–50.

5. "The Terrorist Bonus of Southeast Asia", *Xinhua News Agency*, 1 August 2002.

6. Rommel. C. Banlaoi, "The Role of Philippine-American Relations in the Global Campaign against Terrorism: Implications for Regional Security", paper delivered at the international conference "Dialogue, Competition and Cooperation in Asia Pacific region after China's accession into WTO", organized by the Centre for Asia Pacific Studies of Zhongshan University, Guangzhou, China on 26–29 June 2002.

7. "Asian Financial Crisis and Japanese Aid", trans. by Si Wei, in *Malay Archipelago Data* 2 (1999): 1.

8. Japanese Foreign Ministry, "The Relations between Japan and Thailand", <http://www.mofa.go.jp/region/>.

9. Lim Siang Keat, Raymond, presentation at the ASEAN-Japan Commercial Conference held on 10 October 2002, *Lianhe Zaobao* (Singapore), 11 October 2002.

10. Japanese Foreign Ministry, *ODA 1999*. <http://www.mofa.go.jp>.

11. <http://www.mofa.go.jp/region/>.

12. Ibid.

13. Bhubhindar Singh, "ASEAN's Perceptions of Japan: Change and Continuity", *Asian Survey* 42, no. 2 (March/April 2002): 293–94.

14. Ibid., p. 291.

15. Lee Kuan Yew, presentation of the talk with the editor of *Global Perspective*, *Lianhe Zaobao*, 24 December 1992.

16. "ASEAN-Japan Ties Mature with Security Talks, Says Wong", *Kyodo News International*, 2 August 1999.

17. Hardew Kaur, "Ensuring We're Not Bitten by the Same Dog Twice", *New Straits Times* (Malaysia), 3 October 2000.

18. "ASEAN-Japan Ties Mature with Security Talks, Says Wong", *Kyodo News International*, 2 August 1999.

19. *Yomiuri Xinbun* (Japan), 13 December 2003.

20. Aileen S.P. Baviera, "China's Relations with Southeast Asia: Political Security and Economic Interest", PASCN Discussion Paper, no. 99-17, published by Philippine APEC Study Centre, pp. 8–10.

21. Mohamad Mahathir, "China's Rise: Challenge or Opportunity", *AFP* in Tokyo, 21 May 2002.

22. George Yong-Boon Yeo, "The Increase of Chinese Economy Is Not a Threat, But a Challenge", *Lianhe Zaobao*, 14 September 2002.

23. Lee Kuan Yew, "ASEAN Must Balance China in Asia", *New Perspectives Quarterly* 18 (July 2001), p. 20.

24. Brus Lasita and Hawy Staer, *World Politics*, second edition, trans. by Wang Yuzhen (Huaxia Press, 2001), p. 53.

25. Liang Ming, "What Are the Attempts of Japan to Expand in Southeast Asia", *Liao Wang [Outlook]* (Beijing), no. 18 (2002): 31.

26. Jin Xide, "Japanese Security Strategy are Confronting the Crossroads", *Journal of Japanese Studies*, no. 2 (2002): 15.

10
India's Approach to ASEAN and Its Regional Implications

Hu Shisheng

RECENT DEVELOPMENT OF INDIA-ASEAN RELATIONS

The Phnom Penh ASEAN Summit held in November 2002 can be regarded as a watershed, which divides the development of India-ASEAN relations into two phases.

In the first phase, India-ASEAN relations were mainly tentative and partial. India at this time focused largely on building up her relations with individual ASEAN countries, with different emphases and values for each. For example, in the trade, investment, and science and technology R&D dimension, New Delhi had stronger relations with Singapore, Thailand and Malaysia; in the defence and strategic dimension, India put much stress on her relations with Vietnam and Myanmar; in the area of natural resources cooperation (with energy cooperation in particular), India paid much attention to her relations with Indonesia, Malaysia and Myanmar; while with regard to security cooperation, especially in combating cooperatively against anti-government forces, India attached great importance to her relations with Myanmar and Vietnam. Besides, India has selected Myanmar and Indochinese countries to be its major recipients of economic assistance.

The most outstanding feature of India-ASEAN relations in the first phase is the focus on economic cooperation and trade promotion. From a

Sectoral Dialogue Partnership established in 1992 to a Full Dialogue Partnership established in July 1996, building up close and powerful economic and trade relations and mutual investment had always been the priority between India and ASEAN countries. Thanks to such efforts, bilateral trade and investment had increased rapidly in the first phase. The bilateral trade volume had increased by 16.5 per cent annually, from US$2.9 billion in 1993 to US$9.9 billion in 2001. The investments from ASEAN countries also steadily rose to nearly 15 per cent of the total approved investments in India in 1995. According to India Investment Centre statistics, Indian joint ventures in ASEAN in 1996 numbered 118, with Indonesia 18, Malaysia 39, Singapore 37, and Thailand 24.[1]

During this phase, 1996 was a landmark year for Indo-ASEAN cooperation. In July 1996, at the Fifth ASEAN Summit, India became simultaneously a Full Dialogue Partner as well as a formal member of the ARF at the summit held in Jakarta, Indonesia. The entry into ARF put India at par with Western countries and China *vis-à-vis* ASEAN regional security, and economic and political arrangements.

In the second phase, the relations between India and ASEAN were much more comprehensive and more institutionalized. India's participation in the Phnom Penh ASEAN Summit in November 2002 and the initiation of both "India-ASEAN Summit" and "India-ASEAN Business Summit" have all marked the great-leap-forward of a decade-long "Look East" strategy. It signifies in at least two aspects. One is that ASEAN has acknowledged the economic, political and strategic importance of India; the other is that ASEAN would very much like to deal with India collectively and in unity.

Besides, Indian Prime Minister Atal Bihari Vajpayee's Southeast Asian tour to participate in the ASEAN summit in Bali, Indonesia, in October 2003 was furthermore regarded by India's mass media as opening a brand new chapter of the "Look East" strategy. During this tour, the Indian prime minister signed three landmark documents with ASEAN. The first is the framework agreement for comprehensive economic cooperation between India and ASEAN. The framework agreement spells out a programme for free trade agreements in goods, services, investment, areas of economic cooperation and an "early harvest" programme. Both sides have pledged to formally set up an India-ASEAN FTA by the year 2011. This framework agreement is the most important document signed by India and ASEAN. The second is that India signed the Treaty of Amity and Cooperation in Southeast Asia. This indicates that ASEAN has acknowledged India's significance to ASEAN, believing that India can play a positive role in promoting peace and stability in the region. This would further cement India-ASEAN bilateral relations. The third is that India and ASEAN signed a joint declaration on combating terrorism. Both sides agree that they would strengthen cooperation in the areas of information and intelligence sharing, law enforcement, etc. This is a clear indication that India and ASEAN have broadened their scope of cooperation.

Although the second phase of India-ASEAN relations has just started, there already exist three outstanding features:

1. Institutionalization of Economic Relations

Whether it is the FTA arrangement between India and ASEAN as a whole, or one between India and individual ASEAN members such as Singapore and Thailand, both sides have given high priority to a systematic and institutionalized way to strengthen their economic and trade interactions. The purpose behind such efforts is that both sides want to take advantage of the large scale effect and mutual complementary predominance in their economic and trade developments.

Negotiations on FTA have already started this year. India promised that she will cut down her high tariffs to the same level as ASEAN's before 2005.

2. Broadening the Fields of Cooperation

Both sides have decided to include anti-terror issues into their cooperation. India-ASEAN defence diplomacy has moved gradually to a fast track. Joint military exercises, joint patrolling, joint production of certain weapon systems, and joint R&D in the dual-use technologies have been steadily regularized. India and ASEAN have also stepped up their efforts in jointly tackling non-traditional security issues, especially in strengthening their cooperation on the safeguard of SLOCs and combating terrorists and seaborne pirates. Considering India's unique geostrategic position, greater globalized political and economic influence and being the fourth strongest military force, the widening of bilateral cooperation areas is the inevitable result of the rapid development of India-ASEAN relations.

3. Accelerated Pace of Constructing Physical Connections

Although the construction of physical connections — road, railroad, shipping and air interlinks — between India and ASEAN started in the first phase, it is in the second phase that such construction has picked up speed. India has made unremitting efforts to participate in the building up of comprehensive linkages with ASEAN, including India-Myanmar-Thailand highway linkage, New Delhi-Hanoi (and further stretching into the innerland of Malaysia) railroad connection, the Dawei (Tavoy)-Kanchanaburi road link for ocean-cum-overland inter-modal transit from Indian ports to Myanmar and Thailand, a new plan to link the Andaman Sea and the Gulf of Thailand with an oil/gas pipeline, and to link Port Blair of the Nicobar Islands with Phuket in Thailand in a tourist circuit. Besides, more airline linkages among Indian and ASEAN metropolitan cities are also under consideration. Former Indian Prime Minister Vajpayee declared in the Second India-ASEAN Summit in October 2003 that India would offer a unilateral "open skies" policy to specified Southeast Asian airlines, which will be free to operate daily flights to the Indian metropolitan centres, outside any bilateral aviation pact. In this context, he announced India's unilateral decision to connect all ten ASEAN capitals with four metropoles (New Delhi, Kolkata, Chennai and Mumbai) in India through daily flights without further bilateral discussions.

CALCULATIONS BEHIND INDIA'S EFFORTS TO BUILD ALL-ROUND RELATIONS WITH ASEAN

Thanks to the potential of ASEAN as a collective market, source of and destination for FDI flows to and from India, and especially to ASEAN's political and strategic importance in the larger Asia-Pacific region which can serve as a gateway to the Pacific for India, India has its own economic, political and strategic considerations in strengthening its comprehensive relations and cooperation with ASEAN. Just as Indian Prime Minister A.B. Vajpayee stated on 9 April 2002 in his Singapore Lecture: "This region is one of the focal points of India's foreign policy, strategic concerns and economic interest."[2]

India's geographic adjacence to ASEAN, her pervasive cultural influence in ASEAN and especially the increasing enhancement of India's comprehensive strength has naturally facilitated India's approach toward ASEAN.

1. Economic Consideration

The primary objective and immediate drive of India's "Look-East" policy is economic consideration. At the time when the "Look-East" policy was put forward, the Indian economy was just on the verge of bankruptcy with only US$1 billion in foreign exchange reserves (affording only two weeks' imports). Indian economists and businessmen during that period had been profoundly impressed and influenced by the "miracle economies" of Asia, especially Southeast Asia. Indeed, no other global phenomenon has had a greater impact on the thinking of India's economists and economic policymakers during that time than East Asia and Southeast Asia's rapid economic take-off. When Manmohan

Singh (the present Indian prime minister) started India's economic reforms with marketization, privatization and liberalization as its core content, ASEAN was regarded as a source of both ideas and capital for the development and modernization for the Indian economy. More importantly, there is a mutual recognition of a complementarity-competitiveness continuum between the emerging ASEAN and Indian economies. India's assets include its large diversified and liberalized economy, huge reservoir of manpower and high-quality but cheap scientific talents, natural resources, industrial base and one of the largest, rapidly growing markets, while ASEAN's strengths are demonstrated by its rich natural resources, know-how, infrastructure, social sector development, investible capital, elaborate regional and global linkages in trade and industry and large market. In this sense, New Delhi hopes that stronger economic ties with the ASEAN states would enable it to benefit from the dynamism of the larger economic bloc, and enhance India's comprehensive economic strength. The Indian Government even regards ASEAN as an indispensable partner for India in its quest for new global opportunities and a 7–8 per cent growth rate.[3]

Specifically speaking, the benefit for India to strengthen her economic ties with ASEAN is firstly demonstrated in the increase of bilateral trade volume and frequent economic exchanges. India imports from ASEAN countries mainly vegetable oils, data processing machines, natural rubber, transport equipment, organic chemicals, textile yarns, timber, etc., while exports from India to the ASEAN countries cover the following sectors: pharmaceuticals, computer software, textile machinery components, rubber manufacture, leather goods, agro-products, metal scrap, animal feed, gems and jewellery. With the rapid development of hi-tech industries and services, India finds a much larger cooperative field with ASEAN. The Indian Government hopes that India's advantaged industries and trades such as IT, pharmaceuticals and biological technology would help India to expand her market share in ASEAN. At the same time, such close economic interactions would enable India to introduce advanced administration modes and ideas from ASEAN countries.

Moreover, in recent years, the India-ASEAN arms trade has become an increasingly important part of bilateral trade. Since the 1990s, India's comprehensive capability in R&D in advanced weapon systems has improved substantially. Compared with ASEAN countries, India's weapon systems are not only good in quality, but also inexpensive. Especially with the opening up of the defence production sector for private participation, there is great scope for Indo-ASEAN cooperation in R&D. By actively participating in the maintenance, upgrading and renovating of the existent weapon systems in some ASEAN countries, India has greatly broadened her defence cooperative ties with ASEAN, and also its share in ASEAN's conventional weapons market. At present, Vienam, Malaysia, Thailand and Indonesia have very close defence cooperation and arms trade relations with India.

As a result, India and ASEAN have witnessed a tremendous two-way trade increase, from about US$2.5 billion in 1993–94 to US$12.5 billion in 2002–03. There is little doubt that a vast scope still exists for increasing Indian exports to the ASEAN countries, largely due to the cost advantage that India has *vis-a-vis* Southeast Asian countries in terms of considerably lower manpower costs, and other strengths in terms of industrial experience, technological capabilities, and availability of intermediate inputs and raw materials. That is also why last year the Indian prime minister put forward the ambitious target of US$30 billion two-way trade for 2007.[4]

Secondly, there is rapid increase in mutual investment. India's economic relationship with ASEAN also encompasses an active investment component. In recent years, ASEAN countries are increasingly investing in primary infrastructure sectors, such as roads and highways, telecommunications, ports and airports and tourism, in India. From a negligible investment in 1991, ASEAN investment approvals today in India total over US$2.5 billion, with Singapore, Malaysia and Thailand taking the lead.

Moreover, ASEAN accounts for a large volume of India's investments abroad. The Southeast Asian region is host to a number of Indian joint ventures. Major areas of Indian investment are software development, gems and jewellery, manufacturing, textiles, chemicals, minerals and metals, among which, infrastructure and telecoms formed the thrust areas of cooperation in addition to the traditional high technology sector and pharmaceuticals. Major government engineering firms from India such as the Bharat Heavy Electricals Ltd (BHEL), Bharat Electronics Ltd (BEL) and private IT majors such as Infosys and WIPRO have all invested in Malaysia.[5] Besides, the top twenty Indian information-technology (IT) companies have a presence in Singapore.[6]

More importantly, with the final formation of an ASEAN Free Trade Area (AFTA) by the year 2008, and with the final materialization of a preferential tariff system known as the Common Effective Preferential Tariff (CEPT) scheme, which means by the year 2008, the tariffs of fifteen items of goods in ASEAN (vegetable oils, cement, chemicals, fertilizers, pharmaceuticals, plastics, rubber products, leather products, pulp, textiles, ceramic and glass products, gems and jewellery, copper cathodes, electronics, wooden and rattan furniture) would be reduced by a great margin, there are thousands of reasons for Indian companies to take advantage of the reduced tariffs by establishing joint ventures in the ASEAN region, since India enjoys great advantage in most of the above items.

Last but not least, the diversification of India's energy strategy. In this regard, Indian oil and gas companies are helping Vietnam and Myanmar to explore and exploit petroleum and natural gas. In November 2003, a consortium of South Korean and Indian companies started exploring the waters off the Arakan Coast of northwestern Myanmar. The estimated recoverable reserve of gas is in the range of four to six trillion cubic feet — equivalent to between 700 million and 1.1 billion barrels of oil. It has been accompanied by a blueprint that suggests that the gas will be taken into inner India through an undersea link connecting the Myanmar gas fields to the east coast and an overland line through Bangladesh into northeastern India or West Bengal.[7] India companies also participated in oil exploitation in Indonesia.

2. Stability of Indian Northeastern Region

Ever since India's independence, scores of militia groups have been fighting New Delhi's rule in the northeastern mountainous region. The pervasive backwardness and poverty there have provided fertile soil for the subsistence of those rebel forces. Most of the small states in northeast India lack the capability to develop, even to live, on its own resources. The local governmental finances are completely dependent on the central government's assistance or central financial loan,[8] the local governments lack the money to put into infrastructural construction. Thus in the past five decades, the northeast economy has undergone almost no change. The economic growth rate of the northeast region is far behind the average national level, so northeastern India is also call " India's back lake".[9] Backward economy and geographic isolation make it even more difficult for the governments at all levels to eliminate the ethnic separatist activities there.

Considering the geographic proximity, cultural similarity and historical communications, northeastern states have been calling upon the central government to facilitate their relations with adjacent neighbouring countries and regions. They believe this is the best way to get developed and only through development can they tackle with success the world's longest-running insurgencies. In May 2000, the seven states in northeast India collectively appealed New Delhi to re-link with the Yunnan-Myanmar highway to strengthen their foreign trade relations with China and ASEAN countries. Such appeals and pressure from the northeast regional governments and peoples and the ground reality in the northeast itself finally made the central government more determined to step eastward. As a result, a series of sub-regional economic cooperation organizations, which involves both northeast India and its adjacent countries and regions, came into being. On 6 June 1997, Bangladesh, India, Myanmar, Sri Lanka and Thailand came together to form an economic association called BIMSTEC linking the littoral states of the Bay of Bengal. This economic grouping aims at promoting rapid economic cooperation between members in key areas such as trade, investment, tourism, fisheries, agriculture, transportation and human resources development. In August 1999, India, Myanmar, Bangladesh and China launched the "Kunmin Initiative" to strengthen economic cooperation among these four countries. In July 2000, the foreign ministers of India, Myanmar, Thailand, Laos, Cambodia and Vietnam announced at Bangkok the Mekong Ganga Cooperation (MGC) Project. The six countries also undertook to develop transportation networks including the East-West Corridor project and the trans-Asian highway. Among the above sub-regional cooperation organizations, the BIMSTEC has undergone the most rapid development. On 8 February 2004, economic and foreign ministers from the BIMSTEC countries,[10] led by India, signed a draft agreement that paves the way for the establishment of a trade zone linking India with Southeast Asia. The agreement calls for tariff reductions and the creation of a new free-trade area by 2017. All these efforts have greatly promoted the economic development and social stability in the northeast region. As an Indian scholar, Raj Reddy, once pointed out: "New Delhi's ambition is to change the whole northeast region into one standing point for India's economic entry into ASEAN."[11]

Moreover, in order to deal with the insurgencies effectively, New Delhi has to attach much more importance on the improvement of bilateral relations with Myanmar. India and Myanmar share a 1,650-kilometre border between northwestern Myanmar and India's troubled northeastern states. Among the four states bordering with Myanmar, three have been for a long time troubled by armed separatist unrest, and the rebel forces usually escape the hot pursuit of the Indian Army by disappearing into Myanmar. It is said that the northeast military separatists has the protection of the rebel forces in Kachin, Myanmar. Since the mid-1990s, India has greatly modified her policy toward Myanmar and stepped up her cooperation with Rangoon's military junta. One of the purposes is to ask the Rangoon government to curb such infiltration and flush out their camps there. The primary measure in this regard is to constantly give generous economic assistances and soft loans to Myanmar. In 1997, India provided Myanmar with US$10 million in soft loans; in 1998, US$25 million; in 2001, another US$25 million; and in 2003, India agreed to provide US$57 million credit loan. Most of these loans have been invested into infrastructure sectors. By the end of 2001, the Mora-Kalimu road in the western region of Myanmar was completed under the Indian assistance. On 6 April 2002, India's External Affairs Minister Jaswant Singh visited Myanmar to launch a trilateral highway project linking Thailand and Myanmar with India, which is expected to be completed in two years. India has provided 1 billion rupees for this grand project.

In response, Rangoon in recent years has stepped up its cooperation with the Indian Army in jointly combating the anti-government militias camped on Myanmar's land, and strengthened the border control and management. The two had also signed an anti-terror agreement. And in July 2003, the Myanmar Army destroyed a commanding unit of Nagaland National Socialist Council (a separatist military organization still active in northeast India). On 22 December 2003, Myanmar Foreign Minister U Win Aung told reporters in New Delhi that his country would take "whatever action is necessary" to "flush out Indian insurgent camps" and that his government would "cooperate with the Indian Government" in this matter. In the last week of December 2003, India's Chief of Army Staff, General N.C. Vij, announced that India might launch joint military operations with Myanmar against rebels based in that country. "Army-to-army relations between India and Myanmar have been very good and we have been helping them," he said. This is not the first time Myanmar has cracked down on Indian rebels. It has helped the Indian security forces against the rebels at least three times in the past ten years.[12]

3. Anti-Terror Consideration

In October 2003, India and ASEAN signed a joint declaration on combating terrorism. Both sides agreed that they would strengthen cooperation in the areas of information and intelligence sharing, law and justice enforcement. This is significant not only because that it shows both sides have broadened their cooperative areas, but also indicates that both sides are determined to jointly fight against any security threats.

The above anti-terror joint declaration is all the more significant to India. The Indian ruling elites strongly believe that Indian national interests cover a huge area, stretching right from the Persian Gulf, Afghanistan, Tibet to Southeast Asia, East Asia and Northeast Asia. Such geostrategic conception is inherited from the British India empire. Well-known Indian sea power theorist, K.M. Panikar, once pointed out in his famous book, *Problem of Indian Defence*, "It is quite obvious to all of us, India's security interests cover... Burma, Thailand, Indochina coastlines, certainly including Malaysia and

Singapore."[13] Up till today, India's political elites still strongly hold such a geo-strategic belief. Former Indian Foreign Minister Jaswant Singh once stated in his speech at the Singapore Institute of Defence and Strategic Studies on 2 June 2000, that "considering her size, geographic location and EEZ, India's security environment certainly includes Persian Gulf in the West, Central Asia in the Northwest, China in the Northeast and Southeast Asia."[14] And in a marked departure from the traditionally bland address to the Combined Commanders Conference, former Indian Prime Minister Vajpayee, on 1 November 2003, made some significant observations on record on India's strategic priorities:

> Our security environment ranges from the Persian Gulf to the Straits of Malacca across the Indian Ocean, includes Central Asia and Afghanistan in the North West, China in the North East and South East Asia. Our strategic thinking has also to extend to these horizons, especially to some of the areas of interest that have a bearing on India's security.[15]

It is quite clear that in terms of India geo-security perception, Southeast Asia occupies a most significant position to India. In this regard, India has solid reasons to build intimate and sound relations with ASEAN. Thus, the threats ASEAN faces would also be, to a larger extent, threats to India. At present, various terrorist organizations, extremist forces and organized crimes, such as the Moro Islamic Liberation Front (MILF), the Abu Sayyaf, arch separatist militia, Muslim separatist forces in Southern Thailand, Golden Triangle drug mafia, are still very active in and around the ASEAN region. Furthermore, piracy in and around the ASEAN waters is all the more rampant. All these are more or less threats to India's security and strategic interests, given the great proximity of India to ASEAN regions and especially considering the covert linkages between the illegal forces in ASEAN and the illegal militia in northeastern India, Jammu and Kashmir and other regions and overt spillover effect to India of the drug- and light and small weapons-trafficking by all the above mentioned forces.

And what is really raising the eyebrows of India is the increasingly clear inter-linkages between ASEAN terrorists and the South Asian terrorists. The articles published by the "South Asia Analysis Group" website recently, written by Professor Raman deserve thorough reading. Based on solid proofs, he argued strongly that there are close inter-linkages and interactions between the ASEAN terrorist organizations and South Asian ones.

Professor Raman in his articles pointed out that as early as in the 1980s, cadres of the Moro Islamic Liberation Front and Abu Sayyaf of Southern Philippines had fought along with Pakistani *jihadi* and Afghan Mujahideen groups against the Soviet troops in Afghanistan in the 1980s. The links built up then have been sustained. The Harkat-ul-Mujahideen (HUM) of Pakistan, which is a member of bin Laden's International Islamic Front (IIF), has been training the Abu Sayyaf and providing it with arms and ammunition. HUM leaders claim that many HUM cadres fought against the Filippino security forces along with Abu Sayyaf. In 1998, Abu Sayyaf became a member of IIF. The Jemaah Islamiyah (JI), which has been coordinating pan-Islamic *jihadi* activities in Southeast Asia, sought to be patterned after the IIF. The Pakistan branch of the Tablighi Jamaat (TJ) is very active in Southeast Asia, ostensibly to teach the Muslims of the region to be better Muslims, but it acts as the front organization of the *jihadi* members of the IIF for recruiting local volunteers for training and for funnelling financial and other assistance.[16]

Moreover, many Southeast Asian Muslims have been brainwashed by the *madrasahs* in South Asia. According to reliable statistics, by mid-2002, the total number of students from Southeast Asia studying in various pan-Islamic *madrasahs* of Pakistan was estimated at about 400. Among them, there were 167 Malaysians, 149 Thais and 84 Indonesians.[17]

In this sense, if India wants to make some achievements in its anti-terror war, it is all the more imperative for New Delhi to cooperate with ASEAN in this regard.

At present, India gives particular attention to Thailand and Malaysia in its anti-terrorism cooperation efforts with ASEAN countries. In early June 2003, the Federation of Indian Chambers of Commerce and Indian Industry (FICCI) defence committee chairman K G Ramachandran said there was a need to forge stronger bilateral ties between New Delhi and Bangkok in fighting terrorism. "India and Thailand are natural allies in the global war against terrorism. It is time we intensify our linkage to fight the scourge."[18] India also asked Malaysia to control some of its nationals allegedly collaborating with Pakistan-based terrorists active in the Indian part of Kashmir. According to India many Malaysian youths were encouraged before 11 September 2001, to study at *madrasah* Islamic religious schools in Pakistan and many of them, it became known later, worked closely with the Taliban in Afghanistan.[19]

Besides anti-terrorism, it is also necessary for India to cooperate with ASEAN countries in tackling other non-traditional security threats, particularly drug trafficking, light and small weapons smuggling and piracy. All these threats have already caused a lot of trouble to the safety of India's SLOCs, social stability and economic development. The more dynamic Indian overseas economic activities become, the more urgent India would feel in dealing with the above threats. Thanks to the geographic importance of ASEAN, without ASEAN's cooperation, it would be very difficult for India to deal with such threats successfully and with efficiency. Particularly, considering that the ASEAN waters are the most plagued by piracy worldwide, joint anti-piracy provides another cooperative platform for India and ASEAN.

In fact, before signing the anti-terror declaration with ASEAN, India had already started joint patrolling in the Malacca Straits with the United States. And in recent years, India has also increased its joint military exercises in the Indian Ocean and South China Sea with ASEAN countries, Japan and South Korea. In particular, India has established regular joint military exercises with Singapore, Vietnam and Indonesia. One of the core targets of all these military efforts is to tackle all kinds of non-traditional threats, especially in combating against seaborne terrorism and armed attacks.

4. The China Factor

In his response to the question whether the "China factor" affects India's "Look East" policy, the former Indian Foreign Minister Yashwant Sinha said in a very implicit way, "No. This is the business between India and ASEAN. But even if we had not taken the China factor into consideration, ASEAN countries would do that."[20] However, in fact, one can find the China factor in nearly every development of India's "Look East" strategy.

Strategically, India hopes, through her "Look East" policy, to balance China and to ease the geographic and psychological pressure brought about by the close China-ASEAN relations. Economically, India wants to compete with China in the ASEAN market and to expand substantially India's economic influence in ASEAN.

During the 1990s, China-ASEAN relations have advanced rapidly, and China has successively established forward-looking friendships with Singapore, Malaysia, Thailand and Vietnam. China's influence in ASEAN has increased steadily, especially with its influence in Myanmar becoming all the more pervasive. All these developments have caused great concern to India. New Delhi fears that China, by building close friendships with ASEAN countries, and Myanmar in particular, would encroach into India's traditional sphere of influence and hence "threaten" India's strategic interests. Since India can do nothing about the American military presence in its "sphere of influence", India believes that it could at least balance or counterbalance China's presence there. As Professor Amitab Madhu, in charge of national security research in Nehru University, pointed out in his recently published book on India-

ASEAN relations, "because of the uncertainties in the future, and especially out of her deep concern toward China's future role, Indian ruling bloc wants to see a multi-lateral security order in Asia-Pacific region through building partnerships with ASEAN."[21] It is said that the formally established new Far Eastern Naval Command (FENC) based on the southern tip of Andaman Island in July 2001, was most likely a direct response to China's increased influence in ASEAN countries with Myanmar in particular.

To this end, India in the last ten years or so made great efforts to approach ASEAN, paying particular attention to her relations with two countries — Myanmar and Vietnam.

As for Myanmar, India has been establishing ties with Rangoon in all ways, that is, reinforcing her political, economic and military ties with Myanmar. This is a great shift in Indian foreign policy. In the past, the Indian Government practised a policy of constantly criticizing the generals in Myanmar for subverting democracy. But nowadays, India has adopted a brand-new Myanmar policy of non-interference. Now New Delhi often speaks of reconciliation with Myanmar rather than back Aung San Suu Kyi against the generals. In 2000, Indian relations with Myanmar entered a totally new phase of comprehensive improvement. In January 2000, New Delhi sent both military and ministerial delegations for talks with Myanmar. In November 2000, Admiral Maung Aye, the vice chairperson of the National Council for Peace and Development, paid a landmark state visit to India. Admiral Maung Aye became the first high level political leader of Myanmar to visit India since the military junta took over power in 1988. In 2001, India's Foreign Minister Jaswant Singh paid a visit to Myanmar. He was the first Indian minister to visit Rangoon in the past fourteen years. In early 2003, the state visit of the Indian vice president to Myanmar further promoted the bilateral relations in a substantial way. Especially after 2000, bilateral military relations have increased steadily. Besides mutual exchange visits, India also started to provide advanced military training and MiG-series fighter planes to the Burmese National Army. But the most outstanding features of the close India-Myanmar relations are demonstrated by the large sums of economic assistance and soft loans provided by New Delhi to Rangoon.

At the same time, India has also enhanced its traditional strategic partnership with Vietnam. India regards Hanoi as its only entry into the South China Sea. In 2000, India and Vietnam signed an agreement paving the way for institutionalized military cooperation between the two countries, with Hanoi to train Indian Army officers in jungle warfare and counter insurgency, and regular exchange of security perceptions and intelligence and visits by top military brass, while India agreed to examine and overhaul

Vietnam's Soviet/Russian made fighters. India's Coastal Guard and Vietnam's maritime police would jointly combat against smuggling. In October 2000, India and Vietnam held their first joint military exercises in South China Sea. In 2001, India's prime minister visited Vietnam and promised to provide nuclear science laboratory equipment to Vietnam and train thirty Vietnamese scientists. India even went further to promise to provide short range surface-to-air missiles to Hanoi. On 17 March 2002, Vietnamese Vice President Nguyen Thi Binh visited India. India agreed to give 100 million rupees to set up a software and training centre; the Indian Oil and Natural Gas Corporation Limited (ONGC) to invest 238 million rupees for oil and gas exploration in Vietnam; Tatas to supply 300 truck chassis, India to supply ten locomotives and Ranbasy to start a new project.

Besides the strategic balance against China in ASEAN, India is also intent on countering China's growing economic clout in Southeast Asia. One of the indications is that India in recent years has accelerated the FTA process with ASEAN. Just one month after China declared that in the coming ten years China would establish FTA with ASEAN, India's former prime minister also proposed at the First India-ASEAN Summit that the two sides form an FTA even before the formation of the China-ASEAN FTA arrangement. Driven by this, New Delhi has become increasingly proactive in participating in the transportation networks construction projects connecting India and the ASEAN region. India is determined to speed up the pace in opening the trade corridor with ASEAN countries. The eagerness to compete with China in this regard is also quite clear, especially judging from the shift in attitude of the Indian Government toward the New Delhi-Hanoi railroad, which will run through Myanmar, Thailand, Laos and Cambodia. On 4 September 2003, former Indian Prime Minister Vajpayee disclosed in front of ASEAN economic ministers, that India is "now considering the railway links between New Delhi and Hanoi". However, originally New Delhi was not so keen toward this railroad project. In 2002, during the first India-ASEAN Summit, the Cambodian prime minister suggested that India could help Cambodia build its railroad network and eventually connect this with the Singapore-Kunming Railroad. At that time, India did not give a clear response. But in 2003, when New Delhi noticed with anxiety the Fifth Ministerial Meeting on the ASEAN-Mekong Development Cooperation held in Kunming, where it was finally decided that China and related ASEAN countries would start to build the Pan-Asia Railway which runs from Kunming to Singapore *via* Malaysia, Thailand, Cambodia and Vietnam just next year. India feared that once completed, such a Pan-Asian railway (also called "Golden Corridor") would further enhance China's economic dominance, at least in ASEAN.

This prospect made New Delhi feel much more concerned. So finally, New Delhi decided to kick-start the ten-year New Delhi-Hanoi railway project. The future completion of this railroad would not only end the history of there being no railroad linkage among Vietnam, Laos and Cambodia, but also end the history of there being no railway connection between India and the ASEAN region. More importantly, this railroad would finally be connected with the Pan-Asia Railway and would greatly facilitate the access of India-made products into the ASEAN market. And India believes that the Delhi-Hanoi Railroad would also, to a great extent, change the inferiority of New Delhi while competing with Beijing in the Mekong area.

India contesting with China in this regard can also be seen quite clearly from the formation and development of the Mekong-Ganga Cooperative organization. In 2000, when India decided to form the MGC with Vietnam, Laos, Cambodia, Thailand and Myanmar, New Delhi insisted that this organization should give first priority to the development of tourism, culture and education. New Delhi wanted to take advantage of its traditional cultural linkage with ASEAN countries to exclude China substantially in the Mekong area at least.

Even though India would undergo "healthy competition with China" (as stated by fomer Indian Prime Minister Vajpayee), the perception among India's ruling class that China would be India's tough competitor in the long run cannot be changed fundamentally.

5. Big Power Pursuit

Ever since independence, successive Indian leaders have regarded the acquiring of "big power" status as their first priority. But due to the Cold War, especially due to the long-time stand-off between India and China and long-time confrontation between India and Pakistan, it seemed that India's big power dream in the first four decades had become increasingly remote. By the end of the Cold War, India was even on the verge of bankruptcy economically. Even worse, at the end of the Cold War, India was not a member of any major trade bloc other than the SAARC, which has yet to make a significant impact on the regional economic scene or on global trade. New Delhi really felt that India had been greatly marginalized in the international community.

However, the end of the Cold War created an environment for India to make some changes. On the one hand, New Delhi wanted to increase India's international status through vigorous economic reforms, and on the other hand it wanted to increase India's international influence by overhauling her external policies. Thus, acquiring the status of "big power" has again figured as an important determinant of India's post-Cold War foreign policy, in particular, with its "Look East" strategy. Furthermore, Indian elites believe that ASEAN could serve as a springboard for India to enter into the Asia-Pacific region and would help New Delhi in securing membership to the Asia-Pacific Economic Co-Operation and the Annual Asia-Europe Meeting, which would be helpful for India to garner more bumper economic harvest and hence be helpful to India's big power pursuit. In this sense, it is no surprise to hear former Indian Prime Minister Vajpayee stating at the 2002 Singapore Lecture, that "this region is one of the focal points of India's foreign policy, strategic concerns and economic interest."[22]

THE REGIONAL INFLUENCE OF INDIA'S "LOOK EAST" POLICY

India's "Look East" policy also greatly benefits ASEAN. The close India-ASEAN bilateral relations would certainly be in the economic, security and political interests of the ASEAN region.

Economically, closer relations between ASEAN and India benefit ASEAN in its regional economic development. The economic interest is, in fact, the immediate motivation behind the ASEAN-India mutual approach. Singapore's then Prime Minister Goh Chok Tong, while interpreting ASEAN's new perception on India's economic role in this region, pointed out in a metaphor that if ASEAN were a huge plane, China and India would be the two wings.[23] This metaphor itself reveals vividly the great importance of India to ASEAN's economic prosperity.

There are at least three kinds of gains from the close economic relations between India and ASEAN. First of all, the underdeveloped ASEAN region has benefited a lot. Thanks to the geographic proximity, India's "Look East" policy could not bypass the less developed members of ASEAN (Myanmar, Vietnam, Laos and Cambodia). Moreover, this geographic location has also provided India with the advantage to play a very positive role in these four countries and hence in the whole ASEAN region. So, in this sense, the less developed countries of ASEAN are inevitably the direct beneficiaries of India's Look East policy, compared with other ASEAN members. For Myanmar, Vietnam, Laos and Cambodia, they are most eager to change their backwardness, especially of their infrastructures, but they lack the much needed foreign capital and science and technology, which an emerging India could provide. In fact, in recent years, India's sub-regional cooperation mainly focused on these four economically backward ASEAN members. In November 2002, at the First India-ASEAN Summit, India promised to provide the four countries with privileged, substantial tariff reduction. Besides, these four countries, in particular Myanmar, have in these years benefited substantially from Indian economic assistance and governmental soft loans. The large scale infrastructural constructions completed or undertaken in this region are the best evidence.

Secondly, the formation of a super large integrated market is being accelerated. With the completion of various transportation networks undertaken in ASEAN, South Asia, East Asia and Southeast Asia would be gradually fused into one united geographical community. And still in the future, when India-ASEAN transportation networks finally connect with China-ASEAN ones, a super-sized market with its population at three billion and GDP at US$2.5 trillion would come into being. By that time, the flow of goods, capital, people and ideas would become faster and there would be huge economic and peace dividends for all of the members, a blessing especially to ASEAN countries. ASEAN could certainly make full use of its advanced and applicable technology, rich capital, abundant commercial experiences and high efficiency of administrations to benefit greatly from such an enormous market. Such a huge market is especially conducive for ASEAN to sharpen the edge of its goods in the international markets. Besides, ASEAN would witness a great increase in bilateral trade with China and India. This can be easily testified by the implementation of the China-ASEAN FTA. It is predicted by experts that both China and ASEAN would witness a 50 per cent increase of their two-way trade volume. In fact, in the first year of the China-ASEAN trade agreement, bilateral trade hit a record high of US$78.25 billion, an increase of 42.8 per cent year-on-year, according to Asia Pulse.[24] We may also witness such a prospect for the ASEAN-India trade. In the past ten years, with bilateral economic relations being increasingly close, the bilateral trade volume between ASEAN and India has increased by 16.5 per cent annually, much higher than the growth rate (6 per cent) of the general ASEAN trades with the outside world.

Further, such a huge market would facilitate ASEAN investors to seek more lucrative places and areas to invest. The Indian market itself is worth mentioning. India has 200–300 million middle class people with a total population standing at one billion. The average tariff of India has reduced dramatically from 300 per cent in 1991 to 25 per cent presently. In future, ASEAN would find it much more profitable to invest into such a big emerging market,[25] especially in the infrastructure sectors. Since India's infrastructural construction lags very much behind, the Indian Government intends to carry out big energy and transportation projects with the help of FDI. In fact, in the past years, ASEAN businessmen have been putting large sums of FDI in India in crucial infrastructural sectors such as roads and highways, telecommunications, ports and airports, and tourism. ASEAN has indeed become a major player in the FDI stakes in India with Singapore, Thailand and Malaysia in the lead.

The third gain is the speeding up of FTA negotiations and its final establishment. The frequent interactions between India and ASEAN have served as a catalyst in this regard. As expressed by the ASEAN Secretary General Ong Keng Yong, "we ASEAN are just like a bride, being courted by all of them (big powers). Our negotiation with India (on FTA) has stepped onto a rapid track."[26] At present, more and more outside powers are eager to reach FTA arrangements with ASEAN. Now, China, Japan and India have already signed the FTA, while the United States has also reached a bilateral FTA with Singapore in 2003 and is currently working on similar deals with Thailand and the Philippines. Japan, New Zealand and Australia have also signed FTAs with Singapore. Finally with free-trade agreements (FTAs) to be completed with China in 2010, India in 2011 and Japan in 2012, the ASEAN region would be transformed into a giant free-trade zone by 2020.

The FTA arrangements and finally even the formation of a certain common economic community would enable ASEAN to combat with more confidence and success against any form of financial crisis such as the 1997 financial crisis, and outside challenges.

Still, there are some limitations to the development of the India-ASEAN bilateral economic relations. In fact, the economic linkages between Southeast Asia and Northeast Asia are far closer than India-ASEAN economic relations. The trade volume and investment volume are self-explanatory. The India-ASEAN trade volume in 2003 only occupied two per cent of the total volume of ASEAN trade with the outside world, while ASEAN-China's trade would occupy eighteen per cent of ASEAN's total foreign trade.

As for security, a much closer India-ASEAN relation benefits the security and stability of Southeast Asia. During the Cold War period, the two superpowers had scrambled to win over Southeast Asia. As a result, Southeast Asia had split into two confronting camps. During that time, Southeast Asia's security situation was very bad. The Vietnam War and the Cambodian civil war had greatly damaged the general security and stability in Southeast Asia. But in the post-Cold War period, ASEAN seems more free and independent. In order to increase its security stakes, ASEAN has invited all the big powers, potential or existent, such as the United States, China, Russia, India, and Japan into this region, creating a balance of power. ASEAN wants to maximize its security guarantee through such multi-lateral balance and counterbalance among big powers. The balance of big powers can, to a great extent, ensure that the ambitions of any power or combination of powers are curbed by the combined efforts of others. This is proved to be the best way for small and weak countries or country groups to guarantee their security and stability. So in this sense, India's "Look East" policy not only has facilitated the formation of a certain balance of power in the ASEAN region, but also enhanced the security and stability in ASEAN. As pointed out by Indonesian strategist Djiwnadono: "Indeed, in terms of power politics, the engagement of the two largest nations in the world (referring to China and India), along with the United States, Japan and Russia, might help create a regional balance of power in East Asia and the Asia-Pacific region as part of the global balance that includes the European Union."[27]

Singapore's former Foreign Minister S. Jayakumar once spoke highly of Indian contributions to ASEAN's security and stability by pointing out that considering India's size and her geographic location in the Indian Ocean, India could play some positive role in regional stability.[28] In fact, with the enhancement of India-ASEAN defence exchange and cooperation, ASEAN has gradually diluted her apprehension toward the development of India's deep-sea naval forces, and started to welcome India's counterbalancing role.[29]

Specifically speaking, the closer military relations between India and ASEAN countries have facilitated the defence-building of ASEAN; the joint military exercises have greatly increased the coordination of different services and greatly enhanced their technical and tactic capability; the military training has benefited ASEAN to improve its own military commanders' capability to tackle sensitive issues and emergencies; the R&D cooperation would greatly upgrade the existent weapons systems in ASEAN; and India's arms sale to ASEAN would also help some countries to modernize their weapons systems. Moreover, India has signed defensive agreements or memorandums with Vietnam, Malaysia and Singapore. All in all, India's military engagement with ASEAN countries has played a great role in the modernization of ASEAN's defence.

On the other hand, India's strong military strength encourages ASEAN countries to invite India to act as one of the protectors of its security. With the cooperation of Indian military forces, it would be much easier for ASEAN countries to combat various seaborne evils, such as the terrorism, piracy, organized crimes and other illegal activities.

As for the piracy issue, according to the Worldwide Maritime Piracy Report, Southeast Asia is one of the two hot spots of piracy.[30] It retains its position as the most active with regard to attacks on vessels, accounting for more than half of the reported attacks. And in the recent past, piracy-related incidents, which were more common in the Malacca Straits and South China

Sea, have tended to spill over into the Bay of Bengal and the Arabian Sea. According to the International Maritime Bureau reports, the ranking of the regions or countries most plagued by pirate attacks (including the failed ones) in 2000 were Indonesia, Malaysia, Bangladesh, India, Ecuador, Malacca Straits and Red Sea. In 2001, the ranking was nearly the same with Indonesia (72 reported attacks), Malaysia (11) and Bangladesh (11) being the three most affected countries by piracy attacks. In 2002, the reported attacks around Indonesian waters shot up to 103, followed by Bangladesh (32), India (18), Malacca Straits (16), Malaysia (14), Nigeria (14) and Vietnam (12). In the above three successive years, the reported piracy attacks around the Indian Ocean Rim countries and regions accounted for respectively 64 per cent, 35 per cent and 55 per cent[31] of the worldwide reported attacks. The actual problem of piracy is much more disturbing and serious than what the figures reflect. To make matters worse, the very active illegal militias, terrorist organizations, anti-governmental and insurgent forces and drug mafias are also involved in the maritime armed attacks, some of them even colluding with the pirates.[32] Due to the limitations of defensive strength and even weak economic strength, many ASEAN countries could not cope with such threats from the waters. In this sense, with the militarily stronger India's engagement with ASEAN, especially with the growing military cooperation between India and ASEAN, it would be relatively easier for Southeast Asian countries to tackle such non-traditional security issues, especially the piracy threat.

As for terrorism, since India has a good database on those terrorist organizations — whether in South Asia or in Southeast Asia — and their activities, and has valuable experience in dealing with them, close interactions between the counter-terrorism agencies of India and the countries of the Southeast Asian region would therefore be of mutual benefit.

Frankly speaking, without the substantial involvement of India, it would be very difficult for ASEAN countries to deal with such asymmetrical threats. There was some truth in what Jaswant Singh once declared in the speech made in Singapore on 2 June 2000. He said: "The smooth passing through Malacca Straits and South China Sea should be guaranteed, this bears much significance to both ASEAN and India economies. India has never eroded and will still never erode the strategic space of ASEAN. India's engagement will only contribute to the stability of ASEAN."[33]

Incidentally, a structure of cooperation and peace in which the United States, Russia, China, Japan, India are all engaged and find equally beneficial is necessary for Southeast Asian stability and peace. Presently, with India and some big powers' positive participation in the ASEAN Regional Forum (ARF) process, the ASEAN region and beyond would get the bonus of much more stability. Peace and stability in this region is crucial if economic dynamism is to persist in the twenty-first century.

Of course, India's engagement also bears some negative impact, such as an increasingly obvious arms race in Southeast Asia, although some may call it a normal process of military modernization and weapons system refining and upgrading, one of the grim consequences is that with a much sharper military edge, the settlement of existing conflicts and differences would become more complicated.

Finally, India's "Look East" policy would have a positive impact on ASEAN politically.

Southeast Asia is very diversified in the sense of culture, civilization, religion, language, etc. There is no even distribution of wealth nor equal levels of economic development. There is also no political system that is common to all. The historical legacies and mutual suspicions among ASEAN members themselves and between ASEAN and its neighbours, particularly with the great powers, are too obvious to be ignored. In this regard, the key determinants of regional security would be the balance of power and the nature of relations between the great powers, rather than any regional institution. This political logic and grim geographic reality has forced ASEAN to develop solid and strategic relations with as many big powers as possible. India's "Look East" policy has greatly facilitated ASEAN's effort in this regard. At present, nearly all the significant big powers in the international arena have built very close relations with ASEAN. The geostrategic environment of ASEAN is one of the best in history.

The other concomitant of India's "Look East" policy is that with more big powers entering Southeast Asia, ASEAN's international political influence has also become substantially enhanced. Nowadays, ASEAN is more like an important coordinator among big powers. It is even like a shock-absorber which helps the big powers calm down in their disputes.

Lastly, India's "Look East" policy and its practice would be helpful for the construction of political democracy in ASEAN, especially for ASEAN countries to tackle their ethnic, religious and even political problems. Most ASEAN countries face a common problem: How to build stable, tolerant and secular state structures under conditions of multi-ethnicity, multi-religion and externally-induced complications. In this regard, India may be a valuable source of lessons and experiences to ASEAN. In recent years, a positive development in this regard is ASEAN's modification of its traditional "non-interference" foreign policy, which is demonstrated by the fact that due to the implicit pressure of some ASEAN members, Rangoon has changed its harsh and rigid attitude towards Aung San Suu Kyi.

In short, the India-ASEAN mutual approach has proved, and would still prove, to be a blessing for both sides.

NOTES

1. C.S. Kuppuswamy, "India's Policy — Looking Eastward", South Asia Analysis Group, Paper no. 176, 27 December 2000, <http://www.saag.org/papers2/paper176.htm>
2. "PM's Address at the Annual Singapore Lecture 2002", *Press Information Bureau, Government of India*, 9 April 2002.
3. Ministry of External Affairs, *Annual Report 1998–99*, Government of India, New Delhi, 2000.
4. Sultan Shahin, "India's 'Look East' Policy Pays Off", 11 October 2003, <http://www.atimes.com/atimes/South_Asia/EJ11Df05.html>.
5. Arun Bhattacharjee, "India Airs Grievances against Malaysia", 5 June 2003, <http://www.atimes.com/atimes/Southeast_Asia/EF05Ae03.html>.
6. "Singapore Pushes to Become Indian Trade Hub", 20 February 2004, <http://www.atimes.com/atimes/South_Asia/FB20Df01.html>.
7. Supratim Mukherjee, "Myanmar: Cheers, Jeers over Giant Gas Find", 14 February 2004, <http://www.atimes.com/atimes/South_Asia/FB14Df05.html>.
8. Sreeradha Datta, "What Ails The Northeast: An Enquiry Into The Economic Factors", *Strategic Analysis*, 2001/4, pp. 73–87.
9. Ye Zhengjia, "India's Northeastern Region", *Facing Toward Asia*, January 2001.
10. "B" here refers to Bhutan, not Bangladesh.
11. Assad Latiff, "India Looks Further Eastward", *Sunday Times*, 15 February 2004.
12. Sudha Ramachandran, "Now Myanmar Targets Anti-India Rebels", 17 January 2004, <http://www.atimes.com/atimes/South_Asia/FA17Df04.html>.
13. K.M. Panikar, *Problems of Indian Defence* (London: Asia Publishing House, 1960).
14. *The Straits Times* (Singapore), 15 November 2000.
15. Dr Subhash Kapila, "India Defines Her Strategic Frontiers: An Analysis", Paper no. 832, 4 November 2003, <http://saag.org/papers7/paper832.html>.
16. B. Raman, "Counter-terrorism: The Indian Experience", 1 April 2003, <http://www.saag.org/papers7/paper649.html>.
17. B. Raman, "Terrorism in SE Asia-India's Concerns", 10 March 2004, <http://www.saag.org/papers10/paper980.html>.
18. "India, Thailand urged to Cooperate in Defense", 7 June 2003, <http://www.atimes.com/atimes/South_Asia/EF07Df06.html>.
19. Arun Bhattacharjee, "India Airs Grievances against Malaysia", 5 June 2003, <http://www.atimes.com/atimes/Southeast_Asia/EF05Ae03.html>.
20. Amit Baruah, "Foreign Ministers of India, China, Russia to Meet Again" *The Hindu*, 12 October 2003.
21. Asad Latiff, op. cit.

22. Atal Bihari Vajpayee, "India's Perspectives on ASEAN and the Asia-Pacific Region", Singapore Lecture, 9 April 2002 (Singapore: ISEAS Publications, 2002).
23. Amit Baruah, op. cit.
24. Peter Morris, "Grouping to Check China's Influence", 11 February 2004, <http://www.atimes.com/atimes/South_Asia/FB11Df06.html>.
25. Asad Latiff, op. cit.
26. *Lianhe Zaobao* (Singapore), 23 March 2003, p. 16.
27. Seminar 487: Looking East, March 2000, p. 16.
28. *The Straits Times*, 25 July 1996.
29. Rahul Bedi, "India and China Vie for Regional Supremacy", *Jane's Intelligence Review*, September 2000, p. 38.
30. See <http://www.maritimesecurity.com> and < http://www.specialops associates.com>.
31. <http://www.iccwbo.org/ccs/imb_piracy/piracy_maps2002.asp; <http://www.iccwbo.org/ccs/imb_piracy/maps/2001/maps2001.asp>; <http://www.iccwbo.org/home/ news_archives/2003/stories/piracy%20_report_2002.asp>; <http://www.geocities.com/cdelegas/index.html>, <http://www.piratesinfo.com>.
32. Vijay Sakhuja, "Indian Ocean and the Safety of Sea Lines of Communication", *Strategic Analysis*, 25 no. 5 (August 2001): 689–702, <http://www.idsa-india.org/an-aug-4.01.htm>; Rohan Gunaratna, "Illicit Transfer of Conventional Weapons: The Role of State and Non-State Actors in South Asia", in Jayanth Dhanapala, *Small Arms Control: Old Weapons, New Issues* (Vermont: Ashgate Publishing Ltd, 1999), p. 266; Muhammad Shahedul Anam Khan, "Linkage Between Arms Trafficking and the Drug Trade in South Asia", in Dhanapala, ibid., p. 248.
33. *The Straits Times*, 15 November 2000, p. 17.

11

The Dragon, the Bull and the Ricestalks: The Roles of China and India in Southeast Asia

Chulacheeb Chinwanno

The end of the Cold War in the early 1990s brought about opportunities as well as challenges to the countries in Southeast Asia. It provided the opportunity to establish a new regional order where the countries in the region could co-exist peacefully in spite of different ideologies. It also offered the challenge for the establishment of a new security arrangement in order to manage the extra-regional powers, both the dominant and the rising ones.

The United States, the hegemonic power, had played a significant role during the Cold War in guaranteeing the security of the Southeast Asian region. Japan, the United States' ally, also contributed to the industrialization and economic development of the region through investment and trade. China was then perceived as a menace as she supported the communist insurgencies, while India was looked at with suspicion because she was close to the Soviet Union and sided with the communist regimes in Indochina.

The Sino-Soviet conflict and the subsequent demise of communism in Eastern Europe as well as in Soviet Union altered the strategic landscape in Southeast Asia. The Association of Southeast Asian Nations (ASEAN), formed in 1967 of five Southeast Asian nations, saw the opportunity to enlarge and include the communist neighbours so that ten countries in the region belonged to the same regional organization. ASEAN also realized that it must engage the major powers, all extra-regional ones, including the hegemonic United States, the declining Japan, the rising China and the emerging India, so that the region could be secure, and prosper.

The four major powers — different in size and potentials — could become the four engines of the ASEAN plane. The question is how to manage them so as to maximize the benefits and minimize the risks for ASEAN. This chapter will analyse the roles of two major powers — the rising of China and India, in Southeast Asia. The chapter is divided into two parts, the first will focus on the China-ASEAN relations, the second part on the India-ASEAN relations.

THE ROLE OF CHINA IN SOUTHEAST ASIA

Southeast Asia has always been considered strategically and economically important for China. Since the end of the Cold War, China had cultivated a close relationship with countries in the region, completing the formal diplomatic recognition of all Southeast Asian countries by the early 1990s and moving toward closer economic partnership.

The rise of China had become the major concern among countries in the region. Since Deng Xiaoping's Southern Tour to Guangzhou in 1992 and especially after the yuan devaluation in 1994, the Chinese economy had undergone rapid expansion as a result of foreign direct investment and trade surplus. The Chinese economy in the 1990s grew on an average of 7–8 per cent. During this period, China also increased the defence budget and modernized its armed forces as it witnessed the United States' military

Table 11.1
A Comparison of Four Major Powers

Country	GDP (US$ Billions) 2000 (ppp)	Population (Millions) 2000	Foreign Trade Turnover (US$ Billions) 2000	Defence Expenditures (US$ Billions) 2000	Defence Expenditures (% of GDP) 2000
USA	9645.9	281.6	2010.2	294.7	3.0
China	5023.2	1262.5	474.3	41.2	3.0
Japan	3317.8	126.9	854.5	44.4	1.0
India	2443.2	1015.0	94.0	14.5	3.1

Source: World Bank, 2001*a*; World Bank, 2001*b*; IMF, 2001; IISS, 2001*a*.

superiority in the Gulf War of 1991. China's economic expansion and defence modernization created an image of the "rise of China" as well as the potential "Chinese threat" in Southeast Asia.

Although there was no consensus on the impact of the rise of China on Asia, most Southeast Asian leaders preferred to "ride the Chinese wave" and tried to manage it as best as possible. On the other hand, ASEAN states seemed to have differing views on the extent to which China could become a potential "threat". Vietnam, the Philippines and probably Indonesia tended to support stronger measures to discourage or condemn Chinese misbehaviour, while Thailand and Singapore preferred to engage the Chinese so as to sensitize it to ASEAN concerns.

In order to engage and sensitize the Chinese, ASEAN then set up a multilateral mechanism, the ASEAN Regional Forum (ARF) for regional security discussion and consultation. The first ASEAN Regional Forum met in Bangkok on July 1994 with eighteen founding members, including Brunei, Indonesia, Malaysia, the Philippines, Singapore, Thailand, Japan, South Korea, Australia, New Zealand, USA, Canada, European Union, China, Russia, Vietnam, Laos and Papua New Guinea. The subsequent meetings of the ARF admitted Myanmar, Cambodia, India and North Korea to the group. The ARF became the only regional security framework in which all major players of the world including the USA, Russia, China, Japan and the European Union, were involved. Moreover, it also became the first multilateral forum covering the Asia-Pacific.

The annual ARF meetings involved dialogues and exchanges aimed at promoting confidence-building measures in the first stage, and moved toward preventive diplomacy and conflict resolution at the later stage. The third stage was later changed to the elaboration of approaches to conflict, as China was not comfortable with the original term.[1]

At first, China was suspicious of the motive of any multilateral security attempt and preferred the South China Sea disputes to be dealt with mostly through bilateral diplomacy. Yet China had moderated her adamant rejection to engage in multilateral dialogue on the Spratlys and other security issues. In order to alleviate China's suspicion toward the ARF, ASEAN first took measures to build China's confidence toward the multilateral security dialogue itself, by pursuing its non-confrontational ASEAN-style approach and refraining from pushing for a solution on the South China Sea. China's confidence toward the ARF paved the way for the ARF to bring up the sensitive South China Sea sovereignty issue for discussion. The ARF had become a regional security framework crafted and designed by ASEAN to contain threats without specifically containing any particular power.

In the past, China did not trust the multilateral dialogue on security and preferred to deal with this issue bilaterally. However, China seemed to have more confidence and saw benefits from multilateralism, probably from the good experience with ASEAN. China's new approach to Southeast Asia at present include the following.

1. New Concept of Security

After the end of the Cold War in the early 1990s, China saw the change in the strategic landscape as a result of the demise of communism and the rise of the United States as a hegemonic power. Globalization and rapid changes in technology affected the international environment and security. China began to develop and articulate a new concept of security which expanded the old narrow definition of security to include defence, diplomatic, political as well as economic considerations. Hu Jintao, then China's vice president during his visit to Indonesia in July 2000, advocated a new concept of security at the Indonesia Council on World Affairs:

> ...A new security concept that embraces the principles of equality, dialogue, trust and cooperation, and a new security order should be established to ensure genuine mutual respect, mutual cooperation, consensus through consultation and peaceful settlement of disputes, rather than bullying, confrontation and imposition of one's own will upon others. Only in that way can countries coexist in amity and secure their development...[2]

From the new Chinese perspective, security was not just a matter of military capability. In fact, national security was inseparable from political stability, economic success, and social harmony. Yang Yanyi, Deputy Director General of Policy Planning Department of the Ministry of Foreign Affairs of China, elaborated further that the new security concept "is characterized by mutual trust, mutual benefit, equality and coordination".[3]

China believed that frequent dialogue and mutual briefings on each other's security and defence policies could contribute to bringing up the comfort level and degree of confidence, and fostering goodwill and trust. Besides trust, mutual benefits should also be advocated through multilateral mechanism. China saw to it that while ensuring its own security interests, other countries' security interests were also respected. Equality was also important in the sense that countries, big or small, strong or weak, must subscribe to the same universally recognized norms and principles, especially the principles of sovereign equality, non-interference in each other's internal affairs and peaceful settlement of international disputes. China also placed a premium on dialogue and consultation in place of coercion and confrontation in addressing security issues.

The objective of China's security policy on the Asia-Pacific is composed of three parts: China's own stability and prosperity; peace and stability in the surrounding region; and dialogue and cooperation with other countries in the Asia-Pacific region.[4]

2. Strengthening Bilateral Relations with ASEAN Neighbours

China pursued a good neighbourly partnership with her southern neighbours in Southeast Asia. To enhance further cooperation with ASEAN, China during 1999–2001 negotiated and signed bilateral documents and statements with ASEAN countries on long-term cooperative frameworks. Thailand was the first ASEAN member to sign a Joint Statement on a Plan of Action for the twenty-first century in February 1999, laying out the plan for cooperation in various fields including political, economic, cultural and security.

Later, China with nine other members of ASEAN, signed similar statements, indicating her commitment in promoting regional stability, peace and prosperity. It was significant that all the statements affirmed that the bilateral relations would be based on the basic norms found in the UN Charter, the Five Principles of Peaceful Co-Existence, the ASEAN Treaty of Amity and Cooperation (TAC), and recognized principles found in international law. Bilateral political dialogues including policy dialogue on strategic and security issues between China and each member of ASEAN were to contribute to mutual understanding and trust.

3. Promoting Multilateral Cooperation

The multilateral relations between China and ASEAN have contributed significantly to closer relations and cooperation. Since July 1994, China and ASEAN agreed to open consultation on political and security issues at the senior official level. By February 1997, ASEAN and China formalized their cooperation by establishing the ASEAN-China Joint Cooperation Committee (ACJCC) to act as the coordinator for all ASEAN-China mechanisms at the working level.

China became ASEAN's dialogue partner and participated in the annual ASEAN Post-Ministerial Conference (PMC) consultation process, with other dialogue partners (ASEAN Ten+10) as well as the meeting between ten ASEAN members and each dialogue partner (ASEAN Ten+1). China also participated in another ASEAN multilateral mechanism, the ASEAN Regional Forum, reluctantly at first. Later, China took an active role in the ARF process, especially in the inter-sessional work programme related to confidence-building measures.

Besides the above, the ASEAN-China multilateral relations was expanded and transformed into ASEAN+3 (APT), which included China, Japan and South Korea, and evolved into annual summit meetings at head-of-state level. At the APT summit in Cambodia in November 2002, ASEAN and China signed a Framework Agreement on Comprehensive Economic Cooperation between ASEAN Nations and the People's Republic of China. This agreement aims to establish a free trade area between China and ASEAN, which will be discussed later.

Also in Cambodia, at the Sixth ASEAN-China Summit, the leaders of ASEAN and China signed a Joint Declaration of ASEAN and China on Cooperation in the Field of Non-Traditional Security Issues, agreeing to cooperate in combating trafficking in illegal drugs, people-smuggling including trafficking in women and children, sea piracy, terrorism, arms smuggling, money laundering, international crime and cyber crime. Moreover, China also signed here with ASEAN a Declaration on the Conduct of Parties in the South China Sea. At the October ASEAN 2003 Summit in Bali, Indonesia, China also acceded to the ASEAN Treaty of Amity and Cooperation, becoming the first non-ASEAN major power to do so.

4. Deepening Economic Relationships with ASEAN through Free Trade Agreement

The economic relations between China and ASEAN have become increasingly close. The trade volume had increased from less than US$9 billion in 1993 to about US$55 billion in 2001, making ASEAN China's fifth largest trading partner and China ASEAN's sixth. In 2001 China exported to ASEAN around US$23.8 billion and imported from ASEAN at US$31.5 billion. Among ASEAN members, Singapore was China's largest trading partner, followed by Malaysia, Indonesia and Thailand. Trade with ASEAN increased by 30 per cent over last year and could soar to more than US$65 billion in 2003.

Direct investment between China and ASEAN also increased. Before the financial crisis in Asia in 1997, most investment capital would flow to China. However, since 1997, one saw a reverse trend as Chinese enterprise, state-owned as well as private, started to invest more in the cheaper ASEAN.

China found that the financial crisis had weakened ASEAN considerably and also heightened their fear about ASEAN's ability to compete with

Table 11.2
Chinese Direct Investment in ASEAN

Number of Approved Outward Direct Investment Projects in ASEAN

	1999	2000	2001	2002	Cumulative Value (US$ Millions)
Thailand	3	13	6	15	431.0
Cambodia	1	3	7	3	214.7
Vietnam	2	17	12	20	85.0
Singapore	6	6	3	6	71.1
Myanmar	1	7	3	5	66.1
Indonesia	0	1	2	6	65.0

Source: Ministry of Commerce, Beijing, December 2003.

China economically. This concern plus the worry about China's entrance into the WTO brought about the image that China could become an economic threat to ASEAN. Realizing the importance of expanding economic relations with ASEAN and alleviating its fear, China proposed to conclude a Free Trade Agreement with ASEAN. The ASEAN-China Free Trade Area (ACFTA) would offer ASEAN members an advance opportunity to enter the Chinese market under reduced tariffs before lower rates are extended to all WTO members.

At an ASEAN Summit in November 2001, China and ASEAN agreed to conclude an FTA in the next ten years. At a China-ASEAN Summit in Phnom Penh in November 2002, China and ASEAN signed an agreement outlining the general FTA framework, under which trade in meat, fishery products and vegetables would be liberalized in 2004. Tariffs on other products would be cut and abolished in stages and the FTA could be realized as early as 2015.

China viewed an FTA with ASEAN as an important driver for its economic development in the coming decades, arguing that the western region of China, less developed than the coastal area, could benefit by tapping the market and capital of ASEAN. Moreover, China was also involved in the Greater Mekong Sub-Region (GMS) economic cooperation with Laos, Myanmar, Thailand, Cambodia and Vietnam.

It may be argued that Chinese influence in Southeast Asia has been increasing as a result of many factors, especially the shift in its policy and approach toward Southeast Asia. Although some issues still lingered on such as Chinese territorial disputes with several ASEAN members over territories in the South China Sea, or that China was a major competitor with Southeast Asia for global investment and export markets, they seem to be well contained. China-ASEAN relations are destined toward closer cooperation for mutual benefit.

China in fact sought closer economic and political ties with Southeast Asia after the demise of communism in East Europe, the Tiananmen incident and the fragmentation of the Soviet Union in the early 1990s, but the relationship was complicated by the South China Sea conflict, especially the Mischief Reef incident in 1995. By the end of the decade, the new Chinese leaders from both the third and fourth generation, including Hu Jintao, advocated a new security concept emphasizing multilateral cooperation among states, resolving differences through dialogue and peaceful settlement of conflict.

Moreover, the Chinese leaders were quite attentive to the interests and concern of ASEAN countries in seeking to develop common ground with them. Bilaterally, China pursued a good neighbour policy and signed numerous framework agreements governing relations with individual Southeast Asian states. China was at first reluctant to join the multilateral forum to discuss security issues but later actively participated and came to some understanding with ASEAN on several issues.

The Chinese also tried to calm regional fears over an expanding China through multilateral dialogues and joint statements. The free trade agreement was also a way to alleviate fear and promote mutual benefits. To sum up, the main objective of China in Southeast Asia is to preserve a regional security and economic environment conducive to domestic development and regime stability. This aim is also shared by Southeast Asian nations. Thus the peaceful rise of China could enhance the security and stability of the Southeast Asian region.

THE ROLE OF INDIA IN SOUTHEAST ASIA

India, the world's largest democracy with a population of one billion people, has been regarded in the past by Southeast Asia as merely a regional power in South Asia, with a marginal influence on other parts of Asia including Southeast Asia. During the 1990s, however, two fundamental changes occurred within India that caught the eyes of Southeast Asia.

The first was the economic liberalization initiated in 1991, the success of which had contributed to the GDP growth rate of the 1990s, averaging six per cent. The foreign exchange reserves of India exceeded US$40 billion at the end of 2001. The export sector expanded vigorously as the software brought in more than US$4 billion a year.

The second was the change in India's perception of the world and the change in its strategy toward East Asia. The "Look East" policy reoriented India toward Southeast Asia, whose economy was growing and expanding at that time. India needed new friends and partners as it realized that it could no longer rely upon Russia or East Europe after the demise of communism.

Before then, India's relations with Southeast Asia was lukewarm and inconsistent.[5] After the Second World War, India and many countries in Southeast Asia were struggling for independence from Western colonialism. The shared experiences and the fear of being dragged into the subsequent Cold War conflict, prompted India under Nehru and Indonesia under Sukarno, to push for Asian solidarity by inviting many newly independent countries to the Afro-Asian Conference at Bandung in Indonesia in 1955.

The close relationship between India and Southeast Asia became more and more distant as India championed the Non-Aligned Movement (NAM) in the 1960s, while Southeast Asia was busy with internal insurgencies and allied with the United States for external security. From that time on, India virtually disengaged from the Southeast Asian region and did not re-engage until it launched a "Look East" policy in the early 1990s.

There was a brief attempt for engagement in 1980 when India wanted to become a dialogue partner with ASEAN but India's support of Vietnam's invasion of Cambodia and her subsequent recognition of the Vietnam-backed regime in Cambodia upset ASEAN. Despite the close cultural ties in language, literature and religions — Buddhism and Hinduism, India and Southeast Asia were politically and strategically far apart.[6]

However, India and Southeast Asia began a rapprochement in the 1990s after the end of the Cold War with the launch of its "Look East" policy. Chatchai Choonhavan, the Thai prime minister, saw the opportunity for trade and investment with India, especially the 200 million middle class, visited India in 1989 and the former Indian Prime Minister N. Rao also visited Thailand and other ASEAN countries in 1990. The renewed interest on both sides culminated in India becoming a sectoral dialogue partner of ASEAN in 1992. Indian and ASEAN officials met in New Delhi in March 1993 to identify specific areas of collaboration within the designated sectors such as trade, investment and tourism. In 1994, two additional sectors, science and technology, were added to the list. In 1995, ASEAN upgraded its relations with India to the level of a full dialogue partner.[7]

After 1995, India-ASEAN relations expanded not only vertically but also horizontally. To institutionalize the cooperation, the ASEAN-India Joint Cooperation Committee (AIJCC) was established which held its first meeting in New Delhi in November 1996. "The first AIJCC focused attention on the establishment of institutional mechanism in specific sectors of cooperation as well as discussed ways and means of expanding and intensifying ASEAN-India cooperation in the identified areas of trade, investment, science and technology, tourism, human resource development, infrastructure and people to people interaction."[8]

Institutional linkages between ASEAN and India were further strengthened, with India's participation in the ASEAN Post-Ministerial Conference (PMC) held in Jakarta in July 1996, and also India's membership of the ASEAN Regional Forum (ARF). These institutional linkages were important because it provided regular contact and communication with one another.

However valuable institutional linkage may be in itself, what would make it of lasting value to both India and ASEAN would be the level of economic transactions, and the congruence of political views and strategic perceptions.

Economic transactions between India and ASEAN increased significantly in the past decade. Two-way trade was insignificant at first, with only US$2.22 billion in 1990. It went up to US$5.37 billion in 1995 and exceeded US$10 billion in 2002. Both sides expect that the two-way trade could reach US$15 billion in 2005. Trade was also unevenly distributed between India and members of ASEAN. A breakdown of bilateral trade figures between India and ASEAN members showed that Singapore traded the most with India, followed by Malaysia, Indonesia, and Thailand.

From ASEAN's viewpoint, India's trade with ASEAN was still in its infancy, at only US$10 billion in 2002, compared with other ASEAN trading partners, such as that of China at US$70 billion, Japan at US$116 billion and the United States at US$120 billion. Moreover, the share of ASEAN in India's total trade had gone up from slightly more than 4 per cent in 1990 to close to 10 per cent in 2002, but that of India's share in ASEAN's total trade was only slightly more than 1 per cent.

However, there are ways to increase the trade volume. In 2002, India offered ASEAN a Regional Trade and Investment Arrangement (RTIA) to increase trade and investment ties. The ASEAN-India Task Force on Economic Linkage was set up at the First India-ASEAN Summit in November 2002 to make recommendations. The Framework Agreement for Comprehensive Economic Cooperation between India and ASEAN was later signed at the Second ASEAN-India Summit, Bali, Indonesia in October 2003, spelling out a plan for free trade agreements in goods, services investment, as well as an early harvest programme.

Both sides agreed to set up a negotiating committee and tried to finalize the negotiations by the end of 2004 so that a free trade area could be established between India and the original five ASEAN by 2011 and the others including the Philippines, Laos, Cambodia, Vietnam and Myanmar by 2016. The negotiations to liberalize trade in services and investment should also be concluded by 2007. Moreover, an early harvest package of 105 items whose tariffs would be reduced to zero by 2007 could start being implemented from 1 November 2004.

In order to facilitate increased economic transactions, infrastructure such as land, sea and air transportation and communications must also be developed. The India-Myanmar-Thailand highway linkage would connect Moreli in northeastern India to Maesot in Thailand's Tak province *via* Bagan in Myanmar.[9] Another highway would connect Kanchanaburi in Thailand to Tavoy deep seaport in Myanmar, with shipping links to seaports in India. Two task forces had been set up — one on financing and the other on technical matters — chaired by Thailand and India respectively. The two highways are expected to be completed by 2006.

The highways would go a long way in reviving the traditional economic and people-to-people contacts between India and Southeast Asia, said Indian Prime Minister Atal Behari Vajpayee during his visit to Singapore and Cambodia in April 2002. An equally important link was the undersea cable between India and Singapore which would facilitate another long distance telephony and enhance bandwidth for Internet surfers.

India also offered an "open skies" policy to airlines of ASEAN members so they would be free to operate daily flights to New Delhi, Kolkata, and Mumbai and onward to eighteen other tourist centres in India. The land, sea and air transportation linkages would enhance economic transactions between India and ASEAN.

India's thrust in her effort to intensify the engagement with ASEAN is not only on economic but also security issues. In the past different security perceptions kept them apart. At present there are more similarities than differences. India, by becoming a participant in the ARF, realized the ASEAN way of new security management through engagement and consultation.

India, like China, also acceded to the ASEAN Treaty of Amity and Cooperation, accepting the principle of peaceful settlement of conflict through negotiation. Moreover, the ASEAN-India Joint Declaration for Cooperation to Combat International Terrorism was signed so as to enhance counter-terrorism. Following the September 11 terrorist attacks in New York and Washington and the December 13 attack on the Indian parliament, India found it necessary to cooperate with friends and neighbours in this matter.

Defence cooperation between India and ASEAN have existed for some time on a bilateral basis. India has held naval exercises with Singapore, Malaysia, Indonesia and Thailand regularly. In 1993 India and Malaysia signed a Memorandum of Understanding to expand their defence cooperation. India was very much concerned with maritime security and wanted to cooperate with ASEAN regarding the protection of the Sea Lanes of Communication against piracy and other transnational crimes.

India-ASEAN relations have improved and continue to move forward slowly and steadily. The May 2004 Indian general election result was a surprise as the BJP lost. The new coalition government led by the Congress Party installed Manmohan Singh as prime minister.[10] The relationship between India and ASEAN would not be affected by the change in leadership in New Delhi because it was the Congress Party which started the "Look East" policy more than a decade ago. Moreover, Prime Minister Manmohan Singh was once finance minister who started the liberalization economic policy and valued the economic cooperation with India's Southeast Asian neighbours.

CONCLUSION

China and India are two great neighbours of ASEAN, the sources of regional civilization in the past and the sources of regional prosperity in the future. Both are the rising powers in the twenty-first century, China being the first to rise in the first quarter of the century, followed by India in the second quarter. China seems more prepared than India as it has invested tremendously in developing infrastructure, physical as well as human.

The two rising powers will play increasingly active roles in the region. They can develop into partners as well as competitors, in the economic as well as security arenas. ASEAN must manage the two rising powers and the two hegemonic powers of the United States and Japan in such a way that they would complement each other and learn to respect one another. The ASEAN pilot must not only navigate the rough environment of the twenty-first century but also balance the four engines so that the ASEAN plane will experience a smooth ride to peace and prosperity.

NOTES

1. Michael Leifer, "China in South East Asia: Interdependence and Accommodation", in *China Rising* edited by David S.G. Goodman and Gerald Segal (London: Routledge, 1997), p. 156.
2. Carlye A. Thayer, "China's New Security Concept and Southeast Asia", in *Asia Pacific Security*, edited by David W. Lowell (Canberra: Asia Pacific Press, 2003). p. 91.
3. Yang Yanyi, "A New Approach: China's Perception and Policy on Security Dialogue and Cooperation", *Foreign Affairs Journal*, June 2003, pp. 17–26.

4. Alice D. Ba, "China and ASEAN: Renavigating Relations for a 21ˢᵗ Century Asia", *Asian Survey*, July/August 2003.
5. See Mohammad Ayoob, *India and South East Asia* (London: Routledge, 1990).
6. Kripa Sridharam, "India and South East Asia in the 1990s", *Southeast Asian Affairs 1997* (Singapore: Institute of Southeast Asia Studies, 1998), pp. 47–48.
7. Ibid., p. 50.
8. "First Meeting of the ASEAN-India Joint Cooperation Committee" Joint Press Release, New Delhi, 14–16 November 1996 from <www.asean.or.id>.
9. Dinesh C. Sharma, "India Reaches Out", *The Bangkok Post*, 13 April 2002, p. 8.
10. "India's New Government", *The Economist*, 4 June 2004.

12

Evolving Security Environment in Southeast Asia: An ASEAN Assessment

Jusuf Wanandi

INTRODUCTION

Since the main topic is on the evolving security environment of Southeast Asia, particularly on external security challenges of Southeast Asia, this introduction will include two other problems that are internal security concerns for Southeast Asia. First is the domestic challenges due to the financial crisis (and generally globalization) which put a lot of new pressure on the developing societies of Southeast Asia. They are not only economic in nature but also social, political and even cultural or the values system that have been touched and changed.

The second challenge is the new relations in ASEAN created not only by the expansion of its membership from six to ten Southeast Asian nations, but also by the new challenges of globalization that put a lot more pressure on the relationship. This is due to the expectations of the greater East Asian and Asia-Pacific regions on the regional entity, ASEAN, while the entity could not be advanced or expanded due to the limitations of some of its new members and to the diversity of political systems and economic development among them.

These two internal challenges could be more devastating to Southeast Asia than any external security challenges, because in fact, outside threats directed towards Southeast Asian states are non-existent in the foreseeable future. However, there are developments in the East Asian region that could become sources of instability for the whole region and affect the security of Southeast Asian states indirectly. They are the potential conflicts across the straits between China and Taiwan, and the problem of proliferation of nuclear weapons in the Korean peninsula. Another source is the nuclear stand-off in the sub-continent between India and Pakistan.

In addition, there are new threats and challenges coming to the region (and globally), namely, the problem of global and regional terrorism and the proliferation of weapons of mass destruction (WMD). These new asymmetrical threats are non-state in nature but are very damaging because they are distinct from earlier domestic political terrorism. The terrorists form a global network based on a very extreme interpretation of Islam and they have no qualms about killing innocent people anywhere and in big numbers. They are also well-equipped with high-tech equipment, and have been well-trained in Afghanistan during the war against the USSR and afterwards under the Taliban regime. And they have been able to network with a lot of disgruntled elements in all parts of the world. Most importantly, they have acquired a steady source of finance.

In the longer term the challenges to Southeast Asia's security environment are the challenges for the whole of East Asia, and these are:

- How to cope with a rising China in the East Asian region in the longer term, when China in its own right will become a "superpower".
- How the relationship between the two great powers, China and Japan, is going to evolve. As has been said by Singapore's Senior Minister Lee Kuan Yew, this is the first time we are going to see in the East Asian region both a strong China and a strong Japan.
- Most important is the future relations between China and the United States, the only superpower now. In history it has never been an easy transition between one great power to another great power, or for that matter, to have a new great power to be accepted by the existing one. The worst case scenario for the region would be a potential confrontation between the two in the long term.

SECURITY ISSUES RELATED TO GLOBALIZATION

As stated in the introduction, globalization has put a lot of pressure on every state and society in East Asia. The financial crisis in 1997 brought about by globalization has greatly curtailed the economic exuberance of the region which had lasted for over twenty years. The crisis brought about much misery and also instability and conflicts in some of the developing parts of the region.

Another impact of globalization is on political stability, because political systems have also been pressured to change. And last but not least, changes are happening in the values system or socio-cultural aspect, which pose a challenge to the stability and continuity of a system. In that sense, domestic security problems and instabilities have arisen due to globalization, which should also be considered as a serious challenge where the developing countries are concerned. That is why they also should be supported and assisted to strengthen their political system, to improve their economic well-being, and to have certainty to be able to preserve some of their values system. These are all important to be able to overcome the impact of globalization.

Globalization has also brought about some real problems to ASEAN cooperation, because every member is busy taking care of its own crises, especially Indonesia which, accounting for over 40 per cent of the ASEAN population, has been ASEAN's anchor. The new members who are also dependent on the older members for assistance and support are disappointed. And it has become more difficult for them to catch up with the older members to participate fully in ASEAN activities and development.

IMPACT OF REGIONAL CONFLICTS ON SOUTHEAST ASIAN SECURITY

First, the proliferation of nuclear weapons by the Democratic People's Republic of Korea (DPRK) has become a real threat to East Asia, and it will have a real impact on Southeast Asia. This is because the whole of East Asia has become one region strategically, thanks to economic integration that happened to a very large extent of the region, particularly in trade, investment, and transfer of technology. The Six-Party Talks under the leadership of China have become the instrument to stabilize and overcome this problem of proliferation. The U.S. administration has not been willing to deal with DPRK alone, and has relied on this multilateral effort to seek a resolution. After two meetings no results are in sight yet, and the situation still at a stalemate.

Although ASEAN is not directly involved in the Six-Party Talks, it is important that Southeast Asia gives political support to the efforts of non-proliferation of North Korea, because it concerns the security of East Asia and the Asia-Pacific; and ASEAN's support could be an additional factor that could be important for North Korea to understand that the whole region is behind the non-proliferation effort. This instrument of the Six-Party Talks could also be used in the future to solve other problems and crises in Northeast Asia, which until now has no sub-regional institution to depend upon.

A second issue is the cross-straits relations between China and Taiwan which have worsened under the presidency of Chen Shui-bian because he has not been trusted by the Chinese. Under Lee Teng-hui the people of Taiwan have become more assertive as Taiwanese rather than being Chinese. And in the long term the Chinese could not be comfortable that reunification will happen. Although Taiwanese companies are becoming more dependent on their investments in China in order to remain competitive, and more and more Taiwanese are living in China (up to two million people), economic reasons alone can never be adequate to keep peace between the two parties.

In the short to medium term, the Chen Shui-bian presidency is trying all kinds of political tactics to get more public support for independence democratically and put China in a *fait accompli* through constitutional reforms and by having referenda about many things that relate to independence. And, by increasing arms procurement from the United States and integrating their armed forces with the United States through training and exercises, the Taiwanese think they will be able to prevent Chinese military action against them in the future. They have made China very nervous and scrambling to maintain the *status quo*.

It is important for China to strengthen the understanding of its One-China policy in its relations with the United States, EU, and East Asian countries through a lot of information and exchanges, and to get them to support China's policy instead of being influenced by Chen's capriciousness. While Taiwan should always be reminded of the idea of a greater China, it is obvious that the basic idea of "one country and two systems" proposed by Deng Xiaoping is not acceptable to Chen. A new paradigm to maintain the *status quo* therefore has to be found. China's reaction to Chen's inaugural speech (which was supposedly more responsible but was in reality meant to keep the Chinese guessing what he was going to do next), has led to new proposals such as having Confidence and Security Building Measures (CSBM) activities, and willingness to give space internationally to Taiwan, as long as the idea of one China will be accepted. But since trust has been so limited on both sides, constant attention by East Asians (and the United States) is advisable, since the relationship will become more heated in the future. East Asia has a stake that things do not get out of hand in a very complicated, emotional and dangerous situation. A military confrontation will make the whole region suffer a setback for a long time. The main problem at present is that a credible but direct and low-key level of relations between the two regimes is non-existent. Therefore it is very likely that both sides may misinterpret each other's plans and activities, and increase the possibility of a confrontation. China's resoluteness to see that Taiwan does not become independent has to be taken very seriously. The fourth generation leaders of China, who took over just more than a year ago, cannot lose Taiwan and survive. It is not that they will use military force immediately (when they are not overwhelmingly strong at this stage), but that they have plenty of escalating instruments to punish Taiwan. China will undoubtedly use force against Taiwan if Taiwan declares independence, or prevent Taiwan from becoming independent by using other legal instruments such as constitutional amendment or referendum. On its part, Taiwan should not dismiss or underestimate this resoluteness.

The third issue is the dangerous stand-off between the two nuclear powers in South Asia, namely India and Pakistan. At least for the time being, relations have been stabilized, and talks are going on, while the Congress Party in India has promised to continue with the direct talks. Only the United States is in a position to have some influence on the two parties, and is making positive use of those relations with both of them. Now that Pakistan is a member of the ARF, the confidence-building measures among the two could be enhanced and ASEAN has a supporting role to play in this effort to create strategic stability in the sub-continent.

As a footnote, it should be noted that the overlapping claims in the South China Sea, namely, on the Spratly Islands, which was previously another source of worry, has improved considerably with the signing of the Declaration on the Conduct of Parties in the South China Sea between China and ASEAN. This is no more a source of worry between them.

In fact China, which was considered a threat before, has shown responsibility and goodwill towards ASEAN, in the economic field (FTA and many imports) as well as in the political field (Declaration on the Conduct in the South China Sea and signing the Treaty of Amity and Cooperation (TAC) of ASEAN, the basis for regional order in Southeast Asia) so that its "peaceful" rise as a great power is acceptable to ASEAN.

New threats to the security of East Asia have come in the form of international terrorism. This was inspired and encouraged by Al-Qaeda terrorist groups, who have created terrorist networks all over the world. In Southeast Asia it is the Jemaah Islamiyah (JI). Based on an extreme interpretation of Islam, they are against USA and the West, who are being accused of occupying Saudi Arabia, and being enemies of Islam. They are willing to kill many innocent people without qualms and have created a network of terrorist organizations with local/national organizations through the connection of training and education which started from the Mujahiddin War against the former USSR in the mid-1980s.

These new threats can only be overcome through international and regional cooperation. The most immediate and important effort is to raise the threshold against any attack in the future through regional and international cooperation. The most important cooperation should be in intelligence, police, immigration, financial control, and sometimes among the military, when it is needed.

But in the medium term, efforts should be made to identify the root causes, because in the end it is a matter of how to win the hearts and minds of the Muslim community. This can happen only if the moderates are going to win the debate about the right interpretation of Islam on the issues of society and state. Here is where the region and the international community should assist and support them.

There are several ways to do so:

- The most important is to give support to Muslim nations, or nations with a sizeable Muslim population, to be successful in creating a democracy and a growing economy with social justice. Only if the moderates can show their ability to reconcile Islam and democracy, Islam and modernization, and Islam with a growing economy and social justice, can they convince the extremists that a theocratic state (a *khalifah*) or Islamic laws (*shariah*) is no more relevant in the modern world and should be replaced by a modern and secular state.

- The most emotional issue for Muslims in the international scene is definitely the Israel-Palestine conflict. It has become a self-identification problem for them. They feel how Muslims in general have become oppressed, colonized, abused, faced injustice, degraded, and even killed by the Israelis and the West (particularly the United States) in the last century. The United States has generally been so blatantly pro-Israel that Muslims point their hatred towards the Americans in particular. This "hatred" is no excuse for other matters including their inabilities and backwardness, but is real because it is hurting and putting them in despair. It will not be the only reason why they are against the West and especially the United States, but much of that hatred can be overcome if the United States will not give all-out support to Israel, especially under Sharon, and be more willing to be balanced in their policies towards both sides.

- Stopping the Iraq War is another problem that has become imperative, namely through the process of getting the Iraqis empowered and having the UN give legitimacy to the process of empowerment. American and coalition forces, however, have to stay as long as they are needed to guarantee the security of the Iraqi people and with the consent and request of the Iraqi Government in the future.

- Another matter that should be paid attention to by the United States in fighting international terrorism is to keep to the higher moral ground. That means that a fine line and a certain balance have to be kept in adhering to human rights and the rule of law in the fight against terrorism. Ignoring or putting aside the rule of law in Guantanamo will only produce more terrorists, because people everywhere have no more respect for the United States and the ideals that it stands for and is respected for. Such balance has simply been ignored and dismissed by the United States. That is why the abuses of the Abu Ghraib prisoners are also so damaging to the United States.

- Another important problem is poverty. Directly, it may seem unimportant as a cause for international terrorism because the perpetrators are middle class and some, even well educated. But the foot soldiers and the local cells and cadres they created as the next line of activists or supporting elements are poor people. This happened in Indonesia among the local supporters of the JI who have been involved in the Bali bombing and the Marriot Hotel bombing in Jakarta. Because poverty breeds despair, combined with an extreme ideology, it will create explosive situations all around.

- The problem of WMD is related to the dangers of it being paired with international terrorism. It could involve biological "dirty bombs", using nuclear materials to create real havoc. But the fact is that all the treaties on arms control and non-proliferation have become less secured, because they have allowed proliferations involving: India, Pakistan, North Korea, Libya, and Iran. Therefore, first the regime has to be tightened in the review of the Non-Proliferation Treaty (NPT) and other relevant treaties. It is also important to attempt to abolish nuclear armaments in the longer term, because a non-proliferation regime alone may no longer be adequate. In relation to proliferation, controlling the export of WMD and their delivery systems also has to be strengthened. And the Proliferation Security Initiative (PSI) instrument has to be made more palatable to more countries in the Asia-Pacific. Here the maritime security aspects of the threat is critical and should be paid attention to, especially in relation to the sea lanes of communication (SLOC), where oil and goods are being transported through. Their security has only recently been appreciated and paid attention to.

Although these new threats, namely international terrorism and proliferations of WMD, are real and very serious threats to the region, other threats and challenges, including the pressure of globalization, should not been taken for granted or forgotten. The developing parts of the region in particular are still very vulnerable and not all of them are completely equipped to deal with globalization fully, so assistance and support here is important to them. How could they otherwise pay attention to the threat of international terrorism and WMD proliferation if they become "failing states", because they could not become part of the globalized world?

FUTURE CHALLENGES TO THE SECURITY ENVIRONMENT

The first challenge is how the region will cope with a rising great power in East Asia, namely, China. China is huge and is expected to continue to grow quite dramatically by 7–8 per cent a year for the next twenty years.

Understanding this challenge, China itself has tried very hard to define its development in a peaceful and acceptable way to the East Asian region and the world. It has come up with a new paradigm of a "peaceful rise of China". China tried to assure especially the region, which looked at its growth and development with anxiety, that it is still facing so many problems in its future development such as environmental problems, shortage of water and resources, limited energy and power, and lack of infrastructure in most part of China, that its needs peace in the region and good relations with the region and the international community to be able to continue to grow.

China is also trying very hard to establish a new model of development, which should use resources and energy more efficiently, stress renewable ways to use those limited resources, and stress the need to improve urgently its environmental problems which are limiting its future development.

In principle the efforts of the Chinese to portray its rise as peaceful have to be lauded, because in history the rise of almost all great powers has created instabilities, conflicts, and even wars. The Chinese have tried to show that its rise, while real, is also full of new challenges, making it imperative for it to look for a peaceful way to rise.

But because China is so big and powerful in the region, it would be even better if China could expand on this new paradigm and work it out into a new strategy of development, including in the security field.

To make the new paradigm more credible and acceptable to the region and the world, China has to be willing to place itself within a new East Asian regional institution to enable it to cooperate closely with other members of the region.

China's efforts especially to deal with ASEAN and create a lot of CBMs, in the economic (FTA with ASEAN) and political (Code of Conduct for the South China Sea and signing the TAC) fields are well taken. These have been examples where China has started to implement its new paradigm and strategy on its closest neighbours.

The second strategic question for the future is the relationship between China and Japan, which has not been emotionally normalized. It is the first time in the history of East Asia that both China and Japan are great powers. Both do not know exactly how to overcome their historical burden.

Japan has improved its economic growth and overcome its decade-long economic recession. Besides, Japan is increasingly defining its own role in the security field, in tandem with and within the arrangement of the alliance with the United States, or as invited by the UN. Therefore, they also have increased their power besides China. Japan's role in the Afghan War and in the Iraq War has been accepted by the region as part of the fight against international terrorism.

Before the East Asian region can make real progress for deeper cooperation, especially in the political-security field, normalization between the two great powers should happen.

Despite some low tension between the two societies, often played up by the media, the two economies have been cooperating increasingly and very deeply and quickly, especially in trade, investment and technology in the last few years. In fact, part of the reason why Japan has been able to overcome its economic stagnation is because of its tremendous exports to China.

Perhaps both have to proceed in the way that the relationship between Japan and Korea has moved forward. When the two leaders from both sides, President Kim Dae Jung and Prime Minister Obuchi, met, the emotional strains which have been impeding the relationship were overcome by both sides, breaking the ice that existed between the two nations.

Prime Minister Koizumi, whose decision to visit the Yakusumi Shrine every year is opposed by China, is definitely not the person who can reach out to China. We therefore have to wait until another leader arrives on the Japanese side who is strong enough to face the rising of an extreme right in the political spectrum of Japan, to make normalization with China possible.

On the Chinese side, the fourth generation leadership under President Hu Jintao should be able to show that magnanimity if Japan could do the same. But both sides are aware that normalization is an important issue to be resolved.

Hopefully the region, particularly ASEAN, can assist and support the normalization between the two big countries which are also expected to play a leadership role in East Asia. Here the East Asian cooperation or community-building could be useful in the normalization process.

Third, and the most important future challenge to the security for East Asia, is the long-term relations between China and the United States. Potential confrontation between these two great powers could happen, if in the longer term China is going to become another superpower in its own right (twenty to thirty years to come). The region could be split because each of the two powers could pressure other East Asian countries to take sides.

China is not like the USSR before, which was willing to challenge the United States in all fields. Even in the field of ideology, China's basis of socialism is now more rhetoric than real. And as has been said, it needs peace and stability for its survival and modernization.

But the United States will not easily accept another superpower. And there is always a group in the United States' body politic who is out to find another opponent to the United States to enable it to define its foreign and security policy. If China's new paradigm and strategy of development is indeed being implemented, then China will never be in the same league as the United States, but that of course has yet to be seen.

That is why the East Asian cooperation should provide a certain guarantee for the United States that China is a *status quo* power, recognized and supported as well as guaranteed by its neighbours that it will not confront the United States in the longer term.

CONCLUDING REMARKS

A review of the security environment in Southeast Asia at this particular juncture would produce mixed feelings about the situation and future developments. On the one hand, many things have happened and been achieved after the 1997 crisis, such as reforms of the economic structure; process of democratization; overcoming the worst impact on the social safety net of the small people; and also a small reform of the Armed Forces in Indonesia.

But there are also many problems to be faced due to globalization: Lack of good governance, corruption, unemployment, lack of security and rule of law, limited banking restructuring, political conflicts, and weak leadership. That is why the ASEAN Community idea, in the economic, security and social cultural fields, is so vital for the region to be able to cope with these new challenges.

Regional cooperation such as ASEAN and APEC, has also experienced some setbacks. The new threats of international terrorism have put additional pressures on those countries concerned that have not been able to overcome their multiple crises due to globalization.

International and regional cooperation is needed to face globalization and international terrorism because they are global and regional challenges. The domestic weaknesses due to globalization also have to be addressed at the regional and global level through support and assistance in trade, finance, education, health, etc.

Of the potential crises in the region, the China-Taiwan relations could become the most volatile one and has to be watched constantly. Since China does see that regional countries and the United States could play a role in defusing the crisis and also take care of possible irresponsible acts by Taiwan, this will be an important factor in the future, since the whole region could be affected by a war or conflict in a very negative way for a long time to come. China should give some space to Taiwan as an important gesture.

In the end, the Six-Party Talks on North Korean proliferation will achieve its objectives of defusing the crisis of proliferation because after the presidential elections in the United States, some new impetus could be given to the talk.

The East Asian community-building, started with the ASEAN+3 cooperation, could be the critical regional institution to help achieve the three strategic objectives for the security of the region in the longer term by:

- Absorbing a great power such as China in a regional institution and therefore strengthening the new paradigm of China, namely, the peaceful rise of China.
- Assisting in the normalization of China-Japan relations and making the East Asian region much more conducive for peace and stability.
- Helping to prevent a China-U.S. confrontation in the longer term, especially if China is going to become a real great power in the next twenty to thirty years.

13

Evolving Security Environment in Southeast Asia: A Chinese Assessment

Han Feng

Southeast Asia has been in the process of a comprehensive integration while China, as a regional emerging power, is gradually getting into the international community. Looking around China, Southeast Asia is the most important area for China both at the regional level and bilateral level while other directions are mainly its relations with big powers. And security in Southeast Asia and its changes are eventually becoming more and more influential for China. This chapter evaluates the development of security in Southeast Asia as China becomes more deeply involved and actively integrated into the region.

ASEAN DEVELOPMENT AND SECURITY

During the establishment of ASEAN, the Southeast Asian nations faced great challenges. Since becoming independent, they found it was impossible to deal with the political conflicts at home and in the region only through unilateral or bilateral management and coordination. Some of the conflicts were very serious with complicated backgrounds. Meanwhile, the Cold War made the big powers dominant in Southeast Asia and they were based upon their own global interests rather than the Southeast Asian regional interests. Therefore, the Southeast Asian nations shared the common desire for regional cooperation in the 1960s when regionalism was on the rise.[1]

However, ASEAN was established when the big powers were readjusting their relations in Southeast Asia. The situation made the newly established ASEAN realize that dealing with relations with the big powers was the main task since it concerned ASEAN's existence and development.[2]

Since the regional contradictions were far beyond the coordinating capacity of the newly-born ASEAN in term of their complexity and far-reaching impact, simply wiping out the big powers' presence in the region was obviously not realistic because the geopolitical situation, and the small nations' worries about their survival made it impossible for the Southeast Asian nations to have a common policy towards the outside powers, and many nations continued to strengthen their security relations with the different big powers.

The first time that ASEAN put forward a policy towards big powers may be the Zone of Peace, Freedom and Neutrality (ZOPFAN) in 1971.[3] Though it was weak, it clearly expressed the hope, requirement and way to have a new relation with big powers. And it indicated that ASEAN had begun to formulate relations with big powers through coordination, and to change the way of dealing with the big powers relations individually.

In the 1980s, ASEAN successfully made use of the "Cambodian issue" to strengthen its integration and create a relatively consistent regional security interest while consolidating the regional concept for security.

In the 1990s, with the end of confrontation between the different alliances, ASEAN made a readjustment of its relations with the big powers. ASEAN's cooperation is quite encouraging. The cooperation within ASEAN not only strengthened the regional security and stability, but also balanced the big powers' regional interests successfully and improved the international environment for ASEAN.

ASEAN's successes are as follows: (1) enlarging ASEAN; (2) building the ASEAN Free Trade Area (AFTA); (3) keeping a driving force for the multilateral security cooperation in Southeast Asia, even in the Asia-Pacific region, through the ASEAN Regional Forum (ARF); (4) creating cooperation between ASEAN and the big powers in East Asia.

Enlargement

After enlargement in 1999, ASEAN became the third largest in population. It also had a great impact upon the region's international relations:

Firstly, by facilitating regional stability. Regional differences with their complicated historical and cultural backgrounds would be dealt with in the "ASEAN Way" rather than through confrontation.

Secondly, by reducing external "intervention". Enlargement upgraded ASEAN to a regional cooperation forum from a sub-regional one. ASEAN now covers the whole of Southeast Asia. Therefore, problems in Southeast Asia have become ASEAN's internal issues.

Thirdly, by becoming a new force in the multipolar world. After enlargement, ASEAN will be involved in international affairs representing Southeast Asia. ASEAN nations will not only stress their own regional interests, but also the region's interests, which may be positive for the region's international relations.

Fourthly, by stressing "oriental" characteristics. With a background of Western colonization, ASEAN has been on the road to modernization under globalization. However, ASEAN nations have been canonizing "Asian values" or the "ASEAN Way" for fear of being Westernized.

In short, enlargement of ASEAN strengthened ASEAN's power in balancing the big powers.

AFTA

With the development of globalization and regionalization, ASEAN decided to build the AFTA by 2008.[4] The AFTA could increase the economic cooperation level in Southeast Asia and also enhance ASEAN's position in the larger-scale multilateral cooperation by improving its economic competitiveness.

It is a traditional field for ASEAN cooperation, but also a new motivating force both for cooperation between old and new members, and for ASEAN integration in an era of globalization after the economic crisis in 1997. In addition, the AFTA is a basis for the building up of the ASEAN community.

ARF

ASEAN, as a driving force, has been playing an important role as the only regional security cooperation forum. It is, in fact, in a favoured position as the ARF's main driver. During readjustment of the relations between itself and the region's big powers, ASEAN built up its leading role through forming the ARF's regional security arrangement and avoiding internal conflicts in the Southeast Asian region.

ASEAN+3 and "Ten+1(s)"

At the end of 1997, ASEAN started the informal East Asian summit meeting. It is also called "ASEAN+3" or "Ten+3".[5] All ASEAN members, as a whole for the first time, had a dialogue with the most important East Asian powers — China, Japan and Korea, for a closer cooperative mechanism in East Asia. In addition to the summit meeting, there have been economic, foreign and financial ministers' meetings and heads of central banks meetings, together with some special working groups. The aim of ASEAN+3 is to promote economic growth, sustainable development and social progress in East Asia in the next century. Apart from ASEAN+3, ASEAN has also had successful "Ten+1" arrangements with China, Japan and India respectively.

The key point of the relations between ASEAN and big powers is to maintain stability and prosperity in Southeast Asia. By the enlargement of ASEAN, AFTA, ARF, ASEAN+3 and ASEAN+1, ASEAN can increase its influence as a regional group, as well as promote its political, economic and security integration. The big powers should be constructive and in balance during ASEAN's evolution. Moreover, ASEAN stresses the "Asian power and voice" by promoting the "ASEAN Way" in order to create or keep an equal position with the big powers by the building up of a regional system.

ANTI-TERRORISM AND SECURITY

Anti-terrorism in Southeast Asia is another important security issue. Terrorism is not new in Southeast Asia. Prior to September 11, there had been some terrorist organizations. Terrorism has long been one of the numerous security problems of the region.

The impact of September 11 greatly affected Southeast Asia, and a multilateral approach to fight against terrorism is essential for ASEAN, because:

a) It is difficult for ASEAN to coordinate and conduct a regional military operation.
b) Anti-terrorism is providing ASEAN new room to cooperate among its members and with external powers.
c) The Muslim issue is very sensitive politically in the region and in the individual countries.
d) The centralized economy of big cities in Southeast Asia is more vulnerable to terrorist attack. The region's economic readjustment also needs a stable regional environment.

However, there are still some obstacles for cooperation in anti-terrorism in Southeast Asia since it may:

a) Complicate individual countries' domestic political situation;
b) Create more religion-related political oppositions with the extensive Muslim population in the region;
c) Make regional consensus more difficult because there is no universally accepted definition and root causes for terrorism.

Thus the diversity of national strategic interests will give anti-terrorism different interpretations.

The success of ASEAN's multilateral approach needs a comprehensive multilateral mechanism to deal with the issues both at the regional and international level. Therefore, information sharing, clarity of perception and sincerity of intent, delinking Islam from terrorism, and a national consensus on terrorism are key to ASEAN's future anti-terrorism actions. All these show that anti-terrorism would be a long-term and tough work for ASEAN and its individual members.

Anti-Terrorism in Southeast Asia

Though ASEAN supported the United States' anti-terrorism efforts, it has some different thinking: 1) Joint cooperation of non-traditional security and economic and social development in the region is a better way to deal with terrorism than by military means only. 2) The multilateral efforts in anti-terrorism should also combine international, regional and local cooperation, and better understanding of the politics, cultures and social values. They can facilitate the efficiency of the anti-terrorism movement. Thus, norm-setting, common-grounds building, consensus-building, etc. are also very important and basic.

International Impact

After the Afghanistan War, U.S. President Bush declared that Southeast Asia is the "second battlefield" of the U.S.-led anti-terrorism war. Therefore, Southeast Asia has become one of the focal points of the United States' global anti-terrorism strategy.

When the United States signed the joint declaration on anti-terrorism with ASEAN, it was also trying to improve its relations with ASEAN members.

The United States sent over 600 members of its military force to the Philippines, resumed its military relationship with Indonesia, and strengthened its bilateral coordination and cooperation on anti-terrorism issues with Singapore, Malaysia, and Thailand. The United States has obvious strategic intentions in entering Southeast Asia. However, due to the complexity of the region and the alertness of most countries to U.S. domination, it is not as easy for the U.S. forces to enter the region as it was in the Cold War. The recent dispute among ASEAN members on the U.S. military presence in the Malacca Straits is reflective of the different regional security perceptions.

ASEAN also has cooperation with external powers. In addition to the joint declaration with the United States in August 2002, ASEAN signed a statement with China on cooperation in non-traditional security issues. Meanwhile, ASEAN strengthened the anti-terrorism coordination with the EU countries, and supported the role of UN. ASEAN also discussed certain issues in the ASEAN Regional Forum and the "Ten+3" framework in 2003.[6]

In fact, ASEAN does not believe that terrorism is the main threat to the ASEAN countries. ASEAN is facing three adjustments now: The first is economic, the second is social and political (leadership); and the third is the adjustment within ASEAN. Therefore, the strategic consideration of the ASEAN countries are as follows: Keeping the stability of the authority on the basis of domestic stability; pushing forward the reforms and transitions in the social and political fields on the basis of the well-being of the economy; accelerating the economic integration of ASEAN, and furthermore, conducting institutional adjustment within ASEAN.

Generally, the U.S.-led anti-terrorism war and its expansion of influence in Southeast Asia cannot change the basic international relationships in Southeast Asia. China and ASEAN share common interests in preventing the United States from carrying out its hegemonic strategy through its anti-terrorism campaign.

ASEAN-CHINA SECURITY RELATIONS

The relations between Southeast Asia and China have had a long history, which can be traced back to the second century B.C. Since the nineteenth century, Southeast Asia has had closer trade and business relations with China on account of growing immigrants to Southeast Asia from China. Meanwhile, Southeast Asia and China had both suffered under Western colonial invasions.

In recent years, the economic and political relations between the ASEAN countries and China have entered into a new period of comprehensive and friendly development with the international and regional changes. However, ASEAN-China relations had been tortuous since the establishment of

ASEAN for various reasons, such as ideological differences, historical issues and cultural diversity.

A) Development of ASEAN-China Relations

Confrontation (Establishment of ASEAN to the Mid-1970s)

When ASEAN was set up, ASEAN and China were suspicious of each other, and even treated each other as a threat because of issues with the local communist parties, ethnic Chinese, and some territorial disputes. So under the Cold War atmosphere, ASEAN and China began relations with distrust and confrontation. Though ASEAN tried to be independent politically, ASEAN, in fact, was close to the Western camp.

Reconciliation (The Middle to Late 1970s)

In the 1970s, the United States began reducing its military presence in Southeast Asia and improved its relations with China. Meanwhile, Sino-Vietnam relations deteriorated seriously. Therefore, ASEAN-China relations started to improve. Official relations between ASEAN countries and China began.

Cooperation (The Early 1980s to Early 1990s)

ASEAN and China began their strategic cooperation. China gave up its policy of "exporting revolution" and settled the relations between the Chinese Communist Party and local communist parties.[7] In addition, China adopted a policy of economic reform and opening up to the outside world since the end of the 1970s.

Partnership (After the Cold War)

ASEAN-China relations reached a high point in the early 1990s. After Indonesia restored diplomatic relations with China, Brunei and Singapore also established diplomatic relations with China in the early 1990s. All ASEAN countries (at that time) had diplomatic relations with China. China became a partner of ASEAN during the process involving the ASEAN framework.[8]

B) ASEAN's Strategic Importance to China's Security

The smooth progress of ASEAN-China relations is a result of the desire of both sides, as well as the demands of the international political and economic changes.

For China, ASEAN is closely intertwined with China's security.

As a neighbour to China, Southeast Asia is getting more important to China for the following reasons:

1) Closer economic integration, such as ASEAN+3 and ASEAN+1;
2) Most advanced Chinese economic cities, zones and areas are along the coast facing Southeast Asia;[9]
3) More than half of Chinese sea lanes for foreign trade are connected to the Southeast Asian region.[10]

China's process of joining the international community should be in line with its requirement of domestic modernization, so it should be a small step and would maintain the region's stability, as well as promote economic relations. ASEAN's success, both in its own integration and integration with the region, gives China cause to believe that opening up to the outside world is manageable and beneficial.

ASEAN's experience proved that a multilateral approach to international cooperation is the relevant way for China. After attending the PECC in 1986 and the ARF in 1994, China became more confident in not only joining the multilateral cooperation, but also initiated the cooperation.

Economically, with both sides expanding, economic cooperation is becoming necessary for ASEAN and China's economic development. Broad cooperation between ASEAN and China can make production and resource allocation more efficient, and the economies more competitive. The ongoing economic trend of globalization and regionalization is also an impetus. Take trade for example. In 1975, the bilateral trade was only US$523 million, it increased to US$2 billion in 1980, reached US$6 billion in 1990, and by 2000, was about US$40 billion.[11] In 2004, it reached the highest level, at around US$80 billion. China and ASEAN have agreed that the bilateral trade will be over US$100 billion by the year 2005.

Since the ASEAN and China bilateral economic relations have become more important for both sides, a mechanism for cooperation became necessary. In 2002, "Ten+1" promoted cooperation to a concrete level.

C) Problems

"China Threat"

With the traditional geopolitical influences, ASEAN is still afraid that the process and result of Chinese modernization may be a threat to ASEAN in the form of the economy, politics and military.

Territorial Disputes

Some ASEAN members have territorial disputes with China over the Nansha Islands (Spratly Islands). Since the disputed islands and sea areas are rich in resources and important for international sea routes, the sovereignty disputes became complicated. China has suggested that issues over the disputed island be resolved according to the international law and the sea law of the United Nations. Before that, the concerned countries should "shelf the disputes" and "jointly develop" the islands. Though China had an informal dialogue with ASEAN on the dispute and signed a political declaration of the "Code of Conduct", the Nansha Islands issue is very sensitive and even within ASEAN, it is still a problem.

Economic Barriers

They are mainly in the following areas:

1) Compared with the economic growth of both sides, the bilateral trade has developed slowly;
2) The exporting structure of goods are similar, that is, mostly in resource-intensive or labour-intensive products;
3) Trade markets are also similar, namely the developed countries;
4) Both sides compete for foreign investment from the international capital market.

Generally speaking, ASEAN agrees to leave room for China's development in the region since China may provide opportunities for ASEAN's economies. China is also crucial to balance the United States and Japan, and to compete with the Western countries on the ARF process, human rights, democracy, the APEC agenda, regional integration, etc.

CHINA'S REGIONAL SECURITY PERCEPTION

In the post-Cold War period, the international environment has changed greatly: a multipolar system has been taking shape while the bipolar system has vanished. Isolation and confrontation have given way to economic globalization and deepening interdependence among states.

The various kinds of contradictions and differences, which remain in international relations, have changed in nature and their manifestations. There has also been a change in the ways of handling them. The possibility of a large-scale war arising from the intensification of such contradictions and differences and the possibility of their getting out of control is decreasing. Thus security through cooperation has been widely accepted.

China's security interests may be divided into three levels: 1) The core national interests, including: Domestic stability, unity and security; territorial integrity; social prosperity *via* continuous economic reform; regional peace and stability.[12] 2) The global interests, which are quite limited. 3) Security relations with neighbours. As China defines itself as a regional power, so China's security interests are more focused on the neighbouring area, in particular Southeast Asia. Peace and stability are fundamental and the starting point since they can provide a favourable environment for China's modernization. Furthermore, China believe that security interests have become so diverse that security is transnational with bordering nations. Therefore, "China seeks to build up 'partnerships' with as many neighbours as possible", and "aims at the creation of a vast buffer-zone around the nation (China)".[13] In addition, China realizes that Asia is a region with the most concentration of power, and as a power in this region, the most important regional security strategy is to maintain at least a workable relationship with all the major powers in the region (the United States, Russia, Japan, India) so that it will never become isolated in the circle of great powers again.[14] It is crucial for China to keep the relations among the big powers stable and in balance.

China's regional interests therefore represent much of its global perception and also contain its core national interests.

CONCLUSION

Since the 1990s, the security situation in Southeast Asian has been gradually becoming more stable. In the future, this stability will hopefully be maintained, although there are still some problems. The evaluation is based on the following favourable factors:

a) With the changing situation in Southeast Asia and the world, the traditional causes of regional conflicts have become out of date, such as, ideological confrontation, the possibility of regional expansionism, and serious territorial disputes.

b) Enlargement of ASEAN has offered an institutional guarantee for the peace and stability of Southeast Asia although as a mechanism, ASEAN is still weak in its coordination.

c) Southeast Asia's stability is in line with all related big powers' interests.

In the meantime, the following negative elements are still worthy of attention:

a) Economic instability mainly caused by both instability of the developed economies and ASEAN's economic readjustment.

b) Challenges for the ASEAN key members from political and social changes.
c) Some existing disputes with profound historic and political backgrounds.
d) Threat of terrorism.

Therefore, regional peace, stability and development in Southeast Asia may be brought about if some practical measures are taken as follows:

a) Stabilize the regional economy, in particular, the financial system through individual countries' readjustment of their economy and through regional cooperation, such as "Ten+3" and "Ten+1".
b) Have joint efforts to deal with terrorism and to strengthen the regional non-traditional cooperation.
c) Develop a larger regional concept with ASEAN as a driving force economically, politically and in security.

NOTES

1. There were some forms of regional cooperation among the Philippines, Malaysia and Thailand in 1961 and among the Philippines, Malaysia and Indonesia in 1963. But they were all disbanded mainly because of their domestic differences.
2. The contradictions between China and the former Soviet Union came to the surface publicly in the early 1960s; in 1967, the United Kingdom decided to withdraw half its military forces in Singapore and Malaysia in four years, and would totally withdraw by 1975; the United States put forward the "Nixon Doctrine" to reduce its forces in Asia at the end of the 1960s; the Soviet Union stepped up its expansion in Asia through the "Asian Collective Security System".
3. *Political and Security Cooperation*, <http://www.aseansec.org>.
4. Six ASEAN old members realized AFTA in 2003, while four new members will have an extra three to six years to join in.
5. It was "Nine+3" at that time. Cambodia was not an ASEAN member until 1999.
6. The mid-term convention of ASEAN Regional Forum was held in May 2003. Anti-terrorism issues were discussed. The meeting of the ASEAN+3 ministers responsible for transnational crimes was held in October 2003.
7. Zhao Chen, *ASEAN — Establishing and Developing the Relations with Main Powers [Dongnanya Guojia Lianmeng-Chengli Fazhan tong Daguo de Guanxi]* (China Goods and Materials Press, 1993), p. 235.
8. The Chinese foreign minister was invited to attend the ASEAN Annual Foreign Ministerial Meeting in July 1991; China became a formal "dialogue partner" of ASEAN in July 1996; China set up "facing the twenty-first century, mutual trusted partnership relations" with ASEAN at the end of 1997.
    In addition, China joined the "Nine+3" summit meeting and began "Nine+1" dialogue with ASEAN in 1997. The financial and foreign ministers' meeting dealt with the concrete forms of cooperation.

China participated in the Asia-Pacific regional security cooperation. China supported ASEAN in establishing the ASEAN Regional Forum (ARF) in 1994 and became a member when it was set up. Together with other member nations, China is pushing the ARF forward from the "confidence-building measures" phase to the "preventive diplomacy" phase. Meanwhile, China is also a member of the Council for Security Cooperation in the Asia-Pacific (CSCAP).

9. The GDP of the coastal areas was over 50 per cent of China's total GDP in the early 1990s.

10. Chen Fengjun, *Analysis of Current Asia-Pacific Politics and Economy* (Beijing: University Press, 1999), p. 106.

11. *International Trade* 2 (2001): 62.

12. "Chi Haotian's Speech at University of National Defense, U.S." *People's Daily*, 12 December 1996. "Qian Qichen's Speech on the First Meeting of ARF", *People's Daily* (Overseas edition), 26 July 1994.

13. Robert A. Scalapino, *The People's Republic of China at Fifty*, <http://www.taiwansecurity.org>.

14. Shiping Tang and Zhang Yunling, *China's Regional Strategy: An Interpretation*, CRSS working paper 2004 no. 1.

14

China-ASEAN Maritime Security Cooperation Situation and Proposals

Wang Zhongchun and Li Yaqiang

INTRODUCTION

Security cooperation means that two or more international actors, driven by mutually beneficial interests, take common actions to deal with the national security or regional security affairs in a coordinated way in order to achieve the anticipated goals of their respective national security.

China and ASEAN member countries are important neighbours and strategic partners linked by the South China Sea and the Straits of Malacca to its west. Therefore, this region is of great geostrategic significance to the world. At the same time, China and ASEAN countries are faced with a number of common challenges in their maritime security.

At present, almost all the countries in the region hope to strengthen co-operation in Asia-Pacific affairs, advocate building trust through dialogue, solve differences through consultation and seek security through cooperation.

However, it should be pointed out that regional security cooperation between China and ASEAN falls far behind the regional economic cooperation and development, and does not meet the needs of the developing regional security situation. In fact, China and ASEAN not only need the security cooperation, but have a great deal of common and complementary interests. Therefore, the maritime security cooperation between China and ASEAN has great strategic significance.

The aim of this chapter is to analyse the situation of the China-ASEAN maritime security cooperation with a view to proposing steps to strengthen such cooperation. The following aspects are covered: (a) Geostrategic situation (b) Common challenges in China-ASEAN maritime security (c) A good beginning to the China-ASEAN maritime security cooperation (d) The basic foundation for the China-ASEAN maritime security cooperation (e) Principles of China-ASEAN maritime security cooperation (f) Flexible and diversified forms of ASEAN-China maritime security cooperation.

GEOSTRATEGIC SITUATION

The sea area around China and ASEAN states is at the crossroad linking the Indian and Pacific oceans as well as the Asian and Oceania continents. Since ancient times, this area has been the strategic sea lane of communication (SLOC) between the countries in the East, famously known as the "Silk Road at Sea". With the continued development of economic globalization, this sea area is increasingly important to the global economic and military affairs.

First, these waters house many straits and channels of strategic or sea traffic significance. For example, the Straits of Malacca is the strategic lane of communication linking the Pacific and Indian oceans. It is the communication hub at sea between the Asian, African and European continents and one of the busiest sea routes in the world with 30 per cent of the total world trade and almost 80,000 commercial ships each year running through it.[1] Eighty per cent of China's crude oil imports from the Middle East and Africa passes through the SLOC.[2] Meanwhile, the Taiwan Straits and the Bashi Channel are the major lanes to approach the deep ocean from the littoral seas.

Second, this sea area is rich in marine resources. It is one of the most affluent waters of the world in sea fishery, petroleum, natural gas and other marine mineral resources. It has a huge reserve of petroleum and natural gas and abundant sea resources. There is no doubt that the peaceful utilization of marine resources will play an active role in promoting the region's economic development.

COMMON CHALLENGES IN CHINA-ASEAN MARITIME SECURITY

Differences left over from history still exist. After entering the 1990s, the region has witnessed sustained rapid economic development and tremendous expansion of foreign trade and investment. Against this backdrop, the demands for resources and the security of sea lanes are increasing, the strategic status of the seas is becoming more important. However, there remain some differences among countries in the region on such issues as claim of sovereignty over certain islands in the South China Sea, division of continental shelf, demarcation of exclusive economic zones (EEZs), etc. In the vicinity of the Spratly Islands there have been incidents such as the confrontation of military aircrafts and shooting by troops in outposts towards military aircrafts of other countries. Occasionally there have been intense contradictions on the exploration of fisheries and mineral resources. This area has witnessed occasional occurrences of incidents such as the detaining and hurting of fishermen, interdiction of the rightful survey and exploration of ships, and activities endangering safety of navigation.

Non-traditional security threats have become more outstanding. With the end of the Cold War, global threats have been reduced notably, with a declining possibility of any outbreak of major wars between states. However, non-traditional threats such as terrorism, separatism, extremism, piracy, transnational crimes and arms proliferation are growing rampantly. What makes matters worse is that international terrorism, extremist forces and pirates collude with and exploit one another. Such a merging trend is particularly prominent in the Asia-Pacific region. In the Philippines, activities of the "Abu Sayyaf Group" are frequent; in Indonesia, the Yaqi area has been torn by conflicts for many years; in southern Thailand, bombings happen occasionally. In June 2000, the "Abu Sayyaf Group" kidnapped many foreigners in Malaysia and this incident could not be settled properly over several months. In October 2002, the explosion in Bali shocked the whole world. On 20 March 2003, the Chinese fishing ship "Fuyuanyu 225" was sunk after being attacked by terrorists in the waters close to Sri Lanka and fifteen crew members on board were killed. In February 2004, the explosion and fire of the "Super Ferry 14" berthing at the mouth of the Manila Bay cast a dark shadow on regional security.

Piracy has become increasingly rampant with each passing day. According to the International Maritime Bureau (IMB) statistics, altogether 445 attacks on commercial ships occurred throughout the world in 2003, increasing by 20 per cent over the year 2002. As a result of the pirate attacks, 21 crew members died, 71 were missing, at least 88 were wounded, and 359 crew and passengers were held as hostages. These figures have doubled those of 2002 (10 dead, 38 wounded, 191 hijacked as hostages).[3] Data show that in the above-mentioned maritime attacks on commercial ships, about one third happened in the waters of the Straits of Malacca and the Indonesian archipelagoes, and the sea pirates conducting the attacks were equipped with rifles and semi-automatic weapons.[4]

It is worth noting that in spite of frequent incidents of staggering maritime attacks on commercial ships, the arrest and trial of attackers seem to be rare. If we cannot effectively contain and deter this sort of maritime attacks from taking place today, we have to pay a heavier price of more lives and economic losses tomorrow.

A GOOD BEGINNING TO THE CHINA-ASEAN MARITIME SECURITY COOPERATION

In spite of the late start in security cooperation in this region as compared to other regions in the world, the process has proven to be quite successful in the beginning. At present, almost all the countries in the region hope to strengthen cooperation in the Asia-Pacific affairs, advocate building trust through dialogue, solve differences through consultation and seek security through cooperation. Accordingly, great progress has been made in both the multilateral forum concerning maritime military security cooperation and the bilateral maritime security dialogue and cooperation.

The ASEAN Regional Forum (ARF) with twenty-two member states is the most influential official security forum in the Asia-Pacific. In 2001, the ARF was formally brought into the stage of preventive diplomacy and cooperation was proposed in the non-traditional security areas. Though not a special maritime security forum, the ARF, from its very beginning, has been paying very much attention to maritime security cooperation issues in light of the shared security concerns, for most of the forum members are the countries bordering on the sea. Besides, some special meetings of assisting working groups in between the summits are involved in the issue of the maritime military security cooperation. As early as 1994, the Chinese military participated in the forum activities. In 1996–98, the Chinese Navy also officially participated in two special meetings on the sea search and rescue and confidence-building measures (CBM) held by the assisting working groups in between the summits.

In recent years, China and ASEAN have enjoyed a good momentum in the development of the maritime cooperation in the non-traditional security field:

a) In December 2000, China and Vietnam officially signed the Delimitation of the Territorial Sea, Exclusive Economic Zone and Continental Shelf in Beibu Bay and the Agreement on Fishery Cooperation in Beibu Bay. In October 2003, the two countries decided to conduct joint patrol in Beibu Bay, working together to maintain the order and stability in the stretches of the Beibu Bay. The Beibu Bay Fishery Agreement to reduce maritime and territorial disputes was signed on 29 April 2004.
b) In April 2000 and March 2001, the International Maritime Organization (IMO) held conferences in Tokyo and Singapore respectively on combating sea piracy in the Asia-Pacific.
c) In November 2002, China and ASEAN signed the Joint Declaration on Cooperation in the Field of Non-Traditional Security Issues and the Declaration on the Conducts of the Parties in the South China Sea.
d) In October 2003, China officially joined the Treaty of Amity and Cooperation in Southeast Asia (TAC) and made a joint declaration with ASEAN to establish the strategic partnership for peace and prosperity.
e) As early as 1996, Thailand and Vietnam reached an agreement to conduct joint maritime patrol in the Gulf of Thailand, which has effectively prevented fishery disputes. Both parties agreed, on a joint effort, to combat transnational piracy, drug trafficking and arms smuggling.
f) Singapore, Malaysia, and Indonesia have already established a joint maritime patrol force to safeguard the shipping security of the key sea routes, like the Straits of Malacca.

SOUND AND COMPREHENSIVE FOUNDATION FOR THE CHINA-ASEAN MARITIME SECURITY COOPERATION

Although China and ASEAN have witnessed a good beginning in maritime security cooperation, it is quite necessary to point out that this sort of regional security cooperation falls far behind the regional economic cooperation and development, and cannot meet the needs of the developing regional security situation. In fact, China and ASEAN have not only the need for security cooperation, but have a lot of common and complementary interests, which serve as the foundation for further security cooperation of the two sides.

Politically, China and ASEAN member states are all developing countries. Hence accelerating economic development and promoting social progress are the common desire and the greatest strategic interests for them. In addition, China and ASEAN countries have a long history of friendship. They are similar in values, strategic interests, and share the experience of being invaded and colonized. Although countries in the region vary from one another in terms of size, social system, religious belief and ideology, they all pursue the principles of mutual respect, and non-interference in other countries' internal affairs in their respective foreign policies, and non-military aggression especially for the objective of regime change of other countries. These are not only the prerequisites of guaranteeing regional peace and prosperity, but the political will for security cooperation between China and ASEAN.

Economically, China and ASEAN countries are the world's fastest growing economies since they are located in a region dynamically generating the greatest economic vitality and development potentialities. China and ASEAN complement each other with respective advantages on a wide range of economic issues, along with reasonable competition in between. In recent years, countries in the region have maintained friendly relations of mutual benefit and promotion, with economic and trade exchanges increasing continuously. China and ASEAN witnessed the continued robust growth of bilateral trade in 2002. The total import and export volume reached US$54.767 billion, up by 37.2 per cent over the last year and also ten points higher than the annual average growth rate of the Chinese foreign trade. ASEAN, as a whole, is still the fifth largest trade partner of China. On 4 November 2001, China and the ASEAN countries jointly signed the Framework Agreement on Comprehensive Economic Cooperation between China and ASEAN, which provides the juristic groundwork for the eventual establishment of the "Ten+1" free trade area. When the China-ASEAN Free Trade Area (CAFTA) is established by 2010, it will definitely bring about fundamental influence on the East Asia and world economy at large.

In the security area, there is no essential conflict of national security interests between China and ASEAN. Rather, they are faced with common challenges from the field of non-traditional security issues. Both China and ASEAN countries are opposed to the use of force in settling international disputes, and the seeking of hegemony by any country in dealing with international and regional affairs. They do not advocate the building of political-military alliances directed against any third party, or allow foreign countries to station troops in their territories. Except for the participation in the UN peace-keeping operations (PKO), neither China nor ASEAN countries station troops or establish military bases abroad. As the sole nuclear state in the surrounding area of the South China Sea, China is the only nuclear power which declared to recognize and respect Southeast Asia as a nuclear weapons-free zone. Faced with the complex and profound changes in the international situation in the twenty-first century, the Chinese Government has clearly proposed an eight-Chinese-character principle of "befriending and partnering with our neighbours", and further put forward two key points in pushing forward China's policies towards the surrounding countries, namely, enhancing good-neighbourly relations and strengthening regional cooperation.

PRINCIPLES OF CHINA-ASEAN MARITIME SECURITY COOPERATION

Both ASEAN and China advocate that relations between countries should be established on the basis of the Five Principles of Peaceful Co-Existence, namely, mutual respect for sovereignty and territorial integrity, mutual non-aggression, non-interference in each other's internal affairs, equality and mutual benefit and peaceful co-existence. Faced with the trend of world multipolarity and economic globalization, both ASEAN and China agree that, no country can safeguard its national security and economic development only through military means; national security is a relative and interdependent concept, security of any country should not be built on the insecurity of others; every country should enhance mutual trust through dialogue, and promote common security and development through cooperation. Although ASEAN and China have different opinions on some issues, they share the view on the new security concept of "mutual trust, mutual benefit, equality and coordination", which can serve as a principle for guiding their security cooperation.

a) Mutual Respect

The state is the primary player in the international community. Respect for national sovereignty is the most important principle in security cooperation. Every party in the security cooperation should take into full account the other's fundamental strategic interests, values and nature of society. In security cooperation, all parties should take into full consideration others' presence, interests and requirements on the basis of mutual respect.

b) Mutual Recognition of Interests

In international affairs, common interests are the basis of cooperation. Common interests include identical interests and complementary interests.

However, common interests alone do not necessarily result in united cooperation. Only after all the concerned parties recognize and accept the common requirements of interests, and realize that cooperation is reciprocal, is it possible to carry out security cooperation.

c) Mutual Trust and Mutual Benefit

Seeking maximum national interests is a universal principle of international activities. It is common that every party in cooperation expects to maximize its national interests, but at the same time, we should understand that mutual trust is the basis of cooperation, and mutual benefit the objective of cooperation. Security cooperation can only materialize after mutual trust is built up among all the parties of cooperation. And only when all the parties of the cooperation can obtain their necessary interests, can security cooperation be sustained and carried on effectively.

d) Equal Negotiation and Coordination

Effective security cooperation must be based on equality and consensus, and should be realized through negotiation and coordination. In dealing with differences between states, we should "seek common ground while reserving differences" and object to making present problems more complicated. At least, we should make sure that present differences will not have any negative influence on regular cooperation. Regarding such sensitive issues as the ownership of an island, delimitation of the exclusive economic zone, and protection and exploitation of natural resources, we should put aside disputes and explore the road of joint exploitation.

e) Effectiveness

As we all know, the ASEAN region and China are an area with diversified conditions. There are some differences between the security interests and strategic requirements of different countries. So security cooperation should start from reality and focus on effectiveness. On the basis of consensus, we may carry out flexible security cooperation of various forms in different fields and levels in light of the security requirements and different conditions.

f) Steady Advancement

In security cooperation, it is inevitable that countries have to bear certain responsibilities and duties, and make some compromises and concessions. But every country has to make sure that benefits obtained in the cooperation will be more than what it has paid. It is necessary to point out that although many common interests are shared by all the parties in cooperation, some contradictions of interests and differences exist. So we should not only actively advocate security cooperation, but also push it steadily forward.

FLEXIBLE AND DIVERSIFIED FORMS OF CHINA-ASEAN MARITIME SECURITY COOPERATION

In the field of non-traditional security, ASEAN and China can carry out various forms of maritime security cooperation. They may be as follows:

a) Maritime Security Dialogue

China is an active participant of regional maritime security dialogue. In 1994, representatives of Chinese Navy attended the International Conferences on Maritime Search and Rescue and Confidence-Building Measures (CBM) of the ASEAN Regional Forum (ARF). The Chinese Navy sent delegates to attend the Western Pacific Naval Symposium. These dialogues have been conducive to promoting confidence and reducing misunderstanding. It is the basis of strengthening security cooperation. In the absence of a regular formal mechanism of security dialogue and consultation, it may be possible to advocate developing dialogue and discussion between governments on such issues as shipping security, anti-terrorism and piracy, protection of maritime environment, maritime search and rescue, and humanitarian assistance through the second orbit of unofficial forum.

b) Consultation on Shipping Security

As we are aware, the Asia-Pacific international shipping lines are dense and dangerous, the regional situation is comparatively complicated, and consequently, prone to accidents. Shipping safety has become a common concern to all countries. The United States and Chinese navies have started to consult on the safety of navigation. So, it is necessary for ASEAN and China to consult on how to safeguard the safety of navigation, hold multilateral special symposiums, and actively create favourable conditions for the exchange of information and technical training of personnel and selective exchange of intelligence.

c) Maritime Anti-Terrorism Operation

The day after the "9/11" incident, the Fifty-sixth UN General Assembly passed a resolution, appealing to every country to cooperate and fight against international terrorism. The Chinese Government has objected to any form of terrorism all along, and is making its contributions to international cooperation against terrorism. China has already formulated a policy of anti-terrorism, which is "being based on prevention, taking the initiative to launch an attack, coping with terrorism efficiently, and strengthening international cooperation". Personally, I am optimistic that maritime anti-terrorism cooperation will become a major field of maritime security cooperation between China and ASEAN. China and ASEAN can first carry out substantive cooperation in such areas as anti-terrorism intelligence exchange, cooperation and coordination in handling legal cases, and deportation of suspects, followed by further cooperation such as in scenario and real exercises. However, we should be cautious when conducting anti-terrorism operations with armed forces, and should always obtain the consent of the country concerned.

d) Maritime Search and Rescue

Maritime search and rescue is one of the common interests of the peripheral states of South China Sea. According to the Chinese maritime search and rescue system, the Chinese Navy carries out search and rescue work under the coordination of the National Centre of Search and Rescue, so in international cooperation in maritime search and rescue, the PLA Navy can evade the sensitive problem of command. The International Maritime Organization stipulates that the area in the north of 10° north latitude (shared by China and Singapore) and west of 116° east longitude in South China Sea is China's area of responsibility for search and rescue operations. From 1998, the PLA Hong Kong Garrison has attended many multilateral maritime search and rescue exercises organized by the Government of Hong Kong Special Administrative Region. On 26 September 2001, the Chinese Ministry of Communications and PLA Navy organized the first large-scale joint exercise of maritime search and rescue since the founding of the PRC, which not only displayed Chinese military and civilian capability in maritime search and rescue, but also explored new mechanisms and methods of conducting military and civilian joint search and rescue. All these have laid a fairly sound foundation for China to organize joint search and rescue activities with its neighbouring states.

e) Building up Maritime Military Communication Channels

In the past several years, Asia-Pacific states have witnessed ever increasing exchanges of visits of naval fleets. In 2001, Chinese naval fleets paid their first visit to Vietnam, India, UK, France, Germany, and Italy. At the same time, China received frequent visits of naval fleets of other countries. On the one hand, these exchange visits have deepened the understanding and friendship between the navies of these countries, but on the other hand, they have put the issue of building up maritime military communication channels between different countries on China's agenda. At present, the Western Pacific Naval Forum is active in materializing regional maritime joint military operations and the establishment of communication channels. In order to lay the technological foundation for material maritime security cooperation in this region, ASEAN and China should also discuss the methods of communication in maritime security cooperation.

f) Marine Environment Protection

Protection of the marine environment is a common concern and interest of every country. Because of the special legal status of naval vessels and the specific characteristics of maritime military activities, almost all of the current international conventions on protecting the maritime environment stipulate that "the provisions … regarding the protection and preservation of the marine environment do not apply to any warship, naval auxiliary, other vessels or aircraft owned or operated by a state and used, for the time being only on government non-commercial service". As a result of this, we can find few laws, regulations and principles regarding prevention of maritime pollution which are applicable to naval vessels. In fact, just like all the civilian vessels, naval vessels and their activities will also pollute the marine environment. Pollution caused by naval vessels is caused by oil spills and consumer waste, maritime accident, maritime military activities such as the testing, and use of weapons, etc. So cooperation in protecting the marine environment by the navies of all countries will be conducive not only to the sustainable development of every country, but can also reduce related disputes through confidence-building measures (CBM).

g) Joint Law Enforcement against Transnational Crimes

International maritime criminal activities are rampant in the sea area and sea lanes of communication (SLOC) near China and ASEAN. This area has witnessed frequent occurrences of criminal activities such as piracy, smuggling, drug-trafficking, illegal immigrants, etc., which has posed a real threat to every country's shipping and economic security. In handling these common challenges of non-traditional security, we should discuss and explore methods and ways of law enforcement. Maritime joint law enforcement should be conducted by the national maritime law enforcement agencies in the designated sea area on the basis of consensus of respective countries. Joint law enforcement can not only contain and fight against transnational crimes, but also maintain the orderly exploitation of fisheries and oil and gas, and ensure the safety of maritime navigation.

h) Joint Military Exercises

Military exercise in the form of military training at the highest level. The basic objective of military exercises is to train troops, improve operational theories, and test the combat effectiveness of troops. However the major function of maritime joint military exercises is to strengthen international military exchanges, deter hostile forces, stabilize the region, and promote the establishment of a favourable international order. Maritime joint military exercises may first take search and rescue operations, humanitarian assistance, mine sweeping, and cracking down on drug trafficking as their main forms. Subsequently, we can include counter terrorism, piracy, and fighting other maritime criminal activities.

i) Regional Peace-Keeping Operations and Humanitarian Assistance

China is an active participant of the UN peace-keeping operations. It has assigned many peace-keeping troops and military observers to many countries. In 1996, a PLA engineering team was assigned to Cambodia and transported by the PLA Navy, which was the first participation of China's troops in UN peace-keeping operations. China also sent civilian police to East Timor in 2000. With the development of the regional situation and rise in security issues in the Asia-Pacific region, it is possible that under the request of the UN, the Chinese Navy will attend necessary regional peace-keeping operations, especially some operations of humanitarian assistance.

NOTES

The views expressed in this chapter are entirely that of the authors: Sr Colonel Wang Zhong and Navy Captain Li Yaqiang, and do not necessarily reflect the views of the PLA, China.

1. "The Straits of Malacca: A Strategic Keypoint", *Reference News*, 8 April 2004, pp. 12–13.
2. "China Needs New Thinking in Breaking the Dilemma of the Straits", *Reference News*, 8 April 2004, p. 12.
3. CNN News, "Sea Piracy Hits Record", 28 April 2004, p. 2. <http://www.cnn.com>.
4. "U.S. Attempts to Send Troops to Malacca Straits on the Excuse of Anti-Terrorism", *Reference News*, 8 April 2004, pp. 12–13.

15
ASEAN-China Maritime Security Cooperation

Michael Richardson

How will maritime security cooperation between ASEAN states and China evolve? Clearly, such collaboration is in its infancy when compared to the long-standing and quite well developed naval joint training exercises between some ASEAN countries, and between them and the United States, Australia, New Zealand, Britain and India, or between some ASEAN countries and the Japan Coast Guard. These exercises take place under structured frameworks and formal agreements negotiated by the parties involved. Many of them are also being adapted to include unconventional threats against shipping and sealanes, including pirate and terrorist attacks.[1]

Chinese naval vessels have called at Singapore and the ports of some other regional nations. But that is about the extent so far of maritime security cooperation between China and ASEAN members.

What are the realities of power politics versus the prospects for cooperative security between ASEAN and China? The latter could be based on a common need to protect vital sea lanes and straits used for international shipping from attacks by pirates, terrorists and other potential sources of supply disruption. Whether forms of cooperative security evolve between China and Southeast Asian states will depend to a large degree on the future scale of China's seaborne energy imports; from where Bejing gets them; and, most important of all, how China seeks to secure these vital supplies.

One thing is clear: if China continues to grow at anything like the rate of recent years, it will become increasingly dependent on imports of oil and gas, including liquified natural gas, or LNG, carried over long distances by sea from exporting countries to China's industrial and urban east coast heartland. In 1993, China ceased to be a net exporter of oil and became a net importer. Today, it is the fastest growing user of oil in the world, ahead of energy-efficient Japan and second only to the United States in terms of total consumption and imports.[2]

China's demand for transport fuel is projected to grow sharply while production from its onshore oil fields continue to stagnate or decline. As a result, Chinese oil consumption is expected to rise by almost a third to 300 million metric tons by 2010. But then, imports will amount to 50 per cent of China's total oil supply, up from around one third now. The U.S. Energy Information Administration expects China's net imports of oil to rise to around two thirds of consumption by 2025.[3]

China will not only become more dependent on imported oil and gas for its future economic growth, modernization and prosperity; its reliance on supplies from the volatile Persian Gulf and the wider Middle East region, and from politically unstable North and West Africa, also seem set to increase. Around 50 per cent of Chinese oil imports are currently shipped from the Middle East while nearly 25 per cent come from Africa, which is seen not just by the United States but by China, India and Japan as a major source of oil for the future.[4]

Of course, Japan and South Korea — both almost entirely dependent on imported energy for their current and future growth — are far more reliant on overseas sources of oil and gas than China. Japan draws around 85 per cent of its oil from the Middle East and South Korea nearly 80 per cent. Northeast Asia's future LNG demand will rely on major Middle East exporters as well as Western Pacific producers including Australia, Indonesia and Russia.[5]

This pattern of dependence has many implications. But the most important for China and Southeast Asia is that all the oil from the Middle East and Africa, and the LNG from the Persian Gulf and Oman, will be brought in tankers to Northeast Asia *via* three relatively narrow Southeast Asian maritime arteries, chiefly the Straits of Malacca and Singapore. Flanked by Indonesia on one side and Malaysia and Singapore on the other, the Straits of Malacca and Singapore are congested and shallow in many places.

An average of 140 seagoing ships pass every day through these straits between the Pacific and Indian oceans via the South China Sea and the Andaman Sea. And the waterway is getting busier, largely because of China's supercharged growth and its demand for energy and other raw materials. The two-way shipping channels of the straits is only 800 metres wide at two points south of Singapore. As a result, the channels could be closed to shipping, at least temporarily, by an accident or terrorist attack in which a large vessel containing inflammable, explosive, toxic or polluting cargo was sunk or set ablaze in one of the narrow chokepoints. Ships could be diverted through the Sunda Straits or the Lombok and Makassar Straits in Indonesia. But this would add as much as 1,600 kilometres, or several days steaming and considerable cost, to their voyage.[6]

Japan has long been acutely aware of the strategic importance of the Southeast Asian straits used by international shipping, both commercial and naval. As a leading user, it has largely funded the navigational aids that have improved maritime safety in the Malacca and Singapore straits.

More recently, China, too, has realized that its economic future is closely tied to maintaining freedom of navigation on the high seas and in straits used for international shipping. In a significant move, Beijing ratified the United Nations Convention on the Law of the Sea in 1996. China's decision to do so was a sign of two potentially contradictory impulses: its sense of vulnerability and its interest in safeguarding international norms on freedom of passage. This tension is evident in the way China is handling its territorial and maritime boundary claims in both the South China Sea and the East China Sea.[7]

Early in 2004, offers of bird-watching, holiday cruises and flying tours rekindled tensions over disputed atolls and reefs in the South China Sea. In March, Taiwan built a bird-watching hide on one of the specks of territory it claims in the Spratly Islands. In April, Vietnam launched what it said was the first of a series holiday cruises to cays it occupies in the Spratly chain, which it calls the Truong Sa. Vietnam also began work to bring a disused airstrip on one of the cays back into working order.

Vietnam protested at Taiwan's activity while China protested at Vietnam's moves, taking the opportunity to reiterate its assertion of "indisputable" sovereignty over the Spratlys, which Beijing calls the Nansha Islands. China is rapidly expanding its navy and building a new base for warships on Hainan Island. It held military exercises in the South China Sea in April, sending a signal to rivals to back off. In July, China gave its top oil producer, PetroChina, the right to start oil and gas exploration and production activities in the southern part of the South China Sea near the disputed Spratly Islands. In response, the Philippines called on Beijing to desist from "acts that would go against the grain of peaceful diplomatic solutions to any disputes".[8]

China, Taiwan and Vietnam claim the whole of the widely scattered Spratly archipelago which includes at least 200 small islands, rocks and reefs. Many are partially submerged and unsuitable for habitation. The total land area of the Spratly Islands has been calculated at less than 7.8 square kilometres. But its specks of territory are important because sovereignty claims to them can be used to bolster claims to ownership over huge swathes of the seabed and continental shelf that surrounds them. So whoever is in undisputed or effective control of the seemingly insignificant specks of land may be able to exploit any oil and gas there.

Malaysia, the Philippines and Brunei — the other claimants to parts of the widely scattered Spratlys — were alarmed at the flurry of assertiveness by Taiwan, Vietnam and China, not least because it was in blatant defiance of the spirit of a non-binding joint declaration signed in November 2002 by China and the ten members of ASEAN.

The declaration on conduct of the parties said that disputes should be resolved peacefully and called on claimants to avoid actions that might cause tension. Some ASEAN members hoped that the declaration would prevent any further occupation of atolls and reefs in the Spratlys or new construction on inhabited parts. All the claimants, except Brunei, have military garrisons in the areas of the Spratlys they occupy.

Military clashes and skirmishes in the South China Sea have occured numerous times over the past few decades. The most serious were in 1974, when Chinese forces took the Paracel Islands (north of the Spratlys) from Vietnam, and in 1988, when the Chinese and Vietnamese navies clashed near a reef in the Spratlys. Several Vietnamese vessels were sunk and over seventy Vietnamese sailors killed. China calls the Paracels the Xisha. To Vietnam, they are known as the Hoang Sa.[9]

Why is there a resurgence of tension now, after all the diplomatic effort to damp it down? It can hardly be about ornithology and tourism. A significant part of the answer is the increasing imperative of major East Asian economies, led by China and Japan, to secure disputed maritime frontiers and gain control over natural resources, especially offshore oil and gas, that are seen as vital for future growth.[10]

That is why China and Japan are racing to secure other sources of supply much closer to home, including Central Asia, Siberia and the East China Sea. In the latter, they have failed to agree where the sea border marking their respective exclusive economic zones, or EEZs, should be. Tokyo is contesting Beijing's right to develop the big Chunxiao gas field some four kilometres from the EEZ border claimed by Japan, saying that parts of the gas field beneath the seabed might fall within Japan's zone. China has offered joint development of petroleum resources in the area, as it has in the South China Sea. But how this would work in practice is not clear.[11]

In July 2004, the Japanese Government launched its own seismic survey in its claimed EEZ in the East China Sea, despite a stern warning from China not to risk any action that could upset bilateral relations and regional stability. The Chunxiao field is estimated to contain up to 5.6 billion cubic metres of gas reserves. Japanese officials have indicated the area may also yield sizeable oil reserves. China National Offshore Oil Corp (CNOOC), is jointly developing the Chunxiao field with Sinopec. The offshore field is about 350 km east of Ningbo in China's Zhejiang province. When construction is completed in mid-2005, the gas will be delivered to Shanghai and Zhejiang *via* an undersea pipeline.[12]

A long-standing dispute between China and Japan over ownership of the Senkaku Islands, south of Chunxiao in the East China Sea, also flared again in 2004. The islands are uninhabited but under Japanese control. They are constantly patrolled by Japan Coast Guard vessels. Geological and seismic surveys around the Senkakus have indicated that the continential shelf contains sizeable oil and natural gas reserves.[13]

In March, seven Chinese activists sailed from China and landed on the Senkaku Islands in the East China Sea between southern Japan and Taiwan. The cluster of rocky outcrops, which the Chinese call the Diaoyu Islands, are claimed by Japan, China and Taiwan. Although uninhabited, they are constantly patrolled by Japan Coast Guard vessels. The activists were quickly rounded up and deported to China, amid protests from Beijing which said the islands were Chinese territory.[14]

Lying to the south of the East China Sea and forming the maritime heart of Southeast Asia, the South China Sea has proven oil reserves estimated at about 7 billion barrels. Oil production in the region is currently around 2.5 million barrels per day. Gas reserves and output are larger still. The petroleum producing states include Malaysia (which accounts for almost half the region's total offshore oil output), China, Vietnam, Brunei, Indonesia and the Philippines.[15]

Maps published by China mark its maritime boundary as a broken line extending deep into the South China Sea. The Chinese claim line encompasses not just the Paracel and Spratly islands but many of the offshore oil and gas fields being exploited or explored by Southeast Asian countries in the EEZs within 354 km of their territory.

Are the Spratlys and Paracels the key to control of an untapped petroleum province located near some of the world's largest future energy consuming countries? Despite advances in deep water seismic survey techniques and drilling technology, there has been barely any exploratory drilling around the islands. So there are no proven reserve estimates.[16]

Resource estimates for the region that have been reported in the Chinese media or attributed to Chinese officials vary greatly, from around 100 billion barrels of oil to more than double this amount. A common rule-of-thumb for such frontier zones as the seabed surrounding the Spratlys is that perhaps ten per cent of the potential resources can be economically recovered. Using this rule, Chinese estimates imply potential production levels for the Spratly zone of between around 1.5 million barrels per day to as many as 3 million barrels per day.[17]

China, the world's sixth largest economy, is expected to consume about 5.7 million barrels of oil per day in 2004, up from 5.3 million bpd in 2003. Availability of oil from the South China Sea at the upper end of Chinese estimates could cover China's current import requirements.

However, natural gas may turn out to be the most abundant source of energy in the South China Sea. Most of the fields explored have yielded gas rather than oil. Estimates from the U.S. Geological Survey indicate that around 65 per cent of the region's hydrocarbon resources are gas. Chinese estimates of the gas resources of the South China Sea as a whole range above 56.5 trillion cubic metres, and for the Spratly zone around 900 tcm. The latter implies potential recoverable production of around 0.056 trillion cubic metres annually. This is about the level of Malaysia's current offshore gas output. As with oil, China's optimistic view of the South China Sea's gas potential is not shared by most non-Chinese analysts.[18]

Still, the point is that China evidently sees the South China Sea as a potentially rich petroleum province that is all the more important because it is close to home and could ease China's dependence on increasing energy imports from more distant sources, especially the Persian Gulf.

China may be as much as a generation behind the United States in terms of naval power. But within the next few years, China's naval modernization and expansion programme will probably enable it to launch a successful amphibious invasion of Taiwan should the government in Taipei attempt to seek formal independence. The naval build-up will also help to make China the dominant regional power in the South China Sea, able to enforce its sovereignty claims there against other rivals.

But perhaps the crisis Southeast Asia fears most would be one between China and the United States over Taiwan. The last thing that Southeast Asian countries want is for regional stability to be disrupted and economic growth undermined by a crisis in which they would be under intense pressure to choose sides between these two big powers. Still, both China and America have developed substantial common interests in maintaining cross-straits peace. If a conflict with China was provoked by nationalists on Taiwan, it is far from certain that the United States would feel bound to intervene militarily to protect Taiwan.

However, if an armed conflict did erupt between China and the United States over Taiwan, it could escalate. Would Washington try to impose a maritime embargo on China and cut its vital energy and other seaborne imports in or close to the Southeast Asian straits? Probably not, short of all-out war, which could be catastrophic for both China and the United States, and for Asia as a whole, especially if nuclear weapons were unleashed. Moreover, an embargo would be difficult to implement and affect the vital trading interests of other East Asian countries that Washington would want on its side.[19]

In this context, how can Southeast Asia and China develop a common interest in maintaining freedom of navigation while building maritime security cooperation? Defusing tension centred on Taiwan is clearly vital, or at least keeping any tension at a manageable level.

China's relations with individual Southeast Asian states and with ASEAN have become increasingly close and wide-ranging in recent years. They encompass pretty much the full gamut of "soft power" and include trade, investment, aid, scientific cooperation, diplomacy and cultural diffusion. But China's "hard power" ties with the region, including naval interchange, are weak and lag far behind those the United States and other foreign powers have with Southeast Asia.

It may now be timely for Southeast Asian countries with significant navies to develop a programme of naval training exercises with China that includes a counter-terrorism and anti-piracy component. For its part, China should accept the standing invitation from the United States and Southeast Asian countries to play a bigger role in regional military cooperation exercises with a maritime dimension, such as Cobra Gold, that increasingly focus not on defence from external attack but on peace-keeping, disaster relief and combating terrorism, piracy and other potential threats to safety and freedom of navigation. Such steps would help build confidence between Southeast Asian countries and China.

However, resolving the South China dispute in the most rational way will need far bolder diplomacy from all sides. China could help to pre-empt a potential future conflict over energy and other resources in the South China Sea by formally and finally abandoning its broken-line maritime boundary claim in the area. This claim may not now be active. But it could always be revived. Abandoning it would signal that China bases its claims in the South China Sea on current international law.

China and other claimants to disputed islands in the South China Sea could move beyond their non-binding joint declaration and sign a mandatory code of conduct that would freeze their activities and permit no further occupation of atolls and reefs or new construction on inhabited parts. They could agree to put their rival sovereignty claims to arbitration or adjudication before the International Court of Justice or the UN law of the sea tribunal, as some Southeast Asian countries have agreed to do with their island and maritime boundary disputes.

Of course, if the current emphasis on sovereignty is maintained and China becomes economically and militarily more powerful, it will able to negotiate with other claimants from a position of increasing strength. But this approach is unlikely to lead to greater trust or encourage maritime security cooperation between China and Southeast Asian countries.

NOTES

1. Joint news release of Second Five Power Defence Ministers' informal meeting in Singapore, 7 June 2004.
2. *BP Statistical Review of World Energy*, June 2004; "China's Oil Security Faces Tests of War: News Analysis", *People's Daily*, online edition, 21 October 2002.
3. China country analysis brief, EIA, U.S. Department of Energy, July 2004.
4. "China's Imports of Crude Oil Fell in May as Prices Advanced", Dow Jones Newswires in *Asian Wall Street Journal*, 22 June 2004.
5. "Saudi Arabia May Give Discount to Fend off Russia", Bloomberg News in *The Straits Times*, Singapore, 3 April 2004; "China Acts Now to Secure Supply of LNG for Future", Dow Jones Newswires in *Asian Wall Street Journal*, 23 June 2004.
6. "Shippers Want Better Policing of Straits", *The Straits Times* (Singapore), 10 May 2004; "World Oil Transit Chokepoints", Energy Information Administration country analysis briefs, U.S. Department of Energy, April 2004.
7. Philip Andrews-Speed, Xuanli Liao and Roland Dannreuther, "The Strategic Implications of China's Energy Needs", International Institute for Strategic Studies Adelphi Paper 346, p. 81, July 2002.
8. Charlie Zhu, "PetroChina Gets Licences to Explore in South China Sea", *Reuters*, 7 July 2004; Enid Tsui, "China's Hunger for Oil Sparks Shake-up", *Financial Times*, 13 July 2004; "Philippines Asks China to Desist from Provocative Acts in Spratlys", *AFP*, 10 July 2004.
9. Ronald A. Rodriguez, "Vietnam Reaffirms Sovereignty over Disputed Spratly Islands", *AFP*, 25 March 2004; "The Spratly Islands: Small is Beautiful", *The*

Economist, 22 May 2004; "Conduct Unbecoming in the South China Sea?", *PacNet* 22A, 21 May 2004.

10. Willy Lam, "Beijing's Energy Obsession", *Asian Wall Street Journal* opinion page, 2 April 2004; "China Seas Hold 40 Billion Tons of Oilgas Reserves", *People's Daily* online, 25 February 2004; Michael Armacost, "War Past Shouts, While Business Talks… . Quietly", *The Straits Times*, Singapore, 11 February 2004.

11. Mayumi Negishi, "Japan, China Urged to Cooperate on Energy", *The Japan Times* online, 24 July 2004; James J. Pryzstup, "Not Quite All about Sovereignty — but Close", Pacific Forum CSIS Comparative Connections, Japan-China Relations, April–June 2004.

12. Mariko Sanchanta, "Gas Provokes Japan-China Clash", *Financial Times*, 7 July 2004.

13. Reiji Yoshida, "Is the Senkaku Row about Nationalism or Oil?", *The Japan Times* online, 27 March 2004.

14. Anthony Faiola, "Senkaku Spat Scuppers Sea-Treaty Talks", *The Japan Times* online, 1 April 2004; "Isles Become Focus for Old Antagonisms", *Washington Post* online, 27 March 2004.

15. "South China Sea Region", Energy Information Administration country analysis briefs, U.S. Department of Energy, September 2003.

16. "Asia Looking into the Deep Oceans for Oil", *Reuters* in *Business Times* (Singapore), 10 August 2004.

17. "China's Oil Security Faces Tests of War: News Analysis", *People's Daily* online edition, 21 October 2002.

18. "South China Sea Region", op. cit.

19. "The Strategic Implications of China's Energy Needs", op. cit.

16

ASEAN-China FTA: Opportunities, Modalities and Prospects

Shen Danyang

The Sixth ASEAN-China Summit in Cambodia in 2002 is a milestone of regional economic cooperation for China and for the whole East Asian region. The Framework Agreement on ASEAN-China Economic Cooperation (FAACEC) was signed, and ASEAN and China agreed to establish a Free Trade Area within ten years. This is an institutional response to the leaders' agreement one year ago.

The decision of the leaders to establish a free trade area demonstrates that the economic and political relations between ASEAN and China has been further enhanced, and the mutual trust and the interdependence on each other will be further deepened. The decision by the leaders was a natural response to a number of important global and regional developments during the past decade, such as the dramatic growth in the number of regional trading arrangements, China's economic emergence and the 1997 financial and economic crisis.[1]

One of the most important results in the framework agreement is the "early harvest" programme, which has already taken effect from 1 January 2004. Some significant benefits have already been demonstrated.

This chapter maps out the future direction of the ASEAN-China FTA by reviewing the trade and economic cooperation between ASEAN and China, as well as the benefits achieved from this specific FTA.

DEVELOPMENT OF TRADE AND ECONOMIC COOPERATION BETWEEN ASEAN AND CHINA

The increasingly closer economic and trade relations, besides the active promotion by the leaders, could be considered the basis for reaching consensus on the establishment of the Free Trade Area within ten years.

1. Trade between ASEAN and China Greatly Increased

ASEAN and China are important trade partners for each other. ASEAN is China's fifth largest trade partner, and China is ASEAN's sixth largest partner. From 1990 to 2003, the average annual growth rate in trade between ASEAN and China was 20.82 per cent. China's export to ASEAN increased from the US$3.7 billion in 1990 to US$30.9 billion in 2003, and its import from ASEAN increased from the US$3.0 billion in 1990 to US$47.3 billion in 2003. During these fourteen years, the average annual growth rate of China's import from ASEAN increased by 23.78 per cent, faster than that of China's export to ASEAN.

ASEAN's position in China's market has been on the rise with its proportion in China's total exports increasing from 5.7 per cent in 1991 to 7.1 per cent in 2003 and its proportion in China's total imports rising from 6 per cent in 1991 to 11.5 per cent in 2003. ASEAN is now China's fifth biggest trading partner, next only to Japan, the USA, the European Union and Hong Kong. On the other hand, the share of China in the six older ASEAN countries' exports grew from 2.2 per cent in 1993 to 5.0 per cent in 2000 while the share of China in the six older ASEAN countries' imports grew from 1.9 per cent in 1993 to 6.7 per cent in 2002.

There is potential for further growth in these shares given that both regions' trade are largely oriented to the developed countries. Respective exports to the United States and Japan were 17.68 per cent and 12.55 per cent of ASEAN exports in 2002. In the case of China, exports to the United States, EU and Japan accounted for 21.09 per cent, 16.46 per cent and 13.56 per cent respectively of its exports in 2003.

ASEAN and Chinese leaders have agreed to try to make their trade volume reach US$100 billion by 2005. However, this goal might be achieved this year, one year earlier than expected. In 2003, trade between ASEAN and China achieved a record high of US$78.3 billion, with a growth rate as high as 42.9 per cent. This obviously demonstrates the basis and potential for future cooperation. During the first quarter of 2004, trade between ASEAN and China has amounted to $21.92 billion, 38.4 per cent increase over that of 2003. The growing trend may be seen more clearly in Figure 16.1, Tables 16.1 and 16.2.

2. Trade Structure Improved

In 1993, the top five ASEAN exports to China were oil and fuel, wood, vegetable oils and fats, computers/machinery and electrical equipment. Collectively, the share of these five products amounted to 75.7 per cent of all ASEAN exports to China. In 1993, the top five ASEAN imports from China were electrical equipment, computers/machinery, oil and fuel, cotton and tobacco. Collectively, they made up a little less than 40 per cent of ASEAN imports from China.[2]

By 2003, the trade structure between ASEAN and China had improved greatly. These could be analysed from six ASEAN members — the five older members of Indonesia, Malaysia, the Philippines, Singapore, Thailand and one new member Vietnam (hereinafter referred as ASEAN-6.) China's trade with these six countries accounts for 97.63 per cent of China's total trade with ASEAN. Exports to these countries account for 95.68 per cent, and imports account for 98.90 per cent. So analysis on these six ASEAN members is representative of the structure between ASEAN and China.

In 2003, industrial products took a major share in trade between China and ASEAN-6. China's export of industrial products to ASEAN was US$24.69

Figure 16.1
China's Trade with the World and with ASEAN
(US$100 Millions)

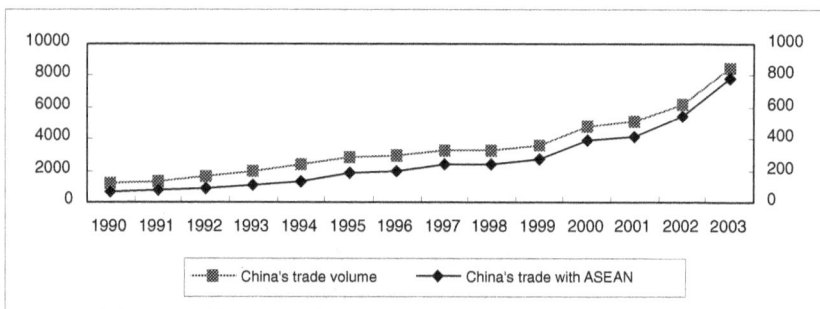

Source: China's General Administration of Customs.

Table 16.1
China's Trade with its Major Partners in Recent Years
(US$ Billions)

	2000		2001		2002		2003	
	Value	Growth %	Value	Growth %	Value	Growth %	Value	Growth %
China's Total	474.31	31.5	509.77	7.5	620.77	21.8	851.21	37.1
Japan	83.17	25.7	87.75	5.5	101.91	16.2	133.57	31.1
USA	74.47	21.2	80.49	8.1	97.18	20.8	126.33	30
EU	69.04	24	76.63	11	86.76	13.2	125.22	44.4
Hong Kong	53.95	23.3	55.97	3.7	69.21	23.7	87.41	26.3
ASEAN*	**39.52**	**45.3**	**41.62**	**5.3**	**54.77**	**31.7**	**78.25**	**42.8**
Korea	34.50	37.8	35.91	4.1	44.07	28.4	63.23	43.4
Taiwan Province	30.53	30.1	32.34	5.9	44.65	38.1	58.37	30.7
Australia	8.45	33.9	9.00	6.4	10.44	16	13.56	30
Russia	8.00	39.9	10.67	33.3	11.93	11.8	15.76	32.1
Canada	6.91	44.9	7.38	6.7	7.93	7.6	10.01	26.2

Source: China's General Administration of Customs.

billion, accounting for 83.43 per cent of its export to ASEAN; China's import of industrial products from ASEAN was US$35.93 billion, accounting for 76.77 per cent. China's ten leading exports to ASEAN-6 amounted to 67.14 per cent of its export to these six countries, and its ten leading imports accounted for 80.38 per cent. Among the ten leading exports and imports of ASEAN-6 and China, five categories of products are the same for ASEAN-6 and China. They are: office machines and automatic data-processing machines; electrical machinery, apparatus and appliances, and electrical parts; telecommunications and sound-recording and reproducing apparatus and equipment; petroleum, petroleum products and related materials; general industrial machinery and equipment, and machine parts. These five categories accounted for 48.38 per cent of China's total export to ASEAN-6, and 62.49 per cent of China's total import from ASEAN-6.

Compared with the early 1990s, the strongest growth has been in the trade of manufactured products, especially these five categories. The fact that these products were both the leading exports and imports of both ASEAN and China suggests the importance of intra-industry trade, brought about by product differentiation and economies of scale.

Table 16.2
China's Trade with ASEAN Members
(US$ Millions)

	2000			2001			2002			2003		
	Total	Export	Import	Total	Export	Import	Total	Export	Import	Total	Export	Import
ASEAN Total	39,522	17,341	22,181	41,615	18,385	23,229	54,766	23,568	31,197	78,252	30,925	47,327
Singapore	10,821	5,761	5,060	10,934	5,792	5,143	14,018	6,966	7,052	19,352	8,869	10,484
Malaysia	8,045	2,565	5,480	9,425	3,220	6,205	14,271	4,975	9,296	20,128	6,141	13,987
Indonesia	7,464	3,062	4,402	6,725	2,837	3,888	7,928	3,427	4,501	10,229	4,481	5,748
Thailand	6,624	2,243	4,381	7,050	2,337	4,713	8,561	2,958	5,602	12,655	3,828	8,827
Philippines	3,142	1,464	1,677	3,566	1,620	1,945	5,260	2,042	3,217	9,400	3,094	6,306
Vietnam	2,466	1,537	929	2,815	1,804	1,011	3,264	2,149	1,115	4,634	3,179	1,456
Myanmar	621	496	125	632	497	134	862	725	137	1,077	908	170
Cambodia	224	164	59	240	206	35	276	252	25	321	295	26
Brunei	74	13	61	165	17	148	263	21	242	346	34	312
Laos	41	34	6	62	54	7	64	54	10	109	98	11

Source: China's General Administration of Customs.

Table 16.3
Structure of China's Export to ASEAN-6 (2003)
(US$ Billions)

Rank	Product (In SITC)	Export Value	Export Share (%)
	China's total exports to ASEAN-6	29.59	100.00
1	Office machines and automatic data-processing machines	4.10	13.85
2	Electrical machinery, apparatus and appliances, and electrical parts	3.93	13.28
3	Telecommunications and sound-recording and reproducing apparatus and equipment	2.77	9.35
4	Petroleum, petroleum products and related materials	2.41	8.15
5	Textile yarn, fabrics, made-up articles, and related products	1.80	6.07
6	Articles of apparel and clothing accessories	1.49	5.03
7	General industrial machinery and equipment, and machine parts	1.11	3.75
8	Miscellaneous manufactured articles	0.81	2.75
9	Road vehicles	0.74	2.49
10	Manufactures of metals	0.72	2.42
	Subtotal	19.87	67.14

Source: China's General Administration of Customs, 2003.

Table 16.4
Structure of China's Import from ASEAN-6 (2003)
(US$ Billions)

Rank	Product (In SITC)	Import Value	Import Share (%)
	China's total imports from ASEAN-6	46.81	100.00
1	Electrical machinery, apparatus and appliances, and electrical parts	15.39	32.88
2	Office machines and automatic data-processing machines	6.94	14.83
3	Petroleum, petroleum products and related materials	4.81	10.28
4	Plastics in primary forms	2.70	5.77
5	Organic chemicals	2.02	4.31
6	Fixed vegetable fats and oils, crude, refined or fractionated	1.58	3.38
7	Crude rubber	1.19	2.54
8	Telecommunications and sound-recording and reproducing apparatus and equipment	1.19	2.54
9	General industrial machinery and equipment, and machine parts	0.92	1.96
10	Cork and wood	0.89	1.89
	Subtotal	37.62	80.38

Source: China's General Administration of Customs, 2003.

Table 16.5

China's Products of Trade Surplus with ASEAN-6 in 2003

(US$ Millions)

Rank	Product (SITC)	Export	Import	Export share %	Import share %	Surplus
1	Telecommunications and sound-recording and reproducing apparatus and equipment	2,768	1,188	9.35	2.54	1,580
2	Articles of apparel and clothing accessories	1,488	35	5.03	0.07	1,453
3	Textile yarn, fabrics, made-up articles, and related products	1,795	507	6.07	1.08	1,288
4	Road vehicles (including air-cushion vehicles)	736	86	2.49	0.18	650
5	Cereals and cereal preparations	687	102	2.32	0.22	585
6	Manufactures of metals	715	172	2.42	0.37	543
7	Inorganic chemicals	513	55	1.73	0.12	458
8	Fertilizers	384	3	1.30	0.01	382
9	Other transport equipment	439	68	1.48	0.14	371
10	Miscellaneous manufactured articles	814	491	2.75	1.05	323

Source: China's General Administration of Customs.

Table 16.6
China's Products of Trade Deficit with ASEAN-6 in 2003
(US$ Millions)

Rank	Product (SITC)	Export	Import	Export share %	Import share %	Deficit
1	Electrical machinery, apparatus and appliances, and electrical parts	3,930	15,391	13.28	32.88	11,461
2	Office machines and automatic data-processing machines	4,099	6,941	13.85	14.83	2,842
3	Plastics in primary forms	105	2,699	0.35	5.77	2,594
4	Petroleum, petroleum products and related materials	2,413	4,812	8.15	10.28	2,400
5	Organic chemicals	395	2,018	1.33	4.31	1,624
6	Fixed vegetable fats and oils, crude, refined or fractionated	12	1,584	0.04	3.38	1,573
7	Crude rubber	20	1,188	0.07	2.54	1,168
8	Cork and wood	8	885	0.03	1.89	877
9	Pulp and waste paper	5	562	0.02	1.20	556
10	Cork and wood manufactures (excluding furniture)	68	522	0.23	1.12	454

Source: China's General Administration of Customs.

Products with the largest trade surplus and trade deficit are also among these five categories. China's telecommunications and sound-recording and reproducing apparatus and equipment enjoys the largest trade surplus, with a value of US$1.58 billion; and China's electrical machinery, apparatus and appliances, and electrical parts has the largest trade deficit, as high as US$11.46 billion.

3. Mutual Investment Expanded

ASEAN is an important source of China's FDI. From 1991 to 2000, ASEAN investment in China increased at an average annual rate of 28 per cent. In 1991, ASEAN investment in China was only US$90 million, and the number reached US$4.2 billion in 1998. Because of the economic crisis, ASEAN investment in China decreased to US$3.3 billion and US$2.8 billion in 1999 and 2000, respectively. By 2001, total ASEAN investment in China increased to US$26.2 billion, accounting for 6.6 per cent of total FDI utilized by China.

China's investment in ASEAN is small compared to ASEAN investment in China, less than US$100 million a year. However, investment in ASEAN also increased sharply. By 2001, China's investment in ASEAN increased to US$1.1 billion, accounting for 7.7 per cent of China's overseas investment (see Tables 16.7 and 16.8).

OPPORTUNITIES FROM ASEAN-CHINA FTA

During the 1990s, the accelerated economic globalization and regionalization has aroused widespread concern throughout the world economies. The WTO-plus ASEAN-China FTA goes a further step than the WTO in terms of the extent of opening up the market and hence creates more advantageous conditions for ASEAN and China to expand bilateral trade and mutual investment. FTA is a successful and effective means of common prosperity and development that has been experienced by EU and NAFTA, because it leads to closer ties and greater interdependence among involved parties. ASEAN and China, both developing countries, are at different economic development levels, but they meet common opportunities and challenges in the rapidly changing world. The healthy and continuous economic growth is determined by whether one country can respond to the world economic trend in time and adjust its direction of development. Establishing a free trade area between the two sides to enhance bilateral relations is a wise decision for the pursuit of new development opportunities.

Table 16.7
ASEAN Investment in China (end 2000)

Country	Number of Projects	Contracted Value (US$ Millions)	Utilized Value (US$ Millions)
Singapore	9,122	35,381	16,992
Malaysia	2,031	4,936	2,203
Indonesia	760	1,591	837
Thailand	2,880	4,971	1,994
Philippines	1,369	2,564	1,029
Vietnam	373	375	86
Myanmar	146	194	34
Cambodia	24	22	7
Brunei	14	36	4
Laos	14	25	5
ASEAN Total by 2000	16,733	50,095	23,191
ASEAN Total by 2001	17,972	US$53.5 billion	US$26.2 billion
Total FDI in China by 2001	390,025	US$745.3 billion	US$395.2 billion

Source: China's Ministry of Commerce.

Table 16.8
China's Investment in ASEAN (end 2000)

Country	Number of Projects	Total Investment (US$ Thousands)	Chinese Investment (US$ Thousands)
Vietnam	41	48,770	31,000
Laos	15	44,040	29,370
Cambodia	50	110,830	85,000
Myanmar	30	146,380	48,580
Thailand	219	201,050	87,980
Malaysia	92	69,340	33,900
Singapore	161	78,350	68,620
Indonesia	50	159,070	59,620
Philippines	34	34,980	14,600
Total by 2000	692	892,800	458,660
Total by 2001	740	US$1.09 billion	US$0.66 billion

Source: China's Ministry of Commerce.

Even if there are challenges in the process of FTA construction, such challenges are only temporary and low cost compared to the long-term benefits. The two sides should work out how to deal with such challenges and pressures, and try to turn such pressures into motivations and minimize the negative impacts through economic restructuring and the FTA construction.

The opportunities from the ASEAN-China construction could be reflected mainly in the following respects.

1. China's Rapid Economic Growth and ASEAN's Recovery from 1997 Crisis Provide Opportunities for Economic Development

According to the simulations conducted by the ASEAN-China Economic Cooperation Expert Group, the FTA between ASEAN and China will increase ASEAN's GDP by 0.9 per cent or by US$5.4 billion while China's real GDP expands by 0.3 per cent or by US$2.2 billion in absolute terms.[3]

These figures are only part of the gains from the FTA construction. If China's commitments to WTO and the economic restructuring are taken into account, the potential opportunities ASEAN could tap from China's liberalization are far greater. With their markets opening to each other, together with China's rapid economic growth and ASEAN's recovery from the 1997 crisis, it could provide the two more opportunities for economic development.

China is the most dynamic economy in East Asia, and its average economic growth rate over the next decade is expected to be 7 per cent annually. China's GDP in 2000 was one quarter of that of Japan's, and one half if calculated in purchasing power. Some scholars expect that China's GDP could at least be the same level as Japan's in the next ten to fifteen years.[4] China has also become a large buyer. In 2003 alone, China's import increased dramatically by US$118 billion. China has bypassed Japan (and the United States) as the main trading partner of virtually every country in the region and has clearly become its growth locomotive, accounting for almost one quarter of the increase in total world trade in 2003 and surpassing Japan as the world's third largest importer.[5] In 2003, China accounted for 5.3 per cent of the total world imports, and increased by 40 per cent over the previous year, the fastest growth rate among all the 30 leading importers.[6] From 1990 to 2000, the share of East Asia's exports going to China almost doubled, from 5.2 per cent to 10.2 per cent, while the share of East Asia's exports going to Japan fell from 14.5 per cent to 12 per cent.[7] Still, from 1990 to 2001, the exports of the ASEAN-5 (Indonesia, Malaysia, Singapore, Thailand and the Philippines) to China grew six times, while their exports to Japan, Europe and the United States grew only two-and-a-half times.[8] And ASEAN's share in China's imports has increased from 6 per cent in 1991 to 11.46 per cent in 2003.

On the other hand, most ASEAN countries have recovered from the 1997 crisis, which had suddenly halted their previous rapid economic growth. As one of China's important trade and investment partner, ASEAN's economic recovery is significant to China.

2. FTA to Further Promote Trade and Economic Relations between ASEAN and China

1) Trade

It is forecast that an ASEAN-China FTA will increase ASEAN's exports to China by 48 per cent and China's exports to ASEAN by 55.1 per cent.[9] However, this model does not reveal their exports to the whole world's markets. After the establishment of the FTA, with the liberalization of trade and investment, and the comprehensive economic and technological cooperation, it will help enhance their production capability, efficiency and product competitiveness, and as a result will create more export opportunities to the world markets. It is true that there is competition between ASEAN and China because of the similarity in their economic structure. But the competition is not because of the FTA. On the contrary, the establishment of the FTA will help overcome the challenges and enhance the competitiveness of both sides.

What should be noted is the "early harvest" programme, which is the early trade liberalization in part of their products. The first batch of liberalization has been implemented from January 2004, and by 2006, all products under the "early harvest" list will reach zero tariff rate for China and the six older ASEAN members. This will cover 500 tariff lines, accounting for about 10 per cent of China's total.

Another set of figures might reflect ASEAN's opportunities from "early harvest" programme: ever since 1992, except for 2000 and 2001, China has always had trade surplus in the "early harvest" products. However, according to the simulation analysis done by CAITEC, after the "early harvest" programme is implemented, by 2006, China's export of the "early harvest" products to ASEAN will increase to US$784–946 million, and China's import from ASEAN will increase to US$838–1,017 million, and China will face a trade deficit of US$125–157 million.[10]

What is more encouraging is the actual development in the first quarter of 2004. According to China's customs, in the first quarter of 2004, the early harvest products China imported from ASEAN was worth RMB 6.154 billion (US$744 million), a 16.1 per cent growth over the same period the previous year. Products enjoying preferential import policy worth

RMB 1.055 billion (US$128 million), accounted for 17.1 per cent of the imports value in the "early harvest" products. Tariffs worth RMB 99.81 million (US$12 million) were exempted. Among ASEAN members, Thailand was the biggest winner after it signed the agreement with China, enjoying zero tariff on vegetables and fruits. China imported in the first quarter from Thailand vegetables worth RMB 556 million (US$67 million), a 38 per cent increase, and fruits worth RMB 240 million (US$29 million), a 80 per cent increase. Tariffs on vegetables and fruits worth RMB 70.36 million (US$9 million) were exempted. China exported to Thailand RMB 44.53 million (US$5 million) vegetables and RMB 64.66 million fruits (US$8 million), 157 per cent and 130 per cent respectively.[11]

The FTA will not only enlarge the trade between ASEAN and China, it will also lessen their exports' over-dependence on developed countries. Although trade between ASEAN and China increased greatly, and they are both among the ten largest trade partners to each other, their exports are heavily dependent on developed countries such as the United States, Japan and Europe. ASEAN's export to the industrial countries amounted to 48.43 per cent, and it is 54.48 per cent for China. ASEAN accounted for only 7.05 per cent of China's export, while China accounted for a mere 5.28 per cent of ASEAN's. For years, the economic performance of the United States, ASEAN's largest export market, has played a very critical role in ASEAN's export and economy. The United States accounted for 17.78 per cent of ASEAN's total export, and Japan 12.55 per cent. For individual ASEAN members, 24.70 per cent of the Philippines' export goes to the United States, and 20.16 per cent and 19.64 per cent for Malaysia and Thailand respectively (Tables 16.9 and 16.10). The sluggish U.S. economic growth is the key factor for ASEAN's unsatisfactory economic performance in 2001. That may be the biggest problem of over-dependence on a single export market. China's accession to WTO and agreement to establish FTA with ASEAN has brought about the further opening of China's market. This would gradually reduce ASEAN and China's over-dependence on the developed countries. Considering these factors, it leaves great room for the future development and expansion in trade between ASEAN and China. In the context of global economic slowdown, and years of recession of the regional economic power Japan, the FTA between ASEAN and China will be especially beneficial to the economic growth of ASEAN and China.

2) Investment

The formation of an ASEAN-China FTA should also attract more investments into the region. More ASEAN and Chinese companies will be willing to

Table 16.9
Share of ASEAN's Export Market (%)

	China	Industrial Countries	USA	Japan
Brunei	6.44	61.75	8.15	40.32
Cambodia	1.28	89.26	59.88	3.92
Indonesia	5.08	52.64	13.25	21.08
Laos	2.21	32.36	0.66	1.54
Malaysia	5.63	47.25	20.16	11.28
Myanmar	4.73	32.44	13.13	3.81
Philippines	3.85	60.09	24.70	15.04
Singapore	5.49	38.74	15.27	7.14
Thailand	5.16	53.76	19.64	14.52
Vietnam	6.45	63.44	14.96	14.63
ASEAN Total	5.28	48.43	17.78	12.55

Source: Direction of Trade Statistics Yearbook 2003.

Table 16.10
China's Share of Trade with ASEAN and Major Developed Economies (%)

	Import and export	Export	Import
ASEAN	9.19	7.05	11.46
USA	14.84	21.09	8.20
Japan	15.69	13.56	17.96
EU	14.71	16.46	12.85

Source: China's General Administration of Customs, 2003.

invest within the integrated market, since market risk and uncertainty are minimized through the preferential arrangement.

For years, ASEAN has been an important source of China's FDI inflows, accounting for 6.6 per cent of the investment utilized by China. The investment has decreased since the 1997 economic crisis. But with the ASEAN economic recovery and the FTA construction, more investment from ASEAN will come to China.

After years of development, Chinese companies have become stronger and more competitive, and their overseas investments have increased fairly rapidly, especially since the mid-1990s. Their investment projects have ranged from purified salt, rubber products, pharmaceuticals, healthcare products, food processing, household electrical appliances and forests products processing to petrochemicals, banking, insurance and shipping. The investment means has ranged from direct investment to technological investment and BOT. With China's further economic growth and industrial restructuring, Chinese companies' overseas investment will no doubt expand. In fact, investment abroad is encouraged by the Chinese Government. ASEAN will be a priority market for Chinese companies' overseas investment in the future due to the geographic closeness and similarity in culture, especially after the establishment of the FTA between the two sides. Chinese companies are likely to select flexible investment approaches in ASEAN according to their own capital size and each ASEAN member's characteristics. For example, some Chinese companies may establish research and development centres in the technology-advanced ASEAN countries, and some may invest in natural resource development projects in those resource-abundant ASEAN countries. And Chinese enterprises have already made substantial progress in this respect: China National Ocean Petroleum Corporation has bought the oil and gas exploitation rights for five oil fields in Indonesia, and this company will become the largest petroleum company operating in the ocean off Indonesia.

On the other hand, the multinational companies from the developed countries, which are interested in making inroads into the Asian market, will also be attracted to invest in the FTA. The integrated market of ASEAN and China can entice more foreign investment, which each alone cannot otherwise attract. For instance, some FDI aiming at China will try to utilize the FTA preferential terms to invest in ASEAN so as to circumvent some of China's existing limitations or restrictions.

3) Services

China is traditionally weak in the service industry, and ASEAN can therefore utilize the FTA opportunities to explore China's huge service market. This is also a chance for China to warm up for full liberalization under the WTO commitment.

China's continuous economic growth has made its people much better off. Their demands for high-quality education, healthcare, and recreational activities have accordingly increased, and will increase by leaps and bounds in the years ahead. It is estimated by Visa International Organization that China's middle-class population will reach 200 million by 2010. This segment of population will be the driving force for high quality services. Tourism is one example. The Chinese State Council has approved twenty-one travel destinations for Chinese citizens' self-sponsored tourism. All the ten ASEAN members are in the twenty-one-destination list, meaning ASEAN accounts for half of the choices Chinese tourists can make. In addition, most Chinese people prefer those places where they have no trouble in language communication. Most ASEAN countries have this advantage. In 2000, of 10,649,455 Chinese tourists travelling abroad,[12] nearly 2.3 million went to ASEAN countries, accounting for 21 per cent. It can also be seen from Table 16.11 that China has replaced Japan in 2003 as the largest non-ASEAN visitor-generating market.

Education and professional services enjoy the same opportunities. China's education market is estimated to be worth US$54 billion, and likely to grow at 20 per cent annually.[13] The joint educational venture has become an important form of China's education cooperation with the world, and it has developed very rapidly in recent years. Currently, there are 657 joint educational ventures/programmes in China, as compared to only seventy in 1995. Since the education systems of some ASEAN countries are influenced by the Western countries and have a relatively high standard of English, Chinese students are willing to choose such joint educational programmes. Besides that, ASEAN has attracted many Chinese students to study there. For example, currently 13,000–15,000 Chinese students are studying in Singapore and about 8,000 in Malaysia.

Table 16.11
Top Ten Visitor-Generating Markets

Rank	1999	2000	2001	2002	2003	2003 Tourist numbers
1	Singapore	Singapore	Singapore	Singapore	Singapore	5,661,459
2	Japan	Japan	Japan	Japan	China	2,003,843
3	Malaysia	Malaysia	Malaysia	China	Japan	1,947,813
4	China	China	China	Indonesia	Indonesia	1,844,286
5	USA	Indonesia	Indonesia	Malaysia	Thailand	1,634,438
6	Chinese Taipei	USA	Chinese Taipei	Thailand	USA	1,362,249
7	Indonesia	Chinese Taipei	USA	USA	Malaysia	1,338,275
8	Australia	Thailand	Thailand	Chinese Taipei	South Korea	1,258,759
9	UK	Australia	Australia	South Korea	UK	1,035,242
10	Thailand	UK	UK	Australia	Chinese Taipei	998,095

Source: ASEAN website.

3. FTA to Enhance the Political Relations between the Two Sides

FTA is just the beginning for the two sides to form a closer and comprehensive economic relation. What should not be ignored is the important role economic integration plays in maintaining regional stability, because it leads to closer ties and greater interdependence among involving parties. The FTA between ASEAN and China is the first FTA China has ever signed with its trade partners. It is one important step in China's regional economic integration strategy in the process of its participation in the multilateral trade mechanism. This is not only an economic agreement, but will also have great significance politically. China has a friendly relationship with ASEAN, and hopes to further strengthen such relationship through a community-like FTA. Closer economic cooperation will help achieve this. The decision of the leaders to establish a free trade area demonstrates that the economic and political relations between ASEAN and China has been further enhanced, and the mutual trust and interdependence of each other will be further deepened.

Thailand has expressed explicitly that it may be too long for ASEAN and China to establish the FTA within ten years, and has proposed to establish the FTA within two years. Some other ASEAN members share the same attitude as Thailand, and also expressed the will to establish a bilateral FTA with China so that they could move faster. This is a good reflection that ASEAN has realized China's role as a strategic partner rather as a straight competitor. Through the FTA, China opens its huge domestic markets to ASEAN, but China will not gain as much as ASEAN in the "early harvest" programme. This in a sense might be to counter the so-called "China-threat" theory. The 1997 crisis has already shown that ASEAN could rely on China to tackle an economic turmoil.

What should be noted are another two agreements China and ASEAN signed after their Framework Agreement of Economic Cooperation: One is the Declaration on the Conduct of Parties in the South China Sea, which has handled well the territorial dispute. The other is the Treaty of Amity and Cooperation in Southeast Asia, and China became the first big nation outside Southeast Asia to sign this treaty. It is believed that these measures will help keep the stability in East Asia, and has created a stable and peaceful environment for economic development for both ASEAN and China. Once their economic interests have overwhelmed any political dispute, China and ASEAN could develop their economies in a harmonious and peaceful environment.

PROSPECTS AND FUTURE DIRECTION OF ASEAN-CHINA FTA

Some Chinese economists have mentioned that the two years after ASEAN and China signed the framework agreement could be a process of warming-up, because the framework commitments will boost the confidence in trade and economic cooperation. After the completion of negotiations and implementation of the "early harvest" programme, bilateral trade and investment could develop by leaps and bounds from year 2004, which will be a strong basis for the future economic growth and stability in East Asia. Even before there is an FTA between ASEAN and China, China has already played a critical role in 1997 and 1998 in the financial and economic crisis by maintaining the stability of its currency. The ASEAN-China FTA would provide another important mechanism for shoring up economic stability in East Asia and drive the economic growth.

As mentioned previously, the "early harvest" programme under the framework agreement has already brought real and visible benefits to ASEAN countries. For any FTA, difficult issues might exist on how to approach the opening up of "sensitive products" in order to protect the domestic industries which are not as competitive. This FTA between ASEAN and China has set a good example on solving the issue of sensitive sectors by carrying out the "early harvest" programme. Through the enforcement of the "early harvest" programme, the elimination of tariff and non-tariff barriers of other products within the agreed ten-year time frame is also likely to be implemented earlier than expected.

Also, influenced by the benefits of Thailand's agreement on vegetables and fruits, more ASEAN members may be interested in signing individual agreements with China. In fact, some ASEAN members have expressed their interest in setting up bilateral FTAs with China, although China has not yet confirmed. It is a possible approach to promote trade between ASEAN and China, and which might also accelerate the ASEAN-China FTA mechanism.

But what China and ASEAN seek should be something based on the ASEAN-China FTA, and also beyond this FTA. Although the establishment of the FTA between ASEAN and China will create an economic region with 1.7 billion consumers, a GDP combination of US$2 trillion and a total trade of US$1.23 trillion, the economic scale of this FTA is still not strong enough and relatively small compared to that of the EU and NAFTA. Under the current trend of globalization, ASEAN and China should integrate themselves into a broader regional cooperation, and the ASEAN-China FTA is only one step towards that end. Cooperation of the whole East Asia should be strengthened through the development of ASEAN-China FTA and two other "Ten+1" cooperation mechanisms.

Regionalization is becoming an important dimension of East Asian economies' overall liberalization strategy, and the tendency is likely to be strengthened in the future. The ASEAN-China FTA has fostered Japan and Korea to carry out similar closer economic cooperation with ASEAN, and the benefits reaped from this FTA will further spur Japan and Korea to accelerate their progress in the FTA negotiation and establishment with ASEAN. The ASEAN-China FTA should be connected and contribute to the future establishment of an East Asian FTA that is much talked about today. The current ASEAN-China FTA, as well as the other two "Ten+1" cooperation mechanisms, should be critical towards the larger scale East Asian FTA. The East Asian Regional Integration based on the current Ten+3 framework, is the future for ASEAN and China, as well as for the whole East Asia.

Economic integration in Asia may be quite different from that of Europe, because of the great variety in economic development level, religion, language, and many other things. But the Asian-wide economic integration should be forward-looking, and should have a near-term target, as well as a long-run goal. It may be relatively easy for the Asian economic integration to start from East Asia, and it has already started from the ASEAN-China FTA. As the first FTA evolved from the "Ten+1" cooperation mechanism, the ASEAN-China FTA is significant to the other two "Ten+1" cooperation mechanisms and the "Ten+3" cooperation, in time frame, modalities, etc. Even if it is not possible to turn the "Ten+3" cooperation into an East Asia FTA immediately, once the three "Ten+1" cooperation mechanisms all evolve into "Ten+1" FTAs, it may be not too far from the realization of an EAFTA.

Reviewing the development of regional economic cooperation in Asia, ASEAN and China are located at the gateway of future large-scale economic integration in Asia or Pan-Asia. ASEAN and China should, on the basis of their "Ten+1" FTA, play an important role in the whole region's economic cooperation in the future. The two should jointly promote the economic integration in East Asia or in the Pan-Asian region.

For political reasons, the regional trade arrangement in South Asia has not made much progress. This has led South Asia's largest economy, India, to shift to East Asia, by proposing to conclude a regional trade and investment treaty or an FTA with ASEAN in the ASEAN-India Summit in 2002. (In fact, the ASEAN-India Summit could also be treated as a "Ten+1".) It shows that India has also begun to take an active approach in regional economic cooperation. Although India is currently only involved in the ASEAN-India Summit, it is quite likely that the current four "Ten+1" will be evolved into a "Ten+4" (China, Japan, Korea and India).

China also has a Shanghai Cooperation Organization with Russia and other five Central Asian countries. Although economic cooperation is not the key sector, closer economic cooperation is inevitable. These Central Asian countries would find great opportunities from the prosperous economic development of China as well as other East Asian economies.

The Bangkok Agreement, a tariff reduction treaty, is another notable regional trade arrangement in Asia that includes six countries — three from East Asia (China, Korea and Laos) and three from South Asia (India, Bangladesh and Sri Lanka). It has special meaning in that it could be a platform to link East Asia and South Asia into a broader regional trade agreement. Except for Bangladesh and Sri Lanka, the other four members of the Bangkok Agreement all have relations with ASEAN — either as an ASEAN member or the "1" in "Ten+1". It might be a bold idea to combine the members of the Bangkok Agreement and the several "Ten+1" into a new Pan-Asia Economic Cooperation Circle.

It might be even bolder to absorb other South Asia Association for Regional Cooperation members and the two countries of the Australia-New Zealand Closer Economic Relations Trade Agreement (CER or ANZCERTA) into this circle. (More economists have tended to include Australia and New Zealand as Asian economies.) If so, it will include a population of three billion, a total GDP of US$7 trillion and a trade volume of nearly US$3 trillion. Greater economic scale in regional economic cooperation may yield greater economic benefits to the involved parties. The diversified economic structures of these countries will make them highly complementary, because this circle includes developed countries like Japan, NIEs like Singapore and Korea, and least developed countries like Laos and Cambodia. Such a large-scale economic organization will also play an important role in maintaining regional stability.

The idea may seem remote for political reasons, but it is not impossible because most of these economies are in the process of or intend to participate in regional economic cooperation. Although difficult, this is the direction of closer Asian economic cooperation and a means to Asian economic integration. Whether it is for an EAFTA or a Pan-Asian Economic Community, the easier part is to carry out bilateral-level cooperation, and a series of intertwined cooperation may help lead to the overall integration. If a closely intertwined state of bilateral FTAs is prevalent in Asia, the closer economic links will make a Pan-Asian FTA, or even a Pan-Asian Economic Community take shape. What should be kept in mind is that all the involved parties must be serious in building an institutionalized and functional RTA or FTA. There is no meaning in building another APEC-like forum in Asia.

NOTES

1. "Forging Closer ASEAN-China Economic Relations in the 21st Century", report submitted by the ASEAN-China Economic Cooperation Expert Group, October 2001.
2. Ibid.
3. Ibid.
4. Tang Shiping and Zhou Xiaobing, "ASEAN, Japan and China Cooperation and the Future of East Asia", *International Economic Review*, November–December, 2001.
5. C. Fred Bergsten, "The Resurgent Japanese Economy and a Japan-United States Free Trade Agreement", paper presented to the Foreign Correspondents' Club of Japan, Tokyo, Japan, 12 May 2004.
6. International Trade Statistics 2003, WTO Website.
7. Susan V. Lawrence, "Enough for Everyone", *Far Eastern Economic Review*, 13 June 2002.
8. Chen Cun, "China Leads East Asia to Exceed Europe and US", *International Herald Tribune*, 14 June 2002.
9. "Forging Closer ASEAN-China Economic Relations in the 21st Century", op. cit.
10. Paper presented at The CAITEC-JETRO FTA Seminar, March 2003, Beijing.
11. *International Business Daily*, 10 May 2004.
12. China National Tourism Administration.
13. Singapore Enterprises Development Bureau.

17

Building ASEAN-China FTA: Opportunities, Modalities and Prospects

Suthiphand Chirathivat

INTRODUCTION

Today ASEAN and China are clearly the world's emerging economies. Both are considered crucial to the future development of East Asia. In general, China is obviously more of a heavyweight in the global economy than ASEAN. In order for their economies to further prosper, they all need consistent integration both in trade and investment and to deepen their interactions with the region and the world. However, most ASEAN countries were weakened by the financial crisis of 1997 before the recent recovery. China's economy, on the other hand, still keeps on growing despite increasing apparent weaknesses related to the strong economic expansion.[1]

Across the world, as much as in the Southeast Asian region, China's economic performance has become a subject of intense debate among the concerned public. China's economic locomotive has dramatically driven the world and even more, the East Asian region, into a new kind of economic interdependence, centred around relations with China's own economic growth.[2] This has led to a new perception of China, which would include seeing China as both economic threat and opportunity. The Southeast Asian region is geopolitically speaking, next to China. It has to take these challenges even more seriously than others as China's future growth path is in direct relation with the region's future development. For sure, the weight of China's economic presence is to be felt more over time, thus causing ASEAN's need to pay attention to these new economic challenges.

At the beginning of the twenty-first century, relations between ASEAN and China have called into increasing focus the signed agreement of the ASEAN-China FTA (ACFTA). Upon China's accession into the WTO, China's growing confidence was displayed in its push toward ASEAN to accept this pact. Willingly or not, all ASEAN members, once accepted, have been busy negotiating with China the new framework.[3] For both parties, this is the first FTA agreed with outsiders. For ASEAN, this agreement has opened doors to negotiate for similar proposals with India, Japan, and others for instance. Amidst the proliferation of bilateral and regional FTAs in East Asia after the financial crisis, it seems valid to ask questions about what this sort of agreement could represent and whether and how it could ensure long-term cooperation between the two sides.

This chapter discusses mainly the potential for much more sophisticated economic exchange between ASEAN and China. As shown in section 2, both ASEAN and China already share growing linkages through trade and investment. There are a number of new issues arising which need special consideration. A closer economic relationship through a free trade initiative or ACFTA is set to influence the policy framework and demand greater smooth negotiations, which imply also the need to look at the economic implications for, and greater competition with, ACFTA as shown in section 3. Section 4 will broaden the focus to look at what is at stake for the joint openness of their markets. It also discusses the evolving context of these economies in the East Asian development. Such efforts between the two should extend far beyond the benefits between the two to cover also their concerns and their unique positions over the new development of East Asian regionalism. The final section will conclude the chapter.

GROWING LINKAGES

ASEAN-China economic relationships have undergone significant changes since the end of the Cold War. On the one hand, Southeast Asia has emerged as ASEAN-10.[4] With the grouping, it has called for more regional policy framework and implemented several regional initiatives to integrate the region further with the global economy. Still, ASEAN remains economically fragmented by integration standards. On the other hand, China's economic reforms since the 1980s have been fruitful. Its economic openness followed by success from the 1990s have had quite a significant impact on others. Together, it seems that China's economic attractiveness is making ASEAN's outlook vulnerable.[5] Things look even worse with the ASEAN economies weakened by the financial crisis, as China turned increasingly with success to the regional and global markets.

Then comes considerations of size. China and ASEAN combined equals a 1.84 billion population, US$2.06 trillion in GDP and US$0.86 trillion in export volume.[6] However, ASEAN's magnitude compared to China would only constitute 42 per cent of the population, 51 per cent of the GDP and similar share of export volume (see Table 17.1). Herein lies the economic asymmetries between the two. Also, by comparison, China is large, rapidly growing, and still expanding.[7] Meanwhile, ASEAN is diverse and economic disparities among member countries still remain important issues.[8] Economic linkages between the two still have to reflect the reality of these economic and social fundamentals and their historical evolution.

Trade in Goods

All the original ASEAN members have long experienced their own economic openness and integration. For at least a decade[9] earlier than China and with the exception of Singapore, these countries' trade patterns have reflected the way in which they carry out export-oriented and investment-driven development strategies, followed by the new members joining ASEAN's integrated region in the late 1990s. China's trade expansion in the 1990s is considered as an engine of economic growth, doubling its per capita income between 1993 and 2002.[10] Within this perspective, ASEAN trade with China has grown over the years and even more so during the years after the crisis of 1997. At present, ASEAN countries export more to China than import from it. China's trade liberalization within the WTO has helped to expose the Chinese market to foreign business, including ASEAN.

In this context, ASEAN-China trade relations have rapidly increased in recent years as detailed in a report by the ASEAN Secretariat:[11]

> "ASEAN-China trade totaled US$39.5 billion in the year 2000. ASEAN's share in China's foreign merchandise trade has been continuously on the rise, increasing from 5.8 per cent in 1991 to 8.3 per cent in 2000. ASEAN is now China's fifth biggest trading partner. Meanwhile, the share of China in ASEAN's trade has grown from 2.1 per cent in 1994 to 3.9 per cent in 2000. China is now the sixth largest trading partner of ASEAN."

Table 17.1
Economic Indicators of Emerging East Asia (end 2003)

	GDP (US$ Billions)	Population (Millions)	GDP/capita (US$)	GDP growth (average 3 years/%)	Exports (US$ Billions)	Foreign reserves (US$ Billions)
Indonesia	216	200	983	3.8	60	34
Thailand	147	64	2,302	6.1	74	39
Malaysia	102	23	4,502	4.9	96	45
Sinapore	92	3.5	26,648	2.9	141	86
Philippines	79	82	959	4.4	35	13
Vietnam	38	81	467	7.1	20	7
Myanmar	9	51	176	4.7	25	–
Brunei	5	0.3	14,305	3.5	3	2
Cambodia	4	13	310	5.7	2	0.9
Laos	2	6	330	6.0	0.3	0.2
ASEAN Total	**694**	**544**	**1,280**	**4.6**	**434**	**227**
China	1,370	1,300	1,050	8.4	436	400
"Greater China"	1,830	1,330	1,400	7.3	680	670
India	500	1,060	471	5.3	55	80

Source: Asian Development Bank and ASEAN Secretariat.

Table 17.2 indicates that China's trade with ASEAN still hit a record high of US$78.3 billion in 2003, surging by 42.8 per cent year-on-year according to the Chinese customs statistics.[12] ASEAN has benefited from its trade surplus with China. Indeed, China's imports jumped to 57.7 per cent to reach US$47.3 billion, leaving a trade deficit with ASEAN of US$16.4 billion in 2003. China bought mainly machinery products and parts, animal fat and plant oil, and mineral and agricultural products from ASEAN countries such as Malaysia, Indonesia, Thailand and Vietnam, and sold machinery and electronic products, chemicals, fabrics and garments. The composition of ASEAN-China trade appears to concentrate on China's needs for raw materials and parts and components[13] as Chinese demand is also pushing up global prices for agricultural products the same way it has spurred a rise in the prices of industrial goods.

Nevertheless, China's trade share among ASEAN's trading partners is still not the most important by far.[14] Table 17.3 shows major trading partners of individual ASEAN members and China. The United States still represents the top export market for five out of the ten ASEAN members, and is also China's top export market. Japan is the top import partner of four ASEAN countries as Japan is also China's top import source. In this

Table 17.2
China's Top Ten Trading Partners
(US$ Billions; Percentages)

	Overall Trade			Exports			Imports		
	Partner	Amount	Share	Partner	Amount	Share	Partner	Amount	Share
1.	Japan	133.6	15.7	U.S.	92.5	21.1	Japan	74.2	18.0
2.	U.S.	126.3	14.8	Hong Kong	76.3	17.4	EU	53.1	12.9
3.	EU	125.2	14.7	EU	72.2	16.5	Taiwan	49.4	12.0
4.	Hong Kong	87.4	10.3	Japan	59.4	13.6	ASEAN	47.3	11.5
5.	ASEAN	78.3	9.2	ASEAN	30.9	7.1	S. Korea	43.1	10.4
6.	S. Korea	63.2	7.4	S. Korea	20.1	4.6	U.S.	33.9	8.2
7.	Taiwan	58.4	6.9	Taiwan	9.0	2.1	Hong Kong	11.1	2.7
8.	Russia	15.8	1.9	Australia	6.3	1.4	Russia	9.7	2.4
9.	Australia	13.6	1.6	Russia	6.0	1.4	Australia	7.3	1.8
10.	Canada	10.0	1.2	Canada	5.6	1.3	Brazil	5.8	1.4

Sources: Ministry of Commerce of the People's Republic of China, "Top Ten Export Markets", "Top Ten Import Sources", and "Top Ten Trade Partners" (all dated 18 February 2004), online at:
<http://english.mofcom.gov.cn/article/200402/20040200183706_1.xml>
<http://english.mofcom.gov.cn/article/200402/20040200183744_1.xml>
<http://english.mofcom.gov.cn/article/200402/20040200182458_1.xml>
Cited from Vincent Wei-Cheng Wang (2004).

Table 17.3
Major Trading Partners of ASEAN Nations and China
(Percentage shares of the country's exports / imports)

	Brunei	Cambodia	Indonesia	Laos	Malaysia	Myanmar	Philippines	Singapore	Thailand	Vietnam	China
Export Partners	Japan (40.3)	U.S. (60.2)	Japan (21)	Vietnam (26)	U.S. (21)	Thailand (31.4)	U.S. (26.2)	Malaysia (17.4)	U.S. (19.6)	U.S. (15.2)	U.S. (21.5)
	S. Korea (12.3)	Germany (9.1)	U.S. (13.2)	Thailand (19)	Singapore (17.4)	U.S. (13)	Japan (14.9)	U.S. (15.3)	Japan (14.9)	Japan (14.9)	Hong Kong (18)
	Thailand (12.1)	U.K. (7.1)	Singapore (9.4)	France (7.5)	Japan (10.9)	India (7.4)	China (7.4)	HK (9.7)	Singapore (8)	Australia (7.1)	Japan (14.9)
	Australia (9.2)	Singapore (4.4)	S. Korea (7.2)	Germany (5.3)	China (6.5)	China (4.7)	Taiwan (5.8)	Japan (7.1)	HK (5.4)	China (6.6)	S. Korea (4.8)
	U.S. (8.1)		China (5.1)		HK (5)		Singapore (5.7)	China (5.5)	China (5.2)	Germany (6.5)	
	China (6.4)		Taiwan (4.2)					Taiwan (4.9)	Malaysia (4)	Singapore (5.5)	
Import Partners	Singapore (30.6)	Thailand (24.8)	Japan (14)	Thailand (59)	Japan (16.9)	China (27%)	Japan (21.6)	Malaysia (18.2)	Japan (23)	S. Korea (12.7)	Japan (18.1)
	Japan (21.5)	Singapore (16.9)	Singapore (13.1)	Vietnam (12.3)	Singapore (15.9)	Singapore (19.5)	U.S. (18.6)	U.S. (14.3)	U.S. (9.6)	China (12.2)	Taiwan (10.5)

sense, trade share between ASEAN and China is not sufficient to explain the ASEAN-China FTA, when comparing ASEAN's trade with the United States and Japan (Wang 2004, p. 4). However, if one takes another view of the growth potential of this trade, it could give a different picture. Table 17.4 shows that from 1993 to 2001, ASEAN exports to China increased seven-fold from US$4.5 billion to US$31.6 billion. During the same period, ASEAN imports from China increased 5.5 times, from US$4.3 billion to US$23.5 billion.

Thus, trade has become more, not less, important in relations between China and ASEAN. This is especially so since the financial crisis that hit the ASEAN economies in 1997–99. A sluggish economy in the United States and the EU had provoked further concern for its markets. ASEAN economies see Japan and increasingly, China, as providing alternatives to its goods to support the future growth. Although ASEAN economies have already begun to face competition from China in the third markets prior to 1997 and following the last renminbi devaluation in 1994, the crisis and later episode allowed ASEAN to reevaluate the economic challenge posed by China, especially its ability to compete and sustain its economic growth.[15] Both ASEAN and China should consider each other as trading partners due to their geographical proximity, strong economic growth, rise of income per capita, and new product diversity and their availability (Chirathivat and Albert 2003).

FDI Flows

Reciprocal FDI flows between ASEAN and China are asymmetrical at the moment. Chinese FDI in ASEAN from 1990 to 2001 represents a total of US$660 million (Chirathivat and Albert 2003, p. 260) or 0.3 per cent out of US$224 billion of FDI in Southeast Asia.[16] Principal destinations of the Chinese FDI are mainland Southeast Asian countries like Cambodia, Laos, Myanmar, Thailand and Vietnam. ASEAN FDI in China, by comparison, is much more substantial. Its accumulated volume in 2001 stands at US$26.2 billion which represents a share of 6.6 per cent of the total FDI in China. And this investment has increased at an annual rate of 2.8 per cent between 1990 and 2000, reaching its peak with an investment of US$4.2 billion in 1998.

Among ASEAN investors, Singapore has a special role to play through its FDI in China. Singaporean investors put US$20.2 billion during the same period, thus contributing around three quarters of ASEAN investment in China.[17] Malaysia and Thailand represent the second tier of ASEAN investors in China, and still concentrate their investments through operations of its conglomerates in China.[18] For Indonesia, the Philippines and other ASEAN

Suthiphand Chirathivat

Table 17.4
ASEAN Trade with China by Country (1993–2001)

Exports (US$ Thousands)

COUNTRY	1993	1994	1995	1996	1997	1998	1999	2000	2001
Brunei Darussalam	–	37.1	152.2	115.4	0.0	0.0	244.2	22,270.0	127,741.3
Cambodia	–	–	–	–	–	–	–	285,985.0	224,984.2
Indonesia	1,249,494.1	1,280,043.2	1,741,717.8	1,867,758.2	2,123,041.2	1,832,034.4	3,338,942.2	4,321,848.9	3,490,998.1
Malaysia	1,202,628.5	1,859,707.4	1,806,866.6	1,519,935.5	1,313,812.7	1,545,082.2	4,595,865.8	6,433,437.9	6,229,130.5
Myanmar	–	–	–	–	–	–	65,076.9	86,525.3	103,700.5
Philippines	173,874.0	163,967.0	212,938.6	327,921.7	244,411.6	343,682.6	2,521,925.8	2,570,611.5	2,372,582.0
Singapore	1,902,697.9	2,000,065.8	2,439,216.6	3,214,704.8	4,195,491.8	4,059,714.3	12,718,557.3	16,236,398.3	16,140,398.9
Thailand	–	–	–	543,696.6	1,291,132.0	1,422,072.6	3,231,764.2	5,077,586.6	2,862,555.1
TOTAL	4,528,694.5	5,303,820.5	6,200,891.8	7,474,132.2	9,167,889.3	9,202,586.1	26,472,376.4	35,034,663.5	31,552,090.6

Imports (US$ Thousands)

COUNTRY	1993	1994	1995	1996	1997	1998	1999	2000	2001
Brunei Darussalam	–	34,931.4	63,336.5	72,500.2	55,090.6	20,620.9	72,415.9	84,958.9	97,356.1
Cambodia	–	–	–	–	–	–	–	364,110.9	203,774.4
Indonesia	935,983.3	1,477,386.7	1,495,223.3	1,235,458.7	1,518,013.9	904,459.4	1,469,664.0	2,364,323.0	2,099,989.6
Malaysia	816,772.8	1,200,709.0	1,516,774.7	1,719,986.8	1,916,805.4	1,685,513.6	3,358,966.0	6,572,884.9	5,129,407.3
Myanmar	–	–	–	–	–	–	223,665.3	261,734.9	394,914.4
Philippines	180,662.9	294,046.6	475,876.6	676,506.8	871,565.5	1,198,911.2	2,265,960.7	1,984,916.9	2,212,320.0
Singapore	2,402,944.9	2,751,912.8	3,578,512.1	4,205,358.5	5,808,553.0	4,853,367.7	8,878,527.6	10,637,225.3	9,982,659.7
Thailand	–	–	–	1,307,809.3	3,312,855.6	2,548,662.2	3,138,797.8	4,210,755.3	3,712,652.5
TOTAL	4,336,363.9	5,758,986.5	7,129,723.2	9,217,620.3	13,482,884.0	11,211,535.0	19,407,997.3	26,480,910.1	23,833,074.0

Note: China including Hong Kong in 1999–2001.
Sources: ASEAN Trade Statistics data query <http://202.154.12.3/trade/publicview.asp>. Cited from Vincent Wei-cheng Wang (2004).

countries, their presence in China is not yet obvious. In general, small and medium enterprises (SMEs) in ASEAN are not financially strong to allow them to start their operations in the Chinese market.

Looking beyond reciprocal FDI between ASEAN and China, ASEAN is concerned more about the Chinese competition for FDI. The tension lies in the widespread perception that investors have left ASEAN for China. As the World Investment Report 2003 highlights for ASEAN:

> FDI flows to Southeast Asia dropped from US$15 billion in 2001 to US$14 billion in 2002, though Brunei Darussalam, Lao People's Democratic Republic, Malaysia and the Philippines received larger flows in 2001. Significant repayments of intra-company loans by foreign affiliates were a feature of the decline, as was the increased competition from China.[19]

Indeed, FDI flows to China rose by 13 per cent in 2002, to US$53 billion, a new record reinforcing China's position as the largest recipient of FDI inflows in the developing world.[20] Given its locational advantages, it is attractive for resource-seeking, efficiency-seeking and market-seeking FDI. Also, this large proportion of FDI comes from the overseas Chinese network and other multinationals, thus contributing to the increase of FDI flows to China.

There is some evidence that China has been drawing the lion's share of Asia-bound FDI, clearly in the 1990s.[21] According to Felker (2003), ASEAN saw its FDI share, headed for development, fall from an average of 40 per cent during the period 1989 to 1994 to a mere 10 per cent in 2000. China's experience was then the opposite. Already in 1998, it received 50 per cent of the FDI headed for developing Asia. In 2000, it received an equivalent of two-thirds of the FDI. Although the decline of ASEAN-bound FDI has been overstated,[22] the perception in Southeast Asia is nevertheless that FDI to China is having a "hollowing out effect"[23] and this perception has contributed to a growing sense of threat across much of the Southeast Asian region.[24]

According to Athukorala (2004), China's FDI figure, through, is of great interest, but has to be interpreted with care as with China's success at the expense of ASEAN. There is a round-tripping FDI between China and Hong Kong[25] and considerable "fat" in Chinese estimates. This has not included certain Chinese linkages and networks underpinning the FDI especially from Hong Kong and Taiwan, the two countries accounting for two thirds of the FDI in China. Finally, there could be a bias in comparison resulting from the exclusion of reinvested earnings. All of these considerations are being dealt with in a number of studies on this specific issue.

Emerging Trends

The magnitude of change in China is starting to affect most aspects of other trading nations. Even before China is likely to overtake the United States economy in size by the mid twenty-first century (Sachs 2004, p. 38), the country is already on its way to becoming a new type of economic entity. Some may see it as the new locomotive of the world economy[26] as developed countries may not be able to strive for a new source of growth so soon. Others may also see a pressure on world deflation[27] as China keeps its price of goods low yet still has great potential to keep the costs at a very competitive basis. This trend puts pressure on other countries' development. So, China's renaissance is called into question (Ohmae 2002). For sure, China has caused a dramatic change in the economic balance throughout Asia and to a certain extent, the world.

In the areas of trade, China has not only fuelled its trade with ASEAN, it has also greatly expanded its trade with the world. While Chinese exports have been growing at about 30 per cent per year, its imports have grown even faster, at about 40 per cent in 2003. China, for example, has replaced the United States as Japan's largest trading partner in 2003, and for the moment, is the third largest trading partner of the United States. It is thus understandable that each country's trade calculus has to bear in mind the rise of China. Japan's reason for economic recovery is strongly related to China.[28] The EU has set out a whole new agenda in foreign policy that is devoted to its economic relationship with China.

With such changes in attitudes toward trade with China, what could be the impact on ASEAN? Recent trends suggest China's need for imports will continue to fuel its growth. That explains why China buys between 20 to 25 per cent of the globally traded volume of many key commodities. This has boosted exports and raised the growth prospects for several emerging nations like ASEAN that rely on commodity exports. The palm oil exports boom of Malaysia has recurred because of the increased demand from China.[29] Rubber exports of Thailand have also benefited from the price increase and export revenue, also due to China.[30] Chinese demand for Indonesian petroleum products, palm oil and rubber has also provided strong prospects for Indonesian economic growth in 2003. Even for a large Latin American country like Brazil, the importance of "commodity-hungry" China has already made it Brazil's Number Three export destination, after the United States and Argentina.

How far will these trends set the future of emerging economies like ASEAN which supply such commodities? The optimists need to tread with care. The question is whether ASEAN economies can continue to grow if and when the overheating Chinese economy starts to cool. The short-term prediction is still on China's rapid manufacturing growth that has increased its reliance on imported industrial commodities. This could also be true for the growing demand for food products from Chinese consumers. For sure, the China factor is increasingly felt in the agricultural and industrial goods market. However, the main concern about the Chinese economy is starting to show in its expansion capacity and weaknesses.[31] The Chinese leaders are struggling to find the right mix of administrative and market tools to cool down an overheating economy and perhaps to meet a soft landing. The global environment like the recent hikes in oil price and U.S. interest rates could put additional pressure on China's short-term growth prospects. Thus, ASEAN countries need to formulate policies to deal with China, in terms of both its strong growth and its possible economic crisis in the years to come.

As for investment between ASEAN and China, ASEAN firms, especially those from more advanced countries, like Singapore, Malaysia and Thailand, are again busy formulating the right strategies to deal with a growing China. For sure, differences among them remain and could vary from industry to industry. But overall, they cannot miss the new opportunities created in an expanded market of ACFTA where other aspects like technology, logistics, inputs, management, and human resources are key to competing, given the pressure from the Chinese firms. ASEAN FDI will continue to flow to China and the whole ASEAN region needs to take a closer look at the future trends.

Chinese investment in ASEAN, on the other hand, has become more noticeable in 2003. Although the flow is still disparate and small, this outward direct investment is rapidly growing. China's neighbours, like the Southeast Asian region, are the earliest beneficiaries of such a changing trend.[32] Indeed, Chinese manufacturers are actually looking at the region for production platforms to penetrate new markets, apart from China's resource-based overseas investments. This trend could be a significant boost to calm down fears in Southeast Asia over losing export income and FDI to China. However, both need to prepare for these new challenges as China is at the point of transforming into a major foreign direct investor in Asia and beyond.[33]

SUBSTANCE OF BLUEPRINT AND POSSIBLE OUTCOMES

Upon understanding the recent ASEAN-China economic linkages, it is natural to ask what substance lies in the ASEAN-China FTA (ACFTA) and what the joint economic blueprint gives us so far as guidelines on the future directions of such a relationship. From the start, Premier Zhu Rongji of

China proposed the ACFTA during the Sixth ASEAN Summit in 2000. A joint study by the ASEAN-China expert group was then called for. A year later, at the following Seventh ASEAN Summit in 2001, the report by the expert group was adopted.[34] The intention was followed with the declaration to create an ACFTA within a decade. Then, in the following Eighth ASEAN Summit in Phnom Penh, Cambodia, on 4 November 2002, ASEAN leaders and Premier Zhu Rongji of China signed a Framework Agreement on Comprehensive Economic Cooperation, which provided the groundwork for the establishment of an ACFTA by 2010 for the original ASEAN members plus Brunei and 2015 for the newer members, including Cambodia, Laos, Myanmar and Vietnam. The latest Ninth ASEAN Summit in October 2003, Bali, saw both sides making the joint declaration on "Strategic Partnership for Peace and Prosperity" in which the ACFTA has become a pillar in the ASEAN-China economic cooperation, apart from political, social, security and regional and international cooperation.

Even Rodolfo Severino, then ASEAN Secretary General, mentioned that he was surprised at the speed at which the process to the framework agreement had taken place, and in such great detail.[35] Also the Chinese Premier Zhu Rongji was enthusiastic about his brainchild initiative as he declared such an agreement would promote long-term relations between the two.[36] For both, such an initiative is of particular note as it pointed to a willingness to address ASEAN needs and concerns. Since the crisis of 1997 and with the economic presence of China in the region, it appears that closer economic cooperation with China is fast becoming less an opportunity than a necessity (Ba 2004). For the ASEAN-China expert group, it is "a natural response to regional and global developments during the course of the past decade".[37] Hence, ASEAN's decision to develop closer relations with China is not for immediate concerns, but rather, a long-term assessment of the smaller economies' need to go forward.

Framework Agreement

The establishment of an ACFTA is an integral part of the "Framework Agreement on Comprehensive Economic Cooperation between the Association of Southeast Asian Nations and the People's Republic of China". It aims to create an ACFTA with special and differential treatment and flexibility to the newer ASEAN members. The leaders also agreed from the beginning that the framework should provide for an "early harvest" in which the list of products and services to be liberalized will be determined by mutual consultation.[38] This Framework Agreement of Comprehensive Economic Cooperation, which provided the ground for ACFTA, contains six major elements,[39] ranging from trade and investment facilitation measures, provision of technical assistance and capacity-building, particularly to ASEAN's new members, down to the expansion of cooperation in various areas and the establishment of appropriate institutions to carry out the cooperation framework, including the establishment of ACFTA.

The framework agreement also provides three phases in its implementation of ACFTA.

- The first phase involves the implementation of an "early harvest" programme, between 2004 to 2006 for ASEAN-5, and up to 2010 for the new members.[40] This would concern the product coverage for tariff reduction and elimination, implementation time frames, rules of origin, trade remedies and emergency measures applicable to the programme.
- The second phase includes the list of "normal track" items, not covered by the "early harvest" programme for which parties could phase out all tariff rates at the end of the framework agreement, from 2005 to 2010 for ASEAN-5 and China, and 2005 to 2015 for new members and the Philippines.
- The last phase includes the "sensitive track" items which are to be kept to a minimum. These items concern industries that need time to adjust, and for them, inclusion in the FTA would be step by step, and respective applied rates reduced and eliminated with time frames to be mutually agreed between the parties.

According to the above principle, both parties should gradually lower tariff rates on globally competitive products at a faster pace than on sensitive products. Also FTA provisions would go beyond reduction of tariffs to cover also the reduction and elimination of non-tariff barriers, liberalization in services and liberalization in investment. However, it will take time to negotiate all these issues in the process of establishing FTA.

At the Ninth ASEAN Summit in October 2003, Bali, ASEAN and China had established a "strategic partnership for peace and prosperity" whereby talks on ACFTA had been integrated as a key pillar in ASEAN-China economic cooperation among other areas such as deepening cooperation in agriculture, information and telecommunications, human resource development, two-way investment and the Mekong River Basin development. China has also supported ASEAN's initiative on reducing the development gap, especially through sub-regional cooperation like the East-West Economic Corridor and opportunity for ASEAN to participate in China's western region developments. The leaders also signed a protocol to amend the framework agreement signed on 4 November 2002 which contains some of the major issues as follows:

- Recognition that any contracting party may accelerate its tariff reduction and elimination for products covered under the framework agreement.[41]
- Incorporation into the framework agreement the rules of origin applicable to the products covered under the "early harvest" programme of the framework agreement.
- Revision of the contents of the framework agreement[42] to include the sub-segment "early harvest" agreements between some ASEAN countries and China and to insert its rules and product descriptions including implementation clarification of the provisions of the "early harvest" programme.

In sum, the leaders agreed on eight articles under this protocol covering:

- Parties unable to complete the appropriate product lists to draw up mutual agreement consistent with the implementation time frame.
- Amendment of article to be substituted by a new Article 2 which provides a contracting party to be fully bound by the commitments under such arrangement with respect to product coverage, tariff schedule, and implementation time frame and its acceleration arrangement.
- Amendment of the rules of origin as set out in Annex 5[43] of the new protocol and its Attachment A with regard to its operational certification procedures for the rules of origin of the ACFTA.
- Prohibition of any individual ASEAN country to enter any agreement with China and/or the rest of the ASEAN countries, outside the ambit of this agreement.

Implications

As the ACFTA is to become an integral part of the future course of ASEAN-China economic relations, one might ask where ACFTA would lead to, what would the potential economic benefits be, and whether the pact is realistic in it goals in implementation and time frame. Certainly, there are strategic interests for both sides to be considered as well.[44] For the moment, it is certain that the ACFTA will be starting with the tariff and non-tariff reduction. For ASEAN-6, average tariff rates on Chinese products are already low at around 2.3 per cent compared to Chinese tariff rates on ASEAN products, at around 7.4 per cent, which are still quite high even with China's accession to the WTO (Chirathivat and Mallikamas 2004). Non-tariff barriers imposed by China against ASEAN are also in general much higher than the reciprocal non-tariff barriers.

In principle, abolishment of trade barriers in the ACFTA will allow trade expansion, which could be realized through trade creation and trade diversion. As ASEAN and China are well adapted to the regional and global competition with its low costs and sufficient efficiency, it is expected that the cost of trade diversion will be low as compared to the benefits gained from trade creation. China, even as a latecomer in industrialization, will pressure ASEAN to do more than just open its region. In any case, there will be even more great adjustments for all ASEAN countries than China as the removal of trade barriers will lower costs, expand intra-regional trade and increase economic efficiency much further along the way to free and open trade areas. Ideally, a real income boost will happen as long as resources continue to flow to efficient and productive sectors. Also non-members of ACFTA might engage in more trade and investment as their economies will be enhanced through market widening, intensified competition and regional economies of scale.[45]

There are, however, also potential concerns associated with the ACFTA. Apart from non-tariff barriers in China, such a free trade area could create significant costs with regard to rules of origin and its administrative surveillance and implementation. This could cause more complications as different countries in ASEAN and perhaps China get involved in an increasing number of separate but overlapping FTAs.[46] A large number of members in separate tracks of ACFTA could create confusion for investors as to which rules, obligations and incentives correspond to which partner. At this point, ASEAN countries and China have just started the long process of negotiations for and implementation of trade liberalization under ACFTA.

There is also the issue of how to take care of the losers in such a trade pact. Each ASEAN country, big or small, is involved with the world's manufacturing workshop, China. By its sheer size and China's economies of scale, a number of manufacturing sectors have to make real adjustments with regard to cost efficiency, production network, and consumer demand. For continental ASEAN with common borders with China, like Laos, Myanmar and Vietnam, these countries have already been invaded by cheap Chinese consumer products. Even Indonesia, the Philippines and Thailand, are also about to face increasing competition with Chinese goods, both in agriculture and manufacturing, and more adjustment in other sectors. Thailand at the moment, has started its "early harvest" phase with China, which calls for more attention, especially for the losers, whether they are farmers or manufacturers in the country.

Potential Results

The effects of ACFTA have been simulated by using the Global Trade Analysis Project (GTAP) as adopted by the Chulalongkorn and Monash General Equilibrium Model (CAMGEM) of Chulalongkorn University, Thailand. The model contains forty-five countries and fifty production sectors (Chirathivat and Mallikamas 2004). In this modelling exercise, it is assumed that the rate of trade protection is reduced to zero with all tariff and non-tariff barriers eliminated.

The results show that China will benefit from ASEAN's tariff reduction, especially for at least three sectors: textiles and apparel, motor vehicles and parts, and electronic equipment. These sectors are expected to gain from improving market access to ASEAN by 31.5 per cent, 16.6 per cent and 49.2 per cent respectively due to lower barriers. There are also gains for sectors like textiles, other food products, motor vehicles and other mineral products from lower inputs costs. Because of China's needs in these sectors, it is expected that ASEAN's complementarities could play an important part in these bilateral exchanges.

The only negative impact on China's trade balance would be its import of ASEAN's agricultural goods, which could cause a decline in outputs due to import substitution. China's rice tariff reduction of 113 per cent will increase its imports from ASEAN by 234 per cent.[47] China's sugar tariff reduction of 26 per cent will increase its imports from ASEAN by 103 per cent.[48] Also, a 35 per cent tariff cut for vegetable oils will lead to a 146 per cent increase in imports from ASEAN, especially by Malaysia.[49] And a 26 per cent tariff cut for imports of poultry and seafood will increase imports from ASEAN by 89 per cent. Countries well placed to benefit from China's import substitution are the Philippines, Thailand and Vietnam for its rice, sugar, seafood and poultry and Malaysia for its vegetable oils. There are also other primary commodities and intermediate inputs which will benefit from China's demand for its manufacturing sector.

As for ASEAN countries, their primary benefits will arise from market access to China for their quality of food exports. They would also gain in exports of primary commodities especially chemicals, rubber and plastic products, textile fibres, vehicles and parts, and electrical components and parts. For example, a 19 per cent cut in chemicals, rubber and plastic products will cause a rise of 77.6 per cent in ASEAN's exports to China. For vehicles and parts, its exports to China will grow by 473.5 per cent as a result of a 20.1 per cent tariff cut. However, ASEAN could face a negative impact from the lower costs of Chinese imports. Vegetable and fruits, apparel and other food, for example, will face higher competition from China.

The overall result of the simulation is that there are trade gains for both ASEAN and China from forming ACFTA. China will increase its imports from ASEAN by 53.3 per cent while China's exports to ASEAN will rise by 23.1 per cent (Table 17.5). The ACFTA will create a slight trade diversion for China as it will decrease its import value from the United States by 2.4 per cent, Japan by 1.3 per cent and the EU by 1.5 per cent. The ACFTA also has an impact not only on external demand but also internal demand. Higher export income and lower commodity prices will increase private consumption, aggregate savings, and private investment, and thus will cause China to possess greater opportunities for its exports.

ASEAN's gains from China will be its access to cheaper imports from China and its export to the Chinese market. However, there will be some trade diversion effects on ASEAN's trade with the world. The intra-ASEAN trade, especially among its members, will significantly decline because of its attention given to the ACFTA. ASEAN's exports to the third markets will face a decline of 1.4 per cent for Japan, 0.8 per cent for the United States, and 1.0 per cent for the EU. China's competition against ASEAN exports in these markets will increase by 0.4 per cent.

Overall, the macroeconomic impact will be a real GDP increase by 0.36 per cent for China and by 0.38 per cent for ASEAN, with differences among its members. Private investment is expected to increase by 0.7 per cent for China and 0.8 per cent for ASEAN. Private consumption and savings will rise by 0.4 per cent and 0.2 per cent respectively for China and by 0.5 per cent and 0.8 per cent respectively for ASEAN (Table 17.6). The major findings here are trade gains for both, for which China will look increasingly at ASEAN as an alternative source of inputs for natural resource-based and intermediate products. China still needs sources of imported inputs to satisfy the needs of its manufacturing sector which domestic suppliers may not be able to meet. With continuing strong growth in China, ASEAN could come to play a crucial role in supplying China's demand for such products. However, ASEAN's industries could face increasing competition from lower costs of Chinese imports, and its exports focused on China could weaken ASEAN's own integration such as in trade liberalization under the AFTA and its third markets.

PROSPECTS FOR ENHANCING FUTURE PARTNERSHIPS

The preceding analysis underlines several key points which should be taken into consideration in assessing the prospects for future relationships. Bilateral trade between ASEAN and China is growing fast in value as compared to FDI. While ASEAN has benefited from China's economic growth, it has to

Table 17.5
Impact of ASEAN-China FTA on Trade Flows (%)

	CHINA	ASEAN	THAI	MALAY	INDO	PHI	SING	VIET	JAPAN	USA	EU	ROW	Total
CHINA	-100.00	23.07	55.01	28.36	23.67	46.58	1.52	91.59	0.04	0.13	0.12	0.07	1.91
ASEAN	53.27	-0.79	64.74	–	–	–	–	–	-1.41	-0.83	-1.04	-1.21	0.76
THAI	63.33	5.45	0.00	-1.42	-4.62	-5.28	0.79	-6.05	-1.82	-1.11	-1.45	-2.38	0.74
MALAY	52.98	–	-2.40	0.00	-1.61	-3.35	0.37	-6.01	-1.51	-0.98	-1.24	-1.58	0.63
INDO	26.85	–	-2.70	-0.71	0.00	-2.94	0.76	-10.06	-0.75	-0.63	-0.72	-0.78	0.46
PHI	31.34	–	-1.17	0.95	0.78	0.00	1.73	-4.80	0.55	2.18	0.91	0.72	1.55
SING	68.58	–	-1.67	-0.55	-0.79	-3.27	0.00	-8.72	-0.83	-0.76	-0.83	-0.85	0.83
VIET	10.06	–	-1.18	9.08	-0.77	3.92	1.20	0.00	1.93	-0.52	4.96	0.51	2.80
JAPAN	-1.31	0.23	-0.81	0.33	-0.27	-0.88	1.24	-5.73	0.00	0.05	0.05	0.03	-0.07
USA	-2.39	0.54	-0.34	0.81	0.00	-0.76	1.19	-3.58	0.02	0.00	-0.02	-0.02	-0.04
EU	-1.50	0.38	-0.25	0.50	0.03	-1.69	1.23	-3.81	-0.02	-0.02	-0.02	-0.03	-0.04
ROW	-2.08	0.63	-0.55	0.62	-0.24	-1.14	1.52	-3.90	0.15	-0.03	-0.02	0.02	-0.09
Total	1.61	1.03	0.95	0.97	0.67	0.43	1.17	1.43	-0.07	-0.05	-0.03	-0.07	0.07

Source: CAMGEM, Chulalongkorn University.

Table 17.6
Macroeconomic Impact of ASEAN-China FTA

Country / Variables	ASEAN			China			Korea	Japan	USA	EU	ROW
	Overall	Internal	External	Overall	Internal	External					
Rental price of capital (%)	0.19	-0.11	0.30	0.00	-0.25	0.24	-0.02	-0.01	0.01	0.01	0.01
Rental price of land (%)	3.64	0.07	3.55	0.23	-0.60	0.83	-0.19	0.07	0.11	0.14	0.18
Labour wage rate (%)	0.97	0.09	0.88	0.61	0.15	0.45	-0.16	-0.06	-0.03	-0.03	-0.05
Average price of primary factor (%)	0.76	-0.02	0.78	0.28	-0.11	0.39	-0.10	-0.04	-0.02	-0.02	-0.01
Price of GDP (market price) (%)	0.55	-0.17	0.72	-0.17	-0.52	0.35	-0.09	-0.04	-0.02	-0.02	-0.01
Import Price (%)	0.03	-0.01	0.04	0.04	0.05	-0.01	0.02	0.04	0.00	-0.01	0.01
Export Price (%)	0.34	-0.11	0.44	-0.11	-0.37	0.26	-0.05	-0.03	-0.01	-0.01	0.00
Terms of trade (%)	0.31	-0.09	0.40	-0.14	-0.42	0.27	-0.07	-0.07	-0.02	-0.01	-0.01
Aggregate capital stock (%)	0.83	0.26	0.56	0.74	0.54	0.20	-0.16	-0.06	-0.05	-0.04	-0.07
Real GDP (factor cost) (%)	0.38	0.09	0.29	0.30	0.18	0.12	-0.07	-0.02	-0.01	-0.01	-0.03
Real GDP (market prices) (%)	0.38	0.12	0.27	0.36	0.24	0.12	-0.08	-0.02	-0.02	-0.01	-0.03
Real private consumption (%)	0.46	0.04	0.41	0.40	0.24	0.15	-0.09	-0.03	-0.02	-0.01	-0.04
Real government consumption (%)	0.52	-0.05	0.57	0.09	-0.09	0.18	-0.05	-0.02	-0.01	-0.01	-0.02
Real investment (%)	0.83	0.26	0.56	0.74	0.54	0.20	-0.16	-0.06	-0.05	0.00	-0.07
Real saving (%)	0.78	0.05	0.73	0.17	-0.06	0.23	-0.10	-0.02	-0.01	-0.01	-0.02
Export volumes (%)	0.95	0.45	0.48	2.37	1.98	0.37	-0.05	0.01	-0.01	-0.01	-0.05
Import volumes (%)	1.27	0.43	0.82	3.44	2.74	0.66	-0.16	-0.11	-0.05	-0.03	-0.08
Trade Balance (millions $)	-177.68	-319.63	147.87	-979.93	-1238.35	267.45	74.37	190.61	233.46	149.70	262.68
Welfare (million $)	2986.22	190.09	2785.73	1787.05	587.59	1191.72	-101.86	-332.42	-118.56	-180.48	-167.15

Source: CAMGEM, Chulalongkorn University.

Table 17.6 – continued

	Thailand			Malaysia			Indonesia			Phillipines			Singapore			Vietnam		
	Overall	Internal	External	Overall	Internal	External	Overall	Internal	External	Overall	Internal	External	Overall	Internal	External	Overall	Internal	External
Rental price of capital (%)	-0.06	-0.30	0.21	0.26	-0.10	0.36	0.22	-0.09	0.32	-0.12	-0.26	0.11	0.15	-0.04	0.19	-0.24	-1.02	0.26
Rental price of land (%)	9.96	0.38	9.71	3.85	0.20	3.70	0.62	0.04	0.57	0.75	-0.55	1.14	2.00	0.16	1.86	2.34	1.82	2.00
Labour wage rate (%)	0.93	0.12	0.87	1.05	0.12	0.99	0.55	0.06	0.54	0.18	-0.10	0.24	1.02	-0.19	1.28	1.95	0.92	0.43
Average price of primary factor (%)	0.77	-0.15	0.92	0.87	0.00	0.90	0.40	-0.01	0.44	0.08	-0.22	0.26	0.56	-0.11	0.70	1.35	0.44	0.56
Price of GDP (market price) (%)	0.40	-0.40	0.77	0.58	-0.17	0.75	0.33	-0.08	0.43	-0.27	-0.55	0.23	0.53	-0.10	0.66	-0.21	-1.80	0.48
Import Price (%)	0.02	0.00	0.02	0.05	-0.01	0.06	0.05	0.00	0.04	0.05	0.00	0.03	0.04	-0.03	0.07	0.11	0.02	0.09
Export Price (%)	0.59	-0.22	0.81	0.36	-0.10	0.46	0.25	-0.08	0.35	-0.18	-0.34	0.12	0.21	-0.05	0.28	0.02	-0.79	0.37
Terms of trade (%)	0.57	-0.21	0.79	0.31	-0.08	0.40	0.20	-0.08	0.31	-0.23	-0.34	0.09	0.17	-0.03	0.21	-0.08	-0.80	0.28
Aggregate capital stock (%)	0.75	0.62	0.23	0.60	0.27	0.41	0.40	0.18	0.26	0.21	0.12	0.08	1.08	-0.23	1.39	1.53	1.37	-0.12
Real GDP (factor cost) (%)	0.33	0.29	0.06	0.46	0.13	0.36	0.18	0.07	0.13	0.08	-0.03	0.07	0.58	-0.12	0.74	0.68	-0.02	0.01
Real GDP (market prices) (%)	0.32	0.34	0.01	0.44	0.15	0.32	0.19	0.08	0.13	0.11	0.02	0.05	0.60	-0.13	0.76	0.78	0.23	-0.03
Real private consumption (%)	0.48	0.21	0.28	0.67	-0.05	0.74	0.18	0.02	0.30	-0.02	-0.39	0.13	0.90	-0.15	0.96	0.67	-1.54	0.19
Real government consumption (%)	0.23	-0.05	0.26	0.67	0.27	0.41	0.30	0.18	0.26	-0.20	0.12	0.08	0.76	-0.23	1.39	-0.10	1.37	-0.12
Real investment (%)	0.75	0.62	0.23	0.60	0.38	0.51	0.40	0.41	0.26	0.21	1.84	0.12	1.08	-0.12	1.15	1.53	5.55	-0.12
Real saving (%)	0.82	0.19	0.65	0.80	0.40	0.78	0.32	0.45	0.56	-0.04	1.05	0.19	0.98	-0.16	1.38	0.73	5.08	0.02
Export volumes (%)	1.05	1.04	0.17	0.79	0.07	0.78	0.62	0.08	0.27	1.68	19.18	-17.94	0.94	11.04	-41.30	2.86	-66.37	9.87
Import volumes (%)	1.45	0.96	0.67	1.05	0.07	0.78	0.92	0.08	0.27	1.07	-0.31	0.21	1.13	-0.17	1.23	2.87	-0.81	0.24
Trade Balance (millions $)	-59.98	-212.86	117.15	-12.13	-55.07	596.16	82.70	-46.66	361.03	-2.76	-115.72	60.17	-31.10	-97.18	638.58	-34.51	-61.19	19.28
Welfare (million $)	422.33	254.20	555.05	113.91	54.33	282.13	135.30	31.89	184.97	-72.62	-0.17	0.10	229.26	-0.18	1.14	-8.09	-0.18	0.11

Source: CAMGEM, Chulalongkom University.

be interpreted with care as for its future trade relationships. There is room for larger FDI flows between the two although both are competing emerging platforms for multinationals. For the moment, China has become much more attractive than ASEAN. The simulation analysis shows the strengths on which to build in sectors that are of mutual interest. Both ASEAN and China have strong opportunities to help develop their trade and industries regionally and globally, and not specifically with each other only. As both ASEAN and China are emerging economies, there is room for larger overall trade flows and increasing investment linkages.

Even though ASEAN and China have agreed to heighten their bilateral interactions to a new level, one has to consider the kinds of regionalization and globalization where these challenges abound. Both sides have evolved differently through the recent economic experiences. These differences have to be taken into consideration as the implementation of the new pact moves ahead.

Policy Options

With the ACFTA put in place, some might argue that with high trade protection and complementary trade, market opening is a significant milestone as compared to the participating countries' bilateral past but the question remains as to how it will be implemented. In principle, the ACFTA's realization comes under the same umbrella as the 2010 liberalization date for ASEAN's old members and 2015 for the new members plus the Philippines. However, China is to negotiate for its implementation with each ASEAN member country, which means each country will have separate and different packages for their trade liberalization. To achieve this, it will require tremendous efforts for all parties concerned. Thus, it comes to the issue again of whether this FTA will not merely translate in the end, into separate preferential trading arrangements (PTAs) of ASEAN countries with China. Rules of origin are one of the issues in which leaders foresee its shortcomings and have tried to embrace possible rules and regulations in its latest protocol at the ASEAN-China Summit in October 2003.

Against this background, there are additional arguments which have to be more widely discussed:

- Market access is one of the major issues involved directly with this pact. Trade liberalization could be delayed as market access is hindered by standards and rules-related factors. China is more protective than ASEAN. Thus, this requires to be dealt with by negotiation and cooperation as well as greater efforts by both sides. Although the relationship in recent years, before free trade came into effect, has been growing, it is reasonable to expect greater benefits will accrue from the reduction and elimination of non-measurable barriers that cannot be easily estimated in the simulation exercise.

- Intra-industry is the basis for trade growth which the ACFTA has to take into consideration. Here, the firms in the same industry will find opportunities to exchange goods and services in which they specialize. ASEAN has developed an interesting degree of intra-industry trade with Japan and Asian NIEs with imports and exports of the same industries, particularly in automobile and electrical and electronic products. China has also caught up quickly with such a trend by increasing intra-industry trade with East Asia. The growth of intra-industry trade between ASEAN and China should follow more closely for industries like textiles, automobiles, chemicals and petrochemicals, machinery, electrical and electronic, etc.

- Mechanisms for resolving disputes will become an essential part to ensure that each party is in conformity with the overall intent of the framework. In principle, trade rules established in an FTA and the dispute settlement mechanisms (DSMs) used to enforce these rules provide a means by which disparities in negotiating strength can be minimized.[50] Imagine a trade dispute arrangement without clear and transparent rules on DSMs: Laos cannot easily find herself comfortable with China in trade disputes. The ACFTA has yet to find a way to depoliticize disputes which could set an important precedent in trade policy.

New Context to East Asian Development

The ACFTA also has to be seen in the broader context of the East Asian development. ASEAN, for example, used to keep up with the regional changing patterns of trade and development until before the recent transformation after the crisis and the emergence of China. China has, since the 1990s, clearly ended its long isolation from its Asian neighbours through trade and investment. If ACFTA is aimed at enhancing their market interaction, one needs to investigate the extent of such a partnership. There remains questions of whether and in what way these increasing links could fit into the transformation of the East Asian economies.

According to recent studies (Lu and Regnier 2003; Felker 2003; Gordon 2003; Ba 2004), economic trends in East Asia suggest a re-orientation of the regional economy around China has already happened, and will increasingly continue to do so. Compared to 1996 and 2002 trade figures, ASEAN's exports to China have increased 138 per cent while ASEAN's exports to the

United States and Japan decreased by 21 per cent and 4 per cent respectively (Ba 2004). To some extent, ASEAN's particular position among the East Asian economies is being challenged strongly by an ascendant China apart from the more advanced Asian NIEs like South Korea and Taiwan. According to Felker (2003) and Ba (2004), ASEAN economies are caught in a "structural squeeze" between China and Asian NIEs, and even more so among the less developed ASEAN countries. China, on the other hand, seems to be progressing well with its low cost exports to most major markets including the ASEAN markets. For China, major markets are still developed countries like the United States, the EU and Japan. ASEAN comes next to supplement its needs essentially in raw materials and intermediate inputs.

The question then is in what way ACFTA can influence such a profile. Southeast Asia (Felker 2003; Ba 2004) needs to find and to "develop more sophisticated production profiles" to fill the gap it has with China. For the moment, ASEAN recognizes China's economic importance will grow, not diminish. But, the issue remains how ASEAN can go beyond just viewing China as having a great potential to stimulate ASEAN growth. As growth alone without prosperity, deepening production networks and industrial linkages like technology transfer and human resources development cannot offer longer-term opportunities to both sides.

This has been argued by the ASEAN-China expert group as well (Ba 2004)[51] as they see the importance of the ACFTA as fostering the development of new regional production networks. Such production networks are not new to the region. These networks exist and are an integral part of Japan's and Asian NIEs' economic presence from the 1980s and the 1990s. The future of ACFTA may be tied to the new networks linking ASEAN and China and these could be within or outside the region. For example, "China is not going to produce everything in electronics on its own. They will also be sourced from countries like Malaysia, Singapore, the Philippines and Thailand" (Ba 2004). A recent study[52] also offered supporting figures for 2001 where China's purchases of parts and components from developing Asia represented up to 20 per cent of those countries' components trade. In a sense, as Felker (2003) put it, "the region's advantages as a node within a networked global production economy will not evaporate in the face of the Chinese challenge, but will evolve in the direction of particular niches and horizontal clusters of multinational activity".[53]

With the ACFTA, Chinese competition is forcing Southeast Asian firms to specialize and become even more efficient. There will be losers and winners, thus this requires one to be especially vigilant in such an industrial adjustment. ASEAN, together with China now, has become part of an existing production network, but could also produce new emerging production networks and have different kinds of dynamics from those that have been known up to the present.

Strategic Interests in Regionalism

ASEAN and China both share a common concern in a global system that neither can control. Of course, China has more influence in world affairs as compared to individual ASEAN countries. Despite this fact, ASEAN has come to play an increasing role in regional affairs (Regnier 2003). Economically, ASEAN has progressed on the ASEAN FTA (or AFTA) since its beginning in 1993, before the recent proliferation of regional and bilateral trading arrangements especially after the Asian crisis. When their leaders talked of bringing ASEAN and China into a common and free trade area, they realized that both "China and Southeast Asia need to have similar progressive goals. Otherwise, political divisions would make cooperation increasingly difficult".[54]

For ASEAN, this is an extended FTA or its AFTA to cover also China. The grouping realizes that China's economic presence will continue to grow, not to diminish, while China had taken particular effort and initiative to respond to ASEAN's concerns. Chinese leaders had been very assuring in proposing such a deal. ASEAN leaders, despite some countries' reservations, decided to move ahead with such an agreement. Thus, it requires ASEAN to open further to other regional initiatives of comprehensive economic partnerships (CEPs) with Japan and India, in particular.[55] At the same time, ASEAN needs to distinguish its own regionalism by growing further to become the ASEAN Economic Community (AEC) in the near future.

Thus, as things stand, the ACFTA seems to have created a renewed interest in ASEAN for its own regionalism and on the part of other players. Some might go further to argue that ASEAN has the potential to be a regional hub for East Asia. For example, Japan also has an increasing interest in ASEAN as it has in China. The ACFTA could be a good complement for Japanese multinationals to work upon.[56] The United States has also expressed its interest in ASEAN by renewing its concept of "Enterprise for ASEAN Initiative". However, there is also the view (Ho 2004) that "ASEAN's small, fragmented markets, are not as attractive to investors as the large Chinese market and more integrated regions elsewhere in the world. Indications point to MNCs' investment strategies as being China+1 rather than ASEAN+1, thus giving priority to China than ASEAN." Counter arguments are that, at least, it is important for MNCs to view the opportunities offered in a connected region. Whatever the major trends will be, ASEAN needs to form its own strategy on economic competition, trade, investment and all other economic aspects, which "will no doubt feature permanently in the relations between China and ASEAN in the foreseeable future" (Ho 2004).

There is another aspect in the ACFTA, that is, that each ASEAN member is too weak to face and confront China. Some countries may feel the Chinese superiority while others are uneasy. These differences could be exploited further by ASEAN itself. Each ASEAN member's bilateral talk with China needs to be synchronized, rather than neglected along the way. To augment their negotiating power, ASEAN members need to pool their resources and capabilities together to overcome contentious issues in their collective action. The sceptic's question for ASEAN is whether "China's real motivation is actually domination, as opposed to integration, and this could see ASEAN not complete full integration, trying instead to cash in on the huge Chinese economy" (Wang Wei-cheng 2004).

China's approach to the ACFTA is a strategic move that should be studied in a broader context beyond economic interests. It is true that economic linkages between the two have broadened much more recently. However, forming an alliance with ASEAN is also obviously China's policy choice to exercise regional influence and leadership and to build further political trust with its neighbours, and thereby strengthen regional security in favour of China. For some (Funabashi 2003; Wang Wei-cheng 2004; Ho 2004), this development shows China's "new diplomacy", "peaceful ascendancy" or peaceful rise" (*heping jueqi*).[57]

This "peaceful ascendancy" is designed to calm down the fears of China's Asian neighbours in a world which is becoming multipolar[58] and China has strongly embraced economic globalization. A "good-neighbour" diplomacy is ideal at a time when the United States is distracted by the wave of terrorism, Japan by its recession and its conservative stance, and ASEAN is still striving with its economic expansion after the financial crisis of 1997. China's diplomatic offensive toward Southeast Asia and also other proposals of forming FTAs in the region[59] has made it much acclaimed for seeking "peace and stability", its style of constructive diplomacy, and its "substance is economics" stance, at least for now (Wang Wei-cheng 2004). Thus, it is evident that geopolitics, rather than purely economic motives, drives China into ACFTA.

CONCLUSION

This study concludes that there is a real need to look closely at the future economic relationship between ASEAN and China. Given the official move to elevate this relationship in a comprehensive manner, it is in the best interest of both sides to deepen and develop their mutual interests in the overall relationship. ASEAN is underway in its economic restructuring and reforms in response to the recent crisis and the forces of globalization. China is growing and is in transition to a full market-driven economy. Potential economic integration between the two provides ample room to develop a new outlook for its future economic relationship.

With regard to liberalization initiatives, both ASEAN and China need to enhance market access and reduce barriers to provide room for more opportunities. To be sure, liberalization will touch upon sensitive sectors and the obstacles to trade and investment, which both sides need to work out. Most ASEAN countries are feeling the weight of the China factor. The issue is how both sides can work upon this integration exercise in order to promote greater specialization as the basis for intra-industry trade between the two parties. There should be room for common interests to be discussed further as both ASEAN and China are still developing regions in connection with the global production networks operating from abroad and within the region.

Of course, things will not move far if the two sides are not paying enough attention to potential opportunities and arising conflicts. At the moment, both sides need to engage in this joint undertaking, continuously and seriously. The groundwork for liberalization and cooperation is key and should be relevant enough for both sides to reflect the industrial restructuring that is underway in response to the forces of globalization and regionalization taking place. Studies show increasing economic interdependence could be further deepened with a proper market-friendly policy framework. In this regard, China needs to show more in deeds rather than in words.

Progress towards an ACFTA should also be consistent with the multilateral and regional liberalization framework. ASEAN has long experienced the WTO process[60] and its regional integration, now known as the ASEAN Economic Community (AEC). China's integration with the global economy is more of a recent phenomena, especially its recent accession to the WTO. The proliferation of bilateral and regional arrangements in Asia, in particular, after the Asian crisis, requires this ACFTA to go beyond its own thrust, and to consider as well what other processes this bilateral commitment could foster.

NOTES

1. China's leaders are struggling to find the right mix of administrative and market tools to cool down an overheating economy. *The Wall Street Journal*, 18 May 2004, p. A17.

2. The locomotive effect of China accounted for 13 per cent of global economic growth in 2003. While Chinese exports have been growing by about 30 per cent per year, its imports have grown even faster, by about 40 per cent in 2003. *Newsweek*, January 26, 2004, p. 35. China is expected to account for 15 per cent in 2004. *The Wall Street Journal*, 18 May 2004, p. A17.

3. 2010, the end-date for the original ASEAN-5 plus Brunei and 2015 for the new ASEAN-4 member countries. The Philippines requested China to postpone the date to 2015.

4. Vietnam joined ASEAN in 1995, then Laos and Myanmar in 1997, and lastly, Cambodia in 1999.

5. Since 1993, a growing China is seen as hollowing out FDI from ASEAN and this trend has become a major complaint among ASEAN members. See the later analysis on the topic.

6. Figure in 2003.

7. China cannot be a region by itself nor does it need to be part of any region (Wang Gungwu 2004, p. 2).

8. ASEAN members remain considerably varied in terms of population, growth, per capita income, economic regimes and levels of economic development, for example.

9. Which started earlier.

10. Which became close to US$1,000.

11. ASEAN Secretariat (2001), "Forging Closer ASEAN China economic relations in the twenty-first century" a report submitted by the ASEAN-China Expert Group on Economic Cooperation, October, p. 1.

12. *Bangkok Post*, 9 February 2004.

13. Quoted as a major reason for this growing deficit. See later in the analysis.

14. Myanmar's import is the only exception. See Wang Wei-cheng 2004, p. 8.

15. ASEAN's less developed economies like Indonesia, the Philippines and Vietnam compete with more directly China. Also, China's economic presence will be felt more intensely in higher technology areas, where ASEAN's more developed economies, Malaysia, Singapore and Thailand have been competitive. Singapore decided to move from hi-tech electronics into the areas of biotechnology. Malaysia and Thailand have yet to come out with a clear programme.

16. *World Investment Report* 2002.

17. Or 16 per cent of the total FDI of Singapore, Department of Statistics, Singapore.

18. As in the case of Charoen Pokphand (CP), an agro-business conglomerate from Thailand that has long established its presence in China.

19. *World Investment Report*, 2003, p. 41.

20. China's large domestic market, strong economic growth, increasing export competitiveness and accession to the WTO are all reasons for investors' interest in locating operations in that country. See *World Investment Report*, 2003, p. 42.

21. Estimates on the percentage of FDI China has received vary but they range from 30 to 50 per cent of all investments bound for East Asia. See Ba (2004), p. 98.

22. As Indonesia accounts for about 60 per cent of the decline in FDI to ASEAN in 2001 registered a net increase over the average annual totals registered from 1990 to 1995. See Ba (2004), p. 98.
23. See Ho (2001), p. 693, cited in Ba (2004), p. 98.
24. See later in the analysis.
25. Estimated to be 15 per cent of total FDI in China.
26. As China will trade and interact more with other countries, this development would be positive for others.
27. China could wipe out a variety of industries in other countries as it could act as the manufacturing workshop of the world.
28. Two-thirds of the reason, as Kenichi Ohmae put it. See Thomas Friedman, *The Ann Arbor News*, 30 April 2004, p. A7. China is literally dragging Japan out of its slump. China is absorbing so many Japanese exports there are not enough ships to bring them over.
29. Malaysia's percentage of world palm oil is 51 per cent, or 6 per cent of its total exports. Malaysia is also the top exporter of the world's US$13 billion palm oil trade. See the *Wall Street Journal*, 21 May 2004.
30. Close to US$3 billion, thus making it the world's largest rubber exporter. *The Wall Street Journal*, 28 May 2004.
31. This has squeezed the cash flow margins of consumer goods manufacturers: On the one hand, they are facing the rising cost of raw materials and intermediate inputs; on the other hand, they cannot increase the price of finished goods, with many of the firms struggling with price falls. Some say China is caught in something that can be described as "bi-flation", a combination of inflation and deflation at the same time. See Shan, Weijian, *the Asian Wall Street Journal*, 19–21 March 2004, p. A7.
32. Thailand, for example, has benefited from Chinese investors using the country as a gateway to the ASEAN market. *Far Eastern Economic Review*, 5 February 2004, p. 26.
33. Several reasons are advanced for this new wave of Chinese overseas investment: Overcapacity in some sectors combining with sluggish domestic demand and declining profit margins forced manufacturers to move overseas. Well-known cases are Haier, the consumer-goods conglomerate, Changhong and Konka, electronics giants. *Far Eastern Economic Review*, ibid, p. 27.
34. A report submitted in October 2001. See <http://www.aseansec.org/newdata/asean_china_bc.htgm>.
35. Declaration made at an international workshop on "China's Entry into WTO: Challenges and Areas of Cooperation", Bangkok, 14–15 November 2002.
36. Declaration made at the ASEAN Summit in Phnom Penh, November 2002.
37. A report on "Forge Closer ASEAN-China Economic Relations in the 21st Century". See pp. 4, 6 and 7. Cited in Ba (2004).
38. See Press Statement by the Chairman of the Seventh ASEAN Summit and the three ASEAN+1 Summits, ASEAN Secretariat, 2001 (unpublished).

39. See further details.
40. The Philippines requested to be placed in the second group of new members which have been accepted by China.
41. Including any commitments covered under the "early harvest" programme under the framework agreement.
42. Existing Annex 1 and Annex 2.
43. With 13 rules including the "ACFTA content" of at least 40 per cent.
44. See the next section.
45. It remains to be seen what is the kind of "dynamic timepath" of such a creation (Bhagwati 1993).
46. Singapore has formalized several bilateral FTAs. Thailand entered similar deals as well as other some other ASEAN countries.
47. As a result, rice output will drop by 3.3 per cent and the sectoral trade balance will decline by US$515.8 million.
48. Sugar output will drop by 6.3 per cent and the sectoral trade balance will decline by US$275 million.
49. Malaysia's palm oil boom from increased demand from China will send a re-configuration of the pecking order of Malaysia that represents 51 per cent out of US$13 million of the world's palm oil trade. *The Wall Street Journal*, 21 May 2004, C.1.
50. Since deliberations assigned to expert panels changed from making determinations on the basis of objective evidence rather than political considerations (Greenwald 1996).
51. One should not assume that the China-ASEAN economic relationship will devolve into one where China exports only primary goods and commodities from Southeast Asia, while flooding it with cheap manufactured products.
52. Krumm and Khanas (2003), The World Bank, p. 11. Cited in Ba (2004).
53. Cited in Ba (2004), p. 279.
54. Wang Gungwu (2004).
55. At the ASEAN Summit in October 2003.
56. Japan's commitment in the region should not be underestimated by ASEAN. So, ASEAN's major challenge is to regain confidence of major foreign investments like Japan, the EU, the U.S. and Asian NIEs, all which have been important partners in the region's development.
57. For China, the word "multipolarity" is suggestive of opposition to U.S. "unilateralism" (Wang Wei-cheng 2004).
58. Chinese Premier Wen Jiabao affirmed that China subscribed to the idea of "*heping jueqi*" and needed a peacful international development and a stable domestic development.
59. With Australia and New Zealand, and some other trading partners.
60. Except a few countries like Laos and Myanmar, and Vietnam, which are not yet WTO members.

REFERENCES

Ba, A.D. "The Role of East Asia in ASEAN-China Relations". Paper prepared for the international conference on "Southeast Asia and China: Global Changes and Regional Challenges", organized by the Centre for Southeast Asia Study, National Sun Yat-sen University, Kaoshung, Taiwan, 4–6 March 2004 (mimeograph).

Bhagwati, J., P. Krisna and A. Panagariya. *Trading Blocs: Alternative Approaches to Analyzing Preferential Trade Agreements* (Cambridge: MIT Press, 1999).

Chirathivat, S. Interdependence between China and Southeast Asian Economies on the Eve of the Accession of China into the WTO. In *China Enters WTO: Pursuing the Symbiosis with the Global Economy*, edited by Yamazawa, I. and K. Imai (Tokyo: The Institute of Developing Economies, 2001).

Chirathivat, S. "ASEAN-China Economic Partnership in an Integrating World Economy". *Chulalongkorn Review* 14 (2002*a*): 98–114.

Chirathivat, S. "ASEAN-China FTA: Background, Implications and Future Development". *Journal of Asian Economics* 13 (2002*b*): 671–86.

Chirathivat, S. and E. Albert. "Resister a la Chine", *Outre-terre*, no. 6 (2003): 257–72.

Chirathivat, S. and S. Mallikamas. "ASEAN-China FTA: Potential Outcome for Participating Countries". Paper prepared for the international conference on "Southeast Asia and China: Global Changes and Regional Challenges", organized by the Centre for Southeast Asia Study, National Sun Yat-sen University, Kaoshung, Taiwan, 4–6 March 2004 (mimeograph).

Day, P. and P. Batra. "China Effect: Food Prices Are Rising". *The Wall Street Journal*, 30 April 2004, p. A13.

Dutta, M. "Asian Economic Community: Intra-Community Macro- and Micro-Economic Parameters". A paper presented at the annual meeting of AEA in Atlanta, GA, 1 June 2002 (mimeograph).

Felker, G. "Southeast Asian Industrialization and the Changing Global Production System". *Third World Quarterly* 24, no. 2 (2003): 255–82.

Funabashi, Y. "China's Long Term Strategy: Peaceful Ascendancy". *International Herald Tribune/The Asahi Shinbun*, 2 December 2003.

Fu-Kao, L, and P. Regnier. *Regionalism in East Asia: Paradigm Shifting* (London: RoutledgeCurzon, 2003).

Gordon, B.K. "A High Risk Trade Policy". *Foreign Affairs* 82, no. 4 (2003).

Ho, K.H. "Rituals, Risks, and Rivalries: China and ASEAN in the Coming Decades". *Journal of Contemporary China* 10, no. 29 (2001): 683–94.

Ho, K.L. "ASEAN+1 or China+1? Regionalism and Regime Interests in ASEAN-China Relations". Paper prepared for the international conference on "Southeast Asia and China: Global Changes and Regional Challenges", organized by the Centre for Southeast Asia Study, National Sun Yat-sen University, Kaoshung, Taiwan, 4–6 March 2004 (mimeograph).

Krumm, K. and H. Kharas. *East Asia Integrates: A Trade Policy for Shared Growth*. The World Bank, Washington D.C., 2003.

Lloyd, P.J. New Bilateralism in the Asia Pacific. *The World Economy* 25 (2002): 1279–96.

Mallikamas, S. *A Study of Thailand's Readiness to Establish Free Trade Areas.* CAMGEM Development Project, Faculty of Economics, Chulalongkorn University, Bangkok, Thailand, 2002.

Regnier, P. "Economic Cooperation in East Asia: Revisiting Regional Concepts and the Subregional Case of ASEAN". In *Regionalism in East Asia: Paradigm Shifting*, edited by Fu-Kao, L. and P. Regnier (London: RoutledgeCurzon, 2003), pp. 52–68.

Sachs, J.D. "Welcome to the Asian Century". *Fortune,* 26 January 2004, pp. 38–39.

Shan, Weijian. "China Must Cool Down to Sustain Growth". *The Wall Street Journal,* 19–21 March 2004, p. A7.

UNCTAD. *World Investment Report 2003*, Geneva.

Vatikiotis, M. "China: Investment Outward Bound". *Far Eastern Economic Review,* 5 February 2004, pp. 24–27.

Wang, Gungwu. "Changes in Regional Perceptions". Paper prepared for the international conference on "Southeast Asia and China: Global Changes and Regional Challenges", organized by the Centre for Southeast Asia Study, National Sun Yat-sen University, Kaoshung, Taiwan, 4–6 March 2004 (mimeograph).

Wang, V. Wei-cheng. "China's FTA with ASEAN Countries: Economic Statecraft of Peaceful Ascendancy". Paper prepared for the international conference on "Southeast Asia and China: Global Changes and Regional Challenges", organized by the Center for Southeast Asia Study, National Sun Yat-sen University, Kaoshung, Taiwan, 4–6 March 2004 (mimeograph).

Zhang, Yunling. "East Asian Regionalism and China". *Issues and Studies* (June 2002): 213–23.

18
China's Business Environment: A Macro Economic Perspective

Yuwa Hedrick-Wong

A macro perspective on China's business environment is important because business executives and investors need to understand what is driving China's growth in terms of both cyclical and structural factors, so that they can plan and manage with better market insights that are anchored in a broader and longer-term perspective. Accordingly, this chapter seeks to answer three key questions, covering both the short and the long term, which could help develop such insights. These questions are:

(i) What is the outlook in terms of the "hard" and "soft" landing debate and what is really driving China's growth?
(ii) What are some of the real bottlenecks to growth?
(iii) What are some of the most critical challenges to China's longer term growth prospects?

OUTLOOK IN TERMS OF THE "HARD" AND "SOFT" LANDING DEBATE AND WHAT IS REALLY DRIVING CHINA'S GROWTH

The whole debate over "hard" and "soft" landing is completely misguided. The primary distinguishing feature of the current economic expansion in

China is that it is led by the private sector. This marks it as completely different from all previous cycles of expansion since the 1978 opening of the economy. The private sector in China today is driven almost entirely by business profitability, which is in turn dependent on buoyant demand. They have had little access to bank financing, and because they invested with their own funds, they are insensitive to either bank credit tightening or higher interest rates. As long as they are enjoying high returns, which they are, they will continue to expand, and there is little the government can do about it. China's private sector entrepreneurs live and die by their profits, and hence are closely tuned to changes in the market.

So what is the big fuss about the government bringing in new measures to curb investment and to "cool" down economic growth? The fact is that the government acted earlier this year in a proactive way to curb excessive investment in the public sector, primarily the state-owned enterprises. This is a reflection of how much the Chinese leadership has taken to heart the lessons learned from the last boom-bust cycle of 1993–94. At that time, the surge in growth was almost exclusively led by massive investment made by state-owned enterprises, with loans from the large state banks. Much of the investment was ill-conceived. Many state-owned enterprises made the investment not because there was a business case to justify it, but just because they could secure the loans to do so. Many managers in the state-owned enterprises treated bank loans as "free" money that they could spend in any way they liked to expand their operations, very often in areas completely unrelated to their core businesses. Thus, government ministries opened hotels, enterprises in heavy industries operated department stores, and construction companies ran restaurants. This inevitably led to over-investment and poor returns, and, worse, accelerating inflation. As the government attempted to rein in inflation by ordering the state banks to tighten credit, it quickly led to an economic downturn. Not surprisingly, many state-owned enterprises defaulted in servicing the bank loans as their investment went sour. In the process, record high non-performing loans resulted in China's banking sector — a legacy that is still haunting the large state banks today. This time around, the government is determined to prevent a repeat of such colossal mistakes, and hence the measures introduced in early 2004 to scrutinize the large loans lent to state-owned enterprises, and instructions to state bank management to curb lending to certain sectors, such as steel, that has experienced rapid increase in production capacity. These are measures aimed proactively to prevent a repeat of the boom-bust cycle of the past, and not to curb growth in general.

So it is the private sector that is driving real growth in China today. The expansion of the private sector is a result of a series of reforms in recent years, which have created a much more welcoming environment to China's private entrepreneurs. The recognition of private property rights is a big step forward, and in many ways a milestone in China's economic reform. The labour market has also been liberalized, especially in terms of the relaxation of restrictions on the movement of migrant labour to urban centres. Most prices have been freed up, which provide better signals to entrepreneurs in terms of supply and demand. Steadily improving transportation and logistics, especially in the interior region, have allowed private businesses to access markets there more efficiently. Rapid urbanization itself has in turn created new and bigger markets.

Perhaps the most important factor of all is the growth of China's new middle class, which is the driving force behind the demand for goods and services that fuels entrepreneurial activities. Defined as someone earning US$5,000 or more per year, the size of the middle class is estimated at about 65 million individuals today, and is expected to double in numbers by 2010. Their growing consumption power is also a key factor behind China's massive rise in imports. We have estimated that domestic consumption destined imports, indexed at 100 in January 1997, rose to 360 by the end of 2003, over three and a half times higher within six years, an astonishing rate of growth.

The structural factors that underpin these new developments and sources of growth can be understood in terms of two long economic cycles that are transforming China's economy. The first is a medium-term cycle, typically around eight to ten years long, driven by a fundamental overhaul of the capital stock and capital expansion. China's economy is in the early phase of this cycle which is seeing rapid replacement of the Soviet era industrial infrastructure by twenty-first century technology and equipment.

Simultaneously there is a second long cycle operating. This is the demographic and urbanization cycle, which is even longer and will run for the next fifteen years or more. It consists of two dimensions. The first is the mass movement of people from the rural to the urban region. The relaxation of the strict residency control in recent years has set this process in motion. Its implication on China's productivity growth is immense. The very same rural migrant, upon arriving at an urban centre and starting work as an industrial worker of some kind, even at the low end of the wage and skill spectrum, is many times more productive than in his previous role in the village as a peasant. The higher income that he earns is then remitted to the home village to support his family's consumption, which in turn helps alleviate rural poverty.

The second dimension is the rapid pace of urbanization itself. Hundreds of small towns are being upgraded to urban centre status through improvement in transportation and communications infrastructure, as well as urban developments within the towns themselves. Based on research that we conducted in 2003 in partnership with the National Economic Research Institute in Beijing in which the drivers of consumption are identified and assessed individually for thirty of China's thirty-one provinces, the pace of urbanization turns out to be the single most important factor next to income — holding income constant, the faster the pace of urbanization, the quicker the rate of growth of private consumption. Thus, the combination of mass rural-urban migration alongside with rapid urbanization is boosting income and raising consumption level for the vast majority of China's rural people, turning millions of them into urban dwellers over the next decade and a half or more.

These structural factors are the bedrocks of China's long-term prospect for continuing high growth, quite separate from the short-term ups and downs and volatility. China's private sector entrepreneurs are tapping into this source of growth to build their businesses, expand their reach, and transform China's business environment in the process.

BOTTLENECKS TO GROWTH

A common refrain repeatedly heard both in the media and among analysts is that China's high rates of growth could come to a crashing halt because of its shaky banking sector. While there is no question that China's state banks are saddled with high levels of non-performing loans, they are unlikely to crash in the foreseeable future to bring down the entire financial sector, nor would they jeopardize China's high growth trajectory in the years to come.

Again, it is important to sort out the myth from the reality. The following table summarizes key items contributing to China's total contingent fiscal liability, thus providing a fuller picture on the fiscal burden of the government, and a basis for better informed discussion.

The first item refers to the level of non-performing loans in China's state banks. Official estimates put the level of non-performing loans at around 25 per cent of GDP. Many independent analysts believe this is too low. Standard & Poor, the credit rating agency, for example, believes that the level of non-performing loans is likely to be at about 40 per cent of GDP. This is because they have serious concerns over the quality of the assets put up by many borrowers as collateral, primarily the state-owned enterprises — many such assets are simply worth much less than what is assumed by the banks. To err on the conservative side, the Standard & Poor's estimate of 40 per cent is used in this analysis.

At the end of 2003, the outstanding liability of the asset management companies (AMCs), to whom the state banks had transferred a great deal of their non-performing loans, is estimated at another 10 per cent of GDP. The government's domestic debt is quite low at 17.2 per cent of GDP. Foreign debt is even lower at 13.9 per cent of GDP. Hence the total contingent liability is estimated at 81.1 per cent of GDP. This is by no means an unmanageable fiscal burden.

China's Overall Contingent Liability	2003 (% of GDP)
S&P NPL estimate	40.0
Liability of AMCs	10.0
Government domestic debt	17.2
Total foreign debt	13.9
Total contingent liability	81.1
Budget deficit	2.2
Foreign reserve	US$405 billion
Growth rate of budget revenue (3-year average)	20% YoY

Source: National Economic Research Institute.

It is important to take into account other aspects of the government's fiscal ledgers as well. Budget deficit remains very low at 2.2 per cent of GDP at the end of last year. Foreign reserve, meantime, is huge at US$405 billion, and is continuing to rise. The tax base is expanding, and the government is also getting better at tax collection — budget revenue has been growing at around 20 per cent per year in the recent past.

So, the often sounded alarm regarding the high levels of non-performing loans is quite manageable as long as China continues on its trajectory of reform and market liberalization. Nor are power and related supply shortages serious bottlenecks to growth. Infrastructure investment continues to be high and many of these supply shortages will be effectively dealt with in the coming quarters, if not months.

From the point of view of private businesses — both domestic and foreign — the real potential bottleneck to growth is likely to occur in a different and unexpected place, human resource. It may sound counterintuitive to suggest that human resource could be a bottleneck to growth in China. Again, we hear all the time in the media and elsewhere the "inexhaustible" supply of labour in China. How could human resource be a potential bottleneck to growth?

It has to do with the quality rather than quantity of China's human resources. It is indeed true that the supply of unskilled and low-skilled labour is virtually inexhaustible in the foreseeable future. The emerging bottlenecks, however, are in the supply of well-trained and skill-intensive labour supply.

It is a feature of China's growth today that the entire spectrum of production, from the low-tech and low-skill end to the high-tech and knowledge-intensive end, is expanding at the same time. In recent years, FDI in the coastal region, especially around Greater Shanghai, has become very technology- and capital-intensive. Correspondingly the demand for highly trained and well educated workers, with good English proficiency, has been rising fast. They are now needed by foreign businesses, domestic SOEs, as well as the private sector businesses alike. It is in this area that bottlenecks have emerged.

According to manpower recruitment agencies in the Greater Shanghai area, wages commanded by Chinese workers with good tertiary education, proficient English, and familiarity with advanced business management structure and tools, have more than doubled between the 2003–04 period. This level of wage increase is clearly unsustainable, and if the trend continues, it would erode much of the cost advantage as well as operational efficiency of the entire coastal region — the fastest growing and most dynamic parts of China.

Furthermore, this shortage of highly trained and skilled manpower is not something that can be rectified overnight. With power shortage, what is needed is more power plants, and once built, they only need to be switched on and the new supply is available. Highly trained and skilled manpower cannot be produced in such a way in a hurry. While enrolment in post-secondary education has been expanding rapidly in recent years, the quality of graduates remains highly uneven. Only a handful of top education institutions have the capability of producing world class graduates, and they remain few. The struggle in the coming years is to improve the quality of higher education itself, which is a long-term proposition. More public and private investment and resources are needed, and participation by international players, including top graduate schools from the United States and Europe, will be necessary to train the next generations of China's scientists, engineers, and business and management executives. Until then, the threat of bottlenecks in the supply of the top-tiered manpower remains.

THE MOST CRITICAL CHALLENGES TO CHINA'S LONG-TERM GROWTH PROSPECTS

Since the 1978 opening of the Chinese economy, a great deal of creative destruction has happened, and a lot more is on the way. The results achieved thus far are beyond dispute. Real per capita income has risen five folds since 1978, from around US$200 to over US$1,100 today, an astonishing feat. Nor is it achieved with a sharp divide between the rich and poor. The World Bank has estimated that in the fifteen years between the early1980s and mid-1990s, some 350 million Chinese were lifted above the poverty line, defined as surviving at one U.S. dollar a day or less. This is equivalent to lifting 70 per cent of the total population of ASEAN-10 from poverty, and is the most successful poverty alleviation effort ever recorded in modern history.

The impact of China's economic growth has been felt globally. Over the period of 1995 to 2003, the U.S. economy dominated in nominal terms in contributing to the growth of the global economy, accounting for about two-thirds of total global GDP growth. When translated into purchasing power parity terms, however, China's contribution looms large at 25 per cent, surpassing the United States' contribution at 18 per cent, rest of Asia's 16 per cent, EU's 14 per cent, and Japan's minuscule 2.5 per cent.[1]

China's economic growth has also been a major factor pulling Asia-Pacific forward. In 2002, for example, China became Korea's largest export market, taking over from the United States. Chinese imports from Japan, especially in machinery and machine tools, have been instrumental in boosting Japanese growth since 2002. China's growing needs for raw materials are firming up commodity prices worldwide, benefiting producers from Southeast Asia to South America. China became the world's largest consumer market for mobile phones in 2001, for steel in 2002, and the world's second largest personal computer market, second only to the United States, by the end of 2003.

Over the period of the first eight months of 2003, a time of high uncertainty because of the Iraq war and the SARS outbreak, China's rapidly rising imports from the rest of Asia was a virtual lifeline to many of the region's struggling economies. Estimates of the impact of China's imports are summarized in the table below.

Given China's current position in the global economy, and what it will likely occupy in the future, it is important to address the question of what are some of the most critical challenges to China's long-term growth prospects.

A remarkable feature of China's economic reform up to now is that it has been tightly controlled from the top-down. A top-down approach is made

| | January – August 2003 | |
Country	Exports to China as % of total exports	% of export growth accounted for by exports to China
Australia	7	37
Hong Kong	34	31
Indonesia	5	11
Japan	10	42
Korea	18	41
Malaysia	5	7
New Zealand	5	8
Philippines	7	11
Singapore	5	19
Taiwan	22	37
Thailand	5	8

Source: Morgan Stanley.

workable with creative destruction because the reform process itself has been compartmentalized. Since 1978, it has been a step-by-step process of the dismantling of the commune, the establishment of the "special export zones", the reduction of the role of the state-owned enterprises, and, finally, the WTO membership and its schedule of market opening and liberalization. In this entire process, the government is in firm control.

In recent years, the power of the private sector has been unleashed. As mentioned above, the private sector today is the real driver of economic growth and business expansion. For the first time since the founding of the People's Republic in 1949, private businesses are legitimized. Even though private businesses had already come into existence in the 1980s, they were surviving in a kind of "twilight zone" up to then. They were more tolerated than embraced by the government. By the early 1990s, however, private business — many of which were a murky blend of ownership of private individuals, bureaucrats, and local governments — had started to flourish.

In the late 1990s, with the reform and downsizing of the state sector gathering steam, private businesses were seen as an indispensable part of reform — they could create jobs for the newly unemployed state workers. Private sector businesses finally stepped out of the twilight zone and became a legitimate plank of the overall reform efforts.

From that point onward, it is increasingly difficult for Beijing to control the pace and scope of reform in a top-down fashion. One very important feature of this new phase of reform is the consumption revolution that has been transforming China in the past several years. At first, the government promoted private ownership of homes as a means to shore up the sagging construction industry. Once the floodgate was open, however, things did not stop with home ownership. Home ownership in turn encouraged purchases of household appliances and furniture, and supported the rapid growth of a whole new industry — home improvement and innovations and the "do it yourself" supplies. With home purchases came mortgage lending and the development of a consumer credit culture. As a result, consumer credit as a percentage of total bank credit outstanding grew from virtually zero in 1998 to close to 15 per cent in 2003 — an astonishing rate of growth, even though it is still far below the level of 40 per cent in the United States.

Viewed from a larger historical perspective, the consumption revolution is a radical and fundamental departure from the policies and ideologies of the past. Under all centrally planned systems, the role of consumption is either ignored outright or relegated to that of an afterthought. The focus is always on production. That is why all centrally planned systems failed. This fixation with production is also true for China even in the first ten to fifteen years in the post-1978 reform period.

Consumption, however, is at the heart of the value creation process, and thus is critically important to efficient resource allocation and productivity, and thereby the welfare of any society. Inputs to production, regardless of how costly, are ultimately meaningless if the final output is not something that consumers want. When consumers are given the rights and choices to select what they want in a multi-participant market, they are then in the driver's seat in value creation. At a given price, their preferences that collectively determine the demand for every product and service are the signals that producers must heed to determine what to invest and how much to invest in order to have the right kinds and levels of product to make a profit. And, as consumer preferences shift, so must producers follow suit if they are to stay in business. So consumption determines value. And consumers "vote" with their wallets on a daily basis in the greatest democracy on earth — the multi-participant market — as they make their purchases.

This represents a complete reversal of the top-down economic management structure of the past in China when the central government decided what to produce and how much to produce, and the state banks lent to the SOEs accordingly to make the investment needed, and whatever was produced was automatically deemed to have value. The absurd extreme of this practice is perhaps exemplified by the disastrous "Great Leap Forward" launched by the Chinese Government in the late 1950s.

Obsessed with steel production, which was seen as a sign of successful industrialization and progress, China's central government in the late 1950s decided to increase steel production massively under the slogan of "catching up to Great Britain in five years". Lacking production capacity to undertake such a Herculean task, Mao decided that, analogous to the "people's war" concept, every village should produce their share of steel and thus contribute to the national effort. A massive campaign was launched and every village in China was instructed to build its "backyard" furnace to make steel. Not surprisingly, not many villages had their own supply of iron ore, so village leaders started to collect cast iron household utensils, window frames in public buildings, gates and bells in ancestral shrines, etc. and melted them down as raw materials for the village furnaces to make steel. Again, not surprisingly, the quality of the "steel" produced, due to the poorly constructed village furnaces and utter lack of expertise of the villagers, was practically useless. Thus, useful items were destroyed to make a useless output, which was then proudly reported to the central government in terms of tons of "steel" produced. The central government then proudly reported to the whole country that the campaign was successful and socialism triumphed once again. Meantime, famine started to sweep across the country, and before the "Great Leap Forward" was stopped when it became plain for all to see that it was a massive leap backward, it is estimated that some twenty million Chinese peasants had died in the resultant famine.

The consumption revolution that was ignited in the late 1990s in China, in contrast, is a genuine great leap forward. There are several distinctive features in China's consumption revolution that are unprecedented. The first is that the domestic private sector has been the primary beneficiary of the consumption revolution. China's private sector, consisting of mostly small and medium-sized businesses, expanded rapidly in recent years. A unique characteristic of China's private sector is that these small and medium-sized businesses got going without bank financing, and were at once launched into an intensively competitive environment, and face high hurdles in product and service quality. Many face competition from imports. This in turn makes those who can survive and prosper in such an environment highly competitive and independent from the government. It is difficult to assess the exact size of the private sector, especially the small and medium-sized businesses. A good proxy measure, however, is in their ability to create jobs. Over the course of 1995 to 2003, roughly some three to five million urban workers were retrenched in the state sector per year. Taking an average of four million per year, this comes to thirty-six million. In spite of this massive influx of the newly unemployed, urban unemployment rate has remained low at around three per cent.[2] This means that private businesses have been able to create at least around four million new jobs per year, not a mean feat given the extremely challenging environment in which they operate. China's new generation of entrepreneurs is clearly a tough and resilient lot. This is confirmed by the high ranking that China receives in the "Total Entrepreneurial Activity Index", compiled by the Global Entrepreneurship Monitor, which places China second only to Korea in Asia, with a score of 12.3, and higher than that of the United States' 10.5.

The second is that the price mechanism is today functioning far more effectively in the private sector. Entrepreneurs tend to respond quicker and better to price signals, and as their investment is based mostly on their own hard earned cash and family savings, they tend to invest more prudently. More effective price signals mean higher capital allocation efficiency. It is therefore encouraging to note that the government is pushing to get the price signals to function better in the state sector as well. In November 2003 Beijing issued new rules explicitly defining and banning cartels and price fixing, which are common practices by SOEs. This move filled a gap in the regulation of the market economy, especially at a time when private sector businesses are increasingly coming into direct competition against SOEs, and thus set the stage for introducing anti-trust laws.

Figure 18.1
China's Great Entrepreneurial Dynamism:
Giving the Small Guys a Chance

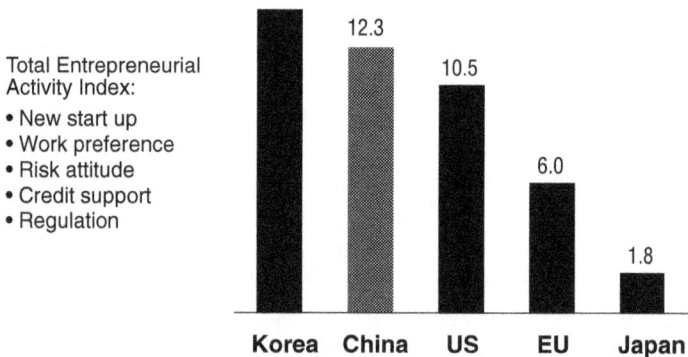

Total Entrepreneurial
Activity Index:
• New start up
• Work preference
• Risk attitude
• Credit support
• Regulation

Korea   China   US   EU   Japan

(Global Entrepreneurship Monitor)

Source: Global Entrepreneurship Monitor.

The consumption revolution in China therefore has ushered in a far less restricted process of creative destruction than ever before. The pace is set to accelerate. Urban property owners are asserting their property rights, challenging local government's unilateral decisions when their rights are infringed upon. Private business owners are increasingly doing the same, encouraged by official recognition of their status as a legitimate segment of the society. The WTO mandated market liberalization schedule, on the other hand, is opening up new business opportunities for private businesses all the time. The state sector is being downsized continuously, which means the SOEs are less and less protected. The scope for creative destruction, driven from the bottom up by entrepreneurs, is being enlarged all the time.

With the private sector, in urban as well as rural areas, emerging as the vanguard of economic growth, and with the consumption revolution placing more and more power in the hands of the consumer, the government's direct control over the economy is steadily eroded. What, then, will govern China's marketplace?

A critical challenge in the coming years is therefore the urgent necessity to build viable, transparent, and effective public institutions that can set and enforce the rules needed for a market economy to function properly. In other words, these are the institutions needed to allow creative destruction to operate effectively with minimum disruptive impact. In China one set of such institutions are the large state owned banks.

The four largest state owned banks[3] collectively employ some 1.4 million employees, have 116,000 branches nation-wide, account for over 60 per cent of total bank loans outstanding, and hold 67 per cent of the country's deposits. The official estimate is that their non-performing loans approach 25 per cent of total loans outstanding. As mentioned above, outside industry estimates put the estimate at 40 per cent of their total loans. These are institutions of monstrous size, and are technically insolvent.

As stated before, they have been used by the central government as policy-driven lending tools, hence their high levels of non-performing loans. Most of their mid-ranking managers, numbering in the hundreds of thousands, have no clue in terms of proper risk assessment and management, and have never worked with private businesses. They will face stiff foreign competition in a few years' time as the financial sector is due to be fully liberalized according to the WTO schedule. Hence they face the daunting twin tasks of cleaning up the bad loans while gearing up for stiff competition. These they must accomplish if China is to avoid a run on its state banks, and the chaos that would ensue.

While a restructured banking sector would immensely assist the development of the private sector, increasingly the focus is on the judiciary. Commercial disputes can only increase with more and more private businesses being created, especially the small and medium-sized ones. As foreign investment continues to grow, disputes between Chinese and foreign business interests are also becoming more commonplace. An impartial, transparent, and effective system for resolving commercial disputes will be one of the critical underpinnings needed to meet the institutional challenges in coping with the creative destruction process.

The challenge of institution development, then, will determine, over the longer term, how successful creative destruction is to become in China. Much has been achieved, often against tremendous odds. But the long-term success can be secured only when this challenge is effectively met.

NOTES

1. Estimates by the Bank Credit Analyst, 2003.
2. This excludes the migrant workers who are rural residents but work in urban centres.
3. They are the Bank of China, Industrial and Commercial Bank of China, Agricultural Bank of China, and Construction Bank of China.

19

Business Environment and Opportunities in Shanghai

Zhang Youwen

RAPID ECONOMIC DEVELOPMENT PROVIDING OPPORTUNITY FOR COOPERATION BETWEEN ASEAN AND CHINA

China's twenty-five years of reform has witnessed rapid development in foreign trade. Since the 1990s, especially with the FTA between ASEAN and China being put forward into the agenda, the economic and trade relationship between the two parties has experienced even more rapid development. Like the United States, Japan and the EU, ASEAN has become equally important and will become an increasingly important trade partner for China.

ASEAN has been one of the most important trade partners of China. From 1995 to 2002, the bilateral trade volume has increased annually at the rate of 19.1 per cent. The high growth rate has been maintained even though the global trend has been moving in the opposite direction as a result of the global economic depression and "9/11" event. In 2002 the bilateral trade volume broke the historical record, reaching US$54.8 billion with the growth rate as high as 31.8 per cent.

According to the statistics, ASEAN has become China's fifth largest trade partner, with the bilateral trade volume accounting for 9.2 per cent of China's entire foreign trade volume, next only to Japan, the United States, EU and Hong Kong (Table 19.1).

Table 19.1
China's Top Ten Trade Partners (2003)

Rank	Country/Region	Volume (US$ Billions)	% of total
	Total	851.21	100
1	Japan	133.57	15.7
2	U.S.	126.33	14.8
3	EU	125.22	14.7
4	Hong Kong SAR, China	87.41	10.3
5	ASEAN	78.25	9.2
6	Korea	63.23	7.4
7	Taiwan Province	58.37	6.9
8	Russia	15.76	1.9
9	Australia	13.56	1.6
10	Canada	10.01	1.2

Note: Ranking by value of trade.
Source: Ministry of Commerce of the People's Republic of China.
<http://www.mofcom.gov.cn/jinchukou.shtml>.

Noticeably, ASEAN has been more important as an import source to China than as an export market. In 2003, while China's export to ASEAN accounted for 7.1 per cent of China's total exports, China's import from ASEAN accounted for 11.5 per cent of China's total imports. China's imports from ASEAN is close to its imports from EU or America (Tables 19.2 and 19.3).

Although ASEAN ranks fifth among China's top ten export markets, the export value is only half that of Japan which ranks fourth and one third that of the United States which ranks as the first. In 2003, China's export to ASEAN was 7.1 per cent of its total value, compared to 21.1 per cent for the United States and 13.6 per cent for Japan (Table 19.4).

However, ASEAN seems more important as China's import source compared with China's export market. In 2003, China's import from ASEAN amounted to 11.5 per cent of its total imports from all countries. The figure is very close to the EU's 12.9 per cent, which is ranked second, and China Taiwan's 12.0 per cent, ranked third, close to two-thirds of Japan's figure, which is ranked first and exceeds the sum of U.S. and Hong Kong imports (8.2 per cent and 2.7 per cent respectively), which are China's two largest export markets (Table 19.5). While the total import growth rate was 39.9 per cent, the import growth rate with ASEAN was 51.7 per cent in 2003.

From the perspective of bilateral balance of trade, among China's top ten trade deficit source countries in 2003, three are from ASEAN: They are

Table 19.2
China's Export Markets (2003)

Continent/Region	Volume (US$ Billions)	% of total
China's Total Export	438.37	100
Asia	222.61	50.8
ASEAN	30.93	7.1
Middle East	16.49	3.8
six countries of the Gulf	8.09	1.8
Europe	88.27	16.5
EU	72.15	16.5
America	110.02	25.1
North America	98.14	22.4
Latin America	11.88	2.7
Australia	7.29	1.7
Africa	10.18	2.3

Source: Ministry of Commerce of the People's Republic of China.
<http://www.mofcom.gov.cn/jinchukou.shtml>.

Table 19.3
China's Import Sources (2003)

Continent/Region	Volume (US$ Billions)	% of total
Total	412.84	100
Asia	272.93	66.1
ASEAN	47.33	11.5
Middle East	15.14	3.7
Europe	69.74	16.9
EU	53.06	12.9
America	53.19	12.9
North America	38.26	9.3
Australia	8.60	2.1
Africa	8.36	2

Source: Ministry of Commerce of the People's Republic of China.
<http://www.mofcom.gov.cn/jinchukou.shtml>.

Malaysia, Thailand and the Philippines. China's deficits to these countries are US$7.85 billion, US$5.05 billion and US$3.21 billion respectively (Table 19.6). Nonetheless in 2003, among the top ten trade surplus source countries, only Vietnam was from ASEAN with a surplus of merely US$1.72 billion (Table 19.7).

Table 19.4
China's Top Ten Export Markets (2003)

Rank	Country/Region	Volume (US$ Billions)	% of total
	Total	438.37	100
1	U.S.	92.47	21.1
2	Hong Kong SAR, China	76.29	17.4
3	EU	72.15	16.5
4	Japan	59.42	13.6
5	ASEAN	30.93	7.1
6	Korea	20.10	4.6
7	Taiwan Province	9.00	2.1
8	Australia	6.26	1.4
9	Russia	6.03	1.4
10	Canada	5.63	1.3

Source: Ministry of Commerce of the People's Republic of China.
<http://www.mofcom.gov.cn/jinchukou.shtml>.

Table 19.5
China's Top Ten Import Sources (2003)

Rank	Country/Region	Volume (US$ Billions)	% of total
	Total	412.84	100.0
1	Japan	74.15	18
2	EU	53.06	12.9
3	Taiwan Province	49.36	12
4	ASEAN	47.33	11.5
5	Korea	43.13	10.4
6	U.S.	33.86	8.2
7	Hong Kong SAR, China	11.12	2.7
8	Russia	9.73	2.4
9	Australia	7.30	1.8
10	Brazil	5.84	1.4

Note: Ranking by value of import.
Source: Ministry of Commerce of the People's Republic of China.
<http://www.mofcom.gov.cn/jinchukou.shtml>.

These basic statistics show that China has become not only ASEAN's important trade partner, but also ASEAN's important export market. China has therefore played an important role in the economic growth of ASEAN countries.

The trade configuration between China and ASEAN demonstrates China's strategy of "Pursuing Mutual Benefits in Asia", which has provided increasingly

Table 19.6
China's Top Ten Deficit Sources (2003)

Rank	Country/Region	China's Deficit (US$ Billions)
1	Taiwan Province	−40.36
2	Korea	−23.04
3	Japan	−14.73
4	Malaysia	−7.85
5	Germany	−6.8
6	Thailand	−5.05
7	Brazil	−3.7
8	Russia	−3.69
9	Philippines	−3.21
10	Saudi Arabia	−3.05

Source: Ministry of Commerce of the People's Republic of China.
<http://www.mofcom.gov.cn/jinchukou.shtml>.

Table 19.7
China's Top Ten Surplus Sources (2003)

Rank	Country/Region	China's Surplus (US$ Billions)
1	Hong Kong SAR, China	65.17
2	U.S.	58.61
3	Netherlands	11.57
4	UK	7.25
5	United Arab Emirates	4.25
6	Spain	2.53
7	Hungary	1.99
8	Vietnam	1.72
9	Nigeria	1.72
10	Mexico	1.59

Source: Ministry of Commerce of the People's Republic of China.
<http://www.mofcom.gov.cn/jinchukou.shtml>.

more opportunities for cooperation between ASEAN and China. On 24 April 2004, China's President Hu Jintao delivered a speech entitled "China's Development and Asia's Opportunities" at the opening ceremony of the annual conference 2004 of the BOAO Forum. In his speech, President Hu stated: "China is a member of Asia. The development of China is closely linked to the prosperity of Asia. China has and will continue to impact actively on the development of Asia."

POSITION OF SHANGHAI AND ITS RELATIONSHIP TO ASEAN WITHIN CHINA'S OPENING

Shanghai has held an important and special position in China's opening towards the outside world. In the thirty years after the establishment of the PRC, Shanghai had been the largest industrial city in the country. In the 1980s, after the doors of China's southeast coastal areas were initially opened, Shanghai experienced a difficult period during the new development. Since the 1990s however, Shanghai identified the development and opening of Pudong as its new target, and started to build on its special position in China's economic system, that is, to be the centre of China's economy, trade and finance. After entering into the new millennium, another target for Shanghai was to develop into a sea transportation centre.

The "Four Centres" target has made Shanghai especially outstanding in terms of its position and function in the Chinese economy. Its importance has not only been justified by the GDP figures and other economic statistics, but also by its being the most important channel of foreign economic relationships.

Shanghai's Special Position in China's Opening

Shanghai is China's major export city. In 2003, its export accounted for 11.1 per cent of the total volume, next to Guangdong and Jiangsu; its import was 15.5 per cent of the total volume, next to Guangdong. Processing of imported materials carries a relatively high weight in Guangdong's export (Tables 19.8 and 19.9).

The Economic and Social Commission for Asia and Pacific (ESCAP) held its sixtieth annual conference in Shanghai from 22 to 28 April. Half a century ago in 1947, the Asian Far East Economic Committee — ESCAP's former form — was established in Shanghai. It was after more than half a century that the organization has returned to its origin of birth to hold its annual conference, where the decision to relocate its headquarters back to Shanghai was also made. The fact shows that Shanghai already held a special position half a century ago; today Shanghai is playing the same role at a much higher level. Since 1949 the headquarters of the organization had been stationed in Bangkok, Thailand, one of the member countries, where most of its annual conferences had also been held. But today, the headquarters has been relocated back to Shanghai, demonstrating China's active involvement in the Asia-Pacific cooperation. China's Vice President Zeng Qinghong in a speech he gave at the conference, recalled the great

Table 19.8
Export Volume and Percentage of Main Provinces in China (2003)

Province	Export Volume (US$ Billions)	% of total
China total	438.37	100
Guangdong	152.94	34.9
Jiangsu	59.12	13.5
Shanghai	48.46	11.1
Zhejiang	41.6	9.5
Shandong	26.56	6.1
Fujian	21.14	4.8
Beijing	16.85	3.8
Liaoning	14.63	3.3

Source: Ministry of Commerce of the People's Republic of China.
<http://www.mofcom.gov.cn/jinchukou.shtml>.

Table 19.9
Import Volume and Percentage of Provinces in China (2003)

Province	Import Volume (US$ Billions)	% of total
China total	412.84	100
Guangdong	130.7	31.7
Shanghai	63.9	15.5
Jiangsu	54.5	13.2
Beijing	51.61	12.5
Zhejiang	19.82	4.8
Shandong	18.08	4.4
Tianjin	14.99	3.6
Fujian	14.19	3.4

Source: Ministry of Commerce of the People's Republic of China.
<http://www.mofcom.gov.cn/jinchukou.shtml>.

changes that had taken place in Shanghai, China, and the entire Asia-Pacific region. He also stated that the Asia-Pacific region has turned into one of the fastest economic growth regions with the largest development potential in the world. Therefore, the relocation of the headquarters back to Shanghai is a symbol of Shanghai's continued importance in the region. No doubt, it will play an active role and contribute to the cooperation of the Asia-Pacific region.

Shanghai's Special Position in the ASEAN-China Cooperation

According to the statistics of China's customs, ASEAN became Shanghai's fourth largest trade partner in 2002, next to the United States, Japan and the EU. The trade volume between Shanghai and ASEAN was US$12.187 billion, an increase of 30 per cent compared with that in 2001. The trade volume between Shanghai and ASEAN in 2002 accounted for 8.5 per cent of Shanghai's total export and import, of which it has the largest trade volume with Singapore, the largest import growth magnitude with the Philippines, and the fastest export growth rate with Malaysia.

The business opportunities from Shanghai to ASEAN do not come from the city itself but from the delta area of the Yangtze River centred around Shanghai. The region has turned into an important investment area to various regions in the world including ASEAN, which facilitates the export of processed imported materials to ASEAN. In 2002, solely foreign-owned investment enterprises accounts for 44.3 per cent of total trade value between Shanghai and ASEAN.

Statistics show that industrial raw materials and information technology products dominate Shanghai's imports from ASEAN. Among the twenty commodities with imports valued above US$50 million, are industrial raw materials such as plastic moulds, lumber and natural rubber. Machine and electronic commodities dominate exports with US$3.954 billion, among which the export of components of auto data processing equipment has increased by 2.8 times, and the export of integrated circuits and microelectronic assembly has increased by 71.9 per cent. As for the traditional commodities, the export of textile threads, weaved products and ready-made products have increased by 43 per cent, the export of clothing and accessories have increased by 29 per cent. Additionally, there is rapid growth in Shanghai's exports to ASEAN in petroleum products, motorcycle and bicycle components.

Presently, the trade cooperation between Shanghai and ASEAN has been well grounded, as demonstrated by the following evidence:

Firstly, there are regular airlines flying between Shanghai and the major cities in ASEAN which have maintained normal communication links, including cities such as Singapore, Bangkok, Yangon and Jakarta. Recently, the airlines linkages have been expanded to newly emerged cities such as Phnom Penh and Bandar Seri Begawan. The newly developed air links have created good conditions for economic and trade relationship between Shanghai and ASEAN.

Secondly, communication between Shanghai and ASEAN has been well established. Enterprises in Shanghai are quite familiar with the Southeast Asian markets compared with that in Africa and South America, and this has enhanced the business understanding of Chinese enterprises. Consequently, the probability of business success between these two parties has been raised.

Thirdly, a few years of success of Shanghai enterprises in Southeast Asia has laid a solid foundation for further business development. Shanghai has signed contracts with some large and important engineering construction projects with successful outcomes, some of which have become the local benchmarks.

Therefore, during the process of building up the FTA between Shanghai and ASEAN, Shanghai as well as the entire delta area of the Yangtze River will be in the frontier.

The significance of Shanghai towards the cooperation between ASEAN and China is multi-faceted and multi-tiered. Generally, China's GDP per capital is about US$1,000, which is close to that of ASEAN countries. Consequently, it can compete with ASEAN countries at the same development level with similar economic structures. However as far as Shanghai is concerned, the situation is different. In 2002, the GDP per capita in Shanghai reached US$5,000 and is expected to grow to US$8,000 in 2007.

Based on the current exchange rate, Shanghai's GDP per capita in 2001 ranked between seventy-fourth and seventy-fifth in the world. Similarly, in 2002, it ranked between seventieth and seventy-first, slightly below the world average level. With the realization of US$8,000, it will rank between fifty-seventh and sixtieth.

The above analysis illustrates that Shanghai is different from ASEAN as a whole, in terms of the development stage. The GDP per capita of ASEAN is slightly higher than that of China but is one fourth that of Shanghai. Shanghai is far below Singapore and Brunei, and slightly higher than Malaysia and Thailand, but much higher than other ASEAN countries. Hence, there exist large complementary factors rather than competition between Shanghai and ASEAN.

Shanghai's objective is to turn itself into a large international metropolis. To enhance its competitiveness in every aspect has also meant enhancing its internationality and openness, which demonstrates its nature as a nuclear city with close linkages to other cities.

Table 19.10
The Position of Shanghai Ranked by GDP per Capita
(in terms of current exchange rate, 2001)

Rank	Country/city/group of countries	GDP per capita (US$)
1	Luxemburg	39,840
5	Japan	35,610
7	U.S.	34,280
	High income average	26,510
13	Hong Kong SAR, China	25,330
14	UK	25,120
20	Germany	23,560
23	France	22,730
25	Canada	21,930
26	Singapore	21,500
	EMU average	20,670
30	Italy	19,390
42	Spain	14,300
54	Korea	9,460
57	Saudi Arabia	8,460
	Shanghai (2007)	8,000
60	Argentina	6,940
70	Czech Republic	5,310
	World weighted average	5,120
	Shanghai (2002)	4,900
71	Hungary	4,830
72	Venezuela	4,760
73	Chile	4,590
	Upper middle income average	4,550
74	Croatia	4,550
	Shanghai (2001)	4,500
75	Poland	4,230
	Lower middle income average	1,230
138	China	890
	Low income	430

Source: World Bank; China Statistics.

SHANGHAI'S ECONOMIC DEVELOPMENT STRATEGY AND NEW OPPORTUNITIES OF COOPERATION BETWEEN ASEAN AND CHINA

Shanghai's rapid development as a dynamic modern international metropolis has drawn the world's attention, especially that of Southeast Asian countries. What Shanghai has achieved since the 1990s has laid a good foundation for today's development, particularly as a conducive business environment for foreign business entities.

Table 19.11
A Comparison of GDP per Capita between China and ASEAN (2002)

Country/Region	GDP per capita (US$)
China	960
Shanghai	4,909
ASEAN*	1,144
Vietnam	439
Thailand	2,043
Singapore	20,515
Philippines	974
Myanmar	104
Malaysia	3,914
Lao, PDR	329
Indonesia	819
Cambodia	299
Brunei	12,090

Source: World Bank: <http://www.worldbank.org/data/databytopic/GNIPC.pdf>; Shanghai Municipal Government Work Report; ASEAN Surveillance Coordinating Unit (ASCU) database; <http://www.aseansec.org/macroeconomic/aq_gdp22.htm>. *As a proxy, combined GDP of ASEAN is computed as the sum of the GDP of ASEAN member countries, and the GDP per capita as GDP/number of population.

Shanghai's opening and its development strategy in the next few years have clearly demonstrated what its business environment and the opportunities can offer to the world. The opportunities that it will provide to ASEAN countries through its development in the next few years will be analysed from the perspective of its development strategy and policies of the Shanghai Municipal Government.

To pursue business opportunities in Shanghai, it is particularly important to pay attention to its development strategies as follows:

1. Making Use of International Industrial Transfers and Structural Upgrading to Build Up New Industrial System

As China's super large industrial city, Shanghai is making full use of the opportunity of international industrial transfers and structural upgrading to develop a group of high value-added modern industries. It is paving a new way towards industrialization so that it can play a larger role in China's industrialization. Shanghai has decided to build up four industrial bases: (1) Microelectronic industry: To develop the microelectronic industry into the largest and highest-quality centre in integrated circuit production and R&D in China. (2) Auto industry: To build up an automobile city and to develop a comprehensive automobile industry including the entire car manufacture, components production, R&D, science and education, trade, car-racing sports and auto-tourism. (3) Modern chemical industry: To develop a Shanghai chemical industrial region and, to establish a modern petrochemical industry with advanced technology and a balanced ecology. (4) Fine steel production: To develop fine steel production and, to become the number one city in production and export in China. In the meantime, Shanghai will introduce international advanced technology, improve its manufacturing ability in complete products and components, to develop rapidly in modern equipment manufacture, to reach an advanced level in the world. Obviously, these production bases will become investment opportunities as well as the major importers and exporters of China.

2. "Prospering the City via Science and Education" as Basic Development Strategy

According to the strategy, the city is making every endeavour to enhance the creativity of its society, accelerate human resource development, construct a public service platform, realize a group of science and technology programmes, and push innovation to attract exports at home and abroad. In order to build up its public service platform, Shanghai is providing large equipment and public experiment rooms in science and technology, and special technology services for R&D such as design, examination and testing, in various industries. Shanghai is also building up a service platform for technology investment, and the government is further playing a role in encouraging the development of various science and technology risk investment. Shanghai is also establishing an information service platform to facilitate R&D, information transmission in R&D transfer, as well as provide complete intellectual property protection services. The strategy of "prospering the city *via* science and education" will therefore provide favourable conditions for foreign investors, as well as local and domestic firms to develop. Shanghai has paid particular attention to attracting talent, and has provided good conditions including various kinds of professional training. Hence, there is a huge opportunity for international cooperation in human resource training. Additionally, the city is able to provide special talents for foreign enterprises in Shanghai. Shanghai is actively facilitating talents from abroad to gather in Shanghai, particularly high-level and rare talents. It is believed that the free and rational talent flow between Shanghai and the rest of the world will benefit the talents themselves and all the countries.

3. Accelerating the Establishment of "Four Centres" to Further Advance Shanghai's Modern Service Level

To hasten the establishment of Shanghai as a financial centre, Shanghai has always been in the forefront in opening up in finance and the development of new financial institutions and products. Hence, banks, non-banking financial institutions, and various financial intermediaries were among the first to experience the opportunities to develop. Particularly, Shanghai has set up financial service institutions under the administration of the government, and has emphasized the regularization of financial administration, which enables it to provide direct, highly efficient and comprehensive services to financial institutions at home and abroad.

4. Comprehensive Planning for the Entire City to Offer Opportunities for Industries and Enterprises

Shanghai has decided to advance the city's entire economic power as its development target. Hence such modern service industries as finance, commerce and trade, information, conference, exhibition and real estate will be developed in Shanghai's central region to reinforce its functions as a large international metropolis. In the suburban area, the plan is to develop it into a nuclear base in modern manufacturing and new high technology, to cooperate with the delta area of the Yangtze River to build up an international industrial region. Hence, Shanghai is a highly comprehensive large city with complete city, government as well as industrial services where all types of industries will find opportunities to develop.

5. Accelerating the City's Development as Information Centre, Regarded as Key to being First to Realize Modernization in China

The objective is to implement a superior information strategy, and push forward the construction of basic infrastructural facilities and the application of information technology to reach the average level of the central cities of developed countries by 2005, and to set up a framework of a "digital city" by 2007. The development target of an information city will create a huge demand for the information industry. Shanghai will enhance and facilitate the application of information technology in companies' R&D, production and management. It aims to develop electronic businesses, promote bank cards business, hasten the development of an "electronic port" and logistic information platform, promote the application of the city's topographic information system, and speed up the establishment of its emergency information system and transport information system. Shanghai will also actively develop the software industry and information service industry, particularly the establishment of software production base. It is believed that as a mega-city as well as China's information centre, Shanghai will create a large demand for the information industry, including huge opportunities for investment, products, services and technological cooperation.

6. Building an Infrastructural System of a Modern City

Although great changes have been achieved in Shanghai's urban development, much more infrastructure has to be developed to form stronger networks for it to function as a central city. Recently, ten projects under construction are: the Yanshan deep port, Pudong international airport — second phase, Shanghai south railway station, central city rail transportation network, city highway network and a few bridges and tunnels across the Huangpu River. No doubt, the huge government investment in these large projects will bring in a great amount of social investment as well as business opportunities in urban planning, construction design and engineering construction and demand for materials.

7. Enhancing the City's Ecological Situation

Shanghai has enhanced its efforts in environmental protection that include the city river, wide application of clear energy such as natural gas, strict control of exhaust gas, construction of more urban green lungs, increasing the green and forested areas, and environmental management of a few major industries. To conclude, the advancement of environmental protection to a higher level provides not only business opportunities in environmental engineering, it also increases the living quality in the city as a whole.

8. Launching a Combined Strategy of "Introducing in" and "Venturing out" (Attracting FDI and Investing Abroad)

In terms of "introducing in", Shanghai's target is to upgrade the quality and level of introducing foreign capital. The government is improving the investment environment, making full use of the comprehensive advantage to service foreign investment. Shanghai is actively introducing foreign projects and facilitating these projects to concentrate in industrial bases and development regions. The increment of capital and expansion of shares of those already invested ventures will be encouraged. Particularly in the past three years, the introduction of foreign companies' headquarters, R&D and purchasing departments has been set as an important strategic target for the opening up and functional development of the city. Consequently, various headquarters have entered into the Shanghai market, where good service and favourable policies will be provided to the business operation and the staff. In terms of "venturing out", large and middle-sized state enterprises with various ownerships have been encouraged to invest abroad in the form of mergers and acquisitions, or establishing strategic alliances with international multinational companies. Firms in Shanghai are encouraged to purchase, or buy shares of, foreign engineering contracting firms, and to set up sales network and R&D organizations abroad. To cultivate a group of large Chinese MNEs and brands is also one of its targets. Southeast Asia is a region that is relatively familiar to entrepreneurs in Shanghai, especially where there are large numbers of Chinese and Chinese firms in ASEAN, which will provide good opportunities for enterprises in Shanghai to invest abroad and will form much closer economic relationships between Shanghai and ASEAN countries.

9. Organizing the World Expo as a Development Opportunity for both Shanghai and China, as well as ASEAN

Shanghai has been authorized to host the World Expo in 2010, for which it is making full preparations currently. From now on, there will be huge amounts of capital at home and abroad gathering in Shanghai: It is expected that there will be US$3 billion invested in the site, and there will be a complete change in both banks of the Huangpu River within the region of the World Expo site. Meanwhile, the construction effects of the World Expo site will extend outwards, creating larger effects. The construction of the site will be linked to the construction of the city development scheme as a whole. The economic, science and culture exchange centre as a result of hosting the Expo will provide services to facilitate long-term and sustainable development. The households and firms that have been shifted from the site will be relocated in production and residential areas, which will bring in a new round of city construction, and cause the development of residential, business buildings, as well as transportation in every region of the city, consequently creating business opportunities in a much wider perspective. Investors at home and abroad have noticed the opportunities and formed a new round of high demand in Shanghai. According to the market price, it is expected that the response would be five to six times the expected direct investment in the site. In the long run, the theme of the Expo — "Better City, Better Life" will draw much attention from the world. "The Expo Effect" will thus create a huge engine for another round of development in Shanghai and also create huge opportunities for the cities surrounding it, including the demand for city construction, as well as the opportunities for tourism and exhibition in 2010. It is expected that the visitors to the Expo will be 70 million, breaking the world record of 63.4 million, and the direct sales related to tourism will be 9 billion yuan, which excludes the consequential business opportunities. All these are the development opportunities not only for China but also for ASEAN countries.

10. Accelerating the Pace in Reforming its Government

The government is becoming more just and transparent, functioning coherently and honestly. A government which is compatible with an open market economic system will be welcomed by the investors at home and abroad. Since joining WTO, the Shanghai municipal government regulates its behaviour as promised, transparency has been improved, the approval system has been improved and simplified, government services improved, and their functions adjusted according to economic principles, market supervision, social management and public service. The investment and development environment in Shanghai has been improved, not only from the perspective of domestic firms, but also that of foreign firms.

CHINA'S PEACEFUL RISE AND THE MUTUAL BENEFIT TO CHINA AND ASEAN

It has been noted that a few scholars and entrepreneurs in ASEAN have observed China's development with both hope and concern. On the one hand, they believe the development of Shanghai has become an engine of growth in the region, a domestic market with thirteen billion consumers will become the source of economic growth in the region at a time when Japan has gone through over ten years of depression. On the other hand, ASEAN countries are also concerned about the large-scale economy and rapid growth rate in China. China has a large and cheap labour market. As a member of WTO, China may grasp the market shares of ASEAN in Europe, America and Japan; China will also receive the international FDI that might flow into ASEAN. Some scholars claim that before the Asian financial crisis, three-fourths of international FDI went to ASEAN countries, with the rest going to China; after the crisis, the opposite situation has happened, with three-fourths of international FDI going to China, and the rest to ASEAN countries.

With a more efficient domestic institution and more complete legal system, China will become more attractive to investors in the world. Hence they are concerned that the development of China will have a negative impact on the development of other countries in the region.

The Chinese leadership has recently clearly put forward a completely new concept of "peaceful rise" or "peaceful development". On 10 September 2003, at Harvard University in the United States, Chinese Premier Wen Jiabao made a speech entitled "Turn your Perspective towards China". He stated that China was a large developing country, would not and could not rely on foreign countries, but should and could only emphasize on its own resources. As China opens increasingly toward the outside world, it should further rely on its own institutional innovation, domestic market expansion, transferring of huge domestic savings into investment, and solving of its resource and environmental problems by improving the population's capacity and advancement of technology. This is the nature of China's peaceful rise. On 26 December 2003, Chinese President Hu Jintao in a speech at a forum commemorating Mao Zedong's 110th birthday, stated:

> We shall insist on the path of socialism with China's characteristics. To insist on this path is to insist on a path of peaceful rise, to be on good terms with all countries on the base of the five principles of peaceful co-existence, to communicate and cooperate with each other on the basis of equal and mutual benefits, make contribution on the cause of peace and development of mankind.

On 24 April 2004, at the opening ceremony of BOAO annual conference, President Hu Jintao stated:

> While the development of China cannot be realized without Asia, the prosperity of Asia needs China. China will follow a path of peace and development, hold highly the banner of peace, development and cooperation, to create a new Asian framework with other Asian countries, to make a bigger contribution to the cause of peace and development of mankind.

On 26 April at the opening ceremony of the Sixtieth United Nations Asia-Pacific Economic Social Conference, Vice President Zeng Qing Hong stated:

> The peaceful development of China will be good for the regional and world's mutual benefit and prosperity. China's persistent, rapid, coherent, and healthy development has not only brought about the welfare for Chinese people, but also opportunities for the people in the region and all over the world; it has not only actively pushed the reorganization of production but also played a constructive role in facilitating the healthy development of the international economy.

While China's foreign currency policy to maintain its exchange rate during the Asian financial crisis has contributed to the stability of the region, the target of a peaceful rise and development will make a deep impact on the region's mutual prosperity.

China has paid great attention to regional cooperation. It has actively pushed the process of regional integration and is negotiating with other Asian countries on FTAs, opening up dialogues on security in various forms, and strengthening cooperation with other countries in the process of Asian regional cooperation. China's huge domestic market is very significant for the ASEAN-China FTA. It is the largest potential market in the world. The market has been developing continuously, the average growth rate of imports having reached over 15 per cent, the third largest in the world and highest in Asia. Recently, the growth rate of direct investment from China to other Asian countries has been 20 per cent on average. In 2003, large numbers of Chinese tourists have selected countries and regions in Asia as their first destination; the population which has gone on cross-border tours has reached twenty million. In 2003, the surplus between China and Europe plus America was US$80 billion. Meanwhile, China's deficit to ASEAN was US$17 billion. China has become a potential market to a large developing country. For instance, in 2003 China's auto sales value was US$4.4 million, an increase of 70 per cent compared with the previous year, when cars entered into households, which indicates that China will become the largest import country for its neighbouring countries. People in China are getting rich rapidly. Undoubtedly, the amazing consumption and purchasing power of China's tourists is the "salvation" for ASEAN countries. By the end of 2001, there were 17,972 ASEAN investment projects in China with foreign capital in negotiation amounting to US$53.468 billion, which accounted for 7.2 per cent of the total foreign investment in China; the realized investment was US$26,175 million accounting for 6.6 per cent of the total foreign investment in China. There are 740 investment projects valued at US$1,091 million from China to ASEAN countries, among which pure investment is US$655 million; the contracted engineering projects and services are worth US$19,581 million, and the value of completed operations is at US$12,443 million.

On 7 April 2004, the financial ministers of ten ASEAN member countries gathered in Singapore and proclaimed that the economic growth rate in the region was increasing, and the expected growth rate would be 5.5 per cent to 5.9 per cent. It has been recognized that the cooperation between ASEAN and China as well as India should be strengthened. At present, ASEAN is negotiating with China on free trade. Six countries including Singapore,

Malaysia, Thailand, Indonesia, Brunei and Philippine may reach free trade agreement by 2010, while Vietnam, Myanmar, Laos and Cambodia are expected to join this agreement by 2015.

"Peaceful rise" or "peaceful development" is not just a new concept but also a strategic path. "Peaceful rise" is not only China's international strategy but also its diplomatic manifesto as well as the strategy and principle that will guide China's development path for a long time in the future.

After reform, China's rapid development has relied on two engines of growth: One is the domestic development potential arising from institutional reform; the other is in the international resource potentials. The reform has released the creativity and desire to get richer among the Chinese people. The opening has allowed China to have access to commodities it needs from the external market, which has become the outside engine for economic development. The nature of "peaceful rise" is thus determined by the development path of these two sources of growth. Domestically, the first objective of development is to get rid of poverty and to enhance the welfare of the people rather than the occupying of land and ruling of other nations. The Chinese have suffered poverty for a long time and have a strong desire to get richer, and increase the national wealth to improve the population's living conditions. Internationally, economic globalization has enabled the free movement of production factors and the degree of opening has been increased. China therefore needs and can achieve its outward development by peaceful means. In the meanwhile, there is no turning back for China's institutional reform and open-door policy because its institutional mechanism has undergone a fundamental change.

Over twenty years ago, Deng Xiaoping saw the development of the world as one of "peace and development" based on his view of a changed world, and the foundation of the development strategy is self-development. For China, "development" has been the theme of all the contemporary countries and "opening" is the condition for development. Therefore, market integration is the mainstay of the world that would create the conditions for "development". This is the international environment in which China could possibly take the path for a peaceful rise. The essence of the development theme is to guide China to seize the opportunity of world peace, and make full use of the global environment to make a fundamental change to its backward situation, and also to help maintain world peace by creating a stable outward environment.

The concept of a "peaceful rise" or "peaceful development" clearly shows that China has already noticed some constraints as well as some friction between China and the world economy, during its process of development. It needs to erase the constraints by means of peace, which is a necessary condition to erase the friction too. The choice for China is to overcome the constraints of resource, environment, capital and market by adjusting its development strategy through scientific development, and to pursue a comprehensive, coherent and sustainable development, in harmony with the world, and to ensure the success of its peaceful rise. The strategy of "peaceful rise" itself demonstrates that China has already clearly identified the problems existing in the development model and the difficulties in the path of future development. The essence of this strategy is to rely on its own capacity which is different from the model of rising superpowers historically, and also different from what some of the countries' concerns are nowadays about China.

The reason that China has generalized its development policy in terms of the "four dependencies" lies in the fact that it will effectively buffer the impact of China's rise on others, as well as create sustainable development space. The "four dependencies" are: To make full use of domestic advantages to create domestic dynamic advantages; to compensate for outside commodity shortages; to further make full use of China's advantage of scale which is getting larger and larger; as well as to create new advantages including institutional, structural, technological, and human resource advantages.

Recently, China has adopted the scientific concept of treating human beings as the basis of a comprehensive, coherent and sustainable development, which is an important stride in China's long-term development path. This stride has not only shown that the development strategy has changed from being extensive to intensive. It also shows that the open-door policy has entered a new stage and become more wide-ranging and more coherent in its international relationship. Hence the development path is also sustainable, and will not stop as a result of any friction with the global economy.

China's "peaceful rise" or "peaceful development" is its diplomatic as well as development strategy. The concept includes diplomatic and domestic aspects, as there is a close relationship between them. China needs a peaceful environment to ensure its development, and to contribute towards world peace. Its rise is the aim of its development which will prosper the population as well as a give China a relatively high international position. The concept of "peaceful rise" shows China's strong belief in the need of a peaceful ascendency, as well as in its possibility. It has been established on the basis of a diplomatic strategy as well as the scientific notion of development, hence it shows the consistency of its diplomatic and development strategy.

Since its open-door policy, China has always tried to integrate with the current international system, and has participated in all aspects of globalization and international cooperation by accommodating the current regulations. Meanwhile, China has played the role of a responsible big nation by means of active participation. The whole process of joining the WTO and the role China has played typically underscores this point. The WTO is the symbol of globalization and representative of the current international system. After fifteen years of hardship, China has moved towards this goal without hesitation. During the process, China has made commitments to reform and an open-door policy through its own efforts and carried out domestic and other reforms to comply with the requirements of WTO, thereby illustrating its attitude towards the current international system. China's joining the WTO and its current activities are evidence of its integrating its own system with the global system rather than challenging it. After joining the WTO, China has actively participated in the negotiations and played roles in completing the multilateral trade system. As a developing country, China's requests will naturally manifest that of developing countries. As a member of the WTO, China will protect its self-interest like other countries. Its objectives in joining the WTO, and its status, role and actions in this organization reflect the basic model of China in its peaceful rise and participation in the contemporary international system.

China's principle of "treating human beings as the basis of a comprehensive, coherent, and sustainable scientific development" is also a development view that recognizes responsibility for the global environment. Sustainable development is a worldwide concept. There is only one globe that can be shared. For certain countries, the continuous development of the national economy may rely on outside resources, but this cannot be the case for mankind as a whole. The scientific development view has demonstrated that China has not relied on the outside world to solve its problems rising from its continuous development. Instead, China is relying on itself and has in fact linked its development with that of the world. There is no precedence in terms of China's responsible attitude as a big country, particularly when China itself is not well developed at present. China's development mission ahead is hard, hence it is not easy for it to emphasize this point, which shows that China is responsible in sharing benefits with the rest of the world.

20

Yunnan's Greater Mekong Sub-Region Strategy

He Shengda and Sheng Lijun

The past decade saw rapid development in the relations between China and ASEAN, especially since the announcement at the ASEAN-China Summit in 2001 in Brunei to build a China-ASEAN Free Trade Area (CAFTA). This CAFTA carries immense significance to the economic cooperation and development in Lancang-Mekong Basin or the Greater Mekong Sub-Region (GMS). This chapter addresses this significance, with the focus on Yunnan's strategy of how to fully tap this development and business opportunity. It ends with some policy recommendations of how best to develop the GMS under the framework of the CAFTA.

OPPORTUNITIES AND CHALLENGES IN YUNNAN'S GMS DEVELOPMENT

Opportunities

In the early 1990s, the Asian Development Bank (ADB) and the six riparian countries of Lancang-Mekong River[1] started a ministerial meeting to kick off the regional cooperation, which has since been known as the "Greater Mekong Sub-Region (GMS) Cooperation". A series of cooperation mechanisms have since been set up, including the (1) ADB-launched GMS

Cooperation; (2) ASEAN-Mekong Basin Development Cooperation; (3) Mekong Committee; and (4) Growth Quadrangle of China, Laos, Myanmar and Thailand. The Framework Agreement on Comprehensive Economic Cooperation between the ASEAN and China, signed at the ASEAN-China Summit in November 2002, identified the GMS cooperation as one of its five priority fields while the Joint Declaration signed at the GMS Summit in 2002 further clarified the key projects of economic cooperation and urged for formulation and implementation of medium and long-term cooperation programmes.[2]

China's Yunnan province has a population of 43 million and area of 394,000 square kilometres which ranks eighth in China. It borders with three Mekong riparian countries with a total borderline of 4,060 kilometres. From ancient times, Yunnan had been an important gateway that linked China and Southeast Asia, called the Southern Silk Road. Now Yunnan has ten first-class port cities (state level) and ten second-class ports (provincial level), eighty-six border passes or trading places along the borders with Myanmar, Laos and Vietnamese, and four big rivers (Dulong-Irrawaddy, Nu-Salween, Lancang-Mekong and Red River) flow from Yunnan through mainland Southeast Asia. This geographical proximity and close relations with these countries give Yunnan a distinct advantage and strong interest in developing the GMS as a backbone of the CAFTA and as a breakthrough in the economic cooperation between China's southwest and ASEAN, and as the linkage connecting East Asia, Southeast Asia and South Asia.

The CAFTA will develop simultaneously along two tracks in terms of economic geography. One is the maritime track, that is, cooperation between maritime ASEAN countries and China's coastal area. The other is the land-track, that is, between continental ASEAN countries and China's southwest. Yunnan is located as an important base or centre in the land track. Its participation in the GMS cooperation started twelve years ago and it has built a variety of cooperation mechanisms such as the ADB-launched GMS Cooperation in 1992, ASEAN-sponsored ASEAN-Mekong Basin Development Cooperation in 1996, and Mekong Committee (1995, with China as its dialogue partner). It has made substantial progress in many fields in cooperation with its neighbours, Cambodia, Laos, Myanmar, Thailand and Vietnam, such as the opening of the international route of the Lancang-Mekong River connecting Yunnan, Laos, Myanmar and Thailand, and the Kunming-Vientiane transnational highway. These cooperations are widely acknowledged as milestones in the regional cooperation.

Yunnan's economic linkage with the GMS countries is reflected in the following figures: In 2002, Yunnan's trade with ASEAN countries (mainly the GMS countries of Myanmar, Vietnam, Laos and Thailand) accounted for 37.5 per cent of its total foreign trade. Its trade with Southeast Asia reached US$1 billion in 2003, of which US$830 million is with GMS countries. ASEAN is Yunnan's largest economic cooperation partner, making up 70 per cent of its foreign contractual projects. The close cooperation can also be found in agriculture, mining, tourism, and science and technology as well. Yunnan has invested US$41 million in non-trade sectors of the GMS countries while ASEAN countries invested in 331 projects in Yunnan, with total contractual investment of US$363 million and actual investment of US$151 million.

Yunnan's participation in the GMS cooperation has greatly improved its infrastructure. In the past ten years, ADB has put in US$775 million in the infrastructure of the GMS countries, of which Yunnan obtained US$150 million for the Chuxiong-Dali Highway and another US$250 million for the Yuanjiang-Mohei Highway.[3] Beijing also put in US$5 million in opening the Lancang-Mekong route,[4] and another US$30 million in building the Laos' section of the Kunming-Bangkok Highway.[5] At the First GMS Summit in November 2002, the state leaders of the six riparian countries approved eleven projects with a total input of US$1 billion for the next ten years, among which the North-South Economic Corridor (from Yunnan to Thailand *via* Laos) and East-West Economic Corridor (from Myanmar to Vietnam *via* northern Thailand and Laos) are counted as priority projects.

Mutual Complementarities

On the other hand, Yunnan's economy has very strong complementarities with those of GMS countries. The GMS countries are rich in natural resources. Though they all (except Thailand) tend to export their natural resources, it is misleading to assume, without looking into the details, that their economies are competitive. They actually complement each other strongly because they possess and export different natural resources (see Table 20.1 for details). Though they all belong to developing countries without one being on top of the economic stream, it is also simplistic to assume that they will naturally compete with each other. A close look will reveal that not only the structures of resources, but also the structures of industries and technologies of the six riparian GMS countries/area are different (see also Table 20.1). What is more, they do not compete with each other in the third international markets and they also complement each other in labour and management.

As for Yunnan, it has its own distinctive advantage in skilled labour, agro-technology, machinery equipment, tobacco, chemical industries, electric power,

Table 20.1
Major Resources & Industries of Lancang-Mekong Riparian Countries/Province

Countries/Province	Myanmar	Thailand	Cambodia	Laos	Vietnam	Yunnan
Resources	Forest, farmland, aquatic products, petroleum, tin, tungsten, gems, copper	Tropical fruits, rice, aquatic products, tin, tungsten, lignite, iron	Manganese, lead, phosphorus, zinc, gold	Forest, farmland, tin, lead, coal	Coal, iron, chrome, tin	Forest, metal, minerals, coal, waterpower
Forest coverage (%)	50	38	40	58	30	25
Major agro-products	Rice, wheat, sugarcane, peanut, beans	Rice, maize, cassava, natural rubber, cotton	Rice, maize, natural rubber	Rice, maize, tobacco	Aquatic products, rice, maize, banana, coconut, pineapple, sugarcane, rubber, coffee	Rice, tobacco, tea, sugar, rubber, fruits and vegetables of temperate zone
Major industries and minerals	Rice grinding, timber process, non-ferrous metals	Mineral melting, construction materials, petrochemical, textile, food processing, automobiles	Food processing, light industry	Power generation, cement, cigarette, cotton spin	Mineral melting, electric power, machinery, chemicals, construction materials, food process	Tobacco, non-ferrous metals, steel, phosphate chemicals, electric power, machinery, hi-tech.

Sources: Collected data about the five riparian countries of Thailand, Myanmar, Vietnam, Laos, Cambodia and Yunnan province.

steel, non-ferrous metals and business administration as well, which the other riparian countries, with their own comparative advantages, do not fully share.

In terms of economic development, as shown in Table 20.2, there is a big gap among the six riparian countries: per capita GDP of Yunnan in 2002 is more than US$600, less than that of Thailand (US$2,043) and higher than the other four riparian countries — Vietnam (US$439), Myanmar (US$104), Laos (US$329) and Cambodia (US$299). Thailand is a newly industrialized country (NIC) with its GDP per capita over US$2,000. Its economy is highly open with half of its manufactured products exported to the world markets. Vietnam's economy has grown rapidly over the past ten years. But the three riparian countries, Laos, Myanmar and Cambodia remain as the world's least developed countries. These economic dimensions and diversification demonstrate the strong complementarities among these riparian countries.

Faced with the ever-increasing challenges from globalization and regionalism, the six riparian countries feel the urgency to seek wider cooperation among themselves to better handle the challenges and fully tap the potential benefits that the China-ASEAN FTA would promise. When proposing the CAFTA, China promised favourable treatment exclusively for those less developed ASEAN states who are also Mekong riparian states. It will include them in its "Early Harvest Package (EHP)" list. Through its Asian Debt Reduction Plan, it has either partially reduced or totally exempted Vietnam, Laos and Cambodia of its debts to China. Besides, it has offered duty-free treatment for goods imported from Laos, Cambodia and Myanmar, and put in US$30 million for building Laos' section of the Kunming-Bangkok Highway. At the first GMS Summit, it joined in the Agreement on the Facilitation of Cross-Border Movement of Goods and People, and signed the Inter-Governmental Agreement on Electricity Procurement in the GMS. It also released a "Country Report" of its participation in the GMS cooperation and brought forward development plans and key projects of the GMS cooperation. It accorded duty-free treatment for exports from Laos, Cambodia and Myanmar and agreed to conduct a research project on the "Improvement of Inner Land Waterway within the territories of Cambodia, Laos, Myanmar and Vietnam". It has also promised to construct and maintain the Kunming-Hanoi Railway so as to support the Pan-Asia Railway. It has accorded the three non-WTO member states of Vietnam, Laos and Cambodia with most-favoured nation (MFN) status equivalent to WTO members. All these measures help promote the GMS cooperation.

Apart from geographical proximity, close economic cooperation, decade-long cooperation mechanisms, strong economic complementarities and strong

Table 20.2
The 2002 Key Indicators of Lancang-Mekong Riparian Countries/Province

Items	Unit	Yunnan	Thailand	Vietnam	Myanmar	Laos	Cambodia	Total
Population	Millions	43.33	63.08	78.69	52.00	5.38	12.30	254.78
Total area	Thousand km²	394	513	329	676	236	181	2329
GDP	US$ billions	25.12	125.0	34.8	16.0	1.7	3.2	205.82
97/98 GDP of SEA	%	/	23.8	4.5	2.1	0.3	0.5	31.2
Per capita GDP	US$	586	1990	436	300	326	260	782
Export-import	US$ billions	2.23	125.24	33.31	5.20	0.84	3.10	136.90

Sources: *Country Report* of Thailand, Vietnam, Myanmar, Laos and Cambodia, The 2002 statistics from EIU; *2003 Yunnan Annual*; *2002 World Development Report*, World Bank.

support from the central government, Yunnan has other favourable conditions, which include:

- Harmonious ethnic relations between the peoples in Yunnan and other bordering states;
- Close bilateral relations: All the riparian states have their consulates in Kunming (Myanmar in September 1993, Laos in October 1993, Thailand in July 1994, Cambodia in March 2004, and Vietnamese in May 2004).
- Beijing's grand strategy to develop its west and consequent mandate given to Yunnan by the central government in Beijing in handling its economic cooperation with other riparian states.

All these favourable conditions give Yunnan a unique opportunity to take part in the GMS cooperation and enlarge its opening to the outside world.

CHALLENGES

Yunnan's participation of GMS cooperation and GMS development is, of course, faced with severe challenges. The riparian states of Laos, Myanmar and Cambodia are the world's poorest nations while Yunnan is one of China's least developed provinces. GMS countries/areas have defective legal systems, lower degree of economic development, large populations of poverty, fragile eco-system and poor infrastructure, and imperfect cooperation mechanism.

Poor Infrastructure

The poor condition of both the road and water transportation between Yunnan and other riparian states pose a severe constraint to its GMS development. Road transportation between China and ASEAN is sparse and the proposed north-south expressway linking China with ASEAN is still under construction. The roads that link other Mekong riparian countries are also in even poorer conditions. Even though there are, for instance, land routes and waterways linking Yunnan with Laos and with Myanmar, a ship on Lancang-Mekong River reaches no further than Houei Say of Laos. Road passage from Kunming to Rangoon is by no means smooth while, in Myanmar especially in north of Mandalay, the road infrastructure is in severely poor condition, being able to open only on fine days. Northern Laos has similar poor road conditions. The railway between Yunnan and Vietnam is over one hundred years old, with narrow passages and poor maintenance. Its current annual freight volume is only 450,000 tonnes, far less than the volume of 1.5 million tonnes as designed in the early 1990s.

Low Competitiveness and Limited Market

The GMS countries and areas, as a whole, are still of a natural and agricultural economy and far from being an open large market (with Thailand as the exception). Thus their participation in the world market and their scale of trade are rather small, especially among themselves. For example, in 2001, China's trade with the other five riparian countries made huge progress but only reached US$9.97 billion, which only accounted for 2.1 per cent of its total foreign trade of US$474.29 billion, and of which more than 66 per cent is out of the Sino-Thai bilateral trade (see Table 20.3). What is more, there is serious imbalance in the trade between China and the four riparian states of Cambodian, Laos, Myanmar and Vietnamese (see also Table 20.3).

Lack of Funds

The GMS development needs tremendous investment. It needs US$15–20 billion in infrastructure development in the next ten years, which GMS countries cannot afford. Apart from Thailand, whose per capita GDP is over US$2,000, the other four riparian countries, together with Yunnan province, are all listed as lowest-income economies. For instance, the per capita GDP of Myanmar, Laos and Cambodia is lower than US$350 while that of Vietnam and Yunnan is somewhere from US$400 to US$700. Most of them run heavy foreign debts. For example:

- By the end of 2002, Cambodia's foreign debt reached US$2 billion with a debt payment ratio of only 1 per cent.
- Vietnam's original foreign debt reached US$20 billion (including interest). After negotiation on debt reduction and exemption, its current foreign debt dropped to US$4 billion (including interest).
- Myanmar's foreign debt has reached as much as US$6 billion, so heavy that it can hardly pay the interest. By the end of 2001, Myanmar owed more than US$100 million of matured debt to firms in Yunnan province. Myanmar's delay of payment of this debt has put a severe capital strain on some Yunnan firms.[6]

Trade and Market Barriers

Most of the GMS countries/areas have just transformed from a highly centralized planning economy to a market-oriented economy only about a decade ago. Therefore their markets are not open enough for deep cooperation. Laos and Cambodia have a long way to go before being able to be accepted into the World Trade Organization (WTO). Myanmar has

Table 20.3
The 2001/02 China-ASEAN Trade Value (US$ millions)

	Countries	2002			2001		
		Export/import	Export	Import	Export/import	Export	Import
Mekong Riparian Countries	Thailand	8,560.70	2,958.40	5,602.30	7,050.30	2,337.45	4,712.85
	Vietnam	3,264.20	2,148.90	1,115.30	2,815.20	1,804.45	1,011.75
	Myanmar	861.70	724.80	136.90	631.54	497.35	134.19
	Cambodia	216.10	251.60	24.50	240.41	205.61	34.08
	Laos	64.00	54.30	9.70	61.87	54.41	7046
	Total	13,026.70	6,138.00	6,888.20	10,799.32	4,899.27	5,900.05
Other ASEAN Countries	Singapore	14,018.10	6,965.70	7,052.40	1,0934.40	5,791.88	5,142.52
	Malaysia	14,270.50	4,974.50	9,296.00	9,425.47	3,220.26	6,205.21
	Indonesia	7,928.30	3,426.90	4,501.40	6,724.61	2,836.54	3,888.07
	Philippines	5,259.50	2,042.30	3,217.20	3,565.53	1,620.31	1,945.22
	Brunei	262.90	21.10	241.80	165.39	17.15	148.24
	Total	41,739.30	17,430.50	24,308.80	30,815.40	13,486.14	17,329.26
	Grand Total	54,766.00	23,568.50	31,197.50	41,614.72	18,385.41	23,229.31

Source: *2002 China Statistical Yearbook*, China Statistics Press, 2003.

long suffered from the economic sanctions by the West though it has long been a WTO member. Some riparian countries still impose high tariffs and keep excessive non-tariff barriers.

Furthermore, the sub-regional economic cooperation is also faced with the difficulties of local currencies and their exchanges because China's renminbi is still inconvertible. And there is a big gap between the official exchange rate and that in the black market such as in Myanmar. As for transportation, high costs of transit duty and tedious procedures of freightage cause high cost of trade. As for foreign investment, some riparian countries set up non-physical barriers for foreign direct investment in certain domestic economic sectors.

Insufficient Attention and Support

To push the GMS cooperation vigorously, there are limits to what a local government like Yunnan can do and therefore stronger initiatives and support by the central government of Beijing are called for. Yunnan, as a less developed province in China, is faced with strong competition from China's coastal provinces, where the economic growth depends more on the Western economies and international market than on China's west such as Yunnan.

Another worrying sign to Yunnan is that the current huge publicity of CAFTA, ASEAN+3 and other forms of East Asia cooperation has helped to enhance international, regional and domestic attention and interest in China-ASEAN trade and investment. But they may also distract international, regional and Beijing's attention and interest in the less developed area of the CAFTA such as the GMS. Private investment could well go to those more developed ASEAN countries and Chinese provinces that promise higher profit returns. Therefore, a stronger support, such as preferential policy, by the central government of Beijing is needed. Beijing has indeed enhanced its effort to develop its west. However, the GMS is only part, but not the whole, of this western region. What is more, this effort now may be balanced, if not distracted, by the initiative from Beijing to develop China's traditional industrial bases in its northeast. It seems that Yunnan, as local province, has to, first of all, depend more on its own efforts to set its own strategy, and to win over the support of the central government of China and the cooperation of GMS countries and international organizations accordingly, which will be discussed below.

YUNNAN'S GMS STRATEGY

In view of the opportunities and challenges as discussed above, Yunnan has set out its strategy to fully tap the promised and potential benefits of the

CAFTA and East Asian cooperation. This strategy is based on its awareness that a rapid development of Yunnan depends heavily on a successful CAFTA and other regional cooperation such as the GMS. GMS should be taken as the pioneer in establishing CAFTA. In this effort, Yunnan should take ASEAN as its key partner and place the GMS cooperation as a top priority in its opening to the outside world.

Yunnan should speed up the opening of international channels to connect with Southeast Asia, as discussed below, and make great effort to build a modern new Kunming as the primary regional centre and foster another three economic centres in the border areas, that is, Jinghong, Hekou and Ruili. By emphasizing on trade and tourism, Yunnan will build three economic corridors, that is, the "Yunnan-Vietnam Economic Corridor", "Yunnan-Laos-Thai Economic Corridor", and "Yunnan-Myanmar Economic Corridor". This grand strategy entails the following ten aspects:

1. Making GMS Cooperation Pioneer of CAFTA

Yunnan will seek the support from Beijing to make the GMS cooperation a pioneer in building the CAFTA in the land track. The CAFTA has promised favourable treatment exclusive to new members of the ASEAN, who happen to be the Mekong riparian states. Yunnan will make full use of this special treatment policy to bring out initiatives that are unique to itself as a contiguous and border province, which other provinces, because of the geographical localities, cannot match. It is easier and advantageous for contiguous areas/states to cooperate economically. Yunnan will make full use of itself being the connecting point between China and other GMS states. It has declared its general principle as "state-guided, market-oriented, enterprise-subjected and legally-guaranteed" and will decentralize its management for a freer and more open market.[7]

2. Building International Channels

Yunnan will coordinate and intensify its efforts in cooperating with other GMS countries to develop the infrastructure such as highways, railways and ports. Top on its agenda is the building of international channels that connect Southeast Asia with Yunnan and southwestern China. It needs to open "two channels".

The first "channel" refers to transportation, that is, to build modern roadways, waterways, railways and airlines that connect with other GMS countries. Its strategic vision is to "take high-level roadways as its basic backbone, airlines as accessory, waterways as complementary and railways as the medium/long-term foundation". The focus is on building roads and waterways, of which two areas are of particular importance. One is the Lancang-Mekong International Shipping Route and the other is the road linkages of the Kunming-Bangkok Highway, Yunnan-Vietnam Highway and Yunnan-Myanmar Highway.

Lancang-Mekong International Shipping Route: This shipping route, opened in June 2001 and known as the "Golden Waterway", is the main artery of water transportation from Yunnan to Laos *via* Myanmar and Thailand. It needs to be upgraded and extended to the downstream of the river to include more GMS countries.

Kunming-Bangkok Highway, Yunnan-Vietnam Highway and Yunnan-Myanmar Highway: These highways are part of the Asian Highway, of which the Kunming-Bangkok Highway is of great significance.[8] It is the most important north-south economic corridor of the Greater Mekong Sub-Region. Yunnan intends to finish upgrading the sections of these three passages in its own province into high-level roadways no later than 2007.

Apart from building roads and waterways, Yunnan will upgrade the Yunnan-Vietnam Railway (the total length is 418 kilometres. The section from Kunming to Yuxi is finished. The section from Yuxi to Hekou, with a length of 315 kilometres, is yet to be completed) as part of the eastern line of the Pan-Asia Railway. It will also build the Yunnan-Thailand Railway and the Yunnan-Myanmar Railway.

The second "channel" refers to further simplification of customs, for which Yunnan will speed up its effort. The Agreement on the Facilitation of Cross-border Movement of Goods and People (of GMS countries) signed in November 2002 stipulated the simplification and harmonization of laws, regulations, systems and procedures of passengers and freights in transit. If carried out, this agreement will boost trade between the Lancang-Mekong riparian countries. Yunnan will make efforts to remove the non-trade barriers. Meanwhile, all the GMS countries should cooperate and should fully implement the agreement. They should try to simplify the customs services. At the same time, authorities of customs, quarantine and frontier defence of all the riparian countries should conduct counterpart tasks or joint negotiations in order to formulate regional laws and bilateral or multilateral agreements. These measures will help simplify customs inspection procedures to further promote efficiency of the transportation system in transit and boost trade and investment in the region to an integrated regional market.

3. Constructing Regional Legal Framework

Yunnan will make full use of the framework agreement of CAFTA and exceptional arrangement of WTO regulations to push for cooperation among the GMS parties, in formulating, coordinating and harmonizing legal systems on trade and investment for a smooth flow of passengers, freight, capital and information in the region. It will also discuss with other riparian countries on sub-regional trade and investment that cover freight, services, investment, finance, foreign exchange and labour.

Yunnan will do this by seeking support from the central government in Beijing, which will negotiate with the central governments of other riparian states to formulate preferential treatments on international trade, foreign investment and economic cooperation in the region and subscribe to the agreement on "avoiding double taxation on mutual investment". Resource-based products exploited by Yunnan enterprises from the sub-region countries should be treated as domestic products and should be exempted from import duty and value-added tax so as to support Yunnan enterprises participating in resource exploitation in other riparian countries.

4. Making Trade and Tourism as the Leading Sectors

In its GMS cooperation, Yunnan should make trade and tourism the leading sectors in order to promote the exchange of peoples, deepen the understanding of each other, connect its domestic market with overseas ones and promote consumption and, consequently, production. This will in turn help promote further regional economic and technological cooperation.

5. Developing Sub-regional Economic Centres

Yunnan should establish sub-regional economic centres, for example in Kunming, as new growth poles. Efforts should also be made to develop port cities and areas along main transportation lines and the borders. Kunming should not only be made the economic centre of the whole province, but also the centre for China's southwest provinces in the GMS cooperation. Kunming should also be made the centre of commerce, manufacturing, finance, transportation, tourism, as well as science, education, culture and health service exchanges between southwestern China and Southeast Asia, especially the GMS countries.

Yunnan province and Kunming city have formulated a programme of constructing a modern and greater Kunming with a total input of RMB200 billion in the next twenty years. Its major projects include "One Lake

(Dianchi Lake) Four Orientations", that is, city-oriented highways, lake-oriented pollution control, lake-oriented ecology and lake-oriented new city. The Yunnan government will conduct a massive development plan to build Kunming into a city encompassing a prime town, eastern town, southern town and northern town. Meanwhile, it will also make great effort to construct other city groups (Gejiu-Kaiyuan-Mengzi New City), central cities along major transportation lines (Dali and Chuxiong) and port cities along the border areas (Jinghong, Ruili and Hekou), and use these cities as the bases for the purpose of both "going out" (for local enterprises) and "inviting in" (of external investment). The border cities that have geographic advantages will enjoy more inputs of capital, technology, and talent from Kunming so as to expand both the internal and external markets.

6. Building Up the Three Economic Corridors

Yunnan will make great effort to build up three north-south economic corridors and a sub-regional economic zone that is based on the Kunming-Hekou-Hanoi Highway (Yunnan-Vietnam Railway), Kunming-Bangkok Highway (Lanchang-Mekong Waterway) and Kunming-Rangoon Passageway. The Eighth Ministerial Meeting of Greater Mekong Sub-Regional Cooperation held in 1998 brought forward the concept of "economic corridors" which, according to the definition given by the Asian Development Bank, means to combine the infrastructural construction with improvement of production and trade and other developmental opportunities. It also means promoting economic development and cooperation between the neighbouring countries and areas. What is more important is the implementation of "Development Strategies of Economic Corridors".

However, the progress of the ADB-initiated north-south economic corridors is falling far behind the development of the east-west economic corridors. The north-south initiatives should therefore be speeded up.

The first economic corridor is the Kunming-Hanoi-Hai Phong Economic Corridor, which is most promising because areas along the corridor are well-developed in both Yunnan and Vietnam, with a vigorous economy and a great number of large and medium-sized cities along it, and the best transportation in the area. Reconstruction of the Yunnan-Vietnam Railway Yunnan section (*via* the Kunming-Yuxi-Hekou section) should be set off at the earliest possible time and a secondary-level highway from Mengzi to Hekou should also be speeded up so as to promote Vietnam's reconstruction of the Laocai-Hanoi-Hai Phong section. As parts of the Kunming-Hanoi-Hai Phong Traffic Corridor, Kunming-Shiling Expressway and Mengzi-Hekou

Secondary-level Highway have been completed while many cities like Yiliang, Kaiyuan, Gejiu, Mengzi and Hekou are fast developing along the Yunnan-Vietnam Railway line.

The second is the Kunming-Bangkok Economic Corridor (also known as the Yunnan-Laos-Thailand Economic Corridor). This is the most important linkage between Yunnan and Thailand, with the Kunming-Bangkok Highway and Lancang-Mekong Waterway as its two major connections. At present, construction of the Kunming-Bangkok Highway is in progress and the Yunnan section will be upgraded to a high-level highway by 2007. There are more than ten large and medium-sized cities along the corridor such as Kunming, Yuxi, Yuanjiang, Pu'er, Simao, Jinghong, Mengla, and Mohan. Compared with the Kunming-Hanoi Economic Corridor, the Kunming-Bangkok Economic Corridor plays a more important part in economic cooperation between Yunnan and mainland Southeast Asia. While Yunnan is speeding up the construction of the Mohan-Xiaomengyang section and Laos' section of the Kunming-Bangkok Highway, construction of the Middle Line (Kunming-Bangkok) of the Pan-Asia Railway should also be put on the agenda.

The third is the Kunming-Mandalay-Rangoon Economic Corridor (also known as the Yunnan-Myanmar Economic Corridor). This economic corridor connects Yunnan with Myanmar and further extends to South Asian countries. The main communication lines of this economic corridor include the Yunnan-Myanmar Highway, north-south highways and railways in Myanmar and the Irrawaddy waterway. The tough task lies in Myanmar's section of the corridor. Joint efforts should be made by Myanmar and the international community to upgrade the Myanmar section of railways and highways. A the same time, both Yunnan and Myanmar should cooperate to connect the Yunnan-Myanmar Highway with the Irrawaddy waterway. The Yunnan section will be upgraded to high-level roads in the late period of "the Tenth Five-Year Plan" (2001–05) and in the early period of "the Eleventh Five-Year Plan" (2006–10).

Along the Yunnan-Myanmar Economic Corridor some large and medium-sized cities have emerged, such as Kunming, Anning, Chuxiong, Xiangyun, Dali, Baoshan, Luxi, and Ruili. This economic corridor is the main linkage between China, Myanmar, and South Asia, and it has a deep impact not only on the economic development along the route from Yunnan to Myanmar, but also on China's economic relations with the South Asian market, which has a total population of 1.3 billion people.

The development of these three economic corridors will be mainly through developing trade, tourism, agriculture and industries which have their comparative advantages.

The three east-west economic corridors, which connect Myanmar, Thailand, Cambodia, Laos and Vietnam, have been approved as the priority projects with a total input of US$740 million since 1998 while the three north-south economic corridors, which connect Yunnan with Myanmar, Laos, Thailand and Vietnam, have also been highly evaluated and supported by the Asian Development Bank. It is now high time to expedite the establishment of the three economic corridors through joint efforts and cooperation. In this respect, Yunnan will actively seek support from China's central government, and cooperate with the neighbouring countries and international organizations to, first of all, construct the Yunnan-Vietnam Economic Corridor, and at the same time promote the Kunming-Bangkok Economic Corridor, and to create favourable conditions for the construction of the Kunming-Mandalay-Rangoon Economic Corridor.

7. An "Outbound" Strategy: Focusing Economic Cooperation on Four Areas

Yunnan should cooperate with other GMS countries in the following four areas:

Agriculture: The GMS countries have abundant land resources while Yunnan has the advantage of high agricultural technology. With this high economic complementarity, both sides should intensify their cooperation. Yunnan will provide expertise, technologies, improved seeds, farming machines, fertilizers and pesticides. The products can be sold both to the local market and at other markets in China. Yunnan could rent, for example, farmland in Myanmar and Laos for plantation and breeding. It will cooperate with Myanmar, Laos, Vietnam, Cambodia and Thailand to exploit tropical bio-resources, for instance, tropical fruits, flowers, crude drugs, natural spices and rubber. It will also expand its tobacco industry and business to Vietnam, Laos, Myanmar and Thailand by setting up branches there.

Mining: Yunnan is widely known as "the kingdom of non-ferrous metals" in China, with high technology and rich experience in prospecting, exploiting, mill running and melting of minerals while other GMS countries are abundant in mineral resources. All should cooperate closely with this high complementarity. For instance, Yunnan should cooperate with Vietnam in exploiting its sylvite, tin and iron; with Laos, its iron, copper and lead; Myanmar, its copper and lead; and Laos and Cambodia, for the exploitation and processing of gems.

Energy: Yunnan is rich in water and coal resources where other GMS countries are poor, and is poor in petroleum and natural gas resources while others are rich, thus there is great potential for their energy cooperation (see Table 20.4 for their electricity consumptions).[9] Yunnan should "go out" to contract projects of hydropower stations and to exploit petroleum and natural gas in its neighbouring countries. It should also participate in petroleum and gas transfusion projects from Thailand, Vietnam and Myanmar to Kunming. It should cooperate with Laos to transfer its power, generated from Jinghong Hydropower Plant, to Thailand *via* Laos. China will pay in the form of export credit to the three northern provinces of Laos.

Industry and Project Contracts: Yunnan should invest more and set up more plants in the sub-regional countries by using its comparative advantages in light industry, machinery, electronics, construction materials, garments, chemicals and medicines. These will be priority sectors for Yunnan to invest in the sub-regional countries for processing trade.

In respect of project contracts, ASEAN has become Yunnan's leading partner of project contracts and labour cooperation. Yunnan intends to expand this cooperation, where it has comparative advantage and favourable geographic conditions, in order to reduce its trade deficit in services and promote commodities export and industrial transference. Yunnan should upgrade the quality of its project construction and reduce costs.

8. Setting Up Five Platforms

Yunnan should develop Kunming as a centre of capital accumulation, commodity mobilization, communication hub, industry traction, technology extension, information delivery, and human resource exchange and management. This strategy will help Kunming become the sub-regional

Table 20.4
Electric Power Consumption of the Five Sub-Regional Countries

Countries	Total consumption (trillion kw)	Per capita consumption (kw)
Cambodia	0.2	19
Laos	0.5	65
Myanmar	4.3	81
Thailand	92.2	1,391
Vietnam	21.8	194

Source: *Asia-Pacific Economic Yearbook, 1999.*

centre of finance, information, trade, culture and technology. With this vision, Yunnan should work to set itself as the following five service platforms:

Financial Platform: GMS countries, especially Vietnam, Laos, Myanmar and Cambodia, have little foreign exchange reserves and low capacity of payment. Thus, Yunnan should develop a new system of bank settlement to smoothen capital flows between Yunnan and these countries, and eventually set up a modernized electronic financial platform with Kunming as its centre for the whole sub-region. For this purpose, Yunnan should take two steps: First, try to introduce international financial institutions to Yunnan, with Kunming as the financial centre. Second, make the capital account of RMB convertible. Yunnan should speed up its reform of the banking system, deal with bad accounts and reinforce financial inspection and prevent financial risks.

Information Platform: Yunnan should establish high-quality and wide-ranging information hubs in the cities of Kunming, Jinghong, Ruili and Hekou, as required to match its status as a regional economic centre.

Trade Platform: Yunnan should upgrade the marketing facilities in the cities of Kunming, Jinghong, Ruili and Hekou for commodity exhibition, trade negotiation and other services, in the expectation of their growing to become the region's leading trade and commodity centres.

Platform for Science, Education and Health: China and ASEAN should enforce an environmental protection system in the GMS and establish prevention systems against infectious diseases such as Aids, rat plague, cholera and malaria. Yunnan should reform its education system by introducing educational experiences from abroad so as to become a centre of education and human resource development (HRD). This centre also targets ASEAN countries through the provision of training courses for GMS cooperation and CAFTA. Yunnan should reinforce cooperation with ASEAN members, especially with the GMS countries, in the fields of science and technology, in order to make Kunming a centre of science and technology.

Cultural Platform and Convention Centre: Kunming has a very favourable climate to build itself into a regional convention centre for conferences and commercial and cultural exhibitions and performances, and as the regional headquarters and residence of foreign companies and diplomatic missions. Now all the five riparian countries have established their consulates in Kunming. Some South Asian countries like India and Bangladesh may also follow suit in the near future. Kunming should make full use of its favourable climate for more international and regional cultural and sporting activities. For example, it could hold Southeast Asia Week, GMS Exhibition Week, etc.

9. Policy of "Going Out" and "Inviting In"

Yunnan should encourage the policy of both "going out" and "inviting in", that is, not only to encourage its own enterprises to "go out" to invest in and trade with ASEAN and GMS countries, but also to further open itself to the outside world by inviting in more investment, not only from abroad but also from China's coastal provinces and the central government.

10. Drug-Replacement Planting

Drug-trafficking is an issue that must be dealt with under both the GMS cooperation and the CAFTA. Yunnan should intensify its drug-replacement planting programme, which should also be listed as a key project for the Lancang-Mekong sub-regional cooperation. It should strengthen its cooperation with GMS countries and international organizations, increase special funds for replacement planting and provide preferential treatment for those domestic enterprises that invest or undertake replacement-planting programmes. They should work together to resolve the related issues such as border transit of materials, personnel and vehicles. They should coordinate with each other and formulate a joint development plan on the replacement planting in northern Myanmar and northern Laos. As for Yunnan, it should encourage its enterprises to "go out" to participate in replacement planting programmes in the sub-region.

POLICY RECOMMENDATIONS

Yunnan is the only province of China that participates directly in the GMS cooperation. As the principal part of China's participation in the sub-regional cooperation, Yunnan should cooperate more actively than other provinces, with the other five countries. However, Yunnan, as a province, is not entitled to formulate laws and national policy, and conduct international (diplomatic) negotiations and consultations, as the other five sovereign GMS countries are able to, for the GMS economic cooperation and integration. However, there is still a lot Yunnan can do on its own part and this author would like to make the following ten policy recommendations:

1. Make Kunming a Liaison Point between China and ASEAN (GMS) Countries

The Annex 4 of the CAFTA framework agreement stipulates that Kunming should be a liaison point between China and ASEAN member countries.

Yunnan hopes, for example, that it can host permanently some China-ASEAN cooperation institutions, convention and exhibition centres and commercial centres.

2. Actively Plan and Construct the "Key Channels"

Yunnan has conducted good research and come out with a programme in the two phases (2004–08 and 2003–15), for its participation in the GMS cooperation. It has proposed the construction of the "key channels"[10] to connect Yunnan with Southeast Asia. It should coordinate with GMS countries in implementing these programmes under the framework of the CAFTA.

3. Incorporate Kunming's Educational and HRD Programmes into the China-ASEAN Educational Cooperation Programme

4. Reform the Financial System and Diversify Ways of Fund-Raising

This includes attracting international assistance and investment with well-selected projects; encouraging foreign enterprises, organizations and financial groups to invest in different ways such as build-operate-transfer (BOT); gaining support from banking institutions; widening market access; issuing bonds; and setting up public companies to attract private and public funds.

5. Open the Finance Sector Wider to the Outside World

Simplify approval procedures for, and offer incentives to, foreign banks to set up their branches in Kunming, strengthen relations with financial institutions of the ten ASEAN members, and encourage Yunnan's local banks to set up branches in ASEAN.

6. Promote Trade Relations with ASEAN Countries and Expand Border Trade

Legal institutions in border areas should be improved to facilitate trade and investment. Government departments in border areas like the military, customs, quarantine stations, police, taxation offices, should work in coordination with other departments concerned to simplify exit and entry procedures, eliminate tariff barriers, reduce trade cost, provide convenience to investors, and make and carry out protocols with Laotian and Vietnamese governments in regard to transportation of goods so that land transport can extend from border areas to Hanoi and Vientiane.

7. Develop Tourism in Cooperation with ASEAN Countries

The tourist route along the Mekong River and other tourist destinations should be developed to form a sub-regional tourist network.

8. Strengthen Cooperation with ASEAN Countries in Environmental Protection and Natural Resource Development

Incentives should be given to encourage more investment, capital, and advanced technology for the regional environmental protection.

9. Upgrade International and Domestic Coordination Institutions

It is hoped that the Chinese central government would upgrade the current Lancang-Mekong Basin Research and Coordination Office into the GMS Cooperation–China Coordination Office (or Leading Group), or China's Committee of GMS Cooperation.

10. Enhance Strategic Planning

More intensive research should be conducted on, for example, short/medium/long-term GMS cooperation plans and measures, the North-South Economic Corridor projects and their operational mechanisms, environmental impact as well as replacement planting and replacement development plans.

NOTES

1. The six countries are Cambodia, China, Laos, Myanmar, Thailand and Vietnam.
2. This GMS Summit also released another two documents for GMS cooperation, namely, the Memorandum on Connection between the Agreement on the Facilitation of Cross-Border Movement of Goods and People and the Appendix, Protocols and Amendment Commitment on the Article 17 of the Agreement; and the Inter-Governmental Agreement on Electricity Procurement in the Greater Mekong Sub-Region.
3. Zhou Xiaojun, "What can Serve as Bridgehead of China-ASEAN FTA", *Economy Daily*, 8 January 2003. These two highways are now open.
4. The route is now partially completed.
5. The construction of this highway will commence soon.

6. Zhu Guolin, "Issues and Counter-Measures in Yunnan's Participation in the Construction of the China-ASEAN FTA", *Fazhan Luntan* [Development Forum], no. 5, 2002.
7. Wang Minzheng, "Facilitating the Lancang-Mekong Sub-Regional Cooperation to a Higher Stage", in *Yunnan Daily*, 20 October 2002.
8. The Kunming-Bangkok Highway will be extended to Malaysia and Singapore.
9. China and Thailand signed two agreements on the sale of Yunnan's electric power to Thailand and on joint construction of Jinghong Hydropower Plant. According to the Thai National Electric Power Development Plan, Thailand agrees to purchase 1.5 million kw from Jinghong Hydropower Plant in the year 2013 and another 1.5 million kw from Yunnan.
10. The "key channels" here refer to the "two channels" mentioned earlier in the text.

21

ASEAN-China Cooperation for Greater Mekong Sub-Region Development

Kao Kim Hourn and Sisowath Doung Chanto

BACKGROUND

It is fortunate that Southeast Asia is politically stable, enabling an environment conducive for regional cooperation and progress towards regional integration. However, while the spirit of regional cooperation is strengthening, the reality is that political and economic disparities exist among nation states in the region, and in general, institutional weakness continues to retard social progress, development and even social relations. Adding to that, as a consequence, it has been evident that Southeast Asia suffers from a high level of poverty which has worsened after the Asian economic crisis in 1997, the slowdown of Japan's and the United States' economies which the region is highly dependent on for export. In addition, it seems that more and more foreign direct investment is going to the region's largest neighbour, China, due in part to its large consumer market and competitive labour market. Now that the economy of the region is somewhat recovering from the crisis and the political environment is encouraging for regional market development, it is fitting that member countries of the region work together with their neighbours to improve regional competitiveness and reduce dependency on external markets and capitals.

This chapter looks at a specific area of cooperation which China could be very influential in promoting the interest of the common good for the region, for example, the ASEAN-China Economic Cooperation for the Greater Mekong Sub-Region (GMS). The central point of this chapter is that developing ASEAN-China relations is necessary for mutual benefit but this cooperative relation should not turn out to be simply that of a core and peripheral relationship. Rather, this cooperative relationship between ASEAN-China on GMS economic cooperation should be that of mutual partnership.

Naturally, given the economic and political rise of Southeast Asia's biggest neighbour, the People's Republic of China, it is only rational that member countries of the region welcome the rapid economic growth of China, its manufacturing and output capacity, technological development and financial power. The hope is that the ASEAN-China Cooperation will be fruitful for the collective good of the region. The rise of China can bring positive changes to the economies of Southeast Asia through trade, investment, and the flow of goods across borders and cooperation in non-traditional security. Politically the interaction between ASEAN member countries and China would strengthen the economic relationship as well as promote greater regional cohesion; therefore, it is logical that the ASEAN-China cooperation is mutually beneficial for the region as well as the citizens in each of the member countries. Conversely, China can take advantage of the region's resources and market for its exports. In addition to that, given the region's dire need for foreign direct investment, China does not have to look far for investment destinations. At the Eighth ASEAN-Summit on 3 November 2002, China expressed the intent of economic cooperation through the ASEAN-China Free Trade Area and at the same time indicated a gesture of goodwill for open trade and market development, although its trade with the GMS countries is minimal compared to its global trade. China had made its position clear on the development of the GMS, that is, the GMS is one of its high priorities in the region, with an emphasis on the Initiative for ASEAN Integration (IAI) to bridge development gaps between the newer members of ASEAN with their older ASEAN counterparts, and it is for this reason that China had made many lenient trade agreements with Cambodia, Laos, Myanmar and Vietnam (CLMV) as stated by Vice Foreign Minister Wang Yi.[1] However, in light of the cooperative relationship, China is an economy in transition, therefore some economic and structural problems still exist in China, namely the overheating of China's economy, governance reform issues, environment and health hazards which could very well affect the regional cooperation.

PROGRESS OF THE ASEAN-CHINA RELATIONSHIP

For the last several years, ASEAN and China had been laying the foundation for the institutional framework for functional cooperation that eventually led to economic and development cooperation. The ASEAN-China relationship started in 19 July 1991. At the time Chinese Foreign Minister Qian Qichen attended the Twenty-fourth ASEAN Ministerial Meeting (AMM) in Kuala Lumpur. The foreign minister expressed China's interest in strengthening cooperation with ASEAN for mutual benefit by identifying and developing specific areas of cooperation, namely, in science and technology. As the progress of cooperation continued to 1993, ASEAN started to prepare initiatives for a formal ASEAN-China relationship. The same year, ASEAN Secretary Dato' Ajit Singh led the ASEAN delegation to Beijing for an exploratory discussion with China's Vice Foreign Minister Tang Jiaxuan. The result of this meeting produced two ASEAN-China Joint Committees: 1) trade and economic cooperation; and 2) science and technology. Subsequent dialogues and meetings in 1997 laid out the institutional framework under which ASEAN-China established a Joint Cooperation Committee (ACJCC). At this meeting, both ASEAN and China agreed, among other things, that the ACJCC would "act as the coordinator for all the ASEAN-China mechanism at the working level"; and to "further consolidate the economic and functional cooperation" between ASEAN and China. In addition, the ACJCC would also promote cooperation in human resource development, people-to-people contacts and cultural exchanges. There was no mentioning of cooperation on the Greater Mekong Sub-Region but at this ACJCC meeting, there was a proposal to consider a development cooperation on remote sensing in the Lancang-Mekong River Basin, which was referred to as ASEAN-COST's (Committee on Science and Technology) Expert Group on Remote Sensing which was basically created to conduct joint operations and cost-sharing on remote sensing, meteorology and earth sciences.[2]

While there has been some consensus on economic and development cooperation, the ASEAN-China Cooperation on the Greater Sub-Mekong Region was not mentioned. It was not until November 2002 that China finally made its first participation in the Greater Mekong Sub-Region Economic Cooperation Summit in Phnom Penh, Cambodia. Within the theme of "Making it Happen: A Common Strategy on Cooperation for Regional Growth, Equity and Prosperity in the Greater Mekong Sub-Region",[3] China shared the vision and joined the commitment of the GMS development programmes. Key initiatives in this joint summit declaration are infrastructure investments needed to strengthen regional competitiveness, enhance consultation and mutual understanding and benefits, and expanding friendly consultations, promoting the foundation of steady regional economic growth and social progress. On the development cooperation side, the GMS countries' government declared that they are committed to invest in infrastructure and eventually making the transport corridors into economic corridors to enable diversification, industrialization and creating employment opportunity. The GMS leaders also declared that they will expedite the Framework Agreement for Cross-Border Movement of Goods and People, which China had agreed to support. Along with China's proposals, the GMS leaders promised to accelerate the implementation of the Inter-Governmental Agreement on Regional Power Trade, telecommunication infrastructure, and improving the investment climate for the private sector and supporting the ASEAN-China Free Trade Area. In all, the GMS ministers strongly endorsed the Ten-Year Strategic Framework for the GMS Eleven Flagship Programmes, proposed by the Asian Development Bank. Therefore to what extent and in what specific areas could China's participation facilitate, accelerate or expedite a common strategy on cooperation for regional growth, equity and prosperity? And what exactly are ASEAN and the GMS countries expecting China to deliver in a common strategy for regional growth, equity, and prosperity in the Greater Mekong Sub-Region?

GREATER MEKONG SUB-REGION: ADB-ASEAN-CHINA

The implementation of the GMS Programme is expected to bring many challenging tasks, particularly in administration, finance, legal system, and custom control. On the positive side, the GMS programmes were designed to promote economic growth that would fuel economic development for the GMS countries. Politically, GMS economic cooperation can contribute to regional stability and better relationships through economic interdependency; therefore, the dividend in economic cooperation is unquestionably an important factor in creating a positive climate for political cooperation. Initially, the GMS Forum was initiated in 1992. It was not until 1994 when the ASEAN economic ministers and Japan's Ministry of International Trade and Industry launched their efforts to develop Cambodia, Laos and Myanmar that the GMS developments became a critical development agenda for ASEAN. The GMS countries shared the same purpose for cooperative development: Both sides seek to foster a good climate and set the necessary conditions for investment and other economic activity, and the idea at the time as it is now has been to integrate markets and infrastructure linkages, leap-frogging the stages of growth.[4] But what is the real strategic value of the GMS? Is the GMS' grand scheme of economic cooperation meant for sustainable development or simply just a mechanism to maintain regional cohesion?

The Greater Mekong Sub-Region (GMS) is composed of the following countries: Cambodia, Lao People's Democratic Republic, Myanmar, Thailand, Vietnam and the Yunnan province of the People's Republic of China. The GMS has a combined land area of 2.3 million square kilometres, and is the habitat for approximately 243 million people. However, the majority of the people live in the rural areas and are living on a sub-subsistence, or semi-sub-subsistence farming lifestyle. For instance, over 75 per cent of the Laos population lives in the Mekong Basin. As for Thailand being the most urbanized of the Mekong countries, the north, and north-eastern part of the country are predominantly living on an agricultural economy in the Mekong Basin. Fortunately, the Mekong Sub-Region is endowed with rich natural resources that are essential for economic development to alleviate poverty and the hardships of rural livelihood. Naturally, residential communities along the Mekong Sub-Region benefit from the agriculture-based economy but the GMS is also enriched with timber, minerals and energy in the form of hydropower, coal and petroleum reserves. The Mekong River supports an agricultural economy and its fisheries stock is a source of food and income; moreover, the ecological environment in the Mekong Sub-Region provides the potential for tourism and natural resource exploration.[5] Regional stability in the region, in combination with economic integration such as cross-border trade, labour mobility and investment, has expanded the economic space across the region. Other economic mechanisms such as the ASEAN Investment Area (AIA), the Initiative for ASEAN Integration (IAI), the Common Effective Preferential Tariff (CEPT), and ASEAN Free Trade Agreement (AFTA), and the ASEAN-China Free Trade Area even further expands the necessary trade mechanisms for facilitating freer flow of capital and goods within the region. Therefore, the process of economic integration is empirically essential in order for ASEAN to be effective in implementing the GMS programmes.

The Asian Development Bank (ADB), being the most active financier of the GMS development, is keen on environmental issues while at the same time giving strong emphasis on human resource development. Since 1992, the ADB has been giving assistance to the six GMS countries — Cambodia, Laos, Myanmar, Thailand, Vietnam and the Yunnan province of China, to enhance economic relations among themselves so as to focus on infrastructure development, promoting freer flow of capitals and goods in the GMS

Programme. The GMS Programme focuses on eight priority sectors: 1) transport; 2) energy; 3) telecommunications; 4) environment; 5) human resource development; 6) tourism; 7) trade facilitation; and 8) investment. The ADB also helped to promote international recognition of the potential growth of the region. Given the priorities of development as listed by the ADB, there are other development projects that are being carried out by private companies within each respective country, especially in the field of energy development. In the case of Myanmar, Japan and Canada are exploring natural gas and petroleum. As for Thailand, power plant projects have become the central issue of concern of the local communities due to the development impact on the environment. The four new members, Cambodia, Laos, Vietnam, and Myanmar are in need of IT and ICT improvement to alleviate the digital divide between the developed and developing ASEAN members.

There are extensive proposed plans and agendas already laid out for the development of the GMS. The list is quite broad and many plans are rather ambitious. Also, it would help to be mindful that Japan has been working very closely with the Asian Development Bank in financing, planning, and designing many components of the GMS programme for sustainable development. Japan has been helping and financing projects for the Mekong River Commission (MRC) in its core programme, support programme and sector programme and China's entrance to the GMS is welcomed. Nonetheless, many areas of the ASEAN-China cooperation also overlaps with the ASEAN-Japan cooperation, which includes the GMS programme. Even though Japan is not a member country of the GMS, their initiatives with the GMS member countries has provided the launching pad for the GMS programme. What this means is that Japan and the ADB have been working towards sustainable development of the GMS programme. Therefore, it is necessary to avoid overlapping development.

On the other hand, while the spirit of regional cooperation of the GMS has been evident, the reality remains extremely challenging. The challenges are not merely the lack of capital to invest in sustainable development, but different levels of institutional functionality and inadequate human resource, financial power, consumption power, and regime types are inherent complications that need to be resolved by individual countries, mainly by that of the GMS countries. These institutional weaknesses slow down coordination, connectivity and competitiveness. To improve coordination among the GMS countries, at the Twelfth GMS Ministerial Conference,[6] the ministers agreed to meet more often to improve coordination and also to increase the participation of the private sector to strengthen development partnerships. In addition to regional coordination, GMS countries are engaging in their own Economic Cooperation Strategy, Emerald Triangle and the Development Triangle.[7] Nonetheless, GMS ministers appreciate the ADB's leadership and requested the ADB to continue their support. Meanwhile, countries such as Japan confirmed their ongoing strong commitment to support the GMS programme while France made new resource commitments. The World Bank indicated its support through its national programmes and expressed a keen interest in actively participating in some of the GMS working groups. Regardless, in order to achieve the fundamental building blocks of connectivity, competitiveness, and community, the challenges need to be addressed by the GMS countries, individually and collectively. First, the economic growth must be sustained through domestic reform and regional cooperation. This means the policy response must emphasize on poverty reduction, inequalities in income and opportunities that weaken economic, social and political gains in the region. Second, the role of the private sector must be facilitated. The indigenous private sector should be developed and strengthened to lay the foundation for competitiveness. Structural reforms and good governance are essential in facilitating the role of the private sector in economic growth. Third, biodiversity and ecological sensitivity of the Mekong River is critical in maintaining the balance of the ecological system for water, irrigation, food, and electricity. Sound management of natural resources is an important prerequisite for sustainable development. Fourth, financial resources need to be improved. Multilateral development institutions still constitute the majority of funding for the GMS programmes. GMS countries have to improve the mobilization of concessional financial resource.[8]

CHINA AND GREATER MEKONG SUB-REGION COOPERATION

The GMS strategy and framework creates economic and political interdependency among the Indochinese countries which helps to stabilize the region. The GMS system rewards state actors who cooperate and set free those who wish to go about their own way. When China signed the agreements listed in the above GMS Joint Declaration, they are theoretically bound to honour the provisions as stipulated. On the other hand, the listed visions and commitments are not very different from what the Asian Development Bank and the governments of the GMS countries have declared many years ago. The flagship programme is distinctly the ADB's concept of sustainable development plan and design, and most of these plans' components are inherently embedded in the idea of sustainable development that requires decentralization and democratic governance. The many outstanding challenges need to be resolved by the individual GMS countries, or collective regional cooperation. Beyond this area, the ASEAN-China Free Trade Area has indicated China's intentions in connecting the GMS countries to its market and institutional framework. For instance, the ASEAN-China Development Fund, the ASEAN-China Trade Negotiating Committee (ASEAN-China TNC), and the Sixth ASEAN-China Summit on Cooperation on Non-Traditional Security all simplify the institutional framework that is fundamental for strengthening regional integration.[9] However, it also appears that the China-ASEAN Cooperation goes beyond the economic interest. The China-ASEAN Cooperation is, rather, a comprehensive security strategy which helps to maintain stability and cohesion of the region by way of economic cooperation with the peripheral states of mainland China. China made it clear that regional security is important for its own national security, national interest and development.[10]

If China adheres to its pledges in the Eighth ASEAN Summit, Sixth ASEAN-China Summit, and the Tenth GMS Summit, its participation in the GMS is contributory to a very strategic setting for regional economic and political interests.[11] From an economic point of view, pending agreement on the provision of the ASEAN-China Free Trade Area, and the ASEAN-China Comprehensive Economic Partnership, China could be the gateway, and market destination for GMS countries and may thus reduce their export dependency on the international market. Likewise, Southeast Asia could become a strategic market space within the region for China. From this scenario, the ASEAN-China economic trade-off seems to be mutual, but the economic parity is by far in favour of China for several reasons. First, China has a much larger export capacity. Second, China has much more human and financial capital. Third, China is more competitive in attracting foreign direct investment. Fourth, China is more technologically advanced. In contrast, nearly all of the CLMV countries are deficient in all strategic resources such as human and financial capital as well as technological availability. Even so, it would be helpful to realize that China still has a high incidence of poverty and not all provinces sustain equitable growth. Moreover, in China, capital management is still problematic largely due to structural issues. This means that China still has overwhelming domestic and social concerns. Nonetheless, within the ASEAN-China Free Trade Area, China has agreed to expand its cooperative activities into five priority areas: 1) agriculture; 2) information and communication technology; 3) human resource development; 4) two-way investment; and 5) Mekong River Basin Development. In the area of agriculture, ASEAN and China signed a MOU between the Ministry of Agriculture of the People's Republic of China and the ASEAN Secretariat on behalf of the ASEAN Member Countries on Agricultural Cooperation on 2 November 2002 in Phnom Penh, Cambodia. This MOU is an agreement on technical cooperation on implementing training programmes for ASEAN participants in China. Specific areas of cooperation include forestry, livestock production, fisheries, biotechnology, post-harvest technology and the field harmonization of quarantine measures and standard conformity of agricultural products. The ASEAN-China cooperation is also extended to the Greater Mekong Sub-Region Framework, ASEAN Mekong Basin Development Cooperation and the Mekong River Commission. China has expressed interest in sponsoring an Initiative for ASEAN Integration (IAI), "Inland Waterway Improvement Project in CLMV Countries".

Between May 2002 and March 2003, ASEAN and China have implemented fourteen projects in the areas of science and technology, ICT, agriculture, transport, social development, HRD, and mass media.[12]

THE FINANCIAL COMMITMENT

There are many projects which the ASEAN-China Economic Cooperation has implemented under the ASEAN-China Free Trade Area framework. However, the idea of the Greater Mekong Sub-Region is sustainable development. In this context, while the prospects seem bountiful, the institutional delivery is still the major constraint, that is thus undermining competitiveness.

In the age of globalization and the acceleration of technology, competitiveness has been defined in terms of creativity rather than capital, intangible assets, such as knowledge, rather than tangible assets. Therefore, to respond to the paradigm shift, it is important that the GMS countries should increase investment in human capital and good governance. Information communication technology has brought about a fundamental change in conducting global trade and finance since national physical boundaries have become less relevant. It is necessary to be mindful that the GMS countries, including China, are still in the process of transition to a market-based economy and for that reason, the priority for the GMS countries is to accelerate the completion of structural reforms. Structural reform in the areas of finance, trade, legal systems, and investment regimes will be critical for sustaining economic growth and investment in human capital is needed. Good governance is mandatory to ensure that the Mekong Sub-Region sustains its competitive edge and provides the best investment environment. In addition to the institutional constraints, the issue of financing projects is still very challenging. In terms of financing, the ADB has been responsible in mobilizing resources to finance the GMS programme. By 2005, the ADB would have provided nearly US$1 billion to support the development in Yunnan province. Japan has always been supportive in providing credit to infrastructure development, institutional-building and human resource development to improve the investment climate for the private sector in the region. China has provided US$5 million through the ASEAN-China Cooperation Fund for human resource development and has provided US$5 million to improve the waterways of the Mekong River. In addition, China will provide US$30 million to fund one-third of the Laos section of the Kunming-Bangkok Highway.

Given the challenging scenario in making it happen, the GMS reality is exacerbated by institutional weaknesses, as well as inadequate financial and human capital. The GMS programme therefore is very much dependent on external resources, namely, the private sector. Structural reform should become a priority in order to strengthen confidence. Structural reform is necessary to progress towards sustainable development. The setback of the GMS scheme is not that the cooperative scheme is impossible but the political commitment to implement structural reform is lagging behind the economic development. Therefore, the most realistic and most practical implementation of the ASEAN-China Economic Cooperation Development is mainly to just focus on the infrastructure sector, and service and human resource development sector. With the fundamental areas of cooperation such as in transportation, human resource development, and governance taking place, such cooperation could promote growth, equity and prosperity to the region.

THE PROSPECTS AND REALITIES: CONNECTIVITY, COMPETITIVENESS, COMMUNITY

The prospects and realities of achieving the development plans in the ASEAN-China relations are not impossible but they require several fundamental phases, which are *connectivity, competitiveness and community*. For instance, *connectivity* is a strategy to achieve the GMS programme by connecting people, for which China provided considerable investment and support in the forms of the Pan-Asia Railway and East-West Corridors. The transport sector connects the region through inter-state transportation. Inter-state transportation is important for several significant purposes. Transportation is a way of connecting people while at the same time serving the economic interests by facilitating the flow of goods across the region, such as transferring heavy industrial machineries, or expanding the labour market to improve the diversity of skilled labour, and improving people-to-people relations such as tourism, or visiting friends and families across the borders. Ground transport also promote field researches in natural sciences beyond borders. Given the geographical and functional significance, the East-West Corridors such as the Singapore-China Railways jointly constructed by Singapore and funded by the ASEAN-China Cooperation Fund is strategically important. The Singapore-China Railways network is immensely and strategically necessary for the region because it facilitates the flow of goods and people.[13] Essentially, the Singapore-China Railways enables access to the Mekong Basin population where air transport is impossible.

Secondly, competitiveness will be achieved through human resource development. The prospect of realizing the GMS depends on the region's internal resources, particularly human resources. Given the advantage of economic dynamism and the diversity of resources, the region's human resource development is inadequate due to the lack of education and access to market information for creating knowledge-based workers. Today's workers need both skills and creativity. Skilled and creative workers are the building blocks in harnessing internal resources and are the cornerstone in building an ASEAN community in nexus to achieve effective regional integration. Education is important for capacity-building, and the utility that can be derived from innovation depends on the prevailing level of education. The paramount goal of education is to empower people by giving them the tools and capacities to engage in globalization such as taking advantage of the increasingly important role of information technology and market information. Equity and access to education remain the prevailing issues among the ASEAN countries and particularly, GMS member countries, although the level and degree of disparity vary. The educational systems of Cambodia, Laos and Myanmar have been severed by internal conflicts, and knowledge-based workers are nearly non-existent. Education is essential for harnessing internal resources. Education has become the building block for creating the economic space. Therefore, to harness its internal resources, ASEAN should focus on two critical strategic components as the strategies to harness external resources, which are the people and the markets.

Thirdly, community. It is the about people, not geopolitics. The China-ASEAN Cooperation in the field of human resource development could improve the confidence-building measures. In this context, it would be encouraging if the AMBDC would focus on substantive strategies as well as it does on economic strategies. People need to have knowledge that would enable them to make informed decisions in improving market development.

Moreover, it enables them to participate in the market system if the system provides "fair and equal opportunities" to access the market economy for all participants. Empowering people with tools to make independent markets and investment decisions is the essence of a market economy. And of course, education can effectively harness and realize the economic opportunities in the global economy if the majority of the people possess the tools to engage the market economy. The correlation in economic access, equity, increase in income and growth is evidently based on the capacity of a nation to meet the supply and demand of the international market. Development growth indicators cannot be measured based solely on income but also on the innovative capacity to create markets, or utilization of capitals. Education should be an issue of regional concern since all members are focusing on the possibility of a greater ASEAN development.

In terms of expanding the economic space and market dimension to attract external resources, to achieve this feat, the region needs to have equity, access, and income growth to sustain the strategy, where again education plays a very important role in enabling "sustainable development."

CONCLUSION

In conclusion, the prospects and realities of the ASEAN-China relations are bright and achievable. But the real issue at hand is not merely the spirit of cooperation for regional integration. Institutional and delivery constraints present a major problem but that could be remedied if there is political commitment. The realities of the GMS programme rests on structural reform that is also needed for sustainable development, which is particularly important since the people of the Mekong Basin depend on a balanced ecological system. Ultimately, the implementation of the GMS programme is about the people and not geopolitics.

NOTES

1. China Through A Lens, "China-ASEAN Relations Advanced", <http://www.china.org.cn/english/2002/Nov/414.htm>.
2. ASEAN-China Dialogue, <http//www.aseansec.org/7585.htm>.
3. Greater Mekong Sub-Region Economic Cooperation Programme, Twelfth Ministerial Conference, Dali City, Yunnan province, People's Republic of China, 17–19 September 2003.
4. ASEAN Secretariat, "Developing the Greater Mekong Sub-Region: The ASEAN Context", 2000, <http://www.aseansec.org/3256.htm>.
5. Mekong River Commission, "For Sustainable Development" (MRC: Cambodia, 2000).

6. Twelfth GMS Ministerial Conference, 17–19 September 2003, (Dali City, Yunnan province, People's Republic of China)

7. The Economic Cooperation Strategy involves cooperation among Cambodia, Lao PDR, Myanmar and Thailand. The strategy is designed to bring about economic integration among the four countries through greater intra-regional trade and investment. The Emerald Triangle involves cooperation among Cambodia, Lao PDR and Thailand in developing tourism along their shared borders. The Development Triangle Initiative (DTI) involves cooperation among Cambodia, Lao PDR and Vietnam. The aim of the DTI is to raise the level of economic activity in the economically disadvantaged regions. A plan to carry this out is currently being formulated by the countries.

8. Jin Liqun, Asian Development Bank, Vice President, Twelfth Ministerial GMS Meeting: "Greater Mekong Sub-Region Economic Cooperation Programme", Dali City, Yunnan province, People's Republic of China, 19 September 2003.

9. Sixth ASEAN-China Summit: "Joint Declaration of ASEAN and China on in the Field of No-Traditional Security", Phnom Penh, Cambodia, 4 November 2002, <http://www.casy.org/Chindoc/chinaasean.htm>.

10. Zhang Bin, "Comprehensive China-ASEAN Cooperation", 2003, <http://www.china.org.cn/english/2003/Jan/53338.htm>.

11. Press Statement by the Chairman of The Eighth ASEAN Summit, The Sixth ASEAN+3 Summit and The ASEAN China Summit, 4 November 2002, <http://www.aseansec.org/13189.htm>.

12. <http://www.aseansec.org/7585.htm>.

13. Gu Xaison, "On The Development of Cooperation Between South China and GMS: Building a Transportation Network of "1 Vertical and 2 Horizontal", presented at a conference held at the Cambodian Institute for Cooperation and Peace, Phnom Penh, Cambodia, 1–2 November 2000.

22

South China Sea: Turning Suspicion into Mutual Understanding and Cooperation

Gao Zhiguo

INTRODUCTION

As one of the major marginal seas in the world, the South China Sea (SCS) is defined by the International Hydrographic Bureau as the semi-enclosed body of water, situated from three degrees south latitude between South Sumatra and Kalimantan (Kalimantan Straits), and to the Strait of Taiwan from the northern tip of Taiwan to the mainland coast of China, and stretching in a southwest to northeast direction. The South China Sea is a semi-enclosed sea bordered by the ASEAN member states (Brunei Darussalam, Cambodia, Indonesia, Malaysia, the Philippines, Singapore, Thailand and Vietnam) and China (including Taiwan). For the purpose of discussion, the South China Sea also includes the adjoining Gulf of Thailand and the Gulf of Beibu (Tonkin).

This chapter aims to examine the recent relationship and cooperation between ASEAN and China in the South China Seas (SCS). To this end, it will proceed in four steps: First, the chapter begins with a brief introduction to the SCS and its importance. Second, it recalls the recent developments and their implications. Third, the chapter proceeds to examine the cooperative activities in terms of confidence-building. Finally, it attempts to sum up some of the major findings and offer some policy recommendations where possible.

IMPORTANCE OF THE SOUTH CHINA SEA

The total area of the waters of Southeast Asia is about 8.9 million square kilometres, accounting for 2.5 per cent of the world's ocean waters, out of which, the SCS, including the Gulf of Thailand, has a total area of about 3.5 million square kilometres. The significance of the South China Sea is characterized by its environmental and ecological value, living and non-living natural resources, and geopolitical and strategic position. It is the world's most diverse shallow-water marine area. Such richness in flora and fauna contributes to the area's high natural rates of primary and secondary production.[1]

First, the coastal sub-regions of the nations bordering the SCS are home to 270 million people, or 5 per cent of the world's population. The population in the region is predicted to increase from 475 million in 1993 to 726 million by the year 2025.[2] In Southeast Asia, more than 70 per cent of the population live in coastal areas, and their dependency on the SCS for resources and transportation is high.

Second, the SCS is a unique and integral eco-system and a repository for valuable natural resources. Fifty-one mangrove and over 450 coral species are recorded from the Philippines, compared with only five mangrove species and some thirty-five coral species found in the Atlantic. Fisheries in the Southeast Asian region represent 23 per cent of the total catch in Asia, and about 10 per cent of the total world's catch in 1992. Captured fisheries from the South China Sea contribute 10 per cent of the world's landed catch at around 5×10^6 tonnes year.[1] The SCS is the main source of protein for the 500 million people who live in the coastal zone of the sea.

Third, it has the world's busiest international shipping lanes. More than half of the world's supertanker traffic passes through the SCS waters. Over half of the world's merchant fleets (by tonnage) sail through the South China Sea every year, thus making its sea lanes one of the world's busiest international sea lanes.

Fourth, the SCS is also an arena for competing national claims for jurisdiction as well as security interests. In addition to the traditional issues of political stability and economic development in the region, it is today central to environmental sustainability and food security for rapidly expanding populations of the coastal and archipelago communities.

Fifth, oil and gas are perhaps the most important and attractive natural resources in the SCS. According to a 1995 study by Russia's Research Institute of Geology of Foreign Countries, the equivalent of six billion barrels of oil may be located in the Spratly Islands area alone, of which 70 per cent would be natural gas. Oil consumption over the next twenty years among developing Asian countries is expected to rise an annual 4 per cent on average, with about half of this increase coming from China. If this growth rate continues, these nations' oil demand will reach 25 million barrels per day, more than double the current consumption levels. It seems obvious that utilizing the oil and gas resources of the SCS remains one of the better choices for the nearby large energy-consuming countries.

Last but not the least, the SCS not only constitutes the maritime heart of the region, but also more importantly, binds southern China, an economically booming region, to Southeast Asia. The sea is of great importance economically, politically and ecologically to its surrounding nations, thus setting out the stage for necessary understanding and cooperation between the member states of ASEAN and China.

RECENT DEVELOPMENTS AND NEW EVENTS

The SCS has been historically a body of calm waters for many centuries. The contest for national jurisdiction over waters and islands between coastal states in the SCS is one of only recent origin. The late 1960s and early 1970s started to witness frequent territorial claims, which culminated in today's military partition of the Spratly Islands and overlapping national claims.[3] The controversial developments in the SCS over the last quarter of the last century may be grouped into the following categories:

First, military occupation of the Spratly Islands. The SCS is beyond doubt the most troubled waters in the world. Six states and parties have made territorial claims to all or part of the SCS islands. China and Vietnam have claimed the whole of the SCS archipelagoes as their territories. The Philippines, Malaysia and Brunei have made claims, all of which are of recent origin, to a portion of the Spratly Islands. All but Brunei have maintained a military presence in the Spratly archipelago area.[4]

Second, regional arms buying spree. The SCS states in general and claimant states in particular have been actively engaged in building up their military naval and air force capabilities, with a view to: First, backing up their territorial claims and military occupation; second, enhancing bargaining positions in future negotiations. Nearly all of the Southeast Asian countries have actively raised their military spending in order to beef up their modest naval and air force capabilities.⁵ As a result, the SCS region witnessed the largest military purchases in the 1990s.

Third, controversial resource developments. The hydrocarbon potentials in the SCS encouraged the littoral states to occupy islands in order to claim rights in future negotiations. Regional, as well as much of the international interests, centres primarily on these potential hydrocarbon resources. Among the many causes for tension in the SCS over the past three or four decades, the petroleum potentials are obviously the most important factor sparking the territorial claims and military partition of the Spratly Islands. Many parts of the continental shelf of the SCS with the best oil prospects have been or are under lease to both home and foreign oil companies. The SCS is becoming one of the most productive offshore oil fields in the world today, with an annual oil production of over 40 million tonnes.

Fourth, regional dialogue on confidence-building measures. Apart from the deteriorating developments discussed in the previous paragraphs, there were also positive deliberations undertaken by the SCS countries. These efforts culminated in a series of informal and semi-informal regional workshops, among which the workshop on Managing Potential Conflicts in the South China Sea, is worthy of mention. The workshop, brokered by Canada and attended by national representatives in their private capacity, was initiated by Indonesia in 1990, with a view to promoting understanding and avoiding possible conflicts in the SCS. The workshop evolved into a formidable regional forum consisting of annual assemblies and special working groups and meetings.

The September 11 terrorist attacks might be cited as another milestone for new events in the SCS, and which gave rise to a changing security configuration in the SCS and new responses to it by the claimant states. The major ones of these new events are briefly summarized below.

Continued Exercises by Claimant States

Despite the overall improvement of the situation, there have been sporadic actions and counter-actions taken by the claimants to bolster their respective maritime jurisdictional claims to the disputed islands and waters in the SCS.

Fishing disputes have been a frequent argument between the Philippines and China. The Philippines has over the last couple of years, continued to expel or arrest Chinese fishing vessels found in the disputed waters, claimed by China as its traditional fishing grounds and the Philippines as its exclusive economic zone (EEZ). Vietnam has quickened its steps to bolster its territorial and maritime jurisdictional claims in the SCS. Actions taken by Vietnam include setting up administrative bodies and resettling people and building logistics bases on the disputed islands in the SCS.[6] Vietnam's Coast Guard often seized Chinese fishing boats operating in SCS waters claimed by Vietnam.[7] Malaysia constructed a two-storey concrete building on Investigator Shoal in the Spratly Islands group in 1999.[8]

Emergence of New Players and their Expansion

Japan has maintained a strong interest in the SCS for a long time. Under its newly passed "Law Relating to Measures for Preserving the Peace and Security of Japan in the Event of a Situation in the Areas Surrounding Japan", the permitted area of activity of the self-defence forces (SDF) has been expanded from Japan's main islands to encompass "peripheral areas" including the SCS.[9] Japan has been making efforts to strengthen the long-range operational ability of its SDFs. Japan's Maritime Self-Defence Force (MSDF) is one of the biggest in the region, and has been strengthening its capabilities at an unprecedented speed. It is reported that, by 2015, Japan will have built either two medium-sized aircraft carriers or a large transport vessel with displacement in excess of 15,000 tonnes.[10] In the form of military exchange visits and joint exercises with countries in Southeast Asia and South Asia, Japan is seeking to play an active role in collaboration on maritime security in the SCS.

India is a dominant power in South Asia. But its sphere of influence and security interest has traditionally been concentrated on the Indian Ocean as its main strategic objectives. Nonetheless, India has lately developed a "southern forwarding strategy".[11] Under this policy, Indian has since 2000 been actively expanding its naval operations east into the SCS and the Pacific Rim. India's recent naval expansion into the SCS certainly increases the number of players in the region. This will in turn have an impact on the balance of power in the SCS. India's southern advance certainly caused some concern in the region, and even to the United States.

It remains to be seen what the impacts and effects of the expansion of Japan's MSDF into the SCS and India's southern policy are on crisis management and the maintenance of peace and security in the region.

Reinforcement of U.S. Military Presence

Like Japan, the United States is by no means a new player in the SCS. But in the wake of September 11, military ties of the United States with its traditional allies such as the Philippines and Thailand, and friendly countries such as Singapore, were strengthened. The relationship between the United States and Malaysia has also improved since the September 11 terrorist attacks.

More importantly, the U.S. security relationship with its past rival, Vietnam, has been considerably improved. The two countries signed a Bilateral Trade Agreement in 2001. Vietnam was invited by the United States to observe "Cobra Gold" in May 2002, the premier regional military exercise for peace-keeping operations in the Asia-Pacific region.

In short, after September 11 "the Americans have achieved what they have always wanted in Southeast Asia. They now have bilateral relations with countries in the region that keep the sea lanes open."[12]

Controversial Foreign Patrol in the Malacca Straits

In addition to recent reinforcement in the SCS region, the United States has lately put forward a proposal to send troops assisting anti-terrorist efforts in the Malacca Strait. This one-sided initiative met with conflicting and confusing messages within ASEAN member states. While Singapore welcomed the possibility of an American naval patrolling role in the straits, Indonesia openly rejected such an involvement.[13] As the key advocate of ASEAN regionalism in the past, Malaysia strongly opposed such a proposal, stating that "we will not agree for Malaysia to make any concessions on issues of sovereignty."[14]

Breakthroughs in Bilateral Cooperation in the SCS

Thanks to the overall improvement of situation in the SCS, two events of major significance have been achieved in the SCS. First, joint development negotiations between China and the Philippines. The two countries signed a memorandum of understanding in December 2003. Three rounds of negotiations have since been undertaken between China National Offshore Oil Corporation (CNOOC) and the Philippines National Oil Company. The oil companies of the two countries are currently working closely on selecting the potential blocks for joint development.

Second, the maritime boundary delimitation agreement between China and Vietnam. Relations between China and Vietnam have improved significantly in recent times. In February 1999, the General Secretaries of the Communist Party of China (CPC) and the Communist Party of Vietnam (CVC) reaffirmed the guiding principles in developing their bilateral relations for the twenty-first century, namely, "long-term, stable, future-oriented, good-neighbourliness and all-round cooperative relations".[15] The two countries signed their Land Border Treaty in December 1999, and the Agreement on Demarcation of Territorial Waters, Exclusive Economic Zone and Continental Shelf and the Agreement on Fisheries Cooperation in the Beibu (Tonkin)

Gulf in December 2000.[16] On 16 June 2004, the National Assembly (NA) of Vietnam approved the demarcation agreement on the territorial waters, exclusive economic zones and continental shelf of Vietnam and China in the Beibu Gulf.[17] It is expected that the treaty will also be ratified by China soon.

The two agreements on joint development by China with the Philippines and on maritime boundaries with Vietnam are, the first of their kind in the SCS in over thirty years. They certainly represent major breakthroughs in the troubled waters of the SCS.

REGIONAL EFFORTS IN MANAGING CONFLICTS

In the recent past, the issue of managing potential conflicts in the SCS has been identified as one of the major topics for discussions in the process of searching for a paradigm for peace and stability in the region. The following paragraphs attempt to summarize the major efforts on confidence-building in the region.

First, the South China Sea Workshop. The most influential regional dialogue processes is beyond doubt the Informal Workshop on Managing Potential Conflicts in the South China Sea (generally known as the SCS Workshop). The SCS Workshop, hosted by Indonesia and financially supported by Canada, devotes its entire discussions to the SCS issues since 1990. The workshops were attended by diplomats, civil servants and professionals in their private capacity. Eleven plenary SCS Workshops were held since 1990, together with a series of technical working group meetings, group of experts meetings, and study group meetings.

Issues discussed at these meetings included legal matters, marine scientific research, safety of shipping navigation and communications, environmental protection, hydrographic data and information exchange, resource assessment, and zones of cooperation in the SCS. Canadian International Development Agency (CIDA) contributed US$4 million over ten years to support the activities conducted by the SCS Workshop process.

There is no question that the workshop series played a positive role in promoting mutual understanding and building confidence among the participants and the countries they represented during the 1990s.[18] The positive contribution of the SCS Workshop was properly acknowledged in the Joint Communique of the Thirty-Fourth ASEAN Ministerial Meeting held in Hanoi, Vietnam, in 2001.[19]

CIDA made a sudden decision in March 2001 to terminate funding of the participants to the SCS Workshop and the relevant meetings. The countries attending the SCS Workshop decided to take over the workshop process and run it by themselves since 2001. It is unclear whether the Track 2.5 nature of the workshop has been maintained or not. But it is widely believed that the momentum of the SCS Workshop process will disappear once it becomes an official talk-shop.

Second, the ARF and CSCAP discussions of the SCS issues. The SCS issues were also raised and discussed at the ASEAN Regional Forum (ARF), the so-called Track I international governmental organization in the Asia-Pacific region dealing with security issues; and the Council for Security Cooperation in the Asia-Pacific (CSCAP), one of the major Track II non-governmental organizations in the Asia-Pacific region. CSCAP has five working groups, including one on maritime cooperation.[20] Discussions of the SCS issues at these two official and unofficial forums were general and less focused on the SCS issues. They are therefore not examined in greater detail here.

Third, active cooperation between China and ASEAN. The SCS has in recent years seen rapid growth in cooperation between ASEAN and China. China was accorded full dialogue partner status at the Twenty-Ninth ASEAN Ministerial Meeting in Jakarta, Indonesia, in July 1996. China has, since then actively participated in a series of consultation meetings with ASEAN such as the ARF, the Post Ministerial Conference (PMC), and the ASEAN-China Senior Officials' Consultations. At the end of 1997, Chinese President Jiang Zemin and ASEAN leaders had their first informal meeting and issued a joint statement in which the two sides decided to establish a partnership of good neighbourliness and mutual trust toward the twenty-first century. At the ASEAN+1 Summit held in Bandar Seri Begawan in November 2001, ASEAN leaders and China endorsed the proposal for a Framework on Economic Cooperation and to establish an ASEAN-China FTA within ten years. The delegates from China and the ten member states of ASEAN met in Beijing in May 2002 to discuss the outline pact that would make the ASEAN-China free trade zone a reality within a decade.

In the political field, China took a positive attitude towards accession to the Treaty of Amity and Cooperation in Southeast Asia and successfully became a party to the treaty in 2004. As far as managing potential conflicts in the SCS is concerned, China and ASEAN were actively engaged in consultations since 1999 with a view to formulating a regional code of conduct in the SCS. At the regional level, two events may be cited as being of significance.

Fourth, declaration on the conduct of parties in the SCS. Another more important move in the region was the slow development of a possible code of conduct in the SCS. The notion of a code of conduct was not alien to the states of the region. In August 1995, China and the Philippines signed a Joint Statement on the South China Sea and Other Areas of Cooperation, in which the two countries agreed to abide by specific principles for a code of conduct in the disputed Spratly area. The Philippines and Vietnam agreed upon a joint agreement in November of the same year, which provides for "basic principles for a code of conduct in the contested areas".[21] Ironically, the two bilateral codes of conduct in the SCS did not succeed in preventing the parties to them from expanding the structures built on the Spratly Islands, and from firing at or arresting fishing boats operating in the disputed waters.

The regional process on a code of conduct first started in the form of informal consultations between ASEAN and China in 1999. During the consultations, ASEAN and China reaffirmed their desire to have the code as a set of general guidelines for managing disputes in the SCS and developing good neighbourliness and friendly relations between China and member countries of ASEAN.[22] In November 2002, ASEAN and China agreed upon a Declaration on the Conduct of Parties in the South China Sea.

The ASEAN-China regional code of conduct in the SCS, if adopted, could help build trust, enhance cooperation, and reduce tensions in the SCS area.

FINDINGS AND IMPLICATIONS

Many changes in the security concept and mechanisms have taken place worldwide since the September 11 terrorist attacks. The overall situation of the SCS and its issues are not an exception to these world and regional evolutions. The following discussion makes an attempt to look at some of the important policy findings from the preceding discussions.

Major Policy Findings

1. Shift in Security Concerns in the SCS

The SCS also witnessed a shift in security concerns among coastal states. Like elsewhere, the new concept of comprehensive security emerged and became accepted by the states of the SCS region. They, too, came to recognize that major threats to national security are more likely to come from non-state terrorist groups, rather than the traditional security threats and dangers of conflicts arising from sovereignty disputes, such as competing national claims in the SCS. As a result, the focus of the security dialogue and mechanisms in the SCS region have, like elsewhere, shifted to anti-terrorism efforts and relevant cooperative measures.

For instance, at the Seventh ASEAN Summit in November 2001, the leaders considered the September 11 terrorist attacks a direct challenge to the attainment of peace, progress, and prosperity of ASEAN. They adopted the ASEAN Declaration on Joint Action to Counter Terrorism in the same year.[23] Three member states of ASEAN — the Philippines, Malaysia and Indonesia — went on to sign an Anti-Terrorism Pact on 7 May 2002, which aims to target potential terrorist threats and devise measures to tackle money-laundering, smuggling, drug-trafficking, hijacking, illegal trafficking in women and children, and piracy.[24]

Security has been a priority issue of the Shanghai Cooperation Organization (SCO) when it was founded by China, Russia, Kazakhstan, Kirgizstan, Tajikistan and Uzbekistan in 2001. The six member-nations of the SCO met in Uzbekistan to discuss mutual security concerns. The focus of the 2004 Summit meeting is to open an anti-terrorism centre in Tashkent. Speaking at a press conference following the SCO, China's President Hu Jintao said, "to realize that target, we must jointly fight the 'three forces' of terrorism, separatism and extremism, deal with transnational threats and curb drug smuggling to maintain national security and social stability of the SCO members."[25]

2. Shift in the U.S. SCS Policy

Since the inception of the SCS issues, the United States had adopted and maintained a position of neutrality towards the SCS disputes. But as the strategic environment changed and the need for anti-terrorism effort increased after September 11, the SCS policy of the United States evolved slowly but steadily from "neutrality to active neutrality, and active concern".

The United States change in its SCS policy may be witnessed by the increasing number and scale of joint military exercises with Southeast Asian countries. These include: "*Balikatan*" (meaning shoulder to shoulder) with the Philippines in 2000; joint military exercise the "Cobra Gold" with Thailand on an annual basis, and in which Singapore also joined in 2000. The United States also conducted its own military exercises using carrier battle groups in the SCS in 2001.[26] The purpose of these joint and unilateral exercises is to — as claimed by the United States — help maintain stability and peace in the Asia-Pacific region, and to ensure the exercise of freedom of navigation in the SCS.

It is this author's view for some time that the United States' switch in its SCS policy will continue further from "active neutrality" to one of "active concern", possibly evolving in the direction of becoming willing to intervene in sovereignty questions.[27] The EP-3 mid-air collision over the SCS in April 2001, and dispute over the U.S. naval vessel "Boditch" conducting military surveys in the nearshore waters off China's coasts in 2002 and 2003, may be viewed as a relevant indicator of the suggested direction.

3. Shift in China's Attitude on SCS Issues

As one of the major claimant states in the SCS, China has been active in searching for a mutually acceptable resolution to the SCS issues. Traditionally, China generally views territorial questions as bilateral issues, and has seldom engaged itself in any group discussions. Nonetheless, this conservative attitude has been slowly improving in recent years, as evidenced by the following movements. For instance, China has in the past expressed its dissatisfaction over, and even opposition to, the joint military exercises held by the United States with Southeast Asian and other countries in the SCS. China attended the U.S.-Thailand-Singapore "Cobra Gold" joint military exercise for the first time in May 2002. The negotiation with ASEAN on the code of conduct and the final adoption of the Declaration of Conduct of Parties in the SCS serves as another best example of pragmatism and openness. Against this backdrop, it can be said that China's recent initiative to approach the territorial disputes with Vietnam and the Philippines through active bilateral talks demonstrates not only its pragmatic attitude and flexibility, but also its fine-tuning in policy toward ASEAN on the SCS issues.

Implications of the New Developments of the SCS Issues

The implications of the new developments in the SCS issues may be briefly noted as follows:

First, the SCS was previously viewed, particularly by many Western commentators, as one of the flash points in Asia. But the view now shared by this author is that the likelihood of serious armed conflict in the SCS arising from overlapping claims and territorial disputes has been further reduced.[28] This assessment can find its support in many of the new developments in the SCS such as the Declaration on the Conduct of Parties, the joint development programme between China and the Philippines, and the maritime delimitation agreement between China and Vietnam. As a result, a more stable situation in the SCS is required by both ASEAN and China.

Second, Japan has historically had an interest in the SCS. It is anticipated that the country will play an increasing security role there since the limitations on its overseas military involvement, set by its peace constitution after the

Second World War, has not only been lifted by the legislation enacted in October 2001, but also expanded by the Japanese Diet in June 2004.[29] India's fresh entry into the SCS increased the number of players in a place that is already crowded and complicated.

Their immediate implication in the SCS area is to give rise to competition, with ASEAN in general, and China and the United States in particular, for political, economic, and strategic influence in the area. The expansion of Japan's more active involvement in regional maritime security matters, and emergence of India as a new player in the SCS will undoubtedly have a strategic influence in the SCS and the direction of the SCS issues in the future.

Third, the most important breakthrough in terms of understanding and cooperation on the SCS is by far the Declaration on the Conduct of Parties in the SCS between ASEAN and China. Despite the fact that this *quasi* code of conduct is political in nature and has no legal binding force, it is, in this author's view, the best result that can be achieved at present. Its significance lies in the following aspects: 1) it provides ASEAN and China with a formal, even if not a legal, framework for understanding and cooperation on the SCS issues; 2) it serves, more or less, as a safety valve to prevent the relevant parties from taking further unilateral actions or counteractions in the disputed waters and area; 3) it provides the parties with a solid basis for the adoption of a formal regional code of conduct, if this is the desire by all the parties concerned.

Fourth, that being said, it is unrealistic or even naive to expect that the adoption of the Declaration on the Conduct of Parties will be able to prevent all unilateral actions or counteraction in the SCS. The arbitrary move of late by one member state of ASEAN in organizing tour visits to the Spratly Islands is not only highly controversial, but also destructive to the declaration itself. It constitutes an open violation of the spirit and letter of the declaration. It has a poisoning effect on the current understanding and cooperation between ASEAN and China. The worst consequence of such a move, if unchecked and unregulated, is that it is likely to reopen a Pandora's Box, that is, igniting another round of spiralling counter-actions, both within and beyond ASEAN, to bolster their respective sovereignty and jurisdictional claims in the SCS.

Fifth, as already noted, the post-September 11 period in the SCS has seen a reinforcement of the U.S. military presence in the SCS area. The recent attempt by the United States to expand its reinforcement in the form of stationing troops in the Malacca Straits under the name of anti-terrorism has caused concern in Southeast Asia, and met with resistance from some ASEAN member states. This brings another aspect of uncertainty to the overall situation of the SCS and its future.

POLICY RECOMMENDATION AND CONCLUSIONS

ASEAN member states and China have been plagued by the ups and downs in the SCS for over the last three decades. It is not an easy task to have the opportunity of creating such a benign strategic environment in the SCS at the beginning of a new century. For this and other reasons, both ASEAN and China should cherish such a rare opportunity and grab it to promote further understanding and cooperation.

As observed, the general situation in the SCS, and the relations between China and ASEAN as well as its member states, have improved in recent years. This trend of understanding and cooperation is likely to continue, at least in the foreseeable future. The implications of the recent developments and events are perhaps two-fold. While the overall trend is positive and encouraging, some aspects of current events in the SCS are controversial causes for legitimate concerns. These incidents include the recently organized boat tour visit by Vietnam to the Spratly Islands, and the United States' proposal to help patrol the Malacca Straits. According to past experiences, these unwelcome and aggressive actions or counter-actions by a few claimant states can be expected. But the likelihood of these actions to erupt into serious armed conflicts or their ability to adversely affect the peace and stability in the SCS has lessened, at least in comparison with the SCS in the 1980s and 1990s.

The long-standing jurisdictional claims and territorial disputes in the SCS have yielded to the concept of comprehensive security in the region. Tackling the non-traditional security issues such as economic and environmental security, piracy, transnational crimes, maritime terrorism, and law and order at sea, requires regional wisdom and collective efforts. All these fundamental changes helped to shape a new strategic environment in the SCS, in which understanding and cooperation are the only way out for ASEAN and China.

As demonstrated by the recent developments in the SCS and analysed in this chapter, history provides ASEAN and China with a rare opportunity for turning suspicion into understanding and cooperation in the SCS. It is our view that the people and governments of the region will not tolerate a deteriorating SCS. Rather, there is much reason to believe that ASEAN and

China are capable of joining forces to create and maintain peace and stability in the SCS in the twenty-first century.

NOTES

1. UNEP, *Strategic Action Programme for the South Chins Sea*, UNEP SCS/SAP version 3, 24 February 1999.
2. World Resource Institute, 1996.
3. For a full discussion, see Z. Gao, "The South China Sea: From Conflict to Cooperation", *Ocean Development & International Law* 25 (1994): 345–59.
4. Ibid.
5. Ibid., pp. 347–49.
6. "Vietnam Evokes Spratlys before China VP Visits", *Reuters*, 16 April 2001 and "China Demands Vietnam Clarify Disputed Isles Move", *Reuters*, 13 February 2001.
7. For example, see "Vietnam Seizes 51 Chinese Fishermen", *Muzi Lateline News*, 13 June 2001, <http://lateline.muzi.net>.
8. See "China Warns Malaysia Off Construction on Spratly Islands", *China Times*, 30 June 1999.
9. The Ministry of Foreign Affairs of Japan, *Diplomatic Bluebook 2000: Toward the 21st Century*, <http://www.mofa.go.jp/policy/other/bluebook/2000/II-1-1.html>.
10. "Japan's SDF Quietly Expanding Its Long-range Capability", *People's Daily* (Online), 13 December 2000. For more information, visit Japan MSDF's website at <http://www.jda.go.jp/ JMSDF/basic/ DEFEN_E.HTM>.
11. "India's Navy Moves into the South China Sea", *Financial News* (China) (in Chinese), 2 October 2000; "India Challenges China in South China Sea", *Asia Times* (Online), 27 April 2000.
12. " 'War on Terror' Ups U.S. Role in the Philippines", *Inter Press Service*, 24 March 2002.
13. *News References* (in Chinese), 6 June 2004, p. 2.
14. Ibid.
15. "China and Vietnam", Ministry of Foreign Affairs of the People's Republic of China, <http://us-mirror.fmprc.gov.cn/eng/4471.html>.
16. Nguyen Hong Thao, "The Settlement of Disputes in Bac Bo (Tonkin) Gulf", Veitnam Law & Legal Forum, January 2001, pp. 15–18.
17. *People's Daily* (Online), 16 June 2004.
18. The Workshop on Managing Potential Conflicts in the South China Sea was the informal multilateral dialogue process organized by Indonesia to address issues, in particular those related to the Spratly Islands and the broader SCS. For more information, See generally Hasjim Djalal, "Indonesia and the South China Sea Initiative", *Ocean Development and International Law* 32 (2001): 97–103 and Ian Townsend-Gault, "Preventive Diplomacy and Pro-Activity in the South China Sea", *Contemporary Southeast Asia* 20 (1998): 171–90.

19. See the "Joint Communique of the 34th ASEAN Ministerial Meeting, Hanoi, 23–24 July 2001", <http://www.aseansec.org>.

20. For an introduction to CSCAP, please visit <http://www.cscap.org/about.htm>.

21. See generally Nguyen Hong Thao, "Vietnam and the Code of Conduct for the South China Sea", *Ocean Development and International Law* 32 (2001): 126–27.

22. See press release, "ASEAN and China Held A Successful Consultation on Regional Code of Conduct in the South China Sea", <http://www.aseansec.org/news/rcc_scs.htm>.

23. For a full version of the declaration, please visit <http://www.aseansec.org/newdata/2001_asean_declaration.htm>.

24. "Fighting Terror in Southeast Asia: ASEAN Cooperation", *The International Herald Tribune*, 22 May 2002, p. 6. *The Straits Times* (Singapore), 8 May 2002, p. 1.

25. *China Daily*, 19 June 2004, <http://www.chinadaily.com.cn.english/doc.2004-0617/content_ 340342.htm>; *BBC News*, 16 June 2004. See also "SCO Vows to Fight Against Terrorism: Statement", *People's Daily*, 7 January 2002.

26. "Carrier Battle Groups Hold Joint Exercise in South China Sea", *USS Constellation* public affairs, posted 27 August 2001, available at <http://www.c7f.navy.mil/news/2001/08/33.htm>.

27. Yann-Huei Song, "The Overall Situation in the South China Sea in the New Millennium: Before and After the September 11 Terrorist Attacks", *ODIL* 34 (2003): 250–52 .

28. Ibid., p. 261.

29. The Anti-Terrorism Special Measures Law was passed by the Diet on 29 October 2001. For a full version of the law, see the homepage of the Ministry of Foreign Affairs of Japan, "Japan's Measures in Response to the Terrorist Attacks in the United States", <http://www.infojapan.org/region/n-america/us/terror0109/policy/measures.htm>.

23

The South China Sea Disputes after the 2002 Declaration: Beyond Confidence-Building

Aileen S.P. Baviera

BACKGROUND TO THE CLAIMS

The South China Sea (SCS) disputes refer to competing territorial and jurisdictional claims over four groups of islands, reefs, and atolls (Paracels, Spratlys, Macclesfield Bank, and Pratas), along with their surrounding waters, lying strategically between China and Southeast Asia. The claimants include China and Taiwan who are believed to claim the entire South China Sea area, and Vietnam, the Philippines, Malaysia, and Brunei whose claims are more limited to certain features and areas. The SCS is strategically important for various reasons, among them the fact that critical sea-lanes traverse the waters, linking northeast Asia and the western Pacific to the Indian Ocean and the Middle East. More than half the world's shipping tonnage reportedly sails through the South China Sea each year, including more than 80 per cent of the oil destined for Japan, South Korea and Taiwan.[1]

The disputes, particularly those over the Spratly Islands, are considered one of the most complex territorial disputes because there are at least three, but potentially as many as six, claimants to different parts of the area, and not all the claimants have clearly delineated their claims nor fully articulated their grounds for such. Moreover, there is a range of interests at stake for the different parties, including the potential for oil and natural gas deposits in the seabed, access to rich fishing grounds, strategic control of the sealanes, security from external threats, and even protection of the immediate marine environment. The patterns of occupation and military presence in the disputed areas — with Vietnam now occupying the largest number of features in the Spratlys at more than 22, China 14, the Philippines 11, Malaysia 10, Taiwan 1 (the largest feature — Itu Aba), and Brunei none[2] — make it nearly impossible to seek a solution based on physical division of the multiple claim areas. Except for a few islands which have been converted into civilian facilities by Taiwan and Malaysia, the rest are occupied by military troops. Armed clashes took place between China and Vietnam in the Paracels in 1974 and in the Spratlys in 1988.

Claimant states have engaged in unilateral assertions of sovereignty over their claimed areas, such as building or upgrading of structures and facilities (whether military or civilian in nature), conducting naval and air patrols, undertaking oil exploration and fishery activities under state protection, enacting national legislation on the use of the seas in total disregard of other claims, and others. These have resulted in episodes of high tension among the states bordering the South China Sea, although no significant armed conflict has taken place since 1988.

Larger events in the East Asian region during the post-Cold War period contributed to the increasing importance of the South China Sea, raising the stakes for those involved. These include the 1994 entry into force of the UN Convention on the Law of the Sea (UNCLOS), which hastened competition for extended jurisdictions over ocean areas; the heightening contest for hydrocarbon and fisheries resources; the rapid growth of intra-regional trade and thus reliance on shipping; as well as the rise of China as a regional power. The reduction in the U.S. military presence in the region has also added an element of uncertainty to the regional security environment. Meanwhile, Vietnam joined ASEAN, with the perhaps unintended result that the South China Sea disputes began to be thought of and increasingly approached as a problem between China (both Beijing and Taipei, assuming they have a common claim) and ASEAN.

Various confidence-building initiatives have been undertaken by the claimants to try to manage the rising tensions. In 1992, ASEAN enunciated the "Manila Declaration on the South China Sea", calling for restraint and urging cooperation among the various claimants. At the bilateral level, high-level exchanges between military and civilian officials of various countries took place, and agreements upholding the need for peaceful resolution were concluded — such as the China-Vietnam delimitation of the Tonkin Gulf and fisheries cooperation agreements in 2000, and the 1995 Philippines-China and 1996 Philippines-Vietnam agreements on "principles for a code of conduct". The latter two agreements called for the parties to undertake confidence-building measures, exercise restraint and refrain from use or threat of force, as well as expressed the need to cooperate for the protection and conservation of marine resources.

Assessing the agreements and exchanges in terms of results, it appears that these bilateral confidence-building measures still fell short of preventing unilateral activities from taking place. For example, the 1995 "code of conduct" between the Philippines and China did not prevent China from upgrading its presence on Philippine-claimed Mischief Reef to more permanent and apparently military-use structures in 1998–99, although China may have been persuaded to try to pre-empt criticism by sending ASEAN prior notification of its actions. Neither did the existing agreements, non-binding as they are, prevent other possible triggers of conflict such as the apprehension of fishermen by foreign navies, military overflights by one country over the occupied territories of another, continuing upgrades of military facilities, or the presence of warships and survey vessels in disputed areas.

There have also been multilateral ASEAN-China efforts to defuse tensions, but here, too, progress has been slow. In the aftermath of China's occupation of Mischief Reef in early 1995, the ASEAN states closed ranks and severely criticized China's actions. Thus, 1995 marked the first time China agreed to discuss the Spratlys dispute multilaterally with the ASEAN claimants. The disputes have since then become part of the agenda of annual China-ASEAN meetings, involving all of ASEAN and not just the claimants. Notably, however, ASEAN claimants have not been able to sustain solidarity on the matter of how to deal with China on this issue, China being the most militarily powerful claimant and the most expansive in its claims, with Vietnam possibly being the most cautious and suspicious of China's intentions, Malaysia apparently the most in agreement with China's position of seeking bilateral rather than multilateral solutions, and the Philippines somewhere in between. For that matter, tensions among the ASEAN claimants arising from actions in the disputed areas have also surged occasionally, such as between the Philippines and Vietnam, the Philippines and Malaysia, and Malaysia and Vietnam.

For many years, the Indonesian Government with the support of Canada also organized a series of confidence-building workshops on "Managing

Potential Conflicts in the South China Sea", where all claimant countries were in attendance. The workshops resulted in a number of proposals for cooperation, but their implementation has been snagged by the reluctance of governments to compromise on the issue of sovereignty.[3] On the other hand, as an indirect result of the workshop, certain parties have been inspired to explore functional cooperation with each other, such as the Philippines and Vietnam, which have held joint oceanographic and marine scientific research expeditions in the disputed areas. Unfortunately, funding for the Indonesian workshops was halted in 2002 after more than a decade, placing the future of the process in question.

In 1997, the top leaders of China and ASEAN also held their first summit and issued a Joint Statement for ASEAN-China Cooperation towards the Twenty-First Century that covered overall relations. On the subject of the South China Sea disputes, the statement said that the two sides shall "continue to exercise restraint and handle relevant differences in a cool and constructive manner".[4] Then in 1998, the ASEAN governments and China resolved to work for a regional code of conduct to prevent the further escalation of conflict.

Following much internal negotiation among ASEAN members and then between ASEAN and China, a regional Declaration on the Conduct of Parties to the South China Sea — not a code as targeted — was finally agreed upon in November 2002. It was the first time China agreed to a formal multilateral agreement on the SCS, and therefore raised some hopes of significant compromise. To some China watchers, this confirmed their analysis that China showed an increasing receptivity to international norms in its foreign policy behaviour.[5] Some noted a shift in approach to ASEAN, which one scholar attributed to China's current need for the diplomatic and economic support of ASEAN states, as well as China's fear of the political costs should it be forced to take unilateral action.[6]

ASEAN-CHINA DECLARATION ON THE CONDUCT OF PARTIES TO THE SCS

What was the significance of the Declaration of Conduct? Most knowledgeable observers are probably sceptical that this new declaration can succeed where other agreements have already failed, owing to its emphasis on principles (which some would call "motherhood statements") and the lack of verifiable commitments. This writer's view of the declaration, however, can be described as neither sceptical nor optimistic, but one that sees the declaration as a challenge to future regional policy *vis-à-vis* the disputes. This chapter thus examines how claimants and other interested parties can use the agreement to push forward the process of ASEAN-China SCS conflict management beyond confidence-building and into the next, vital stage of preventive diplomacy, eventually paving the way for claimants to explore together cooperative approaches to the management of the ocean and its resources.[7]

The official proposal for an ASEAN-China code of conduct came in 1996 from the ASEAN foreign ministers, who during the ASEAN Ministerial Meeting endorsed the need to have such a code "to lay the foundation of long-term stability" with respect to the territorial disputes, using the 1995 Philippines-China code of conduct as a model. At first, China resisted ASEAN's proposal for a code, citing previous bilateral agreements between China and ASEAN countries which already embodied the commitment to peaceful resolution of disputes, and then later arguing that the 1997 China-ASEAN joint statement on twenty-first century cooperation made such a code unnecessary. However, perhaps because of ASEAN's persistence, China finally gave way and in 1999 agreed to discuss the drafting of a code. Ultimately, the agreement reached in November 2002 fell short of some people's original expectations of a more concrete and binding multilateral pact, but it nevertheless should be seen as a building block to peace in the SCS, one whose significance will be determined by the actions taken by the parties to faithfully implement its provisions.

The declaration binds the parties to the usual common principles (those of the United Nations Charter, the UN Convention on the Law of the Sea, the Southeast Asian Treaty of Amity and Cooperation, and the "Five Principles of Peaceful Co-Existence"), as well as to consultative and peaceful processes of dispute settlement based on "equality and mutual respect". Other provisions of the declaration include calls for the exercise of self-restraint; mutual notification of military exercises; exchange of information; and the extension of humanitarian treatment to all persons in situations of danger or distress in the area. The declaration then calls on parties to promote exploration or cooperation in marine environmental protection, scientific research, safety of navigation, search and rescue, and efforts aimed at combating transnational crime.[8]

Most of these provisions are not new and all of them have in one way or another been proposed in various bilateral and multilateral mechanisms involving the claimant states. There are three specific commitments, however, that this writer finds to be of potential significance.

The first is an undertaking to "refrain from action of inhabiting on (sic) the presently uninhabited islands, reefs, shoals, cays, and other features".

Simply put, this means that no new occupation should take place, and implies that there should be a freeze on the status quo of occupations, as far as the effect that "effective occupation" may have on the legality of one's claims under international law. If this commitment is fully complied with, the claimant states should be less anxious about further "creeping expansionism" by other claimants and won't have to be on the constant lookout, and can thus concentrate on defining and limiting the nature of the present occupation to non-hostile, peaceful purposes. The same item of the declaration also contains specific confidence-building commitments such as voluntary notification of joint military exercises in the area and humane treatment of persons in danger or distress. Both appear to be initiatives of the Chinese side, the first with reference to the resumption of joint Philippines-U.S. military exercises and the second in light of the growing number of Chinese fishermen who are being apprehended for intrusion and illegal fishing not just in disputed territories, but in the case of the Philippines, well within the boundaries of the main archipelago.

The second commitment of potential significance is a pledge to continue regular consultations on the *observance* of the declaration (emphasis mine), "for the purpose of promoting good neighbourliness and transparency…and facilitating peaceful resolution of disputes". One problem that arises is how can one tell whether commitments under the declaration are being observed or not? This necessitates efforts by the parties to further operationalize the meaning of or to transform into verifiable indicators such broad concepts as the "threat or use of force", "self-restraint", "activities that would complicate or escalate disputes", and "freedom of navigation and overflight", particularly in the context of the actual state of military and civilian activity as well as in relation to the parties' respective rights and jurisdictions under UNCLOS. For instance, if military aircraft of one claimant state repeatedly flies over an island occupied by another, this may be interpreted as a "threat to use force" by the occupant of the island, but be argued as an exercise of the "freedom of overflight" over its EEZ by the state to which the aircraft belongs. In another example, if fishermen of one country are apprehended for fishing in a disputed area claimed as EEZ by another country, can the act of fishing itself be considered "an activity that would complicate the disputes", or it is the apprehension of fishermen that might be seen as "complicating" or "escalating" the disputes? It appears necessary to come to mutually-acceptable interpretations of such actions, and one must therefore define these concepts in concrete terms. In the process, parties should engage in identifying conflict prevention measures that can provide the basis of each one's rules of engagement as well as for a possible future, binding "code of conduct". Moreover, this process should pave the way for agreement on what constitutes or does not constitute a violation of the Declaration of Conduct, as well as establishing procedures for monitoring and verification of the actions of claimants, and for developing agreement on whatever the consequences of violations should be.

Thirdly, the parties agreed to work for the eventual adoption of a genuine and binding *code* of conduct (as opposed to a *declaration*) on the basis of consensus (emphases mine). The negotiations and drafting process leading up to the November 2002 Declaration already revealed the extent of disagreement among the parties over how prepared they are for more binding instruments (that is, a legal "code" or treaty as against a political "declaration"). In this light, the inclusion of this statement demonstrates an appreciation of the need to gradually strengthen the quality of their commitment to cooperate for the sake of peace and development in the South China Sea. It also sets a new benchmark that the parties should strive to attain. A possible approach to establishing a binding code of conduct would be for the claimants to enter into bilateral incidents-at-sea agreements (INCSEA), eventually linking these into a regional INCSEA. In this writer's view, the most urgent purpose for such a code or agreement would be to institutionalize verifiable measures to avoid any conflicts that could aggravate the situation, rather than to establish regimes of cooperation or delimit areas of control or jurisdiction. This will still rely in great measure on the good faith and unilateral self-restraint of parties, but being a collective agreement, peer pressure and even some form of Asian-style "soft sanctions" might also be allowed to play an important role.

The suspension of new occupation and other provocative acts of sovereignty by the claimants could then lay the ground for establishing mechanisms or institutions that would explore further the possibilities of cooperation and joint management in other transboundary activities of mutual interest to the parties. Such activities may include search and rescue, anti-piracy and anti-smuggling operations, pollution monitoring and control, and the promotion of safety and freedom of navigation, shipping and communications. Eventually, these forms of cooperation may help build models of joint management and cooperation that may be extended to the more sensitive issues of resource conflicts over fisheries and hydrocarbons.

Through these three provisions, the 2002 Declaration points the way forward for the future management of the SCS disputes beyond confidence-building and into preventive diplomacy and even conflict resolution. This may again be summarized as the following measures:

(1) Freezing the *status quo* of occupations, and voluntarily limiting the scope and nature of military presence in the disputed areas;
(2) Implementing specific conflict prevention measures, including adjustments in each party's rules of engagement, and entering into bilateral incidents at sea agreements, and eventually a binding regional INCSEA/code of conduct. Monitoring and verification procedures should also be put in place by common agreement;
(3) Establishing modalities and regular structures for continuous coordination, consultation, and progressive agreement on other issues relating to the disputes, including the possibility of joint development of resources.

Thus interpreted, the declaration then may be said to signal a shift in the South China Sea discourse among claimants from confidence-building to conflict prevention. The following upward flowchart illustrates the envisioned process:

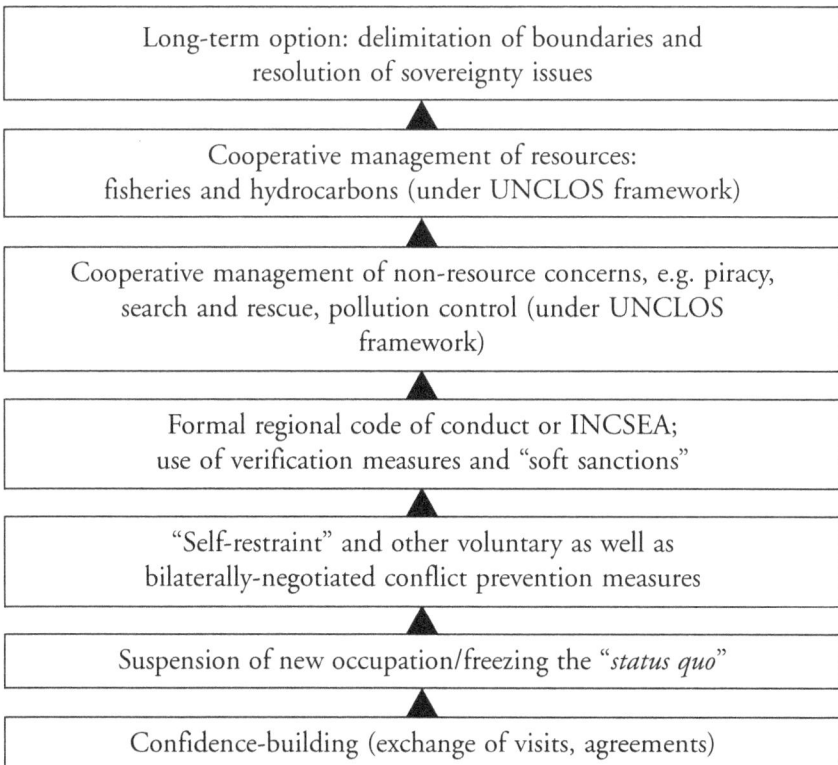

Long-term option: delimitation of boundaries and resolution of sovereignty issues
▲
Cooperative management of resources: fisheries and hydrocarbons (under UNCLOS framework)
▲
Cooperative management of non-resource concerns, e.g. piracy, search and rescue, pollution control (under UNCLOS framework)
▲
Formal regional code of conduct or INCSEA; use of verification measures and "soft sanctions"
▲
"Self-restraint" and other voluntary as well as bilaterally-negotiated conflict prevention measures
▲
Suspension of new occupation/freezing the "*status quo*"
▲
Confidence-building (exchange of visits, agreements)

In addition, the 2002 Declaration may be considered additionally significant from the arguments that:

(1) It was the first formal multilateral agreement entered into by China on the SCS, indicating acknowledgment of the multilateral nature of the disputes and that bilateral solutions, while desirable especially at the initial stages, may no longer be sufficient;

(2) The whole of ASEAN is a party to the declaration rather than only the claimant-states, framing the SCS disputes as a matter of importance to ASEAN-China relations and to security and economic cooperation between the two sides. This also reflects ASEAN's efforts to unite and agree among themselves on a common approach and common norms in SCS dispute resolution; and

(3) Through this agreement China may have succeeded in limiting the "internationalization" of the disputes, in particular the involvement of non-ASEAN parties such as the United States and Japan in its resolution. Therefore, it is important for China that the declaration must be seen as successful, otherwise other claimants may be tempted to bring the disputes to other forums or mechanisms for resolution, including seeking closer security ties with the United States.

Unless the follow-through agenda on the declaration is drafted and agreed on early enough, there is of course, the danger that like previous agreements and declarations, it will fail to help address any of the key issues or prevent further tensions or "triggers of conflict" from taking place. Taiwan, of course, is not happy with the declaration as it was not even a party to the consultations, leading to what appears to be an unfortunate decision by Taiwan to take more unilateral actions to assert its claims.

A series of untoward events shortly after the signing of the declaration in fact already appear to challenge the value of the agreement. Among these: The appearance of new Chinese markers in some features as reported in 2003, the decision of the Philippines to hold bilateral military exercises with the United States in the SCS area, Taiwan's construction of a "bird-watching stand" on Vietnamese-claimed Ban Than Reef, Vietnam's dispatch of a boatload of "tourists" on an eight-day visit to the islands, and China's conduct of a navy drill, apparently intended to signal displeasure at the above-mentioned move by Vietnam.[9]

These incidents underscore the argument that, while confidence-building activities and declarations may help to improve the atmosphere somewhat by encouraging greater dialogue and highlighting the need to take cooperative measures rather than focusing on the intractable sovereignty issues, they are far from adequate. Unilateral assertions of sovereignty have not ceased to take place just because an agreement or, in fact, several agreements have already been signed. Claimants have not become less suspicious of each other just because confidence-building activities have been pursued. As a matter of fact, even some seemingly benign activity such as building fishing shelters, tourist facilities and scientific stations, sending fishing boats and research vessels apart from naval patrols, may be seen as attempts to increase presence or legitimize resource exploitation activities in disputed areas or EEZs of neighbouring states. These types of actions, too, will have to be addressed in the process of discussing rules of engagement and a code of conduct.

BEYOND CONFIDENCE-BUILDING

There are other measures beyond confidence-building that may also usefully be undertaken as other building blocks to peace. The first that comes to mind is for littoral states of the South China Sea (claimants as well as non-claimants) to come to common understandings of the impact of the UNCLOS provisions on the management of the SCS, as well as the impact of UNCLOS on their own jurisdictional claims. After all, the claimants have time and again reiterated their pledge to abide by UNCLOS and other international norms. It may be necessary to "imagine" the South China Sea region as free from all territorial disputes for the purpose of developing cooperative arrangements on combating piracy, marine environmental pollution or on implementing the International Maritime Organization (IMO) responsibilities within the disputed areas.

Another much-needed step is to expand mutual understanding of the fundamental interests of the various claimant states, then exploring areas where trade-offs are possible. For instance, if county A's primary concern is security *vis-à-vis* country B, and B's concern is access to energy resources, then compromises may be built around B guaranteeing non-aggression towards A, and A guaranteeing B access to some part of resources within its EEZ or occupied area. Of course, since there are so many pairs of disputes, a collective or multilateral approach would considerably reduce transaction costs but give the parties less room for bargaining.

Another important step that may be worth considering is for each government of a claimant state to exert efforts to gradually transform opinion among their respective stakeholders and publics away from the emotionalism identified with territoriality and sovereignty, and to assist in building domestic constituencies for peace and cooperation in the South China Sea. It is possible that in most cases, the internal negotiations within claimant states may be even more difficult than the pursuit of dialogue and cooperation among them.

CONCLUSION

The important question for the parties concerned is that, having engaged in confidence-building for over ten years and still failing to prevent tensions and triggers of conflict from taking place, what comes next for the SCS? The foregoing discussion stresses the need for conflict-prevention measures and monitoring mechanisms to be put in place, drawing from the 2002 Declaration. At the same time, this chapter identified a number of other important tasks that hopefully can help move the process forward.

With the present warming of bilateral relations between China and ASEAN as well as between China and individual ASEAN member-states, and with the emphasis in relations shifting to economic cooperation through free trade arrangements and to broader regional cooperation schemes such as the ASEAN+3, things seem to be moving in the right direction. However, there is a risk that the claimants will once more become complacent about the territorial and jurisdictional disputes in the South China Sea, until another crisis or major incident occurs, which could well result in an escalation of the conflict.

The construction of a true and lasting peace between China and ASEAN must proceed by building on what little progress we have already made, moving with patience but with persistence to achieve "peace by pieces" as it were. In this process, we need champions and believers on all sides, not sceptics.

NOTES

1. Brad Glosserman, "Cooling South China Sea Competition", *PACNET Newsletter no. 22A*. Pacific Forum-Center for Strategic and International Studies, 1 June 2001.
2. Hasjim Djalal and Ian Townsend-Gault, "Preventive Diplomacy: Managing Potential Conflicts In The South China Sea", in *Herding Cats: Multiparty Mediation In A Complex World*, edited by Chester A. Crocker (Washington D.C.: United States Institute of Peace Press, 2000), pp. 107–33.
3. For a detailed report of the workshop process and outcome until 1998, see Djalal and Townsend-Gault, *Preventive Diplomacy*. For analysis, see Liselotte Odgaard, "Conflict Control and Crisis Management between China and Southeast Asia: An Analysis of the Workshops on Managing Potential Conflict in the South

China Sea", at <www.stanford.edu/~fravel/chinafp/scs.htm.>, also printed in *ASEAN and the EU in the International Environment*, edited by Dieter Mahncke, et al., Nomos Verlagsgesellschaft, Baden-Baden, 1999.

4. Joint Statement of the Meeting of Heads of State/Government of the Member States of ASEAN and the President of the People's Republic of China, Kuala Lumpur, 16 December 1997.

5. This thesis is expounded in Johnston, Alastair Iain and Paul Evans, "China and Multilateral Security Institutions", in *Engaging China: The Management of an Emerging Power*, edited by Alastair Iain Johnston and Robert S. Ross (London and New York: Routledge, 1999).

6. Leszek Buszynski, "ASEAN, the Declaration on Conduct, and the South China Sea", *Contemporary Southeast Asia* 25, no. 3 (2003): 343–62.

7. According to the ASEAN Regional Forum, conflict management processes are a progression from confidence-building to preventive diplomacy and conflict resolution. In this author's view, the actual implementation of major cooperation proposals in the SCS such as co-management of resources should already be indicative that conflict resolution is underway, which can take place even without addressing the ownership/sovereignty issues.

8. Declaration on the Conduct of Parties in the South China Sea, 4 November 2002.

9. Ronald A. Rodriguez, "Conduct Unbecoming in the South China Sea?", GLOCOM Asia Report no. 66, 24 May 2004, <http://www.glocom.org/special_topics/asia_rep/20040524_asia_s66/>, accessed 10 June 2004.

24
China and Ethnic Chinese in ASEAN: Post-Cold War Development

Leo Suryadinata

INTRODUCTION

During the Cold War, there were two schools of thought regarding the policy of the People's Republic of China (PRC) towards Chinese residents in Southeast Asia, including those in Indonesia. The first school was represented by Harold Hinton,[1] which argued that China would protect the "overseas Chinese" (ethnic Chinese) at all cost; the second school of thought, which was spearheaded by David Mozingo[2] and developed by Leo Suryadinata[3] and others was that China's national interest differed from that of the "overseas Chinese", and it would only protect the "overseas Chinese" if this initiative coincided with the highest priority of China's national interest such as national security, territorial integrity and the survival of the regime.

After the end of the Cold War, as ethnicity and ethno-nationalism was more intensively examined, the view of the first school, in a modified way, re-emerged. This view was that since China wanted to modernize and it recognized the tremendous economic resources of the Chinese communities overseas, Beijing began to stress ethnic ties and encouraged the ethnic Chinese to re-orient themselves toward China. China was also prepared to protect ethnic Chinese interest, as it became part of China's national interests, especially in its pursuit of global dominance. This view was articulated by Western journalists rather than scholars; the examples are Sterling Seagrave, and Lewis M. Simons and Michael Zielenziger.[4]

This chapter examines China's policy towards the ethnic Chinese in Southeast Asia after the end of the Cold War in order to determine whether there have been any significant changes from the earlier findings. What has been Beijing's policy towards the ethnic Chinese in Southeast Asia? What are the responses of Southeast Asian countries to the Chinese overture? Do ethnic Chinese remain as an important factor in Sino-ASEAN relations?

THE EVOLUTION OF CHINA'S POLICY TOWARDS ETHNIC CHINESE: FROM PROTECTION TO NEUTRALITY

The PRC initially inherited the Kuomintang (KMT, the nationalist party) policy of treating ethnic Chinese as the nationals of China.[5] However, as Beijing entered the international community, it realized that to claim all ethnic Chinese to be China's nationals was not only unrealistic but also harmful to the conduct of foreign relations. Beijing began to offer dual nationality treaties to countries, which recognized Beijing or wanted to be friendly with the new communist giant.

The point of departure was in 1955 during the Afro-Asian conference where China initiated a friendly gesture to the newly independent states. Indonesia was the first and only country which signed the treaty, but it was only ratified by the Indonesian parliament in the 1960s. The 1950s and 1960s were the height of the Cold War, and Beijing's primary goals in its foreign policy were to safeguard its "national interests", including the security of the regime. The United States was considered as the prime enemy of China and later, the Soviet Union was also seen as a threat.[6] The policy of the PRC towards Southeast Asia, including Indonesia, should also be seen in this light.

When Indonesia introduced an anti-"overseas Chinese" regulation in 1959 and implemented it in 1960, which banned foreigners (that is, ethnic Chinese) to engage in retail trade, many Chinese livelihoods were threatened. They were forced to move out of the rural areas, which created social upheaval. The PRC intervened by sending ships to repatriate its nationals. But when Beijing discovered that this was detrimental to the Beijing-led anti-colonialist and anti-Western coalition, giving rise to the pro-Soviet faction in Jakarta, it immediately stopped repatriating the Chinese and absorbed the humiliation,[7] indicating that "national interest" reigned supreme in Beijing's policy.

When the abortive coup attributed to the communists took place in Jakarta on 30 September 1965 (G-30-S), Beijing was accused by the pro-U.S. army generals such as A.H. Nasution and Suharto to have supported the Indonesian Communist Party (PKI) in its attempt to seize power, and Sino-Indonesian relations reached its all-time low. The coup was crushed and the new military regime was hostile towards Beijing. Diplomatic relations were eventually frozen from 1 October 1967 and not rehabilitated until 1990, lasting for more than twenty years.

It should be noted that during the period 1965 to 1969, there was a Cultural Revolution in China and radical groups took over in Beijing. China's foreign policy became militant, at least temporarily. After the fall of the radical groups, known as the Gang of Four, Beijing began to reintroduce a moderate policy. It started approaching non-communist ASEAN states, and they responded to the Chinese overture. Malaysia (1974), the Philippines (1975) and Thailand (1975) established diplomatic ties with the PRC for the first time. Despite diplomatic ties, relationships were not yet close, due partly to the ideological problem. Beijing continued to support the communists in Southeast Asia.

It was only after the re-emergence of Deng Xiaoping as the strongman of China in 1977, that Beijing took initiatives to improve relations with its neighbours, probably intended to counterbalance Vietnam, which was moving closer to the Soviet camp. In 1978, Deng Xiaoping visited some ASEAN states, showing China's readiness to cooperate with non-communist states. When he discovered that many ASEAN states were still unhappy with China's policy towards the ethnic Chinese, he promulgated the 1980 nationality law, introducing the first citizenship law since the birth of the PRC, stating that China will only recognize one citizenship. Those Chinese who adopted local citizenship willingly ceased to be China's citizens.

However, Suharto's Indonesia continued to be suspicious of China and purported that China was involved in the 1965 coup. Jakarta demanded Beijing to apologize while Beijing continued to deny its involvement. The diplomatic ties remained frozen. However, with the reduction in tension between the East and the West, and in light of Indonesia's economic problems, direct trade between China and Indonesia was resumed in 1985. Nonetheless, it took another five years before the relations were normalized when the Cold War ended. In 1989, Chinese diplomats met Suharto in Tokyo and decided that the time had come for the two countries to re-establish diplomatic ties.[8] Soon after Indonesia, Singapore followed suit to establish ties with China.

It is worth noting that the normalization of diplomatic relations between Indonesia and China was crucial in China-ASEAN relations, as Indonesia is the largest country in ASEAN and its refusal to rehabilitate ties affected ASEAN's overall relationship with Beijing. Not surprisingly, Beijing was also eager to mend ties. When Indonesia expressed that it was ready to respond to the Beijing overture, Qian Qichen, Foreign Minister of China, met General Murdiono (then Cabinet Secretary) in a hotel room after attending the funeral of Japanese Emperor Hirohito. The discussion went very smoothly and Qian Qichen was soon received by Suharto who was in the next room. Both Murdiono and Suharto no longer mentioned anything about "China's involvement" in the coup, showing that Jakarta was keen for diplomatic normalization.[9] Both agreed in principle to do so. A year later, the two countries announced that Sino-Indonesian ties were officially restored. It should be noted that Jakarta did not insist that Beijing apologize for "its alleged involvement in the 1965 coup".

ETHNIC CHINESE AND THE ASEAN STATES

While in the past, the ethnic Chinese issue often posed as a factor in normal relations between China and some Southeast Asian countries, why was this not a factor in 1990? Many people have observed that the ethnic Chinese in general are quite well integrated into the local scene. Even in Indonesia, most of the Chinese Indonesians had become Indonesian citizens and hence outside the jurisdiction of the PRC. In fact, before Malaysia established diplomatic ties with Beijing, the majority of ethnic Chinese were already Malaysian citizens. Even for the Chinese in the Philippines, Ferdinand Marcos had issued laws allowing ethnic Chinese to become Philippine nationals before the establishment of Beijing-Manila ties in 1975. There was no problem with ethnic Chinese in Thailand as Sino-Thais have been well integrated and there had been no problem between the two ethnic groups. Singapore being a city state with a large number of ethnic Chinese, in order to create a Southeast Asian identity, felt obliged to be the last ASEAN state to establish ties with the PRC.

The ethnic Chinese in many ASEAN countries had often been suspected by the host countries as being oriented, if not loyal, to China. These governments ignored the heterogeneous nature of ASEAN ethnic society and also rapid integration of the Chinese into the local communities.

However, a significant number of ethnic Chinese belonged to the so-called "trading minorities", and they often formed a middle class in their adopted countries and caused jealousy among the less successful "indigenous" population. The Cold War and the previous policy of Beijing towards the communist movements and ethnic Chinese did not help Southeast Asia's Chinese either. Local politicians also used the Chinese issue to gain mileage during political power struggle. As a result, the ethnic Chinese issue was blown out of proportion.

Nevertheless, after the establishment of diplomatic ties between ASEAN countries and China, the ethnic Chinese issue did not completely disappear. Some ASEAN governments continued to be suspicious of their ethnic Chinese group and their orientations towards China. They feared that closer ties between the ASEAN states and China would only benefit China rather than the local populations. Ethnic Chinese investment in China was often considered to be at the expense of their adopted countries. One of the examples was when President Fidel Ramos wanted to bring a Philippine delegation to the PRC in 1993 to foster economic cooperation, he asked six Philippine Chinese tycoons to sign agreements "to form a consortium that would invest in infrastructure projects in the Philippines".[10] A survey also shows that the Filipinos "expressed concern that activities may be contrary to Manila's developmental interest".[11] Meanwhile the Indonesian Chinese were prohibited to invest in China directly as the investment in China was considered to be an "unpatriotic act".[10]

Many ASEAN governments did not see the investments as purely business ventures but an expression of ethnicity. However, with globalization and the economic crisis in Southeast Asia, this perception has gradually changed. The PRC policy towards ethnic Chinese, at least officially, has reinforced the image that even after the end of the Cold War, Beijing remains neutral in dealing with the ethnic Chinese issue and in the domestic affairs of the ASEAN states. One of the test cases was Beijing's attitude towards the anti-Chinese riots.

CHINA AND ANTI-CHINESE RIOTS IN INDONESIA

Towards the last years of Suharto's rule, there were many riots and ethnic Chinese often became the targets for attacks. Many Chinese outside Indonesia criticized the Indonesian Government for poor handling of the situation. Some even suggested that Beijing should protect the Chinese in Indonesia. However, Beijing refused to intervene.

On 19 February 1998 an Australian reporter asked the Chinese Ministry of Foreign Affairs for comments on the anti-Chinese violence in Indonesia. Zhu Bangzao, the Ministry's spokesman, was quoted as saying: "We believe that the Indonesian Government can control the situation, maintain social stability and racial harmony."[13] Clearly, Beijing considered the situation a domestic problem for Indonesia.

Privately, a Chinese diplomat in the United States stated that Beijing would not be able to protest or send ships to Indonesia because "there is no good reason to do so as the majority of the Chinese in Indonesia are Indonesian citizens."[14] To protest or to send ships would mean intervention in Jakarta's domestic affairs. Such intervention would also generate a negative reaction in other parts of Southeast Asia. It could send a signal that China still wanted to protect ethnic Chinese although they are no longer PRC's citizens. And the intervention might also impose greater difficulties on Indonesian Chinese who wanted to continue living in Indonesia.

According to a report filed by a *Lianhe Zaobao* American correspondence, China's Jakarta embassy would help individual Chinese (presumably those who are non-Indonesian citizens) who encountered difficulty on a case-by-case basis.[15] Understandably, the embassy was very cautious in doing this since such action may affect Sino-Indonesian relations.

Beijing-Jakarta ties have been quite cordial in recent years. Beijing does not want to jeopardize the relationship that it had slowly built. To win over Jakarta, Beijing has been willing to help Jakarta solve its financial problem by giving economic assistance. It had contributed USS$1 billion to Thailand under the IMF package and it offered a similar aid to Indonesia.[16] PRC state companies which had invested in Indonesia and Beijing did not want to jeopardize these investments.[17] They also did not want to pull out their investments fearing that such action would have a negative impact on Indonesia's political stability.

BEIJING'S ATTITUDE TOWARD THE MAY 1998 ANTI-CHINESE RIOTS

Perhaps the best example of Beijing's post-Cold War policy towards Jakarta is its attitude towards the anti-Chinese riots. On 12–13 May 1998 anti-Chinese riots took place in Jakarta, Surakarta, Medan and some other cities, resulting in the burning of Chinese property, and the killing and raping of Chinese girls and women. It was considered the worst anti-Chinese riots since Indonesia's independence. The factors that contributed to these riots were complex but the sufferings of the ethnic Chinese drew the attention of Chinese overseas. However, Beijing did not register any protest until two months later.

The first official reaction of Beijing to the May 1998 riots occurred in late July 1998. However, the first reaction by a PRC official to the incident was on 6 July. Chen Shiqiu, the new Chinese ambassador to Indonesia, visited East Kalimantan to investigate the possibility of investing in the area, especially in the palm oil business. During his visit, he was asked by Indonesian reporters on his view of the May riots. He was quoted as saying that China was "concerned with the incident" and wanted the Indonesian Government "to investigate the matter thoroughly".[18] He told the reporters that he met B.J. Habibie twice; the first time when Habibie was still vice-president and the second time, when Habibie was president. During the meeting Chen said that he discussed the riots and "hoped that the riots will not recur".[19] Chen clearly stated that, "according to the international law as well as the law of the two countries, it was the responsibility of the Indonesian Government to protect its own citizens, including the citizens of Chinese descent."[20] There was no official protest on the part of Beijing.

Although in late July a Chinese Foreign Ministry spokesman had used diplomatic channels to express concern over the victims of the riots, only on 3 August, did Tang Jiaxuan, Minister for Foreign Affairs, publicly state that "his government 'expressed concern' about the violence against Chinese women to the Indonesian Government".[21] He also "urged Jakarta to punish those who brutalized the ethnic Chinese minority during violent riots in Indonesia in May".[22] On the same day, the *People's Daily* also published a strong worded commentary urging Jakarta to take "strong steps to punish the lawless and to protect the personal safety and property of the ethnic Chinese, and treat them fairly".[23] Apparently Beijing had been under pressure of the Chinese communities in Taiwan, Hong Kong, Southeast Asia and the West to do something. Nevertheless, China was very cautious in expressing its opinion, as it wanted to behave like a responsible major power.

Indeed, unlike the riots in the 1960s, the May 1998 riots were not anti-PRC. It was targeted at the ethnic Chinese and there was no indication that it developed into anti-PRC riots. Although some PRC citizens might have been affected by the riots, the majority happened to be Indonesian citizens. However, under pressures from world opinion, especially from the ethnic Chinese communities outside China, Beijing appeared to change its attitude towards the matter. Nevertheless, the main policy of non-intervention remained.

POST-CRISIS AND POST-SEPTEMBER 11 ASEAN-CHINA RELATIONS

Southeast Asian countries were seriously hit by the monetary crisis starting in 1997, especially Thailand, the Philippines and Indonesia. China was less affected by this monetary storm. The priority of many ASEAN states had shifted to the economic rather than ideological fields. After a few years, many countries began to recover from the crisis, except Indonesia which took longer than others. On 11 September 2001, the New York World Trade Centre was attacked by terrorists, which shocked the world.

Ironically, the September 11 terrorist attacks offered new opportunity for cooperation between China and the ASEAN states. Zhu Rongji, then Chinese Prime Minister, proposed the concept of a China-ASEAN Free Trade Area at the ASEAN leaders informal meeting in 1999 in Singapore but there was no agreement on the matter. Some ASEAN states, including Indonesia, did not support the concept. However, when Zhu attended the Seventh ASEAN Summit in Brunei and proposed the idea again in early November 2001, the concept was accepted fully by the member-states, including Indonesia, despite its earlier position of maintaining its distance from open approval.

After the summit, Zhu was invited to visit Jakarta by President Megawati. The official visit (7–11 November 2001) by one of Beijing's highest leaders is significant as Beijing promised more assistance and aid to Indonesia.[24] Zhu had also succeeded in gaining Jakarta's cooperation and signed agreements of cooperation in the cultural and economic fields. They also agreed to re-open the branch of the Bank of China in Indonesia.

During a dinner party hosted by President Megawati in honour of Zhu, Taufiq Kiemas, husband of Megawati who is both Member of Parliament and a businessman, was present. It was reported that Zhu had a long discussion with Kiemas. Kiemas was later sent by Megawati to lead an Indonesian delegation to China.[25] It was a successful mission as the delegation managed to conclude a number of projects, including the joint feasibility study of the building of the Java-Sumatra Bridge, tender for importing Liquefied Natural Gas (LNG) from Papua to Guangdong, and the purchase of China-made electric power station equipment.[26]

Indonesia, which was the most critical of the PRC policy, especially Beijing's policy towards ethnic Chinese, has come to terms with Beijing. The state-to-state relations have been dramatically improved. Mutual visits between senior officials have become more often and the ethnic issues appear not to be a factor in the Sino-Indonesian relations, at least for the time being.

CONCLUDING REMARKS

Basically the PRC has been dictated by its national interests in its policy towards Southeast Asian Chinese, especially those in Indonesia. To play a major role in the international arena, Beijing realized that to solve the nationality problem with Southeast Asian countries would be in the mutual interest of China and the ASEAN states. This was especially important during the Cold War era when non-communist Southeast Asian states were suspicious of the PRC. However, since the rise of Deng Xiaoping and his successors, the PRC appeared to have been able to observe the principle of non-intervention, even on matters concerning the ethnic Chinese. After the Cold War, Beijing continued to observe this national interest principle, and had even sacrificed ethnic Chinese interests, if they came into conflict with higher priorities such as the security and well-being of the Chinese state.

Sino-Malaysian relations have also improved since Deng came to power. China's hands-off policy towards local communists earned Kuala Lumpur's trust. In addition, the communists were already defeated and no longer posed any threat to the security of Malaysia. In fact, during the Mahathir administration, Sino-Malaysian ties had also significantly improved. Mahathir even visited China in 1993. In 2003 Abdullah Badawi, then Deputy Prime Minister of Malaysia, visited China and reaffirmed that "China is not a threat." After Abdullah Badawi assumed the prime ministership, he led the largest Malaysian delegation to visit China in May 2004, promoting economic and political relations.[27] An improvement of ties can also be noted between China and Thailand, and between China and Indonesia in recent years. Moreover, the Southeast-Asianization of ethnic Chinese in the last few decades has been quite successful. The problem faced by many ASEAN states, in fact, is not the problem of ethnic Chinese but their own indigenous minority groups.

As the concern of many ASEAN countries is predominantly economic in nature and China appears to have been able to offer economic opportunities for many ASEAN states, the ethnic Chinese in Southeast Asia may be able to serve as a golden bridge between China and ASEAN states, provided that China will not reverse its policy and that ethnic Chinese continue to integrate with local societies. For the time being, the ethnic Chinese factor has not been considered as a negative factor in China-ASEAN relations, a great improvement indeed from the Cold War era!

NOTES

1. Harold C. Hinton, *Communist China in World Politics* (Boston: Houghton Miffin, 1966).

2. David Mozingo, "China and Indonesia", in *China in Crisis*, edited by Tang Tsou (Chicago: University of Chicago Press, 1968), pp. 333–56.

3. Leo Suryadinata, *"Overseas Chinese" in Southeast Asia and China's Foreign Policy: An Interpretative Essay*. Research Notes and Discussion Paper (Singapore: Institute of Southeast Asian Studies, 1978); Leo Suryadinata *China and the ASEAN States: The Ethnic Chinese Dimension* (Singapore: Singapore University Press, 1985).

4. Sterling Seagrave, *Lords of the Rim: The Invisible Empire of the Overseas Chinese* (London and New York: Bantam Press, 1995); Lewis M. Simons and Michael Zielenziger, "Enter the Dragon", *San Jose Mercury News Special Report*, 26–29 June 1994. These journalists also argued that the "Overseas Chinese", as a group, formed an alliance with the PRC, ignoring the diversity of the ethnic Chinese community in Southeast Asia.

5. For a fine study on China's policy towards the "Overseas Chinese" in Southeast Asia, see Stephen Fitzgerald, *China and the Overseas Chinese: A Study of Peking's Changing Policy, 1949–1970* (Cambridge: Cambridge University Press, 1972).

6. On the Sino-Soviet split, see *The Sino-Soviet Dispute*, edited by G.F. Hudson, Richard Lowenthal, and Roderick MacFarquhar (New York: Praeger, 1961); see also Seweryn Bialer, "The Sino-Soviet Conflict: The Soviet Dimension", in Donald S. Zagoria, *Soviet Policy in East Asia* (New Haven and London: Yale University Press, 1982), pp. 93–120.

7. For an excellent analysis, see David Mozingo, *Chinese Policy toward Indonesia, 1949–1967* (Ithaca: Cornell University Press, 1976).

8. Leo Suryadinata, "Indonesia-China Relations: A Recent Breakthrough", *Asian Survey* (July 1990): 682–96.

9. Qian Qichen, *Waijiao shiji* [Diplomacy: Ten Notes]. (The original English title is "The Stories of a Diplomat"), Beijing: *Shijie zhishi*, 2003, pp. 118–26. One of the stumbling blocks of normalization was that Beijing should openly apologize to Jakarta that it was involved in the 1965 coup.

10. Theresa Chong Carino, "The Ethnic Chinese, The Philippine Economy and China", in *Southeast Asian Chinese and China: The Politico-economic Dimension*, edited by Leo Suryadinata (Singapore: Times Academic Press, 1994), p. 216.

11. Willy Laohoo, "Filipino Reactions to Philippine Chinese Investments in China: An Exploratory Survey", *Chinese Studies Journal* 5 (1995): 41, in *China, Taiwan, and the Ethnic Chinese in the Philippine Economy*, edited by Ellen Huang Palanca.

12. Leo Suryadinata, "China's Economic Modernization and the Chinese in ASEAN: A Preliminary Study", in *Southeast Asian Chinese and China: The Politico-Economic Dimension*, edited by Leo Suryadinata (Singapore: Times Academic Press, 1995), p. 203.

13. "Yinni zhengfu neng kongzi jumian" [Indonesian Government can Control the Situation], *Lianhe Zaobao* (Singapore), 20 February 2001.

14. Ruan Ci Shan, "Zhongguo zai Yinni luanjuzhong jintui liangnan" [China is in a Dilemma in Turbulent Indonesia], *Lianhe Zaobao* (Singapore), 25 February 1998.

15. Ibid.

16. According to another source, there was only $0.52 billion, see Xiao Shen, "Yin Zhong bangjiao wushi zhounian qianxi fangwen Zhongguo Zhu Yinni Chen Shiqiu dashi" [An Interview with China's Ambassador to Indonesia Chen Shiqiu on the Eve of the 50th Anniversary of Sino-Indonesian Diplomatic Relations], in *Yinni yu Dongxie* (Jakarta), no. 111 (July 2000): 24.

17. However, PRC's investment in Indonesia has been modest. Between 1967 and January 2000, China's direct investment in Indonesia was only $0.290 billion, constituting 0.13 per cent of foreign investment in Indonesia. Xiao Shen, op. cit., p. 24.

18. "Dubes RRC Sesalkan Terjadinya Perkosaan Saat Kerusuhan" [PRC's Ambassador Deplores Raping during Riots], *Suara Pembaruan*, 7 July 1998.

19. Ibid.

20. Ibid.

21. China: Punish Indonesia Rioters", *The Associated Press*, 3 August 1998, <http://www.huaren.org/focus/id/080398-10.html>; also "China's Foreign Min Urges Indonesia to Investigate Riots", *Dow Jones International News*, 3 August 1998 Document dji0000020010916du8406ktp. Please note that both reports used "expressed concerns" rather than stronger words.

22. Cited in Mary Kwang, "Violence against Chinese", 4 August 1998, <http://www.icanet.org/public/News/n2_080498%20Punish%20the%guilty,%2...>. Also Michael Richardson, "Beijing Watching Indonesia Violence New Attacks Aimed at Ethnic Chinese Viewed as Test for Jakarta", *International Herald Tribune*, 14 August 1998. Please note that Kwang used the word "urged" while Richardson used "demanded" to describe Beijing's appeal to Jakarta.

23. Mary Kwang, "Violence against Chinese".

24. "Zhu Rongji jiang fangwen Yinni" [Zhu Rongji will Visit Indonesia], *Lianhe Zaobao*, 1 November 2001.

25. "Taufiq Kiemas 'Saya harus membela istri dan presiden saya'," ["Taufik Kiemas: 'I have to Defend My Wife and My President'"], *Tempo*, 13 January 2002, pp. 24–25.

26. "Guanxi di Cina, protes di Jakarta" [Connection in China, Protest in Jakarta], *Tempo*, 6 January 2002, p. 26.

27. "Maguo shouxiang jinqi fangwen Zhongguo" [Prime Minister of Malaysia Visits China from Today], *Lianhe Zaobao*, 27 May 2004.

Index